AF361251

Écrire au-delà de la fin des temps ?

Writing Beyond the End Times?

Écrire au-delà de la fin des temps ?

Les littératures au Canada et au Québec

URSULA MATHIS-MOSER & MARIE CARRIÈRE, Editors

Writing Beyond the End Times?

The Literatures of Canada and Quebec

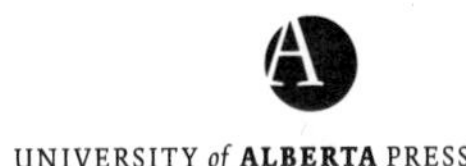

UNIVERSITY *of* **ALBERTA** PRESS

Published by

University of Alberta Press
Ring House 2
Edmonton, Alberta, Canada T6G 2E1
www.uap.ualberta.ca

First published in Austria by Innsbruck University Press

Copyright © 2017 Innsbruck University Press

LIBRARY AND ARCHIVES CANADA
CATALOGUING IN PUBLICATION

Title: Writing beyond the end times? : the literatures of Canada and
     Quebec = Écrire au-delà de la fin des temps ? : les littératures au
     Canada et au Québec / Ursula Mathis-Moser & Marie Carrière,
     editors.
Other titles: Écrire au-delà de la fin des temps ? | Écrire au-delà de la
     fin des temps ?
Names: Mathis-Moser, Ursula, editor. | Carrière, Marie J.,
     1971– editor.
Description: Originally published under title: Écrire au-delà de la fin
     des temps ? [Innsbruck] : Innsbruck University Press, [2017]. |
     Co-published by: Innsbruck University Press. | Includes
     bibliographical references. | Text in English or French.
Identifiers: Canadiana (print) 20190106573E |
     Canadiana (ebook) 20190106603 |
     ISBN 9781772124880 (softcover) |
     ISBN 9781772125078 (PDF)
Subjects: LCSH: Crises in literature. | LCSH: Apocalypse in literature. |
     LCSH: Social change in literature. | LCSH: Canadian literature—
     21st century—History and criticism. | LCSH: Canadian
     literature—21st century—Themes, motives. | CSH: Canadian
     literature (French)—Québec Province—21st century—History
     and criticism | CSH: Canadian literature (French)—Québec
     Province—21st century—Themes, motives
Classification: LCC PS8101.C75 E27 2019 |
     DDC C810.9/355209051—dc23

CATALOGAGE AVANT PUBLICATION DE
BIBLIOTHÈQUE ET ARCHIVES CANADA

Titre: Writing beyond the end times? : the literatures of Canada and
     Quebec = Écrire au-delà de la fin des temps ? : les littératures au
     Canada et au Québec / Ursula Mathis-Moser & Marie Carrière,
     editors.

Autres titres: Écrire au-delà de la fin des temps ? | Écrire au-delà de la
     fin des temps ?
Noms: Mathis-Moser, Ursula, éditeur intellectuel. | Carrière, Marie J.,
     1971– éditeur intellectuel.
Description: Édition originale publiée sous le titre : Écrire au-delà de la
     fin des temps ? [Innsbruck] : Innsbruck University Press, [2017]. |
     Publié en collaboration avec : Innsbruck University Press. |
     Comprend des références bibliographiques. | Textes en anglais
     et en français.
Identifiants: Canadiana (livre imprimé) 20190106573F | Canadiana
     (livre numérique) 20190106581 |
     ISBN 9781772124880 (couverture souple) |
     ISBN 9781772125078 (PDF)
Vedettes-matière: RVM: Crise dans la littérature. | RVM: Fin du monde
     dans la littérature. | RVM: Changement social dans la littérature. |
     RVM: Littérature canadienne—21e siècle—Histoire et critique. |
     RVM: Littérature canadienne—21e siècle—Thèmes, motifs. |
     RVM: Littérature québécoise—21e siècle—Histoire et critique. |
     RVM: Littérature québécoise—21e siècle—Thèmes, motifs.
Classification: LCC PS8101.C75 E27 2019 |
     CDD C810.9/355209051—dc23

First edition, first printing, 2019
First printed and bound in Canada by Blitzprint, Calgary, Alberta.
Editorial assistance by Andrea Krotthammer.

All rights reserved. No part of this publication may be reproduced,
stored in a retrieval system, or transmitted in any form or by
any means (electronic, mechanical, photocopying, recording, or
otherwise) without prior written consent.

University of Alberta Press gratefully acknowledges the support
received for its publishing program from the Government of Canada,
the Canada Council for the Arts, and the Government of Alberta
through the Alberta Media Fund.

Supported by Gesellschaft für Kanada-Studien in den
deutschsprachigen Ländern, Stadt Innsbruck, Zentrum für
Kanadastudien der Universität Innsbruck, Vizerektorat für Forschung
der Universität Innsbruck.

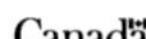
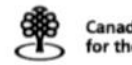
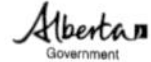

Table des matières – Contents

Table des matières – Contents

Écrire au-delà de la fin des temps ?
Writing Beyond the End Times?

Dans *Vivre la fin des temps*, Slavoj Žižek soutient que « le système capitaliste global approche un point zéro apocalyptique » sous l'effet combiné de plusieurs tendances comme « la crise écologique, les conséquences de la révolution biogénétique, les déséquilibres à l'intérieur du système lui-même (problèmes posés par la propriété intellectuelle, les conflits à venir concernant les matières premières, la nourriture et l'eau), et la croissance explosive des divisions et explosions sociales » (2011, 11). Dans *Murs*, Wendy Brown prétend que nous vivons actuellement « à une époque où les capacités de destruction sont sans équivalent dans l'histoire, de par leur puissance combinée, leur degré de miniaturisation et leur mobilité – de ces corps bourrés d'explosifs aux toxines biochimiques quasiment invisibles » (2009, 15). Bruno Latour, de son côté, avance la notion de modernité en rapport à l'époque géologique de l'anthropocène, d'où l'action humaine exerce une réelle force géologique sur la planète, réalignant ainsi et radicalement les relations sujet-objet, ou encore « ce que signifie être dans un espace [...][,] ce que signifie s'entremêler avec des agentivités animées » (2014, 16 ; trad. M. Carrière). Enfin, si les attaques du 11 septembre 2001, selon Ann Kaplan, ont signalé « un moment cristallisant » pour les États-Unis, le Canada et le monde occidental (2003, 52, 55 ; trad. M. Carrière), elles ont entraîné, suggère Brian Massumi, un « tournant auquel l'environnement-menace a assumé une épaisseur ambiante » (2010, 62 ; trad. M. Carrière).

Dans la tourmente d'une telle anxiété sociale, violence mondiale, agitation culturelle et dégradation environnementale, un sentiment de crise viendrait nous submerger. Cependant, récentes théorisations dans le domaine des études féministes et des affects, comme *Cruel Optimism* de Lauren Berlant (2011), *Le posthumain* de Rosi Braidotti (2016) ou *Matters of Care* (2017) de María Puig de la Bellacasa nous invitent non seulement à repenser nos attachements à des conceptions antérieures de ‹ la bonne vie › – des attachements qui ont en fait mené à nos crises contemporaines –, mais aussi à formuler de nouveaux modes humains et non humains d'être et de relation. Dans ce volume, nous soutenons que les auteures canadiennes et québécoises interviennent de manière des plus profondes et importantes en ces temps de crise, c'est-à-dire, notre temps de ce millénaire plus ou moins nouveau. Sur la toile de fond de l'Après-11 septembre des essais de *L'horizon du fragment* (2004), Nicole Brossard exprime « le goût de recommencer la quête insensée de sens et de beauté » (90), alors que d'autres écrivains font appel à la dérision, l'humour et l'ironie pour illustrer des moyens de « réussir son hypermodernité et sauver le reste de sa vie » (titre de Langelier 2010).

Sur un plan plus général, l'avertissement de Brossard de poursuivre la quête apparemment « insensée de sens » (2004, 90) soulève une question qui, de manière explicite et implicite, détermine la majorité des articles inclus dans ce volume (entre autres : Côté, Defraeye, Fraile-Marcos, Lüsebrink, Mohr, Ravi) : celle, cruciale, de la fonction et de la raison d'être de la littérature à la ‹ fin des temps › que nous vivons actuellement. Dans son texte manifeste « Literaturwissenschaft als Lebenswissenschaft », reconnu sur le plan international et publié en traduction anglaise en 2010, le comparatiste allemand Ottmar Ette définit un cadre de réflexion stimulant qui invite à poursuivre le débat : selon Ette, la littérature doit être perçue comme un ‹ savoir sur la vie ›, un ‹ savoir-vivre › ou « knowledge of life », et les études littéraires comme faisant partie d'un nouveau type de ‹ science de la vie ›, c.-à-d. comme « science for living » (2010, titre). Ette soutient que la littérature représente un medium de stockage de ‹ savoir sur la vie › interactif en constante évolution, qui inclut les expériences existentielles de base telles la naissance, la maladie, l'agonie et la mort, auxquelles nous ajouterons l'expérience de la migration et celle du « ‹ délaissement transcendental › (Lukács) », de l'existence « ‹ sans demeure › (Heidegger) » et « ‹ en transit › » (Meurer/Oikonomou 2009, 12 ; trad. U. Mathis-Moser) du sujet de tous les ‹ post- ›. Toutes ces expériences représentent « des espaces de condensation sémantique » (Ette 2007, 26 ; trad. U. Mathis-Moser), des concentrés polyvalents d'un ‹ savoir sur la vie › – concentrés qui servent à la fois de surface de projection, de laboratoire et d'espace expérimental pour l'écrivain qui est invité à créer de nouveaux mondes et contre-mondes imaginaires, des visions alternatives de l'humain et de la nature, de systèmes de valeur et de leur interaction. Conçue comme auto-réflexion psychosociale et sociopolitique, la littérature – grâce à la langue et à ses procédés esthétiques – peut déranger lorsqu'elle confronte le lecteur et la lectrice à des ‹ logiques nouvelles › inédites ou lorsqu'elle découvre des traces de ce qui a été ‹ enseveli › dans l'oubli. Mais en même temps, elle encourage à aller de l'avant, à transgresser tabous et frontières et à affronter l'inconnu avec courage, tout en (re)découvrant peut-être de nouvelles références éthiques.

Vu sous cet angle, ce recueil de textes constitue une contribution valable au souci général concernant la réorientation de l'homme en ces temps de crise. En même temps, il étudie les manières dont la crise oriente ou transforme les écrits canadiens et québécois d'expressions anglaise et française, et inversement, comment la littérature et la critique s'efforcent de contrebalancer les insécurités sociales, économiques et idéologiques dans lesquelles nous vivons. Nos lecteurs et lectrices pourront identifier des caractéristiques thématiques et même stylistiques marquant ces textes *de* la crise, parfois *en* crise, et encore *au-delà* de la crise. Dans ce projet, nous avons tenté de voir comment l'écriture – au sens large pour inclure le cinéma (Porra) et le théâtre (Defraeye, Dumontet, Mata, Rohrleitner) en plus de la fiction (Bouchard, Côté, Dumontet, Fraile-Marcos, Kühn, Lüsebrink, Mata, Mohr, Poitras, Ravi) et la poésie (Côté, Dolce, Mata, Notard, Rohrleitner) – traite du désordre mondial et quelles stratégies elle emploie pour s'élever contre la hantise de la mort planétaire, des effondrements idéologiques et épistémologiques, des crises financières, des legs contemporains de l'histoire, des désastres environnementaux et de l'ère numérique. Nous posions la question ainsi : comment une écriture de la mobilisation délibérée, de la résistance politique, de la transgression radicale ou de l'agentivité peut-elle contrer la crise, inspirer à l'humanité un nouvel espoir et s'acheminer vers la transformation sociale ? Toutes les formes de récits de vulnérabilité, traumatisme ou dystopie nous intéressaient. Les collaborateurs et collaboratrices à ce volume, qui a été soumis à un processus d'évaluation par les pairs, ont répondu à notre appel et nous offrent désormais les recherches suivantes, souvent à la lumière d'une approche transnationale, transfrontalière, postcoloniale et féministe.

Plusieurs articles réunis dans ces pages abordent apocalypse et dystopie et leurs manifestations littéraires au 21e siècle. Dunja M. Mohr, par exemple, explore la fiction non-mimétique de la trilogie *MaddAddam* de Margaret Atwood, avec son évolution interne d'une narration de l'‹ heure zéro › à un discours « post-anthropocentrique au-delà du sujet humain, basé sur la croyance spéculative en un présent au-delà de la crise » (trad. U. Mathis-Moser). Contrairement à Mohr et contrairement aussi à la conception de l'apocalypse selon Marlene Goldman avec son ‹ avant › et son ‹ après ›, Nicole Côté présente un autre mode de discours de la crise : en comparant trois œuvres de Dionne Brand, Simone Chaput et Nelly Arcan, elle découvre des mondes fictionnels qui paraissent « emmurés dans un présent répétitif » (trad. U. Mathis-Moser), réduisant la marge de manœuvre à une fonction purement testimoniale. Ce présent répétitif qui caractérise les romans d'Arcan est abordé plus en détail dans la contribution de David Boucher qui soutient que l'histoire contemporaine, et plus précisément celle du Québec comme elle est évoquée par Arcan, laisse le lecteur seul face à une société profondément individualiste, hédoniste et néolibérale, une société dépourvue de valeurs et menacée, selon Hannah Arendt, par la « banalité du mal ». À l'instar de Mohr, Nicoletta Dolce interprète les recueils de poésie *Choix d'apocalypses* et *Le livre clairière* de Mario Brassard comme les étapes d'une évolution menant d'un discours dysphorique vers « une écriture d'un espoir lucide et désenchanté », malgré la fragilité indéniable et la vulnérabilité de l'existence humaine.

D'autres articles assemblés ici cernent la répression et l'aliénation sociétales que de nouveaux cadres éthiques de l'amour, du soin et de l'empathie arrivent parfois à surmonter. Se basant sur les catégories aristotéliciennes de l'amour – *agape*, *eros*, *philia*, et *storge* –, Ana María Fraile-Marcos examine *Love Enough* de Dionne Brand et note l'émergence d'une « citoyenneté glocale responsable » (trad. U. Mathis-Moser) au sein d'une métropole ambivalente et indifférente, Toronto ; ce processus s'accompagne d'une éthique de l'amour non romantique, provisoire et vulnérable, répondant ainsi au cynisme et aux défaillances des institutions gouvernementales et publiques de ce 21ᵉ siècle. Avec Wajdi Mouawad, Nicole Brossard et Louise Dupré, Carmen Mata Barreiro choisit trois écrivain-e-s québécois-e-s pour illustrer l'intégrité intellectuelle de l'écrivain et sa disposition à intervenir là où la politique échoue. Lucidité, résistance, empathie et un sens indéfectible de la responsabilité caractérisent les textes choisis en exemples. Émilie Notard, pour finir, consacre son étude au recueil de poèmes *Piano blanc* (2011) de Nicole Brossard, où elle trace une ligne de la théorie du ‹ sens › féministe brossardienne des années 1980 – dirigée contre le « (non-)Sens patriarcal » – à sa forme actuelle – dirigée cette fois-ci contre l'anxiété et le « (non-)Sens nouveau de notre (in)humanité ».

Un troisième groupe d'articles concerne les stratégies créatives et esthétiques utilisées pour atténuer les catastrophes personnelles ou historiques. Piet Defraeye, par exemple, analyse le théâtre de Michel Marc Bouchard qui présente sur scène des personnages ‹ perdus en crise ›, quelles qu'en soient les causes : « vieillissement, trahison, abus, haine, homophobie, dysfonctionnement de la famille, jalousie, sacrifice ou simplement désillusion, mensonge ou dissimulation » (trad. U. Mathis-Moser). En mettant délibérément l'accent sur des ressources mélodramatiques comme l'hyperbole, l'imagination et le jeu, sur la force de la parole et de l'écriture/ la réécriture, Bouchard fait découvrir à ses personnages leurs propres stratégies de résistance. De façon similaire, Véronique Porra présente la nouvelle génération québécoise de cinéastes – Xavier Dolan, Anne Émond, Chloé Robichaud – dont les personnages se trouvent également confrontés à des crises existentielles. Ici, l'aliénation se traduit par la représentation du corps et par la technique de l'encadrement (‹ framing ›) qui « soulignent une nouvelle relation avec l'hypermodernité actuelle, narcissique et dépourvue d'espoir » (trad. U. Mathis-Moser).

Un quatrième axe de cet ensemble de textes concerne la réflexion critique sur « la mémoire », « l'histoire » et « l'oubli », pour citer Paul Ricœur. Marion Kühn choisit trois romans québécois de Jocelyne Saucier, Jean-François Caron et Carl Leblanc pour démontrer le flou des frontières entre histoire et fiction, avec ses instances narratives déstabilisées et déstabilisantes, et entre mémoire individuelle et mémoire collective. Ici, crise signifie inaccessibilité de la vérité (historique) et reconnaissance du caractère « sélectif, construit, voire souvent inventé » de toute narration. De manière analogue, Danielle Dumontet, dans son analyse d'une pièce de théâtre de Wajdi Mouawad et d'un roman de Catherine Mavrikakis, accorde une attention particulière aux défauts de la mémoire et aux traumas de la soi-disant ‹ génération de la post-mémoire ›, que le dénouement prenne une tournure cathartique ou non. Daniel Poitras, pour finir, entreprend une lecture non spatiale, mais temporelle du *Volkswagen Blues* de Jacques Poulin, qui l'amène à la conclusion désillusionnée que désormais il « n'existe plus ni Histoire ni avenir ouvert » (trad. U. Mathis-Moser).

Le dernier groupe d'essais rassemblés dans cette compilation est consacré aux conflits culturels à l'intérieur de la société canadienne et québécoise, faisant ressortir des ‹ attaques › littéraires contre un multiculturalisme sanctionné par l'État, contre des représentations coloniales de la vie Indigène ou des discours anti-immigrants. En tenant compte du genre de l'essai (Monique LaRue) tout comme de celui du roman (Abla Farhoud, Larry Tremblay) Hans-Jürgen Lüsebrink choisit une approche transgénérique dans le but d'évoquer la montée planétaire de fondamentalismes qui minent les cadres éthiques du respect, de la tolérance et de la diversité et rendent indispensable « de repenser et de re-évaluer le multiculturalisme et l'interculturalisme dans les contextes canadien et québécois » (trad. U. Mathis-Moser). L'alerte est également donnée par Srilata Ravi, qui consacre une étude de cas au roman *Uashat* (2009) de Gérard Bouchard. Ravi démontre qu'au lieu de « combler une lacune dans la recherche en sciences sociales », la posture de « compassion bien-intentionnée » vis-à-vis des marginalisés (Innus) « se perd dans le langage eurocentrique du roman » – un diagnostic particulièrement pertinent pour toutes les « pratiques de compassion mondialisée » (trad. U. Mathis-Moser). En dernier lieu, Marion Christina Rohrleitner invite le lecteur à découvrir le champ fertile de la littérature latina canadienne qu'elle situe dans un contexte transnational : le Canada, avance-t-elle, peut se prévaloir d'avoir libéré la littérature latina de la perspective ‹ anti-immigrants › étriquée qui a cours aux États-Unis, et de lui avoir donné la possibilité d'évoluer dans un contexte de solidarité transnational.

La riche étendue des textes et genres analysés étale les répercussions du sentiment de crise traversant les écrits canadiens et québécois de nos jours, notamment les œuvres de Nelly Arcan, Margaret Atwood, Gérard Bouchard, Michel Marc Bouchard, Dionne Brand, Mario Brassard, Nicole Brossard, Jean-François Caron, Simone Chaput, Louise Dupré, Abla Farhoud, Monique LaRue, Carl Leblanc, Catherine Mavrikakis, Wajdi Mouawad, Jacques Poulin, Alfonso Quijada Urías, Nela Rio, Carmen Rodríguez, Jocelyne Saucier, Larry Tremblay, et des cinéastes Xavier Dolan, Anne Émond et Chloé Robichaud. Parfois ces auteurs sont abordés par plusieurs collaborateurs, une indication certaine de la portée profonde de la réflexion critique incitée par ces œuvres.

Enfin, ce livre s'ensuit du premier de deux colloques bilingues (français-anglais) et internationaux tenu à l'Université d'Innsbruck à l'automne 2015, et organisé par le Centre d'études canadiennes (CEC) de l'Université d'Innsbruck et le Centre de littérature canadienne (CLC) de l'Université de l'Alberta. Les deux centres soulignent récemment des événements importants : le CEC célèbre son vingtième anniversaire cette année (2017), et le CLC vient de fêter ses dix ans d'existence (2016). Ce projet ainsi que son axe d'intérêt, sa méthodologie et ses objectifs consistent en un témoignage véritable de la riche et dynamique collaboration de ces deux centres de recherche et du dévouement résolu qu'ils partagent quant à l'avancement des études canadiennes et au rôle de la littérature comme véhicule de connaissance et d'amélioration personnelles, collectives, culturelles et sociales.

***

In *Living in the End Times,* Slavoj Žižek argues that "the global capitalist system is approaching an apocalyptic zero point," comprised of "the ecological crisis, the consequences of the biogenetic revolution, imbalances within the system itself (problems with intellectual property; forthcoming struggles over raw materials, food and water), and the explosive growth of social divisions and exclusions" (2010, x). In *Walled States,* Wendy Brown contends that we currently live with unprecedented "capacities for destruction historically unparalleled in their combined potency, miniaturization, and mobility, from bodies wired for explosion to nearly invisible biochemical toxins" (2010, 20). Bruno Latour, for his part, posits modernity in relation to the geological epoch of the Anthropocene, whereby human action itself wields an actual geological force on the planet, ecologically and thus radically realigning subject-object relations, or "what it means to stand in space […][,] what it means to be entangled within animated agencies" (2014, 16). Finally, if the 9/11 attacks, Ann Kaplan observes, marked a "crystallizing moment" for the United States, Canada, and the Western world (2003, 52, 55), they have led, Brian Massumi suggests, to a "turning point at which the threat-environment took on ambient thickness" (2010, 62).

In the midst of such social anxiety, global violence, cultural unrest, and environmental degradation, a sense of crisis seems to overwhelm us. However, recent theorizations in the field of affect and feminist studies, such as Lauren Berlant's *Cruel Optimism* (2011), Rosi Braidotti's *The Posthuman* (2013), or María Puig de la Bellacasa's *Matters of Care* (2017), prompt us not only to rethink our attachments to previously held notions of 'the good life' – attachments that in fact contribute to our contemporary crises – but to articulate alternative, human and non-human, modes of being that require new relations. It is our contention in this volume that contemporary Canadian and Quebec writers intervene in the most profound and important ways in this time of crisis, that is to say, our time in the not so new millennium. In the post-9/11 backdrop of the essays of *L'horizon du fragment,* Nicole Brossard articulates her "desire to take up again the senseless quest for meaning and beauty" (2004, 90; trans. M. Carrière), while other authors rely on derision, humour, and irony to show ways and means of "how to succeed in one's hypermodernity and save the rest of one's life" (translation of the title of Langelier 2011).

Speaking more generally, Brossard's warning to pursue the seemingly "senseless quest for meaning" (2004, 90) raises a question which – explicitly and implicitly – determines the majority of the following essays (Côté, Defraeye, Fraile-Marcos, Lüsebrink, Mohr, Ravi, and others): the crucial issue of the function and purpose of literature in "end times" such as ours. In his internationally much noted essay "Literaturwissenschaft als Lebenswissenschaft – Eine Programmschrift im Jahr der Geisteswissenschaften" (2007), which was published in an English translation in 2010, the German comparatist Ottmar Ette develops a compelling framework for reflection and further debate on this issue. Ette argues that literature must be comprehended as life knowledge or "knowledge for living" just as literary studies should be considered as part of a new type of life sciences, i.e. a "science for living" (2010, title). Literature, Ette asserts (2004, 231), represents an interactive and ever-changing storage medium for life knowledge, including such crucial existential experiences as birth, illness, agony, and death, to which we suggest to add the experience of migration as well as the "'transcendental homelessness' (Lukács) and 'unhousedness' (Heidegger), the 'being in transit'" (Meurer/Oikonomou 2009, 12; trans. U. Mathis-Moser) of the 'post-everything' subject. All these experiences present themselves as "spaces of semantic condensation" (Ette 2007, 26; trans. U. Mathis-Moser), as multilayered concentrations of life knowledge, which at the same time serve as projection screens, as laboratories, and as experimental spaces for the writer to create new fictitious worlds and counter-worlds, and alternative visions of the human and of nature, of value systems and of their interplay. Literature as psycho-social and socio-political self-reflection by means of language and aesthetic devices may be disturbing when it confronts the reader with unheard-off 'new logics' or when it 'dis-covers' traces of what has been buried and forgotten, but at the same time, it also encourages to go forward, to transgress taboos and borders and to courageously confront the unknown while (re)-discovering possible ethical guidelines.

Seen from this point of view, this collection of essays constitutes a valuable contribution to the global concern of how to reorient oneself in these crisis-ridden times. It also examines how crisis directs or transforms Canadian and Quebec writings in English and French, and conversely, how literature and criticism set out to counterbalance the social, economic, and ideological insecurities we live in. Readers will find identifiable thematic and even stylistic characteristics that mark these texts *of crisis*, sometimes *in crisis*, and indeed *beyond crisis*. In this project, we have sought to explore how writing, understood in a broad sense to include cinema (Porra) and drama (Defraeye, Dumontet, Mata, Rohrleitner) as well as fiction (Bouchard, Côté, Dumontet, Fraile-Marcos, Kühn, Lüsebrink, Mata, Mohr, Poitras, Ravi) and poetry (Côté, Dolce, Mata, Notard, Rohrleitner), deals with global disorder; we look at the strategies it employs to stand up against the hauntings of planetary death, ideological and epistemological collapse, financial breakdown, the contemporary legacies of history, environmental disaster, and the electronic age. How can writing with deliberate mobilization, political resistance, radical transgression, and agency counterbalance crisis, give humanity new hope, and merge towards social transformation? We were interested in all forms of narratives of vulnerability, trauma, and dystopia. The contributors to this peer-reviewed volume answered our call and now offer the following investigations, often in a transnational, cross-border, postcolonial, and feminist light.

Several articles collected in these pages tackle apocalypse and dystopia and their twenty-first-century literary manifestations. Dunja M. Mohr, for instance, explores the non-mimetic fiction of Margaret Atwood's *MaddAddam* trilogy with its internal shift from a narration of the 'zero hour' to a "post-anthropocentric discourse beyond the human subject based on the speculative belief in a present beyond crisis." While comparing three works by Dionne Brand, Simone Chaput, and Nelly Arcan, Nicole Côté comments on a different mode of crisis discourse: Contrary to Marlene Goldman's reading of apocalypse with its 'before' and 'after,' the fictional worlds of the texts chosen by Côté seem to be "walled into a repetitive present," reducing the radius of action to a purely testimonial function. This repetitive present in Arcan's novels is addressed in greater detail by David Boucher, who argues that contemporary history, and more precisely contemporary Quebec history, as portrayed by Arcan, leaves the reader confronted with an utterly individualistic, hedonistic, and neoliberal society, devoid of values and menaced by Hannah Arendt's "banality of evil." Not unlike Mohr, Nicoletta Dolce finally interprets Mario Brassard's poetry collections, *Choix d'apocalypses* and *Le livre clairière,* as manifestations of an evolution from a dysphoric discourse toward "a writing of lucid and disenchanted hope" (trans. U. Mathis-Moser) – in spite of the undeniable fragility and vulnerability of human existence.

A second focus lies on societal repression and alienation which new ethical frameworks of love, care, and empathy sometimes surmount. Based on a brief discussion of the Aristotelian categories of love – *agape, eros, philia,* and *storge* – Ana María Fraile-Marcos' reading of Dionne Brand's *Love Enough* draws attention to the emergence of a "responsible glocal citizenry" in the midst of an ambivalent and indifferent metropolis, Toronto – with an unromantic, provisional, and vulnerable love ethics responding to 21st century cynicism and shortcomings of governmental and public institutions. Carmen Mata Barreiro chooses three Quebec writers,

Wajdi Mouawad, Nicole Brossard, and Louise Dupré, to demonstrate intellectual integrity and the writers' disposition to step in where politics fail; lucidity, resistance, empathy, and an unwavering sense of responsibility pervade the texts Mata cites as examples. Émilie Notard dedicates her study to Nicole Brossard's poetry collection, *Piano blanc* (2011). She traces the line from Brossard's feminist theory of "sense" of the 1980s, which was directed against "patriarchal (non-)Sense," to its contemporary form – now directed against anxiety and "the new (non-)Sense of our (in)humanity."

A third group of essays addresses creative and indeed aesthetic strategies employed to attenuate personal or historical catastrophes. Piet Defraeye, for instance, analyzes Michel Marc Bouchard's theatre, which brings to the stage a number of characters lost in crisis, be it through "aging, betrayal, abuse, hatred, homophobia, dysfunctional family, jealousy, sacrifice, or just plain old disillusionment, lying, or disguise." By consciously placing the emphasis on such melodramatic devices as hyperbole, imagination, and play, and on the power of language and (re)writing, Bouchard's characters define their own strategies of resistance. In a similar way, Véronique Porra introduces a new generation of Quebec film directors – Xavier Dolan, Anne Émond, Chloé Robichaud – whose characters, too, are confronted with existential crises. Here alienation is expressed through the representation of the body and techniques of framing which "highlight[…] a new, hopeless, and narcissistic relationship to present 'hypermodernity'."

A fourth focus of this collection of essays is the critical reflection on "memory," "history," and "forgetting," to borrow from Paul Ricœur. Marion Kühn chooses three Quebec novels by Jocelyne Saucier, Jean-François Caron, and Carl Leblanc in order to explore the blurred boundaries between history and fiction with its destabilised and destabilising narrative instances, and between individual and collective memory. Crisis here means the non-accessibility of (historical) truth and the recognition of the "selective, constructed, and often even invented" (trans. U. Mathis-Moser) character of any narrative. In a similar way, Danielle Dumontet's analysis of a play by Wajdi Mouawad and a novel by Catherine Mavrikakis pays particular attention to the flaws of memory and the traumas of the so-called 'postmemory generation,' whether the final denouement is cathartic or not. Finally, Daniel Poitras undertakes a non-spatial, but temporally informed, reading of Jacques Poulin's *Volkswagen Blues* in which he comes to the disillusioned conclusion that "neither History nor an open future exist anymore."

The last group of essays assembled in this collection examines cultural conflicts within Canadian and Quebec society, highlighting literary affronts to state sanctioned multiculturalism, settler constructions of Indigenous life, or anti-immigrant discourse. Considering both the genre of the essay (Monique LaRue) and that of the novel (Abla Farhoud, Larry Tremblay), Hans-Jürgen Lüsebrink chooses a transgeneric approach to evoke the world-wide rise of fundamentalisms that undermine the ethical framework of respect, tolerance, and diversity and make it necessary "to rethink and reevaluate multiculturalism and interculturalism in the Canadian and Quebec contexts." A warning also comes from Srilata Ravi, who dedicates a case study to Gérard Bouchard's novel, *Uashat* (2009). Instead of "fill[ing] a gap in social science research," Ravi demonstrates, "well-intentioned compassion" towards the marginalized (Innus) gets "lost in the Eurocentric language of the novel" – an insight particularly valuable for all "practices of globalized compassion." Finally, Marion Christina Rohrleitner invites the reader to discover the rich field of Latina/o Canadian literature which she situates in a transnational context: She gives Canada the benefit of freeing this specific literary phenomenon from the narrow anti-immigrant perspective practiced in the US, thus allowing it to evolve in a transnational context of solidarity.

The sheer range of texts and genres analyzed in these pages goes to show the impact of the sense of crisis traversing Canadian and Quebec writing today, particularly works by Nelly Arcan, Margaret Atwood, Gérard Bouchard, Michel Marc Bouchard, Dionne Brand, Mario Brassard, Nicole Brossard, Jean-François Caron, Simone Chaput, Louise Dupré, Abla Farhoud, Monique LaRue, Carl Leblanc, Catherine Mavrikakis, Wajdi Mouawad, Jacques Poulin, Alfonso Quijada Urías, Nela Rio, Carmen Rodríguez, Jocelyne Saucier, Larry Tremblay, and filmmakers Xavier Dolan, Anne Émond, and Chloé Robichaud. Occasionally some of these authors receive the attention of several contributors, a sure indication of the profound range of critical reflection and approach these works incite.

Finally, this book ensues from the first of a two-part, bilingual (French-English), international conference held at the University of Innsbruck in Fall 2015, and organized by the Canadian Studies Centre (CSC) of the University of Innsbruck and the Canadian Literature Centre (CLC) of the University of Alberta. Both centres are marking milestones: the CEC celebrates its twentieth anniversary this year (2017) and the CLC has just feted its tenth year of existence (2016). This project as well as its focus, methodology, and objectives stand as a true testament to the rich and dynamic collaboration of these two research centres and the unwavering dedication they share to the advancement of Canadian studies and the role of literature as a vehicle for personal, collective, cultural, and social understanding and betterment.

Ursula Mathis-Moser – Marie Carrière
Innsbruck/Edmonton – Octobre/October 2017

Bibliographie/Bibliography

Berlant, Lauren: "Cruel Optimism." In: Gregg, Melissa / Seigworth, Gregory J. (eds): *The Affect Theory Reader*. Durham: Duke University Press, 2010, 93-117.

Braidotti, Rosi: *The Posthuman*. Cambridge, UK: Polity, 2013.

Braidotti, Rosi: *Le posthumain*. Fécamp: Nouvelles éditions lignes, 2016.

Brossard, Nicole: *L'horizon du fragment*. Paroisse Notre-Dame-des-Neiges: Trois-Pistoles, 2004.

Brown, Wendy: *Murs. Les murs de séparation et le déclin de la souveraineté étatique*. Trad. Nicolas Vieillescazes. Paris: Les Prairies ordinaires, 2009.

Brown, Wendy: *Walled States: Waning Sovereignty*. New York: Zone, 2010.

Dickner, Nicolas: *Tarmac*. Quebec: Alto, 2009.

Dickner, Nicolas: *Apocalypse for Beginners*. Translated by Lazer Lederhendler. Toronto: Vintage Canada, 2010.

Ette, Ottmar: "Literaturwissenschaft als Lebenswissenschaft – Eine Programmschrift im Jahr der Geisteswissenschaften." In: *Lendemains. Études comparées sur la France. Zeitschrift für vergleichende Frankreichforschung* 125 (2007), 7-32.

Ette, Ottmar: "Literature as Knowledge for Living, Literary Studies as Science for Living." Translated by Vera M. Kutzinski. In: *PMLA* 125,4 (2010), 977-993.

Kaplan, E. Ann: "Feminist Futures: Trauma, the Post-9/11 World and a Fourth Feminism?" In: *Journal of International Women's Studies* 4,2 (2003), 46-59.

Langelier, Nicolas: *Réussir son hypermodernité et sauver le reste de sa vie en 25 étapes faciles*. Montreal: Boréal, 2011.

Latour, Bruno: "Anthropology at the Time of the Anthropocene." Lecture at the American Association of Anthropologists conference. Washington, Nov. 2014, 1-16, http://www.bruno-latour.fr/sites/default/files/139-AAA-Washington.pdf (accessed 22/10/2017).

Massumi, Brian: "The Future Birth of the Affective Fact: The Political Ontology of Threat." In: Gregg, Melissa / Seigworth, Gregory J. (eds): *The Affect Theory Reader.* Durham: Duke University Press, 2010, 52-70.

Meurer, Ulrich / Oikonomou, Maria: "Fremdbilder – Aspekte geographischer und medialer Bewegung." In: Meurer, Ulrich / Oikonomou, Maria (eds): *Fremdbilder. Auswanderung und Exil im internationalen Kino.* Bielefeld: transcript Verlag, 2009, 9-33.

Puig de la Bellacasa, María: *Matters of Care: Speculative Ethics in More than Human Worlds.* Minneapolis: University of Minnesota Press, 2017.

Ricœur, Paul: *La mémoire, l'histoire, l'oubli.* Paris: Seuil, 2000.

Ricœur, Paul: *Memory, History, Forgetting.* Translated by Kathleen Blamey and David Pellauer. Chicago: The University of Chicago Press, 2004.

Viart, Dominique / Vercier, Bruno: *La littérature française au présent.* Paris: Bordas, ²2008.

Žižek, Slavoj: *Living in the End Times.* New York: Verso, 2010.

Žižek, Slavoj: *Vivre la fin des temps.* Traduit par Daniel Bismuth. Paris: Flammarion, 2011.

Apocalypse et dystopie
Apocalypse and Dystopia

Dunja M. MOHR (Erfurt)

Anthropocene Fiction: Narrating the 'Zero Hour' in Margaret Atwood's *MaddAddam* Trilogy

Résumé

Cet article se propose d'analyser comment la trilogie *MaddAddam* de Margaret Atwood raconte la crise, l'‹ heure zéro ›, ainsi qu'un éventuel avenir post-anthropocentrique. Dans un dialogue-*cum*-polylogue complexe, la trilogie passe de la création biotechnologique d'une apocalypse globale aux conséquences immédiates et à une période de transition, puis à une potentielle version utopique et à la cohabitation d'une variété d'espèces sur ce qui reste de la planète. La trilogie est lue comme l'exemple d'un sous-genre naissant de la fiction anthropocénique, c'est-à-dire d'une littérature essentiellement spéculative d'inspiration scientifique qui partage certaines caractéristiques avec les romans du changement climatique ainsi qu'avec la tradition utopique/dystopique. Elle propose une double vision relationnelle de l'opposition culture/nature : l'humain aurait changé et marqué la nature sur toute la planète, c'est-à-dire sur l'anthropocène ; il aurait également causé la transformation et la marchandisation de formes de vie au niveau moléculaire ainsi que la manipulation génétique des animaux, des humains et des post-humains. Le regard d'Atwood sur la crise du présent et sur les avenirs potentiels situés au-delà de l'opposition culture/nature suggère un ‹ post-humanisme hétérophorique › qui met l'accent sur la nécessité de penser le post humain à la fois dans l'avenir et dans le présent. Le récit d'Atwood d'un monde en crise met en relief le lien qui existe entre la survie, la narration et la compréhension de la nature comme réseau dont les humains sont partie prenante.

Dunja M. MOHR

> And although for us the End has perhaps lost its
> naïve *imminence*, its shadow still lies on the crises
> of our fictions; we may speak of it as *immanent*.
>
> (Kermode 2000, 6)

Speculating About the Anthropocene

For the longest time nature has been a fixed background scenario convenient for human existence and exploitation at a whim. However, lasting draughts, (flash) floods, global warming, and increased species extinction rates visibly document climate change caused by human interference. Recognizing the end of the Holocene, Nobel prize winning chemist Paul J. Crutzen and biologist Eugene Stoermer coined the term "Anthropocene" in 2000 to describe this "human dominance of biological, chemical and geological processes on Earth" (Crutzen/ Schwägerl 2011),[1] an impact similar to past epochal changes caused by volcanic eruptions, continent shifts, or a meteorite strike. In the 20th century human mass-exploitation and hyper-consumption, hyper-agriculture, deforestation, the spreading of waste, plastic, pesticides, radionuclides, and large-scale terraforming have left a technofossil stratigraphic geological signature, while biogenetics with synthetic life forms and changed human germlines change nature on a micro level. The (Western) modern tenet of a nature/culture divide has become obsolete: "It's no longer us against 'Nature' [...]. [I]n this new era, *nature is us*." (Crutzen/ Schwägerl 2011; my emphasis)[2] As historian Dipesh Chakrabarty rightly cautions, a more historic-cultural perspective reveals the uneven distribution of global vulnerabilities and responsibilities and the heterogeneity of the (technological) impact of some cultures – often knowingly accepting damaging long-term glocal implications for short-term individual or national profits – as well as the unequally distributed consequences for humanity and all life forms at large.[3]

How does fiction engage with these fundamental challenges? Twenty years ago environmental critic Lawrence Buell called for an ecocentric approach, as the "environmental crisis involves a crisis of imagination" that necessitates "finding better ways of imagining nature and humanity's relation to it" (1995, 2). While constructivism's use of "nature as an ideological theatre for acting out desires" (Buell 1995, 35) cannot address the mimetic crisis,[4] aesthetic representations of the Anthropocene – far from a "faithful mimesis of the object world" (Buell

1995, 84) – can approximate the experience of a post-anthropocentric world.[5] In his landmark study *Anthropocene Fictions* (2015) – which investigates roughly 150 climate change novels of the past 45 years grouped around the topics of (scientific) truth(s), place, politics, and 'eco-nomics' – Adam Trexler convincingly suggests the term 'Anthropocene Fiction' as it "emphasizes the emergence of its subject from a scientific theory [...] to a geological process" (2015, 5) and thus a historical fact, while the 20th century term 'climate fiction' points to a hypothetical future.

A hybrid genre by definition, speculative fiction critically engages with global economic, political, and religious crises, the (post-)apocalypse, climate change, and the potential outcome of bioengineered alterations of species, humans, and other life forms,[6] thus comprising 'cli fi,' solarpunk, Anthropocene fiction, and utopia/dystopia among others. Although sharing the interest in sciences with science fiction, speculative literature differs from generic sf's escapist technophile and anthropocentric inclination.[7] Anthropocene fictions widen the narrative scope by including "new *things* into preexisting genres" (Trexler 2015, 234), returning to the materiality of *all* existence, and imagining life *beyond* anthropocentrism that acknowledges posthuman or other bioform agency.

The Narrative Zero Hour in *MaddAddam*

The *MaddAddam* trilogy (2003-2013), which Atwood classifies as speculative or "ustopian" fiction combining utopian streaks into a dystopian narrative – "each contains a latent version of the other" (Atwood 2011, 66) – critically engages with our world in crisis, focusing on environmentalism, global warming, biotechnology/genetics, consumerism/capitalism, interspeciesism and, in short, undermines humanity's legitimizing claim of superiority over everything deemed non-human.[8] Set in what was the US, *Oryx and Crake* and *The Year of the Flood* narrate life before and during the apocalyptic crisis and its immediate aftermath that affects the whole planet in the near future of our 21st century, while *MaddAddam* focuses on the transition period of establishing a post-anthropocentric network of species. The first book links the privileged male narration (Jimmy/Snowman) predominantly with biogenetic manipulation and a narrative of 'anything goes,' the second book's alternating female voices (Toby and Ren) with victimization and resistance, and the last book increasingly with posthuman perspectives (Blackbeard).[9]

The pre-crisis society, run by neoliberal multinational corpocracies, presents a recognizable though hyperbolic contemporary Western society grounded in consumerist global hypercapitalism, segregation, and the commodification of all life forms reduced to material cut up, rearranged, transplanted, and abused at human whim. Essentially, the *MaddAddam* trilogy narrates how to save an overpopulated world from humanity "like a giant slug eating its way relentlessly through all the other bioforms on the planet" (Atwood 2004, 285), eerily matching thus Alan Weisman's non-fictional *The World Without Us* (2007) documenting a reversal to wilderness (filled with non-biodegradable rubble) of places such as Chernobyl where "life still goes on" (Weisman 2007, 214) and calling for a downsizing of human numbers. In Atwood's story the scientist Crake bioengineers hybrid posthumans (the peaceful Crakers) with 'downsized' needs, desires, aspirations, and resources to repopulate earth devoid of humans after a genetic pandemic Crake designed, the apocalyptic Waterless Flood the sectarian God's Gardeners prepare for in *The Year of the Flood,* connecting the secular apocalypse with the religious motif. Simultaneously more and less evolved, the Crakers' advantageous eco-friendly animal traits – symbolizing the interrelatedness of all life forms and the biosphere – aid their survival in a post-anthropocentric world. Co-evolution and cooperation are the only hope for the few human survivors.

Similar to the *fin de siècle*'s interest in scientific romances linked to the rise of technology, Darwinism, and Victorian degeneration theories, the millennium has sparked a rising (non-)fictional interest in the apocalypse, climate change, and biogenetics, disseminating sf tropes into the collective archive and creating a culture of planetary crisis.[10] Slavoj Žižek thus gloomily warns that

> the global capitalist system is approaching an apocalyptic zero point. Its "four riders of the apocalypse" are comprised by the ecological crisis, the consequences of the biogenetic revolution, imbalances within the system itself [...] and the explosive growth of social divisions and exclusions. (2010, x)[11]

While the Christian doctrine offers redemption after punishment, and many representations of the secular apocalypse skip salvation only to continue the fight against new oppressors and environmental dangers, Žižek sees the apocalypse's potential in its last stage when acceptance initializes an "emancipatory subjectivity" (2010, xii).[12] Addressing all four of Žižek's apocalyptic riders, the trilogy narrates first the very 'apocalyptic zero point,' where the protagonist-narrator Snowman, aka Jimmy, lives in and after the end of times, where civilization's measured time is irrelevant:

> Out of habit he looks at his watch – stainless-steel case [...] still shiny
> although it no longer works. He wears it now as his only talisman. A blank
> face is what it shows him: zero hour. It causes a jolt of terror [...], this
> absence of official time. (Atwood 2004, 3)

Oryx and Crake begins and ends with this collapse of time and civilization, yet while the zero hour of the first chapter marks the end of Jimmy's world and ushers in the post-apocalypse (and his 'rebirth' as Snowman), the zero hour of the last chapter promises a movement forward which the concluding volume then fulfils: "From habit he lifts his watch; it shows him its blank face. Zero hour [...]. Time to go." (Atwood 2004, 433) The zero hour, located in the "terror" of the timeless present, thus ambiguously points to the memory of the lost, "still shiny" measured civilized past – an ambiguity captured in the metaphor of the dysfunctional watch, a token of civilized time, turning into a talisman, a protective magical object, now signifying both the present and the past – and to the active *making* of the future, the necessity to leave the past behind and step out of timeless limbo. The watch acquires also a new function, when Snowman pretends that it establishes a magical contact with Crake: "He holds his watch up to the sky, turns it around on his wrist, then puts it to his ear as if listening to it." (Atwood 2004, 9) Like cultural time the concept of geological time is vanishing: "*Mesozoic.* He can see the word, he can hear the word, but he can't reach the word. He can't attach anything to it. [...] [T]his dissolution of meaning." (Atwood 2004, 43) However, by the end of the third book the ahistorical Crakers have acquired a mythological sense of time and learned the basics of recorded history. Clearly, the survival story is not about heroes, a return, or salvation, but about negotiating new social patterns and alliances along a post-anthropocentric 'pluriversality' (cf. Mignolo 2011, 175-176), giving voice to more species and unlearning human dominance.[13] The utopian element is then not "[t]o make his

[Crake's] perfect world" (Atwood 2013, 334) as Toby scathingly comments, but a post-anthropocentric world of a multitude of species and life forms.

What does it mean then to 'narrate the apocalyptic zero point'? In *The Sense of an Ending* (1967), Frank Kermode argues that humans use apocalyptic narratives to understand an imminent crisis – "inescapably a central element" (2000, 94) of our self-narrations – to provide a larger perspective, "the paradigms of apocalypse continue to lie under our ways of making sense of the world" (2000, 28).[14] The (post-)apocalypse, staple trope(s) of speculative fiction, connotes such a time of crisis, when time has run out and a pivotal historical event impacts on a previously unimaginable scale. The zero hour's *caesura* signifies thus first the fear of extinction or nothingness, secondly, the slim hope for a fresh start, and thirdly, the danger of a circular movement.[15] While much of speculative fiction focuses on a new order of human society, more egalitarian, inclusive, more ecology-minded, communal, and less violent, the *MaddAddam* series narrates all of that, but with a twist. The trilogy marks a desired (self-inflicted intentional) apocalyptic disaster intending a new planetary order *sans* humans (but with eco-friendly posthumans) to ensure the ravaged planet's survival, untangling it from the anthropocentric perspective, and ultimately aims at a larger planetary perspective of material connectivity.

This logic of (self-)erasure for an arguably positive purpose pervades 21st century culture, where zero has become a cultural fetish. De-growth concepts – such as zero growth population, economy[16], consumption, or carbon-emission that environmentalist Bill McKibben or ecologist Paul Ehrlich have promoted for decades and whose exigence Elizabeth Kolbert's recent *The Sixth Extinction* (2014) powerfully documents – pertain to a logic of global survival.[17] Yet on an individual level and in an age of Western decadent plenitude and opulence – brazenly looted from exploited developing countries – hyped cynical concepts of voluntary scarcity (e.g. 'Coke Zero' or 'size zero') are at worst life-threatening.[18] Schizophrenically, Western cultures then promote personal and attack large-scale zero consumption while lamenting zero's symbolism of catastrophe, apocalypse, mass extinction, and the end of civilization.

Initially, the trilogy's use of zero implies a *tabula rasa*, the notion of an ending, where life returns to an imaginary starting or end point.[19] In contradistinction to Kermode's *bonmot*, "[n]o longer imminent, the End is immanent" (2000, 25), Atwood not only narrates the crisis retrospectively from a post-apocalyptic perspective after the immanent end, but places the period of transition *after* instead of before the end, extrapolating an emerging post-anthropocentric order after crisis in the concluding book. Narrating the zero hour focuses here on the apocalyptic turning point and beyond. The trilogy's complex dialogue of apocalyptic and post-apocalyptic narratives, its insistent resistance to provide clear-cut dualism, its twisted plots and complex character motivations (e.g. Crake's nefarious elimination of humanity is also a deep ecology project to save the planet) refute critical claims that dismiss "apocalypticism" on the grounds of reinstating an "extreme moral dualism that divides the world sharply into friend and enemy" nested within "a trans-historical truth" (Garrard [2]2012, 94). *MaddAddam*'s ironic zero space implodes old binarisms, presenting new, if somewhat flawed, relational visions of a culturally/biogenetically changed nature, of transhuman animals, animal humans, and cross-over animal-streaked posthumans.

The mind-boggling potentially very real apocalyptic consequences of the Anthropocene – both elusively abstract (and therefore impalpable) and very concrete in their materiality (and therefore visible and perceptible all around us) – challenge literature into finding responses, making sense of an impending ending (cf. Kermode 2000), without walking into the anthropocentric trap. Giving narrative space to hybrid cross-species voices and other-than-human material realities to make sense of a global post-anthropocentric future is perhaps the greatest artistic challenge.

After the Anthropocene

In the Anglophone Canadian context, nature dominantly figures as an adversarial wilderness – epitomized by the omnipresent yet elusive North – that isolated humans or small communities struggle against. In the trilogy's pre-crisis society, nature is driven by adversarial biotechnology. Rising sea-levels have washed away the Eastern coastal cities, for lack of rain "the Everglades had burned for three weeks straight" (Atwood 2004, 72), and the "coastal aquifers turned salty and the northern permafrost melted and the vast tundra bubbled with methane, and the drought in the midcontinental plains regions went on and on, and the Asian steppes turned to sand dunes" (Atwood 2004, 27). The Anthropocene, as Chakrabarty cautioned, damages predominantly dystopia's "boundless," "porous," and "wide-open" pleeblands, "subject to chance" (Atwood 2004, 231), i.e. the compounds' wild experiments, or the city poor who suffer from pollution, diseases, and food scarcity. The protected corpocracy-run compounds consider nature a theme park providing life forms for (fun) experiments: the escaped "greenish glow[ing]" (Atwood 2004, 109) rabbits' overpopulation, genetically crossed with bioluminescent jellyfish, requires monitoring; out of control bobkittens attack dogs and babies. Without sufficient foresight, myopic humanity engages in uncontrollable biotech games; yet successful 'gaming' requires "parallel strategies: you had to see where you were headed *before* you got there" (Atwood 2004, 45; my emphasis), as Grandmaster Crake sardonically remarks.

"[T]o shut [...] down" this "whole system" (Atwood 2004, 254) of wilful bioform tampering, a guerrilla group of renegade scientists ironically called 'MaddAddam' creates counter bioforms: tar-eating microbes destroy highways; virus-carrying insects infect the epitome of animal objectification, the profitable headless units with multiple chicken parts called ChickieNobs; pesticide resistant insects and small animals interfere with the corpocracies' technologies. The group is also involved in "Extincathon, an interactive biofreak masterlore game" (Atwood 2004, 92), a sardonic extinction marathon showing where the Anthropocene is heading, that unravels history, evolution, and Christianity backwards: "*Monitored by MaddAddam. Adam named the living animals, MaddAddam names the dead ones. Do you want to play?*" (Atwood 2004, 92) Instead of just cataloguing extinct life forms, Crake, a compulsive player, changes the game: "*Adam named the animals. MaddAddam customizes them*" (Atwood 2004, 253), and designs the Crakers as a peaceful human replacement.[20] To end the cycle of violence, Crake (and unwittingly the MaddAddamites aid his ultimate game, the 'Paradice Project') seeks to 'restore' the world to a natureculture neo-prelapsarian state with his superbug, the BlyssPluss Pill, clearing the space for posthumans:

> [T]he end of a species was taking place before his [Jimmy's] very eyes. Kingdom, Phylum, Class, Order, Family, Genus, Species. [...] *Homo sapiens sapiens*, joining the polar bear, the beluga whale, the onager [...], the long, long list. [...] [C]hannel after channel went dead. A couple of the anchors [...] set the cameras to film their own deaths – the screams, the dissolving skins, the ruptured eyeballs and all. (Atwood 2004, 401)

Humankind and not (abused and biogenetically recombined) nature is the source of humanity's downfall.

The cynical internet games Jimmy and Crake play illustrate this wilful abuse of materiality as they re-enact the collective human history of violence and stress the arbitrariness of anthropocentrism, always excluding some from the category of the human. Barbarian Stomp pitches civilization against barbarism, but tellingly allows reversed perspectives: By choice the "Aztecs […] represented civilization, while the Spaniards were the barbarian hordes" (Atwood 2004, 89). The "cosmic" "trading game" (Atwood 2004, 89) Blood and Roses pits atrocities against "human achievements, Artwork, scientific breakthroughs […], helpful inventions" (Atwood 2004, 90). Prophetically, "the Blood player usually won, but […] inherited a wasteland" (Atwood 2004, 91), just as the human Blood players' violation of material reality has begun to create the zero space Crake precipitates. From this perspective, the Crakers are the last pitch of the Roses, a "helpful invention" to ensure the survival of the planet and of human elements. In contrast, the websites Jimmy and Crake visit showcase the individual violated body in pain. The killing sites, live executions, electrocutions, body punishments, assisted suicides (hedsoff.com, alibooboo.com, shortcircuit.com, brainfrizz.com, deathrowlive.com, nitee-nite.com), voyeuristic life-recordings ("At Home With Anna K."; Atwood 2004, 96-97), or sex shows mirror human abjection and depravity as decadent entertainment.

In many ways a human version of the Craker project – sharing the vegetarianism, the color blue (clothes), a cooperative approach, communal singing, and a respectful ecological view – the ecology-driven, science-friendly God's Gardeners *cum* MaddAddamites of *The Year of the Flood* offer a more balanced and reconciliatory attitude to nature and science: "By covering such barren rooftops with greenery we are doing our small part in the redemption of God's creation from the decay and sterility that lies all around us […]. [I]f all were to follow our example, what a change would be wrought on our beloved Planet!" (Atwood 2009, 11) The Gardeners' ritual openings of sermons – "Dear Friends, dear Fellow Creatures, dear Fellow Mammals" (Atwood 2009, 11), "Dear Friends and Fellow Mortals" (Atwood 2009, 89) – point to the post-anthropocentric approach the new post-apocalyptic community of *MaddAddam* must practice to ensure survival. The Gardeners stress human responsibility and the link of life, yet remain within an anthropocentric narrative frame:

> God has given Adam free will [...]. [T]he Names of the Animals were the first words he spoke – the first moment of Human language. In this cosmic instant, Adam claims his Human soul. To Name is – we hope – to greet; to draw another towards one's self [...] [in] loving-kindness and kinship[...]. [That day was] a peaceful gathering at which every living entity on the Earth was embraced by Man. (Atwood 2009, 12-13)

Despite their claim to bioform-equality, the Gardeners struggle with their own human heritage. Reminiscent of the famous quote from Orwell's *Animal Farm* (1945), "All animals are equal but some animals are more equal than others" (2004, 57), the Gardeners' hierarchy satirically allegorizes Christian double standards far from equality: "Adam One insisted that all Gardeners were equal on the spiritual level, but the same did not hold true for the material one: the Adams and the Eves ranked higher." (Atwood 2009, 45)

The post-apocalyptic world is not a new Garden Eden, but an "endless crumbling" (Atwood 2004, 50) of human-made things, a heap of "assorted rubble" (Atwood 2004, 3), where the "sea is hot metal, the sky a bleached blue [...]. Everything is so empty" (Atwood 2004, 13). This legacy of useless things is matched by erased words and concepts devoid of meaning, the "blank spaces in his [Snowman's] stub of a brain, where memory used to be" (Atwood 2004, 5), "the burning scrapbook in his head" (Atwood 2004, 11). In this new world Jimmy's education is useless: "What are all those things he once thought he knew, and where have they gone?" (Atwood 2004, 175) The Crakers have neither use nor a cultural reference point for the beachcombed objects, "a hubcap, a piano key, a chunk of pale-green pop bottle [...]. A plastic BlyssPluss container, empty; a ChickiNobs Bucket O'Nubbins [...]. A computer mouse [...]. [T]ins of motor oil, caustic solvents, plastic bottles of bleach. Booby traps from the past" (Atwood 2004, 7). Instead, things acquire new usage, a "dirty bedsheet" (Atwood 2004, 4) becomes a toga and "ribs of a broken umbrella" (Atwood 2004, 386) turn into pens.

Snowman's lost map, useless in this changed environment, signifies humanity's disorientation in a post-anthropocentric world. Sheltering from a burning sun or afternoon storms with "hailstones as big as golf balls" (Atwood 2004, 49) and searching for food become Snowman's preoccupations. Oblivious to human fate, nature proves its unwavering capacity for adaptation, where civilizational ruins are "overgrown [with] shrubbery" (Atwood 2004, 109), the ocean washes over "tower blocks," and rivers "semi-flood [...] townhouses" (Atwood 2004, 174). Snowman's exasperated scream "'You did this!'" (Atwood 2004, 11) – directed both at the ocean and dead Crake as a proxy of humanity – receives "[n]o answer [...]. Only the waves, wish-wash, wish-wash" (Atwood 2004, 13). Denying human responsibility, Snowman blames nature, the "punishing sun" (Atwood 2004, 6). And his lame excuse, "Things happened, I had no idea, it was out of my control! What could I have done?" (Atwood 2004, 50-51), painfully mirrors contemporary individual and national cop outs from Anthropocene realities. Similarly, Zeb regrets in hindsight having taught Crake hacking and coding, giving him "the keys to the kingdom – the Open Sesames, the back doors, the shortcuts [...]. [A]nd who was to foresee the consequences" (Atwood 2013, 238). Snowman's broken sunglasses with "[o]ne lens [...] missing" (Atwood 2004, 4) epitomize humanity's failure to look at the whole picture. With natural and transgenic animals roaming the former cities, Snowman must acutely prepare to fight off predators, the rummaging highly intelligent pigoons, the prowling wolvogs, and the sniffling rakunks. His environment is filled with animal sounds, chirpings, croaking, whirring, and the sounds of vegetation, wind, rain, and the Crakers' ambiguously "old carboniferous [...] [and] newborn, fragant, verdant" (Atwood 2004, 122) singing. While the new world is chaotic and unpredictable for him, Snowman-the-prophet reinterprets the pre-crisis world from a post-anthropocentric perspective for the Crakers as a chaotic circle of killing and eating animals to which the newly deified Crake and Oryx put an end, "*Let us get rid of the chaos*" (Atwood 2004, 119), installing "the Great Rearrangement" and the "Great Emptiness" (Atwood 2004, 119). Ironically, Crake's Paradice Project involves both a rehumanization in a post-anthropocentric ethical sense and a selective reanimalization catapulting posthumans into a pre-human state. To eradicate violence, Crake aims at destroying human creativity and thus technology, science, art, and religion. Providing the Crakers with an origin myth and teaching the Craker Blackbeard how to read, write, and use language creatively – to record but also manipulate history – Jimmy and later Toby allow the Crakers to reenter the symbolic order, story-telling, and myth-making, yet the Crakers' non-invasive, non-violent culture appears to countercheck any destructive streak.

The posthumans increasingly take over the narrative perspective and story-making in *MaddAddam*: Blackbeard tells the last part of the chapter "Eggshell" and the following chapter "Moontime" alternates between his and the human perspective. He exclusively narrates the last chapter "Book," inheriting the role of historian and storyteller at last. True to the ritual, he puts on the storyteller's 'Red Sox baseball cap,' but instead of eating the fish, he quickly "take[s] it out again" (Atwood 2013, 357), having sufficiently violated the vegan Craker principle in the name of narrative mightiness, "First the bad things, then the story." (Atwood 2013, 358) The only symbolic hunger the Crakers know of is their craving for (ethically sound) stories. In his narrative segments, Blackbeard tells of "the Battle" (Atwood 2013, 358) between the alliance of pigoons, Crakers, and humans against the two remaining Painballers, the epitomes of human violence;[21] of the Painballers' trial for slaughtering and eating two piglets; and how pigoons and humans agree on mutual respect for each culture's necessities. In both the battle and the trial, the Crakers refrain from violence, a concept incomprehensible to them. Empathic even with the Painballers, the Crakers consider trials unnecessary for their folk. Blackbeard also explains the process of writing and reading; he narrates of Kannon-the-Oryx (the Japanese goddess of mercy) and of the Rhizomes-the-Roots, which he takes literally as plant roots, but which also references Deleuze's and Guattari's rhizomatic model of culture, rejecting monocausal origin or chronology and favoring the nomadic "interbeing" or "intermezzo" of unspecific origins.[22] The names of the hybrid Craker-human progeny of multiple parentage, Jimadam, Pilaren, and the twins Medulla and Oblongata, indicate exactly such a new cultural 'interbeing'.[23] As humans recede, the older generation is mythologized but leaves a legacy of interspeciesism: "[W]e [the Crakers] and the two-skinned ones are all people and helpers, though we have different gifts, and some of us turn blue and some do not." (Atwood 2013, 386) While the Crakers cautiously step into culture and subjectivity – they "look behind the mirrors; then […] they realize the people are themselves" (Atwood 2013, 281) – pigoons and humans learn mutual respect, and humans recognize being part of nature's networks.

Heterophoric Posthumanism

Such narratives that cast one eye to a post-anthropocentric *cum* posthuman future and the other to the contemporary biogenetic potentials and their material realities – while negating a popular posthumanism aimed at superelevating humans to perfection or transhumanist digitalization and disembodiment claims –

essentially practice what I suggest to call a *heterophoric posthumanism*.[24] Just as Anthropocene fiction deals with climate change as a historical fact on the planetary macro level, heterophoric posthumanism suggests the reality of changed human nature on the micro level and explores what we need to turn into in relation to other life forms and the sharing of sustainable environments. Such a heterophoric posthumanism could provide the creative leap Rosi Braidotti has called for, moving "forward into the complexities and paradoxes of our times" (2013, 54) in the spirit of post-anthropocentrism, reconnecting the humanities with science and technology, and counteracting a "contemporary bio-genetic capitalism," instead installing "a global form of reactive mutual inter-dependence of all living organisms, including non-humans" (2013, 49).

The *MaddAddam* trilogy employs such a heterophoric posthumanism and narrates the Self's "process of becoming-minoritarian" (Braidotti 2013, 53). In answer to the disturbing question, "What comes after the anthropocentric subject?" (Braidotti 2013, 58), it valorizes the mash-up of species not in terms of human domination and interference, but as a necessary step towards recognizing humankind's evolutionary sharing. Multiple origins link the Crakers with animals and humans (and science), exemplifying the "multiple belongings" (Braidotti 2013, 49) the anthropocentric worldview represses. From a heterophoric posthumanist perspective, the Crakers epitomize perhaps less a perfect human replacement than a changed human nature and therefore altered cultural desires. As the last book's cohabitation of species and co-evolution ('natureculture' in Donna Haraway's sense, 2003) illustrates, global survival necessitates a move beyond anthropocentrism. If the posthuman embodies the "alternative representations of the subject as a *dynamic non-unitary* subjectivity" (Braidotti 2013, 164; my emphasis), the Crakers' initial representation as narrative 'we' suggests a collective subjectivity, while the telepathic communication with the transgenic human neocortex-wired, intelligent pigoons indicates a multifarious connectivity. In *MaddAddam* multiple paternal origins of the new human-posthuman hybrid offspring (with Craker and human fourfathers) illustrate a step into that direction. While Snowman, the "doomed protagonist" (Atwood 2004, 123) from the past, remains outside the Craker mating circle in the first book, humans become part of the circle in *MaddAddam*. A network of species, respect for nature and the Other, communication and cooperation are the pillars of Atwood's post-anthropocentric world where humans share intelligence with other species and learn to appreciate other biological/animal conditions. Her heterophoric posthumanism is less interested in the elimination of the biological body through science or in valorizing and enhancing human intelligence than merging a mindful technology with a life-respecting, sustainable ethics that refrains from turning the Other into an object. "*Her* back. The Pigoons were not objects. She had to get that right. It was only respectful" (Atwood 2013, 351), Toby muses. Atwood's narration illustrates how difficult such an ethic is. We only get the pigoons' perspective via Blackbeard's telepathic translation; the narration keeps objectifying the pigoons or other animals ('it'); and the remaining humans joke about the Crakers' limited intelligence and cultural habits, doubting their human status, and belittle the pigoons. Just as the trilogy began with a human male point of view, it ends with a male Craker voice. We get Blackbeard's male perspective, not a Craker chorus or various Craker perspectives, despite the concluding ritual singing. The ustopian possibilities of the postanthropocentric world are imaginable, but obviously hard to narrate. As much as Anthropocene fiction widens the discursive space of a globally oriented, heterogeneous, twenty-first-century speculative fiction – already embracing diverse ethnic, cultural, and other interrogations of reality – to include post-anthropocentric voices, it necessarily must struggle with politics of representation: How to narrate non-human animal characters' perspectives? Atwood's use of mediatory agents (the Crakers) to access such mental states – reminiscent of critical anthropomorphism but substituting hypothesizing with blurred translations that prevent human *knowing* – requires the readers' readiness for a cognitive empathy of approximation that willingly and imaginatively expands ethics to non-human animals and nature in a relational way. Such narrative opacity disrupts an anthropocentric narrative discourse, rejecting human appropriation of the non-human animal's discourse, ultimately expressing a "postmelancholic anthropomorphism" (Danta 2013, 85) that uncouples non-human animal identity/agency from human agency.

Speculative fiction's cognitive estrangement steers us then towards questioning the anthropocentric bias of narrations and, like heterophoric posthumanism, directs one eye to the fictional future and the other to the material realities of relationality. A twenty-first-century understanding of speculation fiction – not as a distinct generic marker but as a porous term for a broad non-mimetic (cultural) field in Pierre Bourdieu's sense – posits us thus on the threshold between fiction and reality. As fictional and real time scales coalesce, speculative anticipations of future potentialities and real repercussions in a present held hostage by an increasingly dominant future indicate perhaps less a "crisis of imagination" (Buell 1995, 2) than fuzzy boundaries. Such coalescences of fiction and speculation with reality we already see realized in the no longer distinct terms of culture and nature, in the Anthropocene, the post-biological set-up of (post)humans, and in economics, as Joseph Vogl has cogently traced in his literary rendition of economic history and theory in *Das Gespenst des Kapitals* (2010), where fiction as speculation influences the supposedly rational logic of finances, in fact based on utter irrationality in an autopoietic loop. Ever since the dissolution of the Bretton Woods system, an unreliable future has replaced materiality and the economic system relies on risk speculations about the future, ultimately investing in hope.[25] Where the desire for 'taming the time' ("die Zähmung der Zeit"; Vogl 2014, 109; trans. D. Mohr)[26] permeates the material world, narration shapes the perception of time. In other words, if we transfer this autopoietic loop of investing in hope to Anthropocene fictions' narratives of risks speculation and crises, the *MaddAddam* trilogy futurizes a post-anthropocentric discourse beyond the human subject based on the speculative belief in a present beyond crisis: We invest in hope as we narrate.

1   In 2016 the International Commission on Stratigraphy has declared the Anthropocene epoch.

2   The eco-minded Gardeners's lifestyle in *MaddAddam* meets Crutzen's and Schwägerl's three approaches to dealing with the Anthropocene's challenges: First, a "mindful, and less material lifestyle"; second, a staunch turn to renewable energies, "bioadaptive waste," recycling, a "green infrastructure" for biodiversity and "bioeconomy"; and third, a cultural adaptation that recognizes humans as part of an eco-network in Humboldt's sense of a "world organism" (Crutzen/Schwägerl 2011). The suggested "shift […] from crusade to management," however, caters to the anthropocentric Christian 'stewardship,' while the proposed move from "enslaving the formerly natural world" (Crutzen/Schwägerl 2011) to a symbiotic coexistence correlates with the trilogy's interspecies alliance.

3   Climate change, Dipesh Chakrabarty writes, "spell[s] the [recent] collapse of the age-old humanist distinction between natural history and human history" (2009, 201) and is profoundly linked with specifically located global capital, a responsibility

which the "all-inclusive terms [...] *species* or *mankind*" obliterate (2009, 216). For Chakrabarty, the impending universal catastrophe necessitates "a global approach to politics without the myth of a *global identity*" (2009, 222; my emphasis).

4   For an excellent overview of ecocriticisms, cf. Greg Garrard's "Introduction" in *The Oxford Handbook of Ecocriticism* (2014).

5   Discussing the 'scaling strategies' in Ian McEwan's *Solar* (2010), Maggie Gee's *The Flood* (2005), and Indra Sinha's *Animal's People* (2007), Roman Bartosch argues for a transcultural world literature "as a semiotic force" to address "the challenges of complexity posed by the Anthropocene" (2015, 67) that respects fiction's need to diversify into "global, national and individual dimensions" (2015, 69).

6   Critical posthumanists emphasize that a "new alliance between the arts and the sciences" (Braidotti 2013, 183) can provide the badly needed critical framework to counterbalance the too often anthropocentric and technophile approach of life sciences. A number of special exhibitions have addressed the human intermeshing with nature and human collective responsibilities, juxtaposing planetary and human-made socio-political-cultural-economic history in such an alliance of artistic and scientific terms. Cf. the interdisciplinary *Anthropocene Project,* including an Anthropocene Campus, at the Haus der Kulturen der Welt in Berlin (2013-2014); the Serpentine Galleries' two day forum *Extinction: Visions of the Future Marathon* in London in October 2014 that created a dialogue between writers, film-makers, activists, scientists, and theorists with installations, performances, films, and talks; or the *Welcome to the Anthropocene: The Earth in Our Hands* exhibition at the Deutsche Museum in Munich (2014-2016). In response to the planet in crisis, it is then the artist's role as the 'prophet of visions of futures' (cf. Manemann 2014, 11-13) to narrate, paint, perform, or videotape the end and beyond in response to pressing questions, such as: What happens after mass extinction? "[W]ho and what [are] we [...] actually in the process of becoming?" (Braidotti 2013, 12)

7   Trexler's assertion that the "Anthropocene challenges science fiction's technological optimism, general apathy towards life sciences, and patriotic individualism" (2015, 15), however, disregards a bulk of classical sf texts, such as Frank Herbert's soft sf *Dune* saga (1965-1985); Joan Slonczewski's ecofeminist *A Door Into Ocean* (1986), the first of the Elysium cycle series (1986-2000); or Kim Stanley Robinson's *Mars* trilogy (1993-1996); that critically engage in future terraforming, climate change, species cooperation, genetic engineering, and human evolution.

8   The first of the two epigraphs in *Oryx and Crake*, taken from Jonathan Swift's *Gulliver's Travels*, 'grounds' the series in reality: "I could perhaps like others have astonished you with *strange improbable tales*; but I rather chose to relate *plain matter of fact* in the simplest manner and style; because my principal design was *to inform you*, and not to amuse you." (Atwood 2004; my emphasis)

9   From a Genetteian vantage point, narrating the zero hour might presuppose a zero focalization, an omniscient narrator, yet the *MaddAddam* trilogy branches out into polyperspectivism, intertwined narrations, zooming in and out of focalizers.

10   Brett Josef Grubisic, Gisèle M. Baxter, and Tara Lee diagnose an "Apocalypse Industry" (2014, 1) and list over twenty books concerned with the apocalypse, as well as multiple websites, TV shows, films, and commodities (cf. Grubisic/Baxter/Lee 2014, 1-4; 18, fn 3).

11   Drawing on Elizabeth Kübler-Ross's grief theory, Žižek sees the collective consciousness responding to catastrophe in the five classical stages of grief: denial, anger, bargaining, depression, and acceptance. We move from "ideological denial" to "anger at the injustices of the new world order" to bargaining for very small changes to hopefully keep things as they are, to "depression and withdrawal," "the zero point," until "the subject no longer perceives the situation as a threat, but as the chance of a new beginning" (Žižek 2010, xi-xii). While the first two books address the fourth stage, *MaddAddam* deals largely with the fifth stage.

12   Terry Gilliam's *12 Monkeys* (1995) or Andy and Larry Wachowski's *The Matrix* (1999) are prime examples of the abundant post-apocalyptic films where the respective heroes save humanity from a human-induced crisis – e.g. a pandemic virus (*12 Monkeys*), or intelligent machines (*The Matrix*) – aiming at a re-installation of human superiority.

13   The trilogy extends Walter Mignolo's anthropocentric call for reducing Western civilization and paradigms to "one among many options" (2011, 176) within postcolonial discourses to the species level, where humanity is *one*, but not the dominant option. If "[p]luriversality means unlearning […] modernity" (Mignolo 2011, 176) and thus a negation of all universals (except for a universal pluriversality), post-anthropocentric narrations must decenter humans' narrative focus and envision multispecies societies.

14   Frank Kermode argues that "[a]pocalypse depends on a concord of imaginatively recorded past and imaginatively predicted future" (2000, 8) in order to narrate (literary) endings and thus transformation (cf. Kermode 2000, 5-6). However, as Kermode writes in his analysis of biblical and other texts, we "in the midst" (2000, 17) too often

get stuck in between what he calls the *saeculum* and the end, a period he calls the "myth [...] of transition" (2000, 12).

15 Criticizing Christianity's claim to human dominion over earth, the trilogy foregrounds the apocalyptic Christian motif. The Lacanian or Sartre's zero as 'nothingness' would be equated with being, the 'être-pour-soi' aka consciousness, pointing to atheism; in Buddhism nothingness as emptiness (*Sunyata*) describes a desirable mental state of intense focusing geared towards transcendence.

16 For a recent Canadian perspective on (unlikely) economic de-growth, e.g. the Canadian Low Grow simulation model to cut carbon emissions, cf. Peter A. Victor (2011).

17 McKibben was among the first to address irrevocable climate change and global warming. In *The End of Nature* (1989) he describes the levelling of the formerly oppositional human-nature correlation, where nature is increasingly a human-driven force that returns the negative effects of human (ab)use of nature. This notion of the ongoing blending of nature and culture has branched out into new materialism, e.g. Karen Barad's famous (albeit in a sense notorious) claim that humans "*are a part of that nature*" (2007, 26) and participate in its (and their own) shaping from a position of immersion, and the shared concern of ecocriticism, critical animal studies, and posthumanism about the blurred boundaries of organic/inorganic, human/animal, and nature/culture, e.g. in Donna Haraway's seminal "A Cyborg Manifesto" (1985/1991) and her co-evolutionary 'natureculture' concept in *The Companion Species Manifesto* (2003).

18 Zero signifies absence and emptiness and can take an inferior place in the numerical and symbolic order. "It takes two to make a binary," the British cultural theorist Sadie Plant wrote in her gender critical study of technoculture, *Zeros + Ones*, linking the binary code with past (but still prevalent) gender models based on binary gender differences that associate women with Zero, the void or "gap, a space" waiting to be filled, and men with One, because "one is everything" (1998, 35). While fashion's size zero asks annihilation of women, 'bloke coke's' Coke Zero is gender-targeted at young male consumers as a reward for tough guys. For the connection between food pathology, gender, and creativity, cf. Isabelle Meuret's analysis of writing processes linked with the self-starvation epidemic in the 21st century in *Writing Size Zero* (2007).

19 In the light of post-9/11 narrations, the 'zero hour' also recalls 'Ground Zero,' the locus of the most devastating destruction after an explosion, which has become shorthand for the former World Trade Centre site reduced to a pile of rubble, despite its actual 'filling' with a memorial and the One World Trade Centre.

20 "All the real Gardeners believed the human race was overdue for a population crash. It would happen anyway, and maybe sooner was better." (Atwood 2013, 330)

21 Deemed "not quite human" (Atwood 2013, 368), stripped of language and cultural, ethical restraints, the Painballers represent humanity reverted *beyond* animality, killing for pleasure and not out of necessity.

22 "A rhizome has no beginning or end; it is always in the middle, between things, interbeing, intermezzo." (Deleuze/Guattari 1987, 25) Toby, who teaches Blackbeard about plants and reading and writing, represents this link between humans and earth: "Her own hands [...] stiff and brown, like roots." (Atwood 2009, 16)

23 I have explained elsewhere the twin's names referencing "the oldest and basic (reptilian) part of the central nervous system that connects body and brain, linking the brainstem and the spinal cord and dealing with autonomous functions" (Mohr 2015, 295) as a critique of old-fashioned Cartesian thinking.

24 My use of *heterophoric* is not based on Ian Watt's (1960) interpretation of Joseph Conrad's *The Shadow Line* (1916) that distinguishes between an external 'heterophoric' and an intrinsic 'homeophoric' *interpretation*, but on a textual reaching beyond the present that is simultaneously grounded in its materiality. *Heterophoric* stresses here the necessity to simultaneously locate the posthuman in the future *and* the present.

25 As Vogl (2010, 94) explains, speculation and fiction replace a reality-based economy: "Jemand, der eine Ware nicht hat [...], verkauft diese Ware an jemanden, der diese Ware ebenso wenig erwartet [...] und auch tatsächlich nicht bekommt" ("Somebody who doesn't have a product [...], sells this product to somebody, who likewise doesn't expect this product [...] and indeed never receives it"; trans. D. Mohr), creating what he calls "Wertgespenster" (2010, 157; "ghosts of value"; trans. D. Mohr).

26 Vogl (2014, 109) speaks here of the "transformation of uncertainty in predictability" ("Transformation von Ungewissheiten in Erwartbarkeiten"; trans. D. Mohr).

Bibliography

Atwood, Margaret: *Oryx and Crake*. London: Virago, 2004 [2003].

Atwood, Margaret: *The Year of the Flood*. London: O.W. Toad, 2009.

Atwood, Margaret: *In Other Worlds: SF and the Human Imagination*. Toronto: McClelland & Stewart, 2011.

Atwood, Margaret: *MaddAddam*. London: Bloomsbury, 2013.

Barad, Karen: *Meeting the Universe Halfway: Quantum Physics and the Entanglement of Matter and Meaning*. Durham: Duke University Press, 2007.

Bartosch, Roman: "The Climate of Literatures: English Studies in the Anthropocene." In: *Anglistik* 26,2 (2015), 59-70.

Braidotti, Rosi: *The Posthuman*. Cambridge: Polity, 2013.

Buell, Lawrence: *The Environmental Imagination: Thoreau, Nature Writing, and the Formation of American Culture*. Cambridge: Harvard University Press, 1995.

Chakrabarty, Dipesh: "The Climate of History: Four Theses." In: *Critical Inquiry* 35,2 (2009), 197-222.

Crutzen, Paul J. / Stoermer, Eugene F.: "The 'Anthropocene'." In: *International Global Change Newsletter* 41 (2000), 17-18.

Crutzen, Paul J. / Schwägerl, Christian: "Living in the Anthropocene: Toward a New Global Ethos." In: *Yale Environment 360* (2011), http://e360.yale.edu/feature/living_in_the_anthropocene_toward_a_new_global_ethos/2363/ (accessed 20/04/2016).

Danta, Chris: "The New Solitude: Melancholy Anthropomorphism and the Molecular Gaze." In: *English Studies in Canada* 39,1 (2013), 71-86.

Deleuze, Gilles / Guattari, Félix: *A Thousand Plateaus: Capitalism and Schizophrenia*. Translated by Brian Massumi. Minneapolis: University of Minneapolis Press, 1987.

Garrard, Greg: *Ecocriticism*. London: Routledge, ²2012.

Garrard, Greg: "Introduction." In: Garrard, Greg (ed.): *The Oxford Handbook of Ecocriticism*. Oxford: Oxford University Press, 2014, 1-26.

Grubisic, Brett Josef / Baxter, Gisèle M. / Lee, Tara: "Introduction." In: Grubisic, Brett Josef / Baxter, Gisèle M. / Lee, Tara (eds): *Blast, Corrupt, Dismantle, Erase: Contemporary North American Dystopian Literature*. Waterloo: Wilfrid Laurier University Press, 2014, 1-26.

Haraway, Donna: *Simians, Cyborgs, and Women: The Reinvention of Nature*. New York: Routledge, 1991.

Haraway, Donna: *The Companion Species Manifesto: Dogs, People, and Significant Otherness*. Chicago: Prickly Paradigm, 2003.

Kermode, Frank: *The Sense of an Ending: Studies in the Theory of Fiction*. Oxford: Oxford University Press, 2000 [1967].

Kolbert, Elizabeth: *The Sixth Extinction: An Unnatural History*. London: Bloomsbury, 2014.

Manemann, Jürgen: *Kritik des Anthropozäns: Plädoyer für eine neue Humanökologie*. Bielefeld: Transcript, 2014.

Mayer, Sylvia: "Literary Studies, Ecofeminism, and the Relevance of Environmentalist Knowledge Production in the Humanities." In: Gersdorf, Catrin / Mayer, Sylvia (eds): *Nature in Literary and Cultural Studies: Transatlantic Conversations on Ecocriticism*. Amsterdam: Rodopi, 2006, 111-128.

McKibben, Bill: *The End of Nature*. New York: Random, 1989.

Meuret, Isabelle: *Writing Size Zero: Figuring Anorexia in Contemporary World Literatures*. Brussels: Peter Lang, 2007.

Mignolo, Walter D.: *The Darker Side of Western Modernity: Global Futures, Decolonial Options*. Durham: Duke University Press, 2011.

Mohr, Dunja M.: "Eco-Dystopia and Biotechnology: Margaret Atwood, *Oryx and Crake* (2003), *The Year of The Flood* (2009) and *MaddAddam* (2013)." In: Voigts, Eckart / Boller, Alessandra (eds): *Dystopia, Science Fiction, Post-Apocalypse: Classics, New Tendencies and Model Interpretations*. Trier: wvt, 2015, 283-302.

Orwell, George: *Animal Farm*. [s.i.], 2004 [1945], https://wikispooks.com/wiki/File:Animal_Farm.pdf (accessed 24/04/2016).

Plant, Sadie: *Zeros + Ones: Digital Women + the New Technoculture*. London: Fourth Estate, 1998.

Rozelle, Lee: "Liminal Ecologies in Margaret Atwood's *Oryx and Crake*." In: *Canadian Literature* 206 (2010), 61-72.

Trexler, Adam: *Anthropocene Fictions: The Novel in a Time of Climate Change*. Charlottesville: University of Virginia Press, 2015.

Victor, Peter A.: "Growth, Degrowth and Climate Change: A Scenario Analysis." In: *Ecological Economics* (2011), doi:10.1016/j.ecolecon.2011.04.013 (accessed 27/01/2016).

Vogl, Joseph: *Das Gespenst des Kapitals*. Zürich: Diaphanes, 2010.

Vogl, Joseph: "Im Sog der Zeit. Ein Gespräch zwischen Joseph Vogl und Philipp Ekardt über Spekulation." In: *Texte zur Kunst: Spekulation/Speculation* 93 (03/2014), 109-126, https://www.textezurkunst.de/93/im-sog-der-zeit/ (accessed 18/11/2016).

Watt, Ian: "Story and Idea in Conrad's *The Shadow Line*." In: *Critical Quarterly* 2,2 (1960), 133-148.

Weisman, Alan: *The World Without Us*. New York: Thomas Dunne, 2007.

Žižek, Slavoj: *Living in the End Times*. New York: Verso, 2010.

Nicole CÔTÉ (Sherbrooke)

Nouvelles représentations de la crise dans les littératures québécoise et canadienne

Summary

The representation of crisis seems to have undergone a major change in twenty-first century Canadian literature. The Apocalypse pattern that, according to Marlene Goldman, structured many Canadian fictions, offering a temporal map of a world in search of meaning, is much less common. The fictional works as well as the critical articles studied here show that there is very little of that temporal map left, characters seeming to be walled into a repetitive present. The general feeling is that the only action left is to bear testimony to various crises. The fictions studied in this essay – one Anglo-Canadian (Dionne Brand's *Ossuaries*), one Franco-Canadian (Simone Chaput's *Un vent prodigue*), and one Franco-Quebecker (Nelly Arcan's *À ciel ouvert*) – are written from that perspective. Each work offers a diagnostic on the planet and its inhabitants from a Canadian or Quebec viewpoint, but situating it on a world map with the motifs that they share.

Or, si l'imaginaire de la fin contemporain se détache de ses prédécesseurs […], c'est bien dans la multiplication et la réitération des situations de crise, provoquant une mutation fondamentale de son dynamisme même. C'est notre conception du temps qui en ressort perturbée. (Gervais 2009, 212)

Introduction et cadre théorique

Les littératures canadiennes, dont celle du Québec, ont été, dès les débuts de la colonie et comme l'a montré Atwood (*Survival*), préoccupées par la survie. De fait, Marlene Goldman (*Rewriting Apocalypse*, 2005) affirme que, dès la seconde moitié du 20e siècle, les auteurs canadiens, pour représenter les diverses crises qui ont secoué cette période, ont repensé la tradition de l'Apocalypse depuis le récit biblique, où un monde ancien corrompu est remplacé par un nouvel ordre, après qu'une catastrophe en a eu annoncé la fin abrupte. Toutefois, on sait que la tradition littéraire canadienne est peu à l'aise avec ces divisions binaires, entre autres, d'un avant terrestre et d'un après céleste. D'ailleurs, certains chercheurs ont noté que plusieurs œuvres publiées depuis le début du 21ᵉ siècle montrent une réduction de la temporalité à un présent itératif. Selon Bertrand Gervais (2009, 212), l'imaginaire de la fin contemporain en littérature qui se serait esquissée à la suite de crises sociales et culturelles répétées se caractériserait par une réduction de la temporalité à un présent élargi. Cet imaginaire se distinguerait donc des crises envisagées précédemment en ce qu'il abolirait à peu près les notions du passé et de l'avenir. Tout se passe comme s'il ne restait d'autre pouvoir à la littérature que celui de *témoigner* des signes du monde courant à sa perte.

La question du témoignage nous paraît essentielle à la compréhension de la crise. Le témoignage rend compte d'un événement ou d'une série d'événements qui échappent aux cadres conceptuels existants, comme le montrent Shoshana Felman et Dori Laub, qui définissent ainsi un état de crise :

> Nous soulignons la question du témoin et du témoignage comme des *prismes conceptuels* inhabituels à travers lesquels nous tentons d'appréhender – et de rendre tangibles à l'imagination – les divers échecs de nos cadres culturels et les catégories préexistantes qui déterminent et limitent notre perception de la réalité à rendre compte de la magnitude des événements de l'histoire contemporaine. (Felman/Laub 1992, xv ; trad. N. Côté)

Il s'agit, comme ces auteurs le mentionnent encore, de souligner « le rôle crucial de la préservation de la vérité, du savoir et de la réalité, de même que de contribuer à la survie psychologique afin de soutenir la vie après les catastrophes » (Felman/Laub 1992, 5 ; trad. N. Côté).

Par ailleurs, Felman et Laub montrent que par le processus de raconter et d'écrire, le témoignage se double d'un processus de cognition et d'apprentissage. Mais, selon eux, ce témoignage demeure partiel, le témoin ne comprenant pas toujours entièrement l'ampleur ni même la nature de l'événement qu'il décrit. En effet, Judith Butler se demande « si, en ressentant, en percevant, quelque chose comme la pensée n'est déjà en marche, si en agissant, nous ne sommes déjà agis, et si, en entrant dans la zone du je qui pense et parle, nous ne sommes déjà radicalement formés tout en apportant une contribution » (Butler 2015, 16 ; trad.

N. Côté). Témoigner serait donc un acte heuristique, qui permettrait de mieux saisir l'état présent des choses ; le témoignage viendrait d'abord d'une perception, d'un sentiment de vivre, de l'inédit avant d'être mis en mots, et ferait en quelque sorte le pont entre être agi et agir. Plus encore, le témoignage peut être considéré comme un acte de langage non seulement constatif mais également performatif, en ce que témoigner de la réalité veut dire aussi la modifier. On sait que c'est ainsi que la littérature fonctionne : son témoignage est à la fois conscient et inconscient. Issue du corps et de ses perceptions et sensations, l'écriture nécessite l'esprit pour sa mise en forme ; en disant l'inédit, elle crée une poétique, comme la racine grecque de poétique en témoigne (*poien* = faire). Écrire l'inédit, c'est non seulement en témoigner, mais également transformer la manière dont la réalité jusque-là était perçue ; c'est la refaire.

Conservant ces considérations comme cadre d'analyse, je m'attarderai donc à trois œuvres canadiennes emblématiques de leur époque et de leurs groupes culturels, une québécoise (Nelly Arcan, *À ciel ouvert*), une franco-canadienne (Simone Chaput, *Un vent prodigue*) et une anglo-canadienne (Dionne Brand, *Ossuaries*, que j'ai traduit en français) en tentant de relier les questions de crise et de son témoignage à la question de la temporalité. Ce sont donc des œuvres testimoniales – qu'elles soient poésie (*Ossuaries*) ou romans (*À ciel ouvert, Un vent prodigue*) – pour lesquelles la possibilité même d'une transfiguration recule à l'arrière-plan. Le seul acte offrant quelque rédemption est le témoignage de ce monde en rapide mutation, monde qui détruit à mesure les signes de son histoire. Les trois textes choisis contiennent les scories d'une certaine pensée apocalyptique qui visait à donner sens au fouillis de l'histoire en lui assignant une pensée binaire et une portée téléologique, mais on a vu que cette pensée s'est muée dans plusieurs œuvres post-millénaires en un imaginaire de la fin qui n'entrevoit pas d'*après* aux crises qui secouent le début du 21ᵉ siècle.

Dionne Brand, *Ossuaries* (poésie)

Selon Dionne Brand, la tâche de la poésie serait de « soigner la conscience abîmée et brutalisée des peuples opprimés » (trad. N. Côté ; MacDonald 2013, 93), comme elle le remarque dans son essai *A Kind of Perfect Speech*. En fait, Brand a toujours, dans ses écrits, mêlé le politique et le poétique. *Ossuaries* (2010), dans le droit fil de l'exigeante et singulière œuvre de Dionne Brand, est un poème narratif de 15 chants qui poursuit l'inventaire du 19ᵉ siècle entamé avec les recueils de poésie précédents, *Thirsty* (2002) et *Inventory* (2006). Mais cette fois, l'inventaire est plus sombre que jamais. La protagoniste d'*Ossuaries*, Yasmine, fuit son destin tout aussi sans avenir que celui des grandes villes qu'elle traverse, devenues ossuaires de leurs cultures. Le titre du recueil fonctionne donc à la fois comme constat des restes d'une culture et de la nature et comme rite funéraire en mémoire d'êtres aimés, comme témoignage de ce qui a déjà existé. Le poème présente un diagnostic de l'état de l'Amérique. Généralement, les os qui jonchent les poèmes d'*Ossuaries* constituent en particulier un rappel sinistre des atrocités commises en Amérique, en commençant par la traite des esclaves. Les os du titre sont entre autres ceux des Africains du Passage du milieu, dont le souvenir est éparpillé comme leurs os. Mais les os constituent également l'armature du corps ; ils en sont le signe une fois qu'ils sont vidés de vie. Un ossuaire est toujours déjà témoignage, et en tant que nom collectif, il évoque les pertes humaines à grande échelle.

La cartographie du poème offre de nombreux repères culturels et géopolitiques, que Brand saborde toutefois sans cesse, d'abord en opérant une défamiliarisation par le biais du désancrage des mots : ceux-ci, délestés de leurs contextes immédiats, bardés d'images contradictoires, font perdre pied au lecteur, démantelant à mesure les itinéraires possibles dans la cartographie des conventions de lecture, faisant ainsi ressentir le monde dangereux dans lequel circule la narratrice. Yasmine, la voix du poème, dresse une cartographie des zones sinistrées et rapproche les corps humains et animaux, vulnérables dans leur soumission aux aléas du marché. La protagoniste Yasmine sauve de l'oubli, en mettant en mots, leurs vies, humaines, animales, végétales – artéfacts d'un monde englouti par cette grande hécatombe qu'a créée la marchandisation planétaire avec son obligatoire homogénéisation culturelle et technologique.

Afin de faire ressentir les conséquences de l'empiètement de la technologie sur le monde naturel et la lutte toujours possible contre son pouvoir néfaste, Brand emprunte abondamment à la terminologie scientifique tout en sabordant le sens littéral de son lexique : en effet, détournant le sens dénotatif de nombreux termes, elle force le discours scientifique vers une sphère subjective. Cette connotation émotive qui entoure la description clinique des effets de la science liée à l'économique et au politique contribue à remettre en question le prestige lié à un domaine du savoir qui ouvre les portes du pouvoir. Cette nouvelle nomenclature permet à Brand de mieux traquer les effets du néo-libéralisme et de la mondialisation sur les corps humains et animaux ainsi que sur la planète, tout en enrichissant l'expression poétique. En quelques pages on trouve « the lightning geometry » (Brand 2010, 18) ; « lumens of ache » ; « multicellular runnels » ; « its precipitation / and grand arithmetics, the segments / the latitudes of where, where and here » ; « the bodies' symptoms of algebraic floods » (Brand 2010, 19) ; « a lover's clasp of violent syntax and the beginning syllabi of verblessness » (Brand 2010, 20), qui ne sont que quelques-uns des exemples où des terminologies empruntées à des champs très variés sont détournées afin d'enrichir l'expression. Brand utilise tous les langages à sa disposition, passant par exemple du lexique de la grammaire à celui de la géologie dans le même tercet : « I had nights of insentient adjectives / shale nights, pebbled nights, stone nights, / igneous nights, of these nights, the speechlessness. » (Brand 2010, 14)

Comme le note Libe García Zarranz, c'est un corps de femme qui circule au centre du recueil et qui devient emblématique de la vulnérabilité de la vie. Par ailleurs, selon Zarranz (2012, 63-64), cette femme témoigne du monde contemporain, archivant sur son corps les expériences décloisonnées que suscitent les effets de la mondialisation, particulièrement sur les minorités visibles. On voit ici un corps humain écrit par l'histoire, comme Foucault l'avait suggéré. L'auteure dresse un inventaire des deuils de la nature et des cultures, cet inventaire se situant principalement en Amérique du Nord, témoin de néo-colonialismes répétés, particulièrement dirigés contre la population noire.

Généralement, l'ampleur de la dévastation présente dans *Ossuaries* est telle que la voix narrative lutte même pour témoigner de l'état des choses, selon Anne Quéma (2014, 6/15). On a vu que la narration défait à mesure les itinéraires possibles de sa cartographie. Les ironiques « as usual », « of course » semblent être les seuls marqueurs de stabilité dans la vie de Yasmine. La syntaxe malmenée, déstabilisée, présente un autre aspect de la forme qui rend compte du sentiment de perte d'agentivité du citoyen en lutte contre ces forces impersonnelles. Cette syntaxe peu orthodoxe se traduit plus précisément par la rareté des verbes dans la seconde partie du premier chant – fait commenté ainsi : « I lost verbs, whole, like the hull of almonds. » (Brand 2010, 14) Immédiatement après cette confession, c'est-à-dire dans la seconde partie du premier chant, les verbes de fait disparaissent au profit de déictiques et de listes précises, comme l'a finement remarqué Quéma

(2014, 7/15). Ironiquement, ces déictiques et précisions visant l'établissement de repères ponctuels, dérobés avec le départ des verbes, ne font que souligner l'absence de repères. Les préfixes et suffixes à valeur privative, signifiant la perte et le deuil, complètent le tableau du sentiment de déstabilisation que Yasmine ressent en traversant diverses villes, fuyant son passé tourmenté.

Bien qu'il témoigne richement du monde, le lexique, ayant absorbé une terminologie scientifique, ne peut à lui seul ancrer le récit. En outre, la réécriture de l'histoire du point de vue des exclus, si nécessaire soit-elle, ne passe que minimalement par le récit, car le temps ne semble plus se déployer, ce dont l'absence de verbes dans une grande partie du poème témoigne. On n'a donc pas sous cet aspect non plus un récit bien ancré. La voix narrative suggère vraisemblablement que les mots ne suffisent pas pour créer une histoire, ou encore l'histoire : « [T]hese names would help / here, but / such, such did not create the world or fix time. » (Brand 2010, 53)

D'ailleurs, *Ossuaries* refuse le récit linéaire. L'une des techniques de superposition des époques les plus remarquables est peut-être celle qui met en scène de mornes petites villes modernes des États-Unis dont les noms font écho à de grandes cités antiques, et qui de ce fait deviennent hantées par la violence du passé colonial, comme le montre l'exergue au chant XII d'*Ossuaries* qui présente la séparation du trio ayant commis le vol de banque : « one will leave at Corinth, one will make way at Utica, / one at Syracuse, one split another highway, / she'll take Utica, deluged in a thousand years of silt. » (Brand 2010, 90)

On voit là une scène où cette voix oraculaire issue d'un futur indéterminé commente un geste posé dans la jeunesse de Yasmine, et qui déterminera le cours de sa vie : celui de braquer une banque dans le but de redistribuer l'argent. Le chant X propose une narration moins elliptique, qui éclaire l'œuvre le temps d'établir de brefs repères. L'assurance déployée par Yasmine, qui s'arrime à une soudaine possibilité de récit, ne dure pas. Même la violence vraisemblablement triomphante de la narration – « justice pumped through their veins, history will see » (Brand 2010, 72) – est défaite au chant XII par la superposition du regard ironique de la narration sur les conséquences de l'acte du trio. Ce regard est d'autant plus distant qu'il projette un avenir où les actes posés deviennent insignifiants parce que ne demeurent que des ruines du monde présent : « [S]he knows what no one here will know / how in four millennia only one wall or two will survive. » (Brand 2010, 92)

Quéma appelle ce temps « mythopoétique » (2014, 8/15) parce qu'il se situe dans un espace-temps distendu. Ce temps distendu, où la récurrence des violences passées menace, suggère la nécessité de survivre en se fondant dans le décor, ce que tente de faire Yasmine : « [H]ere we morph as twig and ice and bark / and butterfly, weed and spider, vespids, hoping against predators / convergent mimesis, all means, / stand still and hope it passes, the diatonic, / ragged plumage of our disappearances. » (Brand 2010, 89)

Aussi cette voix future est-elle pure conscience, témoin de catastrophes tant reconnues, historiques, que prévues, et ne présume pas nécessairement de la survie de l'humanité. Les catastrophes prévues sont entrevues dans leur accumulation. *Ossuaries*, dans cette optique, débusque la violence dans les pratiques les plus banales : « Some damage I had expected, but no one / expects the violence of glances, of offices / of walkways and train stations, of bathroom mirrors. » (Brand 2010, 10)

Des fragments de la vie de Yasmine, dont apparaissent de touchants instantanés dans le chant XII, lient les motifs du trio ayant braqué la banque (auquel appartient Yasmine) à la pauvreté de leur enfance et au sort de toute une collectivité. Ainsi un souvenir de l'enfance de Yasmine brièvement évoqué et ayant à voir avec le manque, élargit l'image à tous les Noirs grandissant dans cette pauvreté et à la quasi-impossibilité de se prémunir contre l'inévitable :

> All the spherical tumult of former fears return / the ones in childhood tenements, / in gazes through low hallways, / food smells, in their oily jackets / […] And here no dreaming except to jump off […] / to hold back the inevitable concrete storms, / of waste / and drift / too much for them this job of catching air / with butterfly nets / of stopping water with bottomless jars / too much collecting the sloughed skins / of this world's eyelids. (Brand 2010, 99-100)

Le dernier chant, le chant XV, ne propose aucune résolution à cette crise mondiale, mais laisse entendre une voix ostensiblement collective. Les corps sont ici aussi présentés selon un lexique de captivité. Cette fois, des os fragiles du pied, les métatarses, suggèrent de longues marches forcées, des esclaves ou des soldats sans chaussures ou soutien approprié, métaphore de la fragilité des corps (MacDonald 2013, 106). *Ossuaries* se termine donc en refusant quelque clôture que ce soit.

Comme le disait Brand à la fin de *A Kind of Perfect Speech*, « le changement n'est désormais qu'une négociation avec la mémoire » (Brand 2008, 27 ; trad. N. Côté).

Nelly Arcan, *À ciel ouvert* (roman)

Dans *À ciel ouvert*, l'avenir, tant personnel que collectif, est bloqué. L'ouverture signifiée par le titre est selon moi à la fois ironique et symbolique, la seule ouverture envisagée étant verticale, mais dépourvue de la transcendance qu'évoque le mot *ciel* : c'est celle de l'absence de limites qui se remarque chez les personnages, la démesure de leur désir de rester jeune, une *hubris* toute païenne en ce qu'elle ne suppose de rédemption que dans l'amélioration infinie des corps. En effet, le monde se concentre sur la jeunesse, et Julie, la protagoniste, en tant que femme, voit son capital corporel diminuer à vue d'œil après 33 ans, l'âge du Christ, comme elle le dit (cet âge étant celui de la mort du Christ). Du point de vue collectif, dès l'*incipit* du roman, la planète est présentée comme invivable en raison de son système fondé sur la verticalité d'une compétitivité toujours plus féroce. Car s'y tailler une place, c'est monter l'échelle jusqu'en haut, défi qui relève d'une lutte épuisante : « [D]es milliards d'existences à côtoyer en un voisinage planétaire [...], ses bilans de morts [...], ses incessantes manifestations à repousser si l'on tenait à la vie. » (Arcan 2007, 7)

Cette réalité est à proprement parler apocalyptique, Julie se représentant le monde comme « tourné vers l'enfer » (Arcan 2007, 7) : « Jamais le soleil n'avait paru plus près de la Terre qu'en ce jour-là. Il faisait même peur à voir, donnait l'impression de s'être agenouillé, prosterné sur le corps de Montréal en géant débile qui méconnaît sa force. » (Arcan 2007, 11) La menace est à la fois réelle et symbolique : Julie croit fermement que la chaleur du soleil aura raison de la planète. On voit se profiler ici une pensée apocalyptique en ce que le soleil est associé au père, lui-même lié à Dieu le père, selon un système métonymique dont la verticalité, on l'a vu, souligne ironiquement la perte de spiritualité tout en évoquant les lois du marché. Dès l'*incipit* se profile l'image d'un dieu faiblard, un vieux père demeuré, qui, loin de sauver le monde, contribue à sa perte. Le dieu d'*À ciel ouvert* est un dieu vengeur, qui, semble-t-il, brûlera l'humanité plutôt que de l'inonder.

La protagoniste d'*À ciel ouvert*, voyant la planète vouée à une fin proche, en témoigne par son travail de documentariste. Julie filme l'horizon qui se referme sur les corps retravaillés pour le plaisir de l'œil. Cela permet de faire diversion, car la réalité semble murée dans le présent. Le roman baigne dans un état d'urgence généralisé, que Martine-Emmanuelle Lapointe a étiqueté « syndrome de la fin » (Lapointe 2008, 143). Dans ce compte-rendu, Lapointe discute, peu après la parution d'*À ciel ouvert*, et donc avant le suicide d'Arcan, à la fois de la mort dont est imprégné ce récit, et de l'impression générale de fin du monde qui filtre à travers le tissu du texte. Chez Arcan, comme son dernier ouvrage (*Paradis, clef en main*) et son suicide en font foi, l'Apocalypse se fera sur la terre, et surtout, rien ne la suivra, car Dieu est un père jaloux et incestueux qui consume littéralement l'humanité de son désir pervers.

Fait intéressant, si Rose, son alter ego et sa *nemesis*, et Charles, leur amant, travaillent sur les images de mode et créent des fictions avec des gens réels – Charles étant photographe de mode, et Rose étant habilleuse – pour faire acheter des vêtements et des corps parfaits, Julie, presque aussi esclave de son apparence que Rose, se targue de filmer la vérité. Malgré sa position ambiguë de jeune femme qui dénonce l'excès et qui le pratique en témoignant des images que sont devenues les femmes accros à la chirurgie, par des photos, mais des photos non retouchées de corps inlassablement retouchés, Julie rend l'enfer qu'elle vit tolérable et donne quelque sens à son expérience. La position ambigüe de Julie semble inévitable du fait de sa conscience du règne des apparences. Julie elle-même dit n'avoir plus d'âme, l'âme représentant la profondeur. Il est mentionné dans le roman que le Christ est mort à 33 ans, l'âge de Julie qui, « ne voulant pas lâcher le Christ » (Arcan 2007, 9) lie par télescopage la mort du Christ, la mort de Charles – sorte de bouc émissaire – et la fin du monde :

> De toute façon changer le monde ne la concernait plus à ce moment-là de
> sa vie, [...] depuis qu'elle n'avait plus de cœur, ou d'âme si on préfère ;
> et elle s'en taperait encore plus du sort de son monde qui prenait feu sur
> toute la surface de la planète après avoir tué l'homme qui avait pourtant
> voulu lui redonner le jour et qu'elle avait cru aimer. (Arcan 2007, 10)

Chez Arcan, semble-t-il, le religieux – ici d'ascendance catholique, avec Dieu le père et son fils – n'est jamais très loin sous la surface, mais son Dieu le père est un pervers (père-vers ?), et son Dieu le fils, un désespéré tué par la bêtise ambiante des temps derniers. La transcendance s'étant éclipsée, il reste le témoignage, et quoi de plus approprié pour cette époque de la surface, des images de corps parfaits imprimées sur toutes les rétines, que de filmer le processus par lequel ces corps deviennent parfaits, et par là, génériques ? Témoigner, c'est démonter la supercherie des corps de femmes remodelés pour elles-mêmes afin d'archiver la folie du temps ambiant. Et le témoignage, ici, filme de la peau de femme, de la surface qui devient texte travaillé par une idéologie que Rose et Julie assument en partie consciemment, et dont Julie témoigne.

Simone Chaput, *Un vent prodigue* (roman)

Autre œuvre qui prend un des éléments du monde naturel pour titre, *Un vent prodigue*, présente le vent comme principe invisible liant le sort des humains à celui de la planète. Chez les Premières Nations, le vent est souvent associé à l'esprit de Dieu, ou d'un dieu. Mais c'est ici un vent de déperdition, d'entropie, qui souffle : celui de la disparition de valeurs, de paysages, de langues, dont chacun témoigne différemment selon la génération ou le sexe auxquels il ou elle appartient.

Ainsi, Yvan, le père, ingénieur dans la soixantaine, confond sa mort et celle de la planète, faisant de la conservation du monde l'enjeu de sa propre survie. Comme Anne Sechin (2015) l'a montré avec beaucoup d'à-propos, le regard d'Yvan est en mode de domination : en tant que sujet, il parle presque toujours depuis le centre du monde. Yvan, lorsqu'il est sur l'autoroute, ouvre son regard à tous les autres dans de minuscules autos fumantes et imagine une humanité pullulante, son regard effectuant une sorte de travelling panoramique de l'échelle humaine à l'échelle planétaire. La responsabilité environnementale qu'Yvan ressent se mue en désespoir devant l'immensité de la tâche à accomplir pour redresser les comptes : « La glace fond, les mers montent, les forêts brûlent, les lacs s'assèchent, les villes s'engorgent, l'air empeste, l'eau se corrompt, les déchets s'accumulent, et moi, moi, je composte, je recycle. » (Chaput 2013, 37) Sechin (2015, §15) suggère que les préoccupations écologiques d'Yvan sont pénétrées d'une symbolique chrétienne, en raison d'un « champ lexical de l'enfer, de la punition, de la toxicité ». Ce sont de toute évidence des images apocalyptiques qu'évoque Yvan, et il lutte pour aménager la sauvegarde de la planète.

Adrienne, l'ethnolinguiste conjointe d'Yvan, ressent également une responsabilité démesurée face à la tâche de sauver la planète, comme son rêve récurrent, lui aussi lié à une symbolique chrétienne, le prouve : « Toujours le même, mon rêve, une *pietà*, une *mater dolorosa*. Je porte la Terre dans mes bras, et, comme un corps criblé de blessures, elle fuit. » (Chaput 2013, 11) Adrienne veut rescaper non seulement l'environnement, mais une culture Dénée qui entretient toujours un lien étroit avec la nature. Toutefois, le rapport au monde d'Adrienne est tout autant décentrement d'elle-même, dilatation de son univers, qu'action. Elle accueille ce qui reste de beauté du monde et en témoigne à sa façon, en préparant un ouvrage sur la langue menacée de ce peuple, et en notant tout, la beauté de la nature comme celle de ce peuple, dans son journal.

Cette position « périphérique » (Sechin 2015, §54) de l'ethnolinguiste parle le langage de la révélation : « L'exposition à la révélation suppose le relâchement de la volonté, surtout de la volonté intellectuelle. » (Sechin 2015, §54) En dépit de l'extraordinaire élargissement de perspective que permet une telle position, cette esthétique/éthique qui veut que le sujet féminin se dissolve dans le cosmos se situe à l'extrême du spectre des comportements appris de la féminité, car elle laisse toute la place à l'autre, s'effaçant devant sa grandeur, ici un grand Autre cosmique. Paradoxalement, cette absence de contrôle rend Adrienne encore plus apte à témoigner : elle réussit à noter la langue de cette population éloignée, et capte dans son journal la beauté du monde.

C'est pourquoi les discours sur eux-mêmes – savoirs forcément situés, donc sexués – que tiennent les personnages de cette génération d'âge moyen, cachent leurs réelles actions : ainsi, malgré qu'Adrienne semble demeurer en périphérie du monde actif, elle réussit visiblement sa mission de sauvegarder, en la déchiffrant, la langue en voie de disparition d'une tribu Dénée isolée. En revanche, Yvan, désormais professeur d'université à la retraite, malgré sa mission de sauver le monde naturel, voit son champ d'action limité à son potager.

Par ailleurs, chez la jeune génération, tant chez Miguel que chez sa sœur Magali (ce sont les enfants d'Adrienne et d'Yvan), se profile la perte d'un horizon naturel ou social qui accentue le repli sur soi, niant la criante crise écologique. Le seul mode de relation que les enfants d'Yvan et d'Adrienne semblent entretenir reste celui de la séduction hétérosexuelle, un *modus operandi*. Bien qu'aucun des personnages sous la loupe de l'auteure n'en ressorte moralement indemne, Chaput semble suggérer que la jeune génération restreint son champ de vision devant l'imminence du désastre environnemental et ne pense, naturellement, pourrait-on dire, qu'à sa survie – dont on ne sera pas surpris de constater qu'elle gravite vers la reconnaissance de soi et l'auto-gratification. On peut se demander quel rôle joue la mémoire, ou plutôt son absence, dans ce repli, car ces jeunes vivent au jour le jour, dans ce présent itératif dont j'ai parlé plus haut. Ils meublent de moments somme toute agréables ce présent d'une jeunesse ressentie comme éternelle, bien que tous deux aient à faire face aux petites crises qui ponctuent l'existence : chez Miguel, la maladie et la mort entrevue de sa conjointe ; chez Magali, quelques déceptions quant à ses relations sexuelles – à escient, je n'utilise ici pas ‹ amoureuses ›, qui serait un qualificatif trop fort, faisant référence à un attachement investi et prolongé.

Quant au monde naturel ou au patrimoine culturel dans lequel ils vivent, ni Miguel ni Magali n'ont de velléités de témoigner de ces mondes en voie de disparition. Si on peut supposer qu'ils ont connu, enfants, ce monde, puisqu'ils sont des rejetons d'écologistes et d'amants de la culture, ils semblent trop préoccupés par leur monde immédiat pour lui accorder quelque importance. Il s'agit vraisemblablement d'un mécanisme de défense face à l'imminence ressentie du désastre. Néanmoins, Magali peut être considérée bien malgré elle comme un témoin de son époque puisque, ingénieure de son, elle capte des musiques en mouvement (elle en composera), et même, contre son gré, le son de baleines au large d'Haida Gwaii pour un vieil océanographe chaviré par la beauté du monde. Sechin (2015) a montré avec brio comment Magali évite toutes les fenêtres sur le monde pour se retourner sur elle-même. Chez elle, le témoignage est donc presque entièrement inconscient et réside dans la trame sonore des mondes naturels et culturels qu'elle capte en échange d'un salaire.

Les parents, Adrienne et Yvan, ont effectivement connu l'ancien monde, l'ampleur de leur perte se mesurant à la nostalgie ressentie pour sa disparition par fragments. Cependant, comme on l'a vu, Yvan, trop préoccupé de gestion du territoire, témoigne peu de son époque sinon par ses vitupérations. Adrienne, par son travail d'annotation d'une langue Dénée menacée et, plus personnellement, par son journal sur la beauté du monde naturel, témoigne de monuments culturels et naturels en voie de disparition.

Conclusion : petites fins des temps ou du temps

Goldman affirme que les auteurs canadiens ont longtemps invoqué les tropes de l'Apocalypse pour mettre en lumière les changements de paradigmes historiques souvent représentés dans les récits comme des tempêtes qui menacent de détruire toute trace de l'histoire humaine (cf. Goldman 2005, 20). Cependant les récits étudiés ici ne contiennent que les scories d'une certaine pensée apocalyptique, pensée qui visait à donner sens au fouillis de l'histoire en assignant à cette dernière une portée téléologique. Dans le cas des œuvres ici étudiées, cette pensée se serait muée en un imaginaire de la fin, parce que n'est entrevu aucun *après* à la série de crises qui secouent le début du 21ᵉ siècle.

On a vu qu'*Ossuaries* présente un lexique qui détourne le scientifique, lié à l'objectivité et lié à l'objectivation. Il offre ainsi un témoignage de la marchandisation tant des corps humains et animaux que celle des ressources planétaires. Les points de vue, depuis des corps humains et même parfois d'oiseaux, convergent vers une Yasmine parfois incarnée dans un corps accusant les contrecoups de la fuite perpétuelle à laquelle elle se voit forcée, étant donné le braquage de banque qu'elle avait effectué avec ses comparses dans sa jeunesse. Ce corps, témoin des atrocités commises par l'humanité, porte les marques de sa prise de conscience. Les deux œuvres francophones ont aussi pour principaux témoins des femmes (Julie, Adrienne, et dans une moindre mesure, Magali) qui offrent des commentaires d'ordre sociologique : *À ciel ouvert* découvre les mécanismes de la survie à la marchandisation des corps de femmes grâce au témoignage que Julie offre sous la forme d'un documentaire ; dans *Un vent prodigue*, Adrienne note une langue autochtone et la beauté du monde naturel avant qu'elles ne disparaissent ; Magali est témoin de son époque par ses enregistrements de musique contemporaine, et par les sons de baleines au large de la côte ouest du Canada.

Dans le corpus provisoire présenté ici, chaque œuvre établit un diagnostic de la situation de la planète depuis le Canada, anglais ou français, ou depuis le Québec, mais en le situant très clairement sur l'échiquier du monde. Les trois œuvres offrent ainsi des témoignages précieux sur le début du 21ᵉ siècle, qu'elles présentent comme la fin d'*un* monde.

Nicole CÔTÉ

Bibliographie

Arcan, Nelly : *À ciel ouvert.* Paris : Seuil, 2007.

Brand, Dionne : *A Kind of Perfect Speech.* Nanaimo : Institute for Coastal Research, 2008.

Brand, Dionne : *Ossuaries.* Toronto : McClelland & Stewart, 2010.

Butler, Judith : *Senses of the Subject.* New York : Fordham University Press, 2015.

Chaput, Simone : *Un vent prodigue.* Montréal : Leméac, 2013.

Felman, Shoshana / Laub, Dori (éds) : *Testimony. Crises of Witnessing in Literature, Psychoanalysis, and History.* New York/Londres : Routledge, 1992.

Gervais, Bertrand : *L'imaginaire de la fin. Temps, mots et signes. Logiques de l'imaginaire.* Vol. 3. Montréal : Le Quartanier, 2009.

Goldman, Marlene : *Rewriting Apocalypse in Canadian Fiction.* Montréal et al. : McGill-Queen's University Press, 2005.

Keller, Catherine : *Apocalypse Now and Then. A Feminist Guide to the End of the World.* Minneapolis : Fortress Press, 2005.

Lapointe, Martine-Emmanuelle : « Le syndrome de la fin ». In : *Voix et Images* 33,2 (2008), 144-149.

MacDonald, Tanis : « ‹ Rhetorical Metatarsals › : Bone Memory in Dionne Brand's *Ossuaries* ». In : Kilbourn, Russell / Ty, Eleanor (éds) : *The Memory Effect. The Remediation of Memory in Literature and Film.* Waterloo : Wilfrid Laurier University Press, 2013, 93-106.

Quéma, Anne : « *Ossuaries,* Songs of Necropolitics ». In : *Canadian Literature* 222 (2014), 52-68, https://canlit.ca/article/dionne-brands-ossuaries-songs-of-necropolitics/ (consultation 12/10/2015).

Sechin, Anne : « Lectures de l'espace dans *Un vent prodigue* de Simone Chaput ». In : *Temps Zéro* 10 (2015), http://tempszero.contemporain.info/document1379 (consultation 22/03/2017).

Zarranz, Libe García : « Toxic Bodies that Matter : Trans-Corporeal Materialities in Dionne Brand's *Ossuaries* ». In : *Canada and Beyond* 2,1-2 (2012), 55-68, http://rabida.uhu.es/dspace/bitstream/handle/10272/13316/Toxic.pdf?sequence=2 (consultation 29/05/2015).

David BOUCHER (Montréal)

L'apocalypse selon Nelly Arcan

Summary

The novel *Exit* by Nelly Arcan, previously published as *Paradis, clef en main*, can be classified as dystopian and describes a near future in which an underground enterprise, 'Paradis, clef en main,' offers made-to-measure suicide assistance to its clientele. Candidates are to be chosen following a series of ordeals imposed by the company's committee. Specifically, it tells the story of Antoinette Beauchamp, a now paraplegic victim of the 'false paradise' proposed by Mr. Paradis, owner of the morbid company. Yet another level of interpretation demonstrates the plot symbolically focusing on the cultural and political upheaval of the 1960s' Quiet Revolution in Quebec. It offers a glimpse of the lost utopian hopes of this period. With a special interest in the representation of place in the novel, this article aims to highlight a catastrophic vision of historical and cultural evolution where individual liberty has led to an individualistic, not to say hellish, society of death. With Mikhaïl Bakhtine's chronotope concept, together with Friedrich Nietzsche's and Jean Baudrillard's notion of nihilism (linked to the sociological 'death of God'), and also in the light of different aesthetical issues linked to intertextuality (the representation of hell in Arcan's novel, which is borrowed from the work of Dante and Memling), it is possible to highlight a forewarning for today and onward from one of Quebec's best postmodern authors.

Introduction

Récit cauchemardesque d'une nouvelle étape d'évolution sociale, *Paradis, clef en main* invite à une réflexion critique sur le suicide assisté, tout en annonçant une forme prochaine de réification. Par l'anticipation, le roman diagnostique une crise sociétale liée à l'échec de l'utopie des libertés individuelles et collectives issue de la Révolution tranquille, en décrivant un monde nihiliste où l'individualisme et le capitalisme sont roi et où la mort est à vendre. Cela apparaît d'abord à la lumière du concept bakhtinien de chronotope : l'itinéraire spatial d'Antoinette, le personnage principal, retrace symboliquement celui d'un Québec en transformation depuis 1960 jusqu'à aujourd'hui. Dans le même ordre d'idées, le roman d'Arcan pense la question du nihilisme autant à partir du ‹ Gott ist tot › de Friedrich Nietzsche que de l'hyperréalité de Jean Baudrillard, pour mieux décrire la crise sociétale en question, qu'elle soit présente ou à venir. Cette dernière se déploie finalement dans l'image de l'enfer, révélée par différentes références intertextuelles et intermédiales, qui prédisent le « pire » (Faye 1993, *Dans les laboratoires du pire. Totalitarisme et fiction littéraire au XXe siècle*).

Un lieu de rendez-vous avec l'histoire

Au sujet de *Paradis, clef en main*, Martine-Emmanuelle Lapointe (2010, 133) dénote « la sensation d'asphyxie, l'impression d'enfermement qui traversent le roman ». Les lieux de rendez-vous relèvent effectivement de la spirale abyssale, car ils sont toujours doublés par une deuxième destination inattendue pour Antoinette, comme des gouffres qui se prolongent. Primo, lorsqu'elle arrive au Nautilus Plus[1], cette destination se révèle ne pas être le véritable lieu de rencontre fixé par la compagnie (la suicidaire doit tout de suite se rendre à un bâtiment abandonné où l'attendent les membres du comité de ‹ Paradis, clef en main ›). Secundo, quand elle constate que les danseuses du bar Chez Paré sont de connivence avec la compagnie, elle est invitée à aller dans une église vide où l'attend non pas un prêtre mais un psychiatre incapable. Tertio, lorsqu'elle gagne la partie de poker au zoo contre ce psychiatre, elle remporte en même temps son dernier voyage vers un château Walt Disney où ses bourreaux l'attendent pour son exécution. L'enjeu de ce dédoublement ne doit pas uniquement être compris comme une stratégie de brouillage de pistes pensée par la compagnie clandestine ‹ Paradis, clef en main ›, mais aussi comme un labyrinthe d'emprisonnement dont le centre à trouver est un Minotaure qui figure autant la mort-suicide que l'allégorie d'un passé en héritage.

Le chronotope bakhtinien, défini comme « la corrélation essentielle des rapports spatio-temporels, telle qu'elle a été assimilée par la littérature » (Bakhtine 2013, 237), aide à mieux saisir cette logique du double. Considéré dans la totalité de sa complexité, c'est-à-dire en tant qu'*espace-temps*, le lieu représente en effet plus que sa propre image, à savoir une sorte de verticalité qui pointe dans deux directions opposées : l'anticipation (le futur) et la généalogie (le passé). En amont de tous les endroits à visiter tout juste décrits se trouve le cauchemar d'une société dystopique à venir où le suicide est devenu une pure transaction, la vie et la mort étant fondamentalement monnayables et ayant la même valeur d'échange. En aval de chaque lieu se révèlent allégoriquement les causes de ce monde cauchemardesque, enfanté par la perversion du projet émancipateur de la Révolution tranquille : le premier rendez-vous survient dans un Nautilus Plus, symbole du narcissisme contemporain qui réduit tout au paradigme du paraître et qui est tributaire d'un certain hédonisme hippie ; le deuxième rendez-vous se déroule dans un bar de danseuses nues, symptôme d'une société où la logique de la sexualisation s'affirme partout en dogme, comme autant d'échos de la révolution sexuelle des années 1960 et 1970 ; le troisième rendez-vous est fixé dans un zoo, ultime image d'une société déstructurée par les slogans d'autrefois – comme le fameux : « Il est interdit d'interdire ! » (Meuleau 2010, 210) – enclenchant une régression généralisée vers le règne des pulsions (de vie comme de mort).

Le dernier lieu, celui du suicide raté, confirme l'idée d'un parcours plus allégorique qu'initiatique, car il matérialise de façon convergente tous ces éléments critiques dans un château Walt Disney. Derrière les portes de ce bâtiment plus ‹ Dracula › que ‹ Mickey mouse › se trouve la guillotine, objet sanguinaire et symbolique à situer spatialement et temporellement dans la France de 1789. Le spectre de la Révolution française est renforcé par le nom du personnage principal, Antoinette Beauchamp, cette dernière allant jusqu'à dire : « J'étais Marie-Antoinette. » (Arcan 2009a, 201) La dame en costume d'époque qui accueille cette Marie-Antoinette plus québécoise que française à son arrivée au château établit un autre lien entre l'histoire révolutionnaire de la France et du Québec via le fleurdelisé sur fond bleu : « Une femme en robe bleue fleurdelisée s'est approchée de la voiture, elle a déverrouillé la portière pour que j'en sorte. » (Arcan 2009a, 200) Le lien à faire entre la mort réifiée et un certain héritage de la révolution des années 1960 au Québec s'impose subtilement. Ce qui apparaît dans cette scène de la guillotine est donc bel et bien le chronotope bakhtinien, car ce château d'une autre époque dit l'histoire de la Belle Province et le legs de sa Révolution tranquille, à savoir que les droits et libertés, dans la nouvelle perspective de la mort désacralisée, pourraient un jour faire des victimes.

Présentée comme dérive individualiste des libertés néolibérales, la position pro-choix relative au suicide, c'est-à-dire celle basée sur l'idée que « ni l'État, ni la religion, ni la société, ni la famille, ni les amis ne doivent s'interposer entre les corps et l'énergie vitale qui les anime » (Arcan 2009a, 18), est même associée à une forme nouvelle d'obscurantisme dans les mots de la narratrice, comme pour montrer qu'un extrême et son contraire mènent au même :

> Je n'ai pas tout saisi de la complexité de l'enjeu et des nuances idéologiques du discours de monsieur Paradis. Au contraire. Dans mon désir de mourir, le désir de mourir des autres était le dernier de mes soucis. La guerre des valeurs et des droits, je l'ai toujours laissée aux autres. Ainsi sont la plupart des suicidaires : bouffés par l'urgence de s'en aller loin des autres, de prendre la porte du monde ; réduits à leur petite personne détestée, penchés sur leur grande noirceur. (Arcan 2009a, 18)

L'expression « grande noirceur » ici n'est aucunement fortuite, car elle renvoie à un subtil idéologème, concept défini par Cros (2003, 165) comme « un micro-système sémiotico-idéologique sous-jacent à une unité fonctionnelle et significative du discours ». Foncièrement péjorative, « grande noirceur » décrit, depuis 1960, la période clérico-duplessiste précédant la Révolution tranquille, que les acteurs de cette dernière usèrent pour raconter l'histoire. Associée au sujet suicidaire contemporain libre de passer à l'acte comme bon lui semble, cette même expression redit, à l'inverse, par la fiction de l'anticipation, « la subversion des idéaux de la Révolution tranquille » (Meunier/Warren 2002, 87), en conjuguant le passé au futur.

La mort sociologique de Dieu

La fonction de ce chronotope s'apparente à celle d'un miroir qui reflète l'image du passé dans celle du futur, avec les reflets du nihilisme contemporain. Dans sa conception nietzschéenne, cette idée est liée à l'effondrement des croyances et à celle que « Dieu est mort » (Nietzsche 1995, 21), événement sociologique entamé en 1789 en France et survenu subitement durant les années 1960 au Québec, tel qu'évoqué par la narratrice de *Folle* à partir des théories de son grand-père :

> Il disait qu'au Québec, Dieu était mort plus vite qu'en Europe, il disait qu'en Europe Dieu avait agonisé pendant plusieurs siècles alors qu'ici il

était mort subitement. Ici, on l'avait carrément abattu, d'ailleurs son cadavre était encore chaud, la preuve en était qu'on retrouvait des curés hy-
pocrites et abuseurs d'enfants dans tous les téléromans. (Arcan 2005, 140)

Le roman *À ciel ouvert*, quant à lui, résume ce fait en évoquant la croix du mont Royal comme « un fossile, la trace que par là un dieu avait existé » (Arcan 2009b, 211). Par différents indices, *Paradis, clef en main* dit que cette rupture totale et subite – qui se traduit entre autres par la négation des croyances anciennes et des valeurs d'antan – est l'un des facteurs favorisant l'avènement d'une société dystopique en perte de repères, sinon celui de l'argent et de son règne, comme en font foi les amalgames entre l'absence de Dieu et sa substitution par la compagnie ‹ Paradis, clef en main › tout au long du récit (à commencer par le symbolique titre du roman). Divers exemples s'inscrivent dans cette logique (celle d'un constat de l'absence et de la substitution) : la peinture qui se trouve dans l'église en remplacement du « Christ en croix » (Arcan 2009a, 83) – à savoir celle représentant monsieur Paradis – déifie littéralement l'homme d'affaires machiavélique, d'autant plus que son regard est décrit comme celui « infiniment triste de Dieu sur sa création » (Arcan 2009a, 83) ; le comité des treize membres de la compagnie ‹ Paradis, clef en main › constitue, quant à lui, une parodie carnavalesque des apôtres via l'image d'une « dernière cène bureaucratique » (Arcan 2009a, 66), etc. Dans tous les cas, les repères religieux tournent à vide par le faux-semblant.

Sorte d'angle mort de tout le récit, cette référence répétée à la liquidation du catholicisme au Québec durant les années 1960 et 1970 ainsi que son remplacement par une société marchande en quête (ou en manque) de dieux nouveaux, éclaire autrement la symbolique des lieux de rendez-vous durant l'intrigue. Cette liquidation apparaît certes comme *la* cause rendant possible le suicide assisté (sans la mort sociologique de Dieu, tout n'est pas permis) ; bien plus, elle semble mettre en évidence tacitement les facteurs qui sont la cause des nombreux suicides du Québec postmoderne[2] (évoqués dans l'*incipit*) par chaque endroit visité à partir de son envers : derrière le narcissisme, l'hypersexualité, l'hédonisme individualiste évoqués précédemment se trouvent en décombre et en souffrance le corps, la sexualité, la famille, tout ce que le sacré investissait de ses codes et qui, aujourd'hui mis à mal, tourne à vide, laisse seul, devient marchandise. La narratrice d'*À ciel ouvert* résume clairement cette idée dans un passage qui se déroule – sans hasard aucun – aussi au Nautilus Plus :

> De nos jours tout le monde était sa propre vedette et il n'y avait plus de
> public. Dieu qui était mort avait vidé ses créatures de leur capacité à adorer
> autre chose qu'elles-mêmes, et ces créatures avaient ensuite dû se remplir de
> santé mentale et physique, se recoudre à l'hygiène. La place vide de Dieu
> avait dû être remplacée par un milliard de pacotilles, et les gens couraient
> désormais sur des tapis vers le contrôle, la stabilité et la célébration de leur
> corps, vers leur éternité, la brillance à perpétuité. (Arcan 2009b, 129-130)

Quelques pages plus loin, la narratrice renchérit :

> Après l'effondrement des institutions morales et religieuses, après la table
> rase historique du devoir, du sacrifice, de l'abnégation de soi-même, bref,
> de l'ordre établi, il ne restait plus que la beauté pour unir les êtres, et aussi
> l'argent, qui avait tendance à s'accumuler autour des êtres beaux. Sur le
> plan social l'amour ne s'opposait plus à la prostitution, et la prostitution,
> qui marchandait les êtres, sélectionnait les plus beaux, c'était la logique
> darwinienne, le retour aux sources, aux trophées, aux babouins. (Arcan
> 2009b, 144)

Lieu de conditionnement autant physique qu'idéologique, le Nautilus devient la
prison contemporaine du corps et de son image, les deux réifiés parce qu'exploitables monétairement. À l'image du babouin primitif se substitue ainsi celle du
hamster de laboratoire courant sur sa roue de Sisyphe.

Ce constat de la vacuité doit toutefois être interprété avec nuances. *Paradis, clef en main* ne peut aucunement être considéré comme un roman vaguement
catholique, militant pour un retour à la foi, car Nelly Arcan est bel et bien une
écrivaine athée, la croyance religieuse étant souvent présentée comme irrecevable
ou littéralement naïve par ses personnages principaux. Un commentaire de la
narratrice suffit à le prouver :

> Partout, la normalité des églises abandonnées se donnait à voir, avec son lot
> de clairs-obscurs et de désertion, sa hauteur obsolète laissée à elle-même,
> ses fioritures et ses vitraux, ses représentations comiques de la divinité, sa
> conception naïve d'un autre monde où les anges sont des hommes qui
> volent dans le ciel avec des pénis d'enfant. (Arcan 2009a, 83)

N'en demeure pas moins qu'au-delà de ces réflexions d'Antoinette, l'œuvre d'Arcan dit les conséquences de la perte du « [f]ragile absolu » judéo-chrétien, pour parler comme Slavoj Žižek (2008, *Fragile absolu. Pourquoi l'héritage chrétien vaut-il d'être défendu ?*), tout en imaginant la décadence pour une société caractérisée par le présentisme et dont la mémoire collective fut marquée par l'amnésie du jour au lendemain de sa Révolution tranquille. D'où l'idée de dystopie de Tzvetan Todorov :

> De nos jours, il est fréquent d'entendre formuler une critique des démocraties libérales de l'Europe occidentale ou de l'Amérique du Nord, leur reprochant de contribuer au dépérissement de la mémoire, au règne de l'oubli. [...] [C]oupés de nos traditions et abrutis par les exigences d'une société des loisirs, dépourvus de curiosité spirituelle comme de familiarité avec les grandes œuvres du passé, nous serions condamnés à la vanité de l'instant et au crime de l'oubli. Ainsi, de manière moins brutale mais finalement plus efficace, car ne suscitant pas notre résistance, faisant de nous au contraire les agents consentants de cette marche vers l'oubli, les États démocratiques conduiraient leur population au même but que les régimes totalitaires, c'est-à-dire au règne de la barbarie. (Todorov 2010, 657)

En d'autres mots, par le thème du religieux, et sans la foi ou la nostalgie chrétienne, le roman critique le règne de l'oubli que la société des loisirs post-religieuse ‹ comble › par la quête d'un bonheur monétaire, entre autres. Dystopie rime donc, chez Arcan, avec oubli et barbarie.

La technologie et le miroir

Le nihilisme qui se donne à lire dans le roman et qui, selon Arcan, caractérise le Québec dystopique d'aujourd'hui et de demain doit aussi être compris à partir des théories de Jean Baudrillard, celles relatives à l'hyperréalité, car le lieu dans *Paradis, clef en main* est aussi celui de la technologie et du miroir. Dans *Simulacres et simulation*, ce nihilisme se définit par un horizon technologique qui est nôtre et qui instaure un rapport nouveau à l'image et au réel, celui de l'hyperréalité : « Aujourd'hui l'abstraction n'est plus celle de la carte, du double, du miroir ou du concept. La simulation n'est plus celle du territoire, d'un être référentiel, d'une substance. Elle est la génération par les modèles d'un réel sans origine ni réalité : hyperréel. » (Baudrillard 2002, 10) Le nihilisme qui en découle n'est pas étranger à la ‹ mort de Dieu › nietzschéenne, bien que son fonctionnement ne procède pas tellement du désespoir de la perte, mais plutôt d'une prison 2.0, située derrière l'œil :

> Le nihilisme est aujourd'hui celui de la transparence, et il est en quelque sorte plus radical, plus crucial que dans ses formes antérieures et historiques, car cette transparence, cette flottaison, est indissolublement celle du système, et celle de toute théorie qui prétend encore l'analyser. Quand Dieu est mort, il y avait encore Nietzsche pour le dire – grand nihiliste devant l'Éternel et le cadavre de l'Éternel. Mais devant la transparence simulée de toutes choses, devant le simulacre d'accomplissement matérialiste ou idéaliste du monde dans l'hyperréalité (Dieu n'est pas mort, il est devenu hyperréel), il n'y a plus de Dieu théorique et critique pour reconnaître les siens. (Baudrillard 2002, 227)

À mi-chemin entre le miroir et l'ordinateur, le plafond-écran d'Antoinette s'inscrit dans cette logique, entre autres parce qu'il donne l'illusion de la liberté et de la déité à son utilisatrice, qui le décrit comme une « artillerie technologique » qu'elle fait « fonctionner comme Dieu a bâti le monde : par des ordres. Par la force du Verbe » (Arcan 2009a, 21). Antoinette s'y mire en s'y racontant, elle dessine virtuellement la carte de son existence pour mieux faire de sa vie une sorte d'hypertexte à lire, un fantasme technologique d'intimité révélée dont la trajectoire ne lui donnera malheureusement pas la toute-puissance divine, mais seulement la transparence de son discours mélancolique.

Cette logique est celle d'Écho et Narcisse, lequel n'est pas sans lien avec l'imaginaire dystopique d'un point de vue psychanalytique :

> [A]ujourd'hui, la dénommée personnalité narcissique nous incline à conclure qu'il y a un pacte direct entre le surmoi et le ça au détriment du moi. Les puissances sociales, représentées par les pressions surmoïques, manipulent directement les pulsions obscènes du sujet, en court-circuitant la rationalité et l'autonomie incarnée par le moi. Voilà la leçon élémentaire à tirer des ‹ totalitarismes ›. (Žižek 2008, 91)

Dans le roman, la transparence de Baudrillard peut ainsi être comprise, à la lumière des réflexions de Žižek, comme la prison du narcissisme (celui d'Antoinette) et comme l'espionnage du voyeurisme (celui de sa mère) jusqu'à ses ultimes conséquences : la mort libre donnée en spectacle, avatar d'une société qui rappelle, de façon inversée, les totalitarismes d'autrefois. Même si le suicide raté d'Antoinette ne survient pas devant son plafond-écran sous le regard de sa mère, il procède du même principe : « On jouerait avec ma vie, j'avais fait de ma mort un divertissement » (Arcan 2009a, 198), affirme-t-elle, commentaire qui n'est pas sans rappeler celui relatif au suicide de son oncle Léon, qui a aussi fait affaire avec ‹ Paradis, clef en main › : « Le suicide de Léon est l'un de ceux dont on a parlé dans les médias. Quand l'histoire est sortie, il y a eu une onde de choc. La presse s'exaltait, elle avait entre les mains un *reality show* de la mort organisée. » (Arcan 2009a, 152) Le roman fait donc bien plus que simplement critiquer une dérive possible du Québec postmoderne, il dit la barbarie qui prolifère technologiquement sur le cadavre de Dieu et dans l'atrophie *infernale* d'un moi en spectacle, cette idole décevante.

L'enfer, c'est nous autres[3]

Dans la tradition de certains romans dystopiques, et surtout à la manière des écrivains qui ont tenté de nommer l'expérience totalitaire du 20ᵉ siècle, Arcan établit différents rapprochements intertextuels entre la société de demain et l'enfer, ce lieu de la damnation spirituelle : « Avec plus ou moins de dextérité et de liberté, sciemment ou inconsciemment, les auteurs d'Enfers ont, au XXᵉ siècle, souvent pris modèle sur Dante. » (Faye 1993, 176) Dans le roman, l'enfer constitue l'envers du décor, celui du paradis annoncé dès le titre, autant qu'il incarne la crise sociétale présente et future : « Dans son dernier roman publié en 2009, *Paradis, clef en main*, Nelly Arcan va continuer d'arpenter l'enfer montréalais », affirme Gilles Dupuis (2014, 35-36), ce à quoi il rajoute, au sujet de l'intertextualité présente dans le récit : « À l'instar de *La Divine Comédie*, l'enfer se trouve à l'envers dans la mesure où il débouche sur les toits, c'est-à-dire sur le ciel. » (Dupuis 2014, 35) Différents indices romanesques abondent dans le sens de ces propositions, de la simple expression ponctuelle « illusion d'optique diabolique » (Arcan 2009a, 49) pour décrire le premier lieu de rendez-vous entre Antoinette et les responsables de ‹ Paradis, clef en main ›, jusqu'au rapprochement inusité entre la mère de cette dernière et un hideux démon : « Quinte de toux venue des entrailles de l'enfer, montée de son cul de fer, de feu, de cris brûlés et éternels. » (Arcan 2009a, 213) Mais c'est en définitive par le caniche que le parallèle gagne en substance et dynamise symboliquement le récit, car l'animal en question constitue une sorte de signe sémiotique qui permet la porosité entre l'ici sociologique et l'ailleurs théologique.[4] En effet, l'animal guide et tourmente Antoinette dans les lieux de rendez-vous fixés par ‹ Paradis, clef en main ›, à la manière d'un Virgile animalier errant d'un cercle infernal à l'autre, voire d'un petit diablotin perché sur son épaule, et ce, afin de l'inciter à la faute : « caniche miniature, surexcité, satanique » (Arcan 2009a, 172), l'animal est aussi décrit comme « chien de la mort » (Arcan 2009a, 207), expression à un mot près d'‹ ange de la mort ›. C'est d'ailleurs lui qui incite Antoinette au suicide à la fin en « jappant à tout rompre en décrivant des cercles, en allant se frapper aux meubles, couinements, grognements, halètements » (Arcan 2009a, 208). La narratrice va même dire : « Si le caniche n'avait pas été là, je n'aurais peut-être pas appuyé. Qui sait, je n'aurais peut-être pas posé le geste » (Arcan 2009a, 208), réflexion à mettre en relation avec son tout premier contact avec ce petit démon frisé dans l'édifice à plusieurs étages, comme autant de cercles infernaux : « Quelle était la signification de la présence de ce caniche-ci en ce lieu ? » (Arcan 2009a, 68) La réponse à cette question[5] pourrait être qu'Antoinette ne réalisait pas qu'en cognant aux portes de ‹ Paradis, clef en main › (comme à celles du futur), elle pénétrerait dans un enfer où tout espoir d'en sortir était vain, le chien en étant l'indice caché, le déjà-là.

L'intertextualité avec l'enfer dantesque coexiste avec un phénomène d'intermédialité, concept défini par Jürgen Ernst Müller de la façon suivante : « Un produit médiatique devient intermédiatique quand il transpose le côte à côte multimédiatique, le système de citations médiatiques, en une complicité conceptuelle dont les ruptures et stratifications esthétiques ouvrent d'autres voies à l'expérience. » (Müller 2000, 113) La fonction du caniche en tant que signe intermédiaire avec un hors-texte théologico-symbolique converge vers un chef-d'œuvre de la peinture médiévale : l'animal rappelle non seulement l'enfer, mais plus spécifiquement la vanité, car il conjure non seulement Dante, mais aussi Memling. Le célèbre triptyque de ce peintre flamand intitulé *La vanité terrestre et la salvation divine*, « une peinture de chute de damnées vers les enfers » (expression tirée d'*À ciel ouvert* [Arcan 2009b, 178]), cadre exactement avec l'imagerie de *Paradis, clef en main*, autant par son iconographie que par sa morale : par le biais d'Antoinette, qui a survécu à son suicide et qui s'est réconciliée avec la vie, le roman indique implicitement qu'il faut choisir la vie et non pas le suicide, expression déclinable de différentes façons chez Memling (il faut choisir le bien et non pas le mal, Dieu et non pas Lucifer, etc.). De plus, l'un des motifs de cette toile semble être subtilement repris par Arcan :

> Le second tableau représente les tourments de l'Enfer [...]. Un monstre à la gueule béante attire irrésistiblement les damnés qui se tordent de douleur dans les flammes. Un démon danse sur leurs corps, en brandissant une bannière où se trouve écrit : IN INFERNO NULLA EST REDEMPTIO. Un autre panneau symbolise la Vanité [...]. Une jeune femme toute nue, entourée d'un griffon et de deux lévriers, tient à la main un miroir qui reflète ses traits [...]. Et voici, peinte sur un fond noir, la mort victorieuse ! Elle se dresse fièrement à côté d'une tombe où gît un squelette. (Dumont 1966, 74)

Ce qui manque à cette description du tableau de Memling, c'est le petit caniche blanc visible à la gauche de la jeune femme vaniteuse qui « tient à la main un miroir » (Dumont 1966, 74), laquelle rappelle spécifiquement Antoinette, son chien et son plafond-miroir, ainsi que tous les personnages principaux d'Arcan, comme autant d'« enfant[s] dans le miroir » (Arcan/Bourguignon 2007) perdus dans la vanité de leur image. À la manière du tableau de Memling dans sa représentation de l'enfer, *Paradis, clef en main* se présente comme un *memento mori* littéraire, genre esthétique dont le mot d'ordre oscille entre deux significations connexes : « [L]'expression (proprement : ‹ souviens-toi de la mort ›) est [...] souvent traduite par un ‹ souviens-toi que *tu* vas mourir › qui redouble l'implication personnelle de l'enjeu. » (Delmotte 2010, 9) En cela, ce roman posthume reste fidèle au projet d'écriture tacite fixé dans l'*excipit* de *Putain*, c'est-à-dire celui d'une romancière qui « interpelle la vie du côté de la mort » (Arcan 2001, 187). Bien plus, il dit l'enfer de la vanité individualiste comme l'envers du décor du Québec d'aujourd'hui, blessé depuis quelques décennies par l'un des plus hauts taux de suicides au monde.

David BOUCHER

La banalité de la mort

En définitive, *Paradis, clef en main* s'approprie originalement le genre de l'anticipation pour nommer la crise sociétale québécoise liée à l'héritage de sa modernité accélérée et à sa condition définitivement postmoderne, et ce, en fustigeant les dérives nihilistes liées aux récentes avenues du libéralisme et aux nouvelles opportunités du capitalisme, plus précisément celle de l'euthanasie à vendre. Un premier indice de cette critique réside dans le caractère double des lieux de rendez-vous fixés par la compagnie ‹ Paradis, clef en main ›, qui indiquent symboliquement le devenir funeste de certaines revendications du Québec des années 1960 et 1970 : hypersexualité, hédonisme, narcissisme sont autant d'expressions imagées qui dénoncent la foire aux vanités qu'Arcan associe au monde d'aujourd'hui, relégué à l'autrefois par le chronotope de la guillotine de 1789. Sans la nostalgie ou l'apologétique, son roman dit aussi la vacuité engendrée par ‹ la mort de Dieu ›, que le technologique et le monétaire ont comblé implicitement par un nouvel énoncé post-nietzschéen : ‹ Ich bin Gott ›. Le roman affirme finalement, par le thème du suicide, que les portes du paradis de la liberté individuelle s'ouvrent de plus en plus sur l'enfer d'une société néolibérale en perte de repères et guettée par la banalité du mal. Cette notion[6], formulée par Hannah Arendt pour décrire l'instrumentalisation de la barbarie nazie de façon consensuelle dans les institutions et la population allemandes à l'époque d'Hitler, est sans doute la mise en garde ultime d'une anticipation dystopique qui pourrait réellement devenir, dans un proche avenir, maître chez nous.

1   Nautilus Plus renvoie ici à un centre de conditionnement physique du Québec.

2   Dans cette perspective de la ‹ mort de Dieu ›, la postmodernité évoquée ici renvoie à la définition qu'en donne Lyotard (2002, 7), celle de « l'incrédulité à l'égard des métarécits », en l'occurrence, chez Arcan, celui du christianisme, tombé en désuétude après la Révolution tranquille.

3   Nom d'une émission de télévision populaire au Québec (*talk show*) durant les années 1990, forgé à partir d'un jeu de mots en référence à Sartre.

4   Tel qu'évoqué par Cécile Hanania (2010), le caniche comporte aussi une dimension intertextuelle forte, celle liée à *Alice au pays des merveilles*.

5   Michel Peterson (2010, 78), pour sa part, répond à cette question par une autre question : « N'est-ce pas la fidélité à la mort que vient signifier cet animal ? »

6   Hannah Arendt (2002, 1296) affirme au sujet d'Adolf Eichmann : « C'est la pure absence de pensée – ce qui n'est pas du tout la même chose que la stupidité – qui lui a permis de devenir un des plus grands criminels de son époque. Et si cela est ‹ banal › et même comique, si, avec la meilleure volonté du monde, on ne parvient pas à découvrir en Eichmann la moindre profondeur diabolique ou démoniaque, on ne dit pas pour autant, loin de là, que cela est ordinaire. »

Bibliographie

Arcan, Nelly : *Putain*. Paris : Seuil, 2001.

Arcan, Nelly : *Folle*. Paris : Point, 2005.

Arcan, Nelly : *Paradis, clef en main*. Montréal : Coups de tête, 2009a.

Arcan, Nelly : *À ciel ouvert*. Paris : Point, 2009b.

Arcan, Nelly / Bourguignon, Pascale : *L'enfant dans le miroir*. Montréal : Marchand de feuilles, 2007.

Arendt, Hannah : *Les origines du totalitarisme. Eichmann à Jérusalem*. Paris : Gallimard, 2002.

Bakhtine, Mikhaïl : *Esthétique et théorie du roman*. Paris : Gallimard, 2013.

Baudrillard, Jean : *Simulacres et simulation*. Paris : Éditions Galilée, 2002.

Cros, Edmond : *La sociocritique*. Paris : L'Harmattan, 2003.

Delmotte, Benjamin : *Esthétique de l'angoisse. Le memento mori comme thème esthétique*. Paris : Presses universitaires de France, 2010.

Dumont, Georges Henri : *Hans Memling*. Alleur : Marabout université, 1966.

Dupuis, Gilles : « Arcanes de Montréal : la métropole dans les romans de Nelly Arcan ». In : *Études littéraires* 45,2 (2014), 27-40.

Faye, Éric : *Dans les laboratoires du pire. Totalitarisme et fiction littéraire au XXe siècle*. Paris : José Corti, 1993.

Hanania, Cécile : « Arcan, Nelly. *Paradis, clef en main* ». In : *Dalhousie French Studies* 90 (2010), 174-175.

Lapointe, Martine-Emmanuelle : « Dans la fiction, absolument ». In : *Voix et Images* 36,1 (2010), 133-136.

Lyotard, Jean-François : *La condition postmoderne*. Paris : Les Éditions de Minuit, 2002.

Meuleau, Maurice : *L'histoire de France en 100 mots célèbres*. Paris : Armand Colin, 2010.

Meunier, Emmanuel-Martin / Warren, Jean-Philippe : *Sortir de la ‹ Grande noirceur ›. L'horizon ‹ personnaliste › de la Révolution tranquille*. Sillery : Septentrion, 2002.

Müller, Jürgen Ernst : « L'intermédialité, une nouvelle approche interdisciplinaire : perspectives théoriques et pratiques à l'exemple de la vision de la télévision ». In : *Cinémas* 10,2-3 (2000), 105-134.

Nietzsche, Friedrich : *Ainsi parlait Zarathoustra*. Paris : Folio, 1995.

Peterson, Michel : « Ce qui se tient là derrière ». In : *Spirale* 234 (2010), 76-78.

Todorov, Tzvetan : *Le siècle des totalitarismes*. Paris : Bouquins, 2010.

Žižek, Slavoj : *Fragile absolu. Pourquoi l'héritage chrétien vaut-il d'être défendu ?* Paris : Flammarion, 2008.

Nicoletta DOLCE (Montréal)

La poésie de Mario Brassard : au-delà de l'heure violacée des exécutions

Summary

Mario Brassard, a young Quebec writer, has so far published three collections of poems: *Choix d'apocalypses* (2003), *La somme des vents contraires* (2006), and *Le livre clairière* (2012). In *Choix d'apocalypses*, some undefined slaughters that take place are not mentioned directly: there is only a cross-border land illuminated by an agonizing sun, where human beings 'practice' to die. It is a day of war chanted by the voice of a solitary subject. The same deadly wind crosses *Le livre clairière* that in the first section welcomes a sick subject whose body becomes "l'étendue des dommages de notre siècle éventré" (Brassard 2012, 12). As to the second part of the same collection, it is supported by a *we* whose history written in the imperfect is consumed in the shadow of a collective disaster. What strikes in the last part of the collection is the unexpected emergence of a subject who, juggling with death, imagines himself "conjugué au futur" (Brassard 2012, 63). This article will show how certain textual and thematic devices build the apocalyptic landscape in *Choix d'apocalypses* and *Le livre clairière*. It will enable us to penetrate into a universe where dysphoric writing paradoxically drifts towards a writing of lucid and disenchanted hope.

Introduction

Mario Brassard, jeune écrivain québécois, a trois recueils à son actif : *Choix d'apocalypses* (2003), *La somme des vents contraires* (2006) et *Le livre clairière* (2012). Les deux premiers ont été finalistes à sept prix littéraires différents alors que, pour le dernier, le poète a reçu le prix Émile-Nelligan. Dans *Choix d'apocalypses*, des carnages indéfinis ne sont pas évoqués directement : il ne reste qu'une terre transfrontalière, éclairée par un soleil agonique, où les êtres humains s'exercent à mourir. C'est un jour de guerre scandé par la voix d'un *je* solitaire. Le même vent mortifère traverse *Le livre clairière* qui, dans la première section, accueille un *tu* malade dont le corps devient « l'étendue des dommages de notre siècle éventré » (Brassard 2012, 12). Pour ce qui est de la deuxième partie du même recueil, elle est soutenue par un *nous*, dont l'histoire, retracée à l'imparfait, se consume à l'ombre d'une catastrophe collective. Toutefois, ce qui frappe dans le troisième volet de l'œuvre, c'est le surgissement imprévu d'un *je* à l'élan vitaliste qui, jonglant avec la mort et se réclamant fils de la mémoire, s'imagine « conjugué au futur » (Brassard 2012, 63). Cet article montrera par quels dispositifs textuels et thématiques ce paysage apocalyptique se construit autant dans *Choix d'apocalypses* que dans *Le livre clairière*. De plus, il tentera de répondre à l'interrogation suivante : l'écriture dystopique de Mario Brassard remplace-t-elle le besoin de nouvelles utopies ?

Choix d'apocalypses

De prime abord, ce qui frappe dans les deux œuvres en question, ce sont bien les titres. Arrêtons-nous sur *Choix d'apocalypses*, recueil dans lequel le deuxième terme est au pluriel, afin de revenir rapidement aux origines de ce mot. Du grec *apo* (préfixe privatif) et *kalupsis* (qui signifie ‹ cacher ›), il renvoie premièrement à une révélation, notamment à la révélation faite à Saint Jean dans le livre canonique du Nouveau Testament. Dans l'acception contemporaine, il réfère à un événement d'une extrême brutalité qui bouleverse le cours des choses. Quelle que soit la signification donnée à ce terme, le pluriel qu'il arbore ici désoriente. Correspondrait-il à un effet de style, en fait à une synecdoque, dont la fonction serait de noircir l'horizon d'attente du lecteur ? Ou exprimerait-il plutôt un état de crise endémique, une situation terrible évoquée par le constat : « Ici on fabrique une mort sans égale » (Brassard 2003, 52) ?

Dans ce vers incisif, l'indétermination autant du déictique « [i]ci » que du pronom « on » suggère une condition planétaire incomparable (« sans égale »). Révélatrice est aussi la présence du verbe ‹ fabriquer ›, référence explicite à l'expression « fabrication de cadavres » employée par Hannah Arendt qui, elle, en donne une explication exhaustive dans son ouvrage *Le système totalitaire*[1] (Arendt 2005, 190). La fabrication de la mort, dans ce cas, implique un processus de dénaturalisation de celle-ci, autrement dit, le fait de fabriquer la mort, de la programmer scientifiquement, ôte à tout individu le droit de mourir humainement, tue, selon Arendt, la mort qui nous humanise.[2] Toutefois, le syntagme « [c]hoix d'apocalypses » renferme quelque chose de dérangeant, d'inapproprié. En fait, ‹ avoir le choix › suppose une situation qui précède l'événement, implique un ‹ avant ›, un espace-temps où plusieurs possibilités sont encore envisageables. Avoir le choix suppose que l'on puisse faire ou ne pas faire une chose donnée, alors que l'apocalypse nous plonge dans l'immédiateté, dans la calamité. Elle nous tombe dessus sans nous laisser de choix. Autrement dit, il s'agit d'un titre trompeur qui alimente une illusion, rapidement dissipée lorsqu'on plonge dans une lecture plus attentive du texte. Et pourtant l'idée de l'existence d'un ‹ avant › émerge ailleurs dans le recueil. Premièrement, dans le péritexte, où le poète écrit : « À Marilène Gill, avant même cette dédicace. »[3] Ensuite, elle jaillit ailleurs, prenant des nuances mortifères dans le poème « Faire des dragons » : « Mourir déjà empaillé / Avec quelques allumettes / Et un réflexe de pendu au bout du feu. » (Brassard 2003, 20)

L'action de mourir, énoncée par l'infinitif – mode sans aucune indication de personne ni de temps – suggère, par le truchement de l'adverbe « déjà », un état de mort ‹ avant › la mort, une condition de perte de la lymphe vitale. Alors les êtres humains, bourrés de paille, insensibilisés, ne gardent que leur forme, mise en péril par la présence de cette source de feu : autant les allumettes que le réflexe de ce pendu transmettent une idée de précarité. De plus, le fait d'être empaillé renvoie à l'individu qui n'est pas maître de son existence, qui vit passivement, ce qui va à l'encontre de l'image de ‹ l'homme rapaillé › proposée par Gaston Miron dans son célèbre recueil, qu'on trouve en filigrane dans *Choix d'apocalypses* : dans *L'homme rapaillé* en effet l'homme, grâce à la poésie, se prend en main et se refait par lui-même à partir d'éléments épars (cf. Miron 1994).

En réalité, une telle ‹ non-vie pré-mortem › est évoquée ailleurs dans le recueil de Brassard : « On apprend à l'instant à mourir / Sans se servir de son corps. » (Brassard 2003, 12) Le deuxième vers, porté par l'effet traînant des fricatives sourdes, nous oriente vers une mort intérieure partiellement assumée par le *je* lyrique dans les vers suivants : « De l'autre côté de l'océan où je vais / Il vaut mieux être sec et bourré de paille / C'est là que se trouvent les dragons. » (Brassard 2003, 31) Ce dessèchement intérieur est-il primordial afin de se garantir une sorte de survie ? Et ces dragons, nommés deux fois dans le recueil, à qui renverraient-ils ? Ce sont des questions auxquelles le texte ne donne pas de réponses explicites. L'indétermination plane également sur les deux déictiques spatiaux, le « [i]ci » (« Ici on fabrique une mort sans égale ») et le « là » du poème précédent, car aucune indication géographique n'est jamais fournie. Cependant, l'idée que cet endroit, imprécis et lointain, demeure dangereux, comme l'est du reste l'*ici*, surgit ailleurs dans le recueil, et plus précisément alors que le *je* constate qu'« [à] l'autre bout du monde le plafond cède » (Brassard 2003, 54).

Choix d'apocalypses contient une suite de quarante-six poèmes, d'instantanés possédant chacun un titre. Ils se tiennent sur une page et n'ont pas de liens évidents entre eux. Le temps est décliné en trois dimensions (passé, présent et futur) et les pronoms personnels varient. Divisés en strophes, ces poèmes révèlent un style assez similaire, puisque dans la majorité des cas la coupe syntaxique correspond à la coupe lyrique. Néanmoins, cette simplicité apparente est déjouée, parfois, par la profusion de figures rhétoriques, qui complexifient la lecture. Par ici et par là, des déictiques spatiaux et temporels (« [i]ci », « [l]à-bas » ; « à l'instant », « bientôt », « aujourd'hui », « autrefois », Brassard 2003, 9, 12, 14, 24, 28) donnent l'illusion d'une certaine concrétude, alors que, dans les faits, tout baigne dans le vague. L'apocalypse n'est nommée qu'une fois, au pluriel, dans le titre, et le mot ‹ catastrophe › n'y apparaît jamais. Les carnages ne sont pas évoqués non plus. Les dispositifs textuels et thématiques mis en œuvre dans ce recueil tendent vers une écriture épurée, privée de toute image attribuable à des faits circonstanciels connus. Dans ce paysage dénudé, une voix anonyme retentit : « Aujourd'hui c'est un jour de guerre / On le voit au vêtement des hommes / Ces rides sont des tranchées. » (Brassard 2003, 24)

Ce tercet, où les coupes lyriques et syntaxiques coïncident, ne comporte aucune fioriture. Il s'agit d'un constat suivi d'une description, les deux étant dépourvus d'adjectifs et d'adverbes. Chaque vers s'articule autour d'un seul verbe, ‹ être › et ‹ voir ›, et le champ lexical demeure concret. Une seule métaphore clôt cette séquence : elle associe le corps vieillissant (corps malade aussi, car les rides peuvent découler de la fatigue ou de la souffrance) à la terre aux allures de champ de bataille sur lequel « le sang coule » (Brassard 2003, 15). Il s'agit d'un paysage surplombé par un « ciel vide » (Brassard 2003, 22), dans lequel un *je* lucide entrevoit la déperdition de l'humain, alors qu'un *vous* indéterminé demeure indifférent (« Tout suivrait son cours vous n'auriez rien vu », Brassard 2003, 18). Ici, les objets et les êtres ont perdu leur fonction originaire : des humains empaillés, des chevaux acéphales et des couteaux sans dents le composent (cf. Brassard

2003, 15). Cette dénaturation serait-elle le présage d'un bouleversement imminent ? Le distique suivant semble le sous-entendre : « Partout le paysage fait des fautes / Bientôt les forêts au fond des mers. » (Brassard 2003, 17) Les deux vers, au rythme rapide donné par l'enchaînement de consonnes labiodentales (f) et dentales (t/d), renvoient à la signification originaire du mot catastrophe. *Kata* en grec signifie ‹ en bas › et *strépho* renvoie au verbe ‹ tourner ›. Autrement dit, il s'agit de ‹ tourner vers le bas ›, de ‹ subvertir l'ordre constitué ›, et « les forêts au fond des mers » évoquent manifestement un tel bouleversement. Bouleversement présent également dans *Le livre clairière*. En outre, cette subversion s'infiltre davantage dans la trame textuelle, car elle figure aussi dans la facture de certains vers qui, tout en reprenant des expressions figées, les chamboulent. « Ne partez pas le *cercueil* ne fait que commencer »[4] (Brassard 2003, 26), s'exclame le sujet qui, ailleurs dans le recueil, enjoint à un *vous* imprécis de partir vite, car « *[i]l y a des vies où il vaut mieux ne pas s'arrêter* »[5] (Brassard 2003, 30).

Le livre clairière

Comme pour *Choix d'apocalypses*, le titre du *Livre clairière* attire notre attention, car il contient deux substantifs apposés.[6] Le livre alors, en tant que tel, représente une clairière ; il est la clairière en question, ce lieu ouvert dans une zone boisée où la lumière du soleil arrive jusqu'au sol. Cette clarté cependant tardera à poindre, puisqu'elle ne se manifestera que dans la troisième partie de l'œuvre.

Dans l'exergue, l'auteur rend hommage à l'un de ses maîtres, Fernando Pessoa, en y inscrivant un vers tiré des *Œuvres poétiques d'Álvaro de Campos* (1944) : « J'ai besoin de vérité et d'aspirine. » (Brassard 2012, 7) Par une tournure frôlant l'absurde, le côté sérieux de cet adage se double d'un côté drolatique, désopilant. Le prosaïsme de Campos, l'un des hétéronymes de Pessoa, représente ce qu'il y a de plus moderne dans l'œuvre de cet écrivain. En fait, les lecteurs reconnaissent dans cette poésie l'insurmontable difficulté d'exister. Et d'ailleurs, cette aspirine aura-t-elle le pouvoir de l'endiguer ? En d'autres termes, Campos représente le 20e siècle : ses angoisses, ses névroses, son cynisme et sa disponibilité pour la contradiction. Un tel exergue donne décidément le ton du recueil de Brassard.

Celui-ci est divisé en trois sections rédigées entièrement en prose poétique : « La distance dévorée par les loups », « Le cahier blanc » et « Autoportrait à la clairière ». Au début de la première, traversée par la présence d'un *tu* indéterminé, nous lisons : « Un siècle sans pluie ou le désert en sens inverse. Jardins éventrés, jardins vidés jusqu'à la lie. Tu hoches faiblement la tête : partout des mèches. Tu deviens l'étendue des dommages [...]. » (Brassard 2012, 12) Dans ce passage, la présence d'un corps en crise s'associe à l'image de la subversion de l'ordre naturel, le terme ‹ crise › étant entendu ici dans sa plus ancienne acception, la phase décisive d'une maladie. Ce corps en souffrance reflète la maladie du siècle, soit l'affaiblissement de l'humain, puisqu'il devient sa manifestation concrète et pathologique. Comme Hugues Corriveau (2013) le remarque dans le journal *Le Devoir* : « Avec une grande force d'évocation, le poète s'approche de la douleur et de la soumission de l'autre, le cœur en berne, la voix cassée. » Il est important de souligner que si *Choix d'apocalypses* était parcouru par cette idée d'un ‹ avant › (la mort avant la mort), *Le livre clairière*, quant à lui, suggère un ‹ après › assez sinistre. Ces deux extraits le montrent explicitement : « Tu ne sais plus qui de toi ou de ton cadavre fait peur aux enfants » (Brassard 2012, 20), « Me réveiller pour assister à mon départ, cadavre dans mes valises » (Brassard 2012, 62).

Nous sommes déjà dans l'après-mort, lorsque le corps a cessé de vivre. Car si le corps de *Choix d'apocalypses* était empaillé, privé de ses fonctions originaires, l'auteur présente ici la phase suivante, celle de la décomposition. Ce concept revient : « Combien de nuits à laver tes mains, à conjuguer le sang que l'on étire sur deux générations, pour te réveiller en sueur à l'heure violacée des exécutions ? » (Brassard 2012, 22) À la lecture de ce passage une question jaillit : est-ce bien l'heure qui est violacée ou plutôt les exécutions ? Cet adjectif qui signifie, entre autres, « [d]evenu plus ou moins violet sous l'effet d'une cause physique »[7], a été déplacé, par le biais d'une hypallage, afin de créer un effet déroutant. Souvent, la couleur violacée est attribuée au *livor mortis*, à ces lividités visibles sur un cadavre à partir de la deuxième heure après la mort. Ce sont bien les morts qui l'arborent et non pas les exécutions, comme cette métonymie – dans ce cas, la cause pour l'effet – le sous-entend.

Après la première section, portée par une tonalité élégiaque – la mort, le passage du temps – nous entrons dans une deuxième section, « Le cahier blanc », foncièrement différente, dont le registre est épique. Trente-et-un poèmes en prose y figurent, tous numérotés et écrits dans un style narratif. Il y a un *nous* et aussi un narrateur qui adhère à ce *nous* incertain. De plus, ce *nous* accomplit des actions dans un laps de temps linéaire, scandé par des phases. L'âge des illusions (du temps, de l'immortalité ainsi que de l'infaillibilité) est suivi de l'âge de la prise de conscience de la précarité de l'existence et de l'émergence des conflits : « Le soir, la radio donnait le *pointage* des guerres. »[8] (Brassard 2012, 37) Une troisième phase s'ensuit, correspondant à la guerre qui se répand inexorablement : « Minuit passé, on égrena le chapelet *des premières bombes.* »[9] (Brassard 2012, 40) Les conflits, l'exode et la mort déferlent jusqu'à la perte de tout point de repère, jusqu'aux meurtres collectifs et à l'horreur des cadavres empalés ou entassés vers le ciel. L'âge de la capitulation clôt cette partie. À la différence de *Choix d'apocalypses*, aux images rares et épurées, « Le cahier blanc » foisonne de tableaux de guerre, de défaite, de mort (« crâne ouvert », « fosses creusées », « villes désertées », « cadavres empalés », « épidémies », Brassard 2012, 41, 44, 45, 45, 52). Toutefois, un élément les relie, l'image de l'homme empaillé : « [S]urtout ne pas bouger, ignorer la faim, rester calmes, si calmes qu'à la fin de la saison, n'être plus que des épouvantails sous un ciel rempli d'avions. » (Brassard 2012, 47)

Avec surprise, le ton et les intentions changent dans « Autoportrait à la clairière », la section finale. Débutant par une image de lumière, elle laisse présager la découverte d'un passage, d'une voie de sortie : « À l'orée du livre, j'avance bouche ouverte. Ni fleuve de salive ni puits raconté dans mes larmes : je ne parle que l'esquif. Ma voix d'enfant barbu dit les rides d'un pays couleur peau, le cœur déjà froid de la pomme. » (Brassard 2012, 57) Ici revient distinctement, par le truchement de la métaphore initiale, l'identification entre le livre et la clairière. Et ici émerge également un *je* lyrique, un adulte à l'énergie et à l'enthousiasme d'un enfant, exprimant son agentivité, soit sa capacité à agir sur le monde et à l'influencer. Bien que sa langue soit ‹ frêle et légère › (comme un esquif), il se place au centre de l'acte créateur en se proclamant à la fois peintre et ennemi (cf. Brassard 2012, 61). Et cette dualité s'installe par le biais d'un double pronom personnel *je/tu*, où le *tu* n'est que l'hypostase du *je*. Il est intéressant de remarquer, dans l'extrait cité, le retour de l'association entre le corps vieilli (malade ou fatigué) et la terre, le pays.

Tout en étant « né avec un nom de deuil » (Brassard 2012, 58), métaphore exprimant le poids d'un siècle à la dérive, le *je* lyrique se nomme « phénix » (Brassard 2012, 59, 60, 62), cet oiseau mythologique doué d'une extraordinaire longévité, qui avait le pouvoir de renaître de ses cendres (symbole de la résurgence cyclique). Ses propos sont clairs : « J'habite une vie à blanc. » (Brassard 2012,

61) De l'expression « à blanc » découlent plusieurs images. ‹ Saigner à blanc ›, c'est-à-dire « soutirer quelque chose jusqu'à l'épuisement »[10], ‹ couper à blanc ›, notamment utilisé pour indiquer une « [c]oupe rase n'épargnant aucun arbre »[11], ‹ cuire à blanc ›, renvoyant à la cuisson d'une croûte vide, ou encore ‹ une balle à blanc ›, soit une balle qui ne peut faire de mal, qui ne peut tuer. Toutes ces locutions, à l'exception de la dernière, réfèrent à un état de dénuement. À vrai dire, l'enchaînement de deux métaphores, l'image qui en dérive ainsi que le rôle de peintre spéléologue que le sujet s'attribue (cf. Brassard 2012, 63), me rappellent le tableau *Carré blanc sur fond blanc* (1918) de Kasimir Malevitch, le père du suprématisme. Celui-ci proposait une peinture libérée de toute représentation figurative où l'image, n'étant que pure sensation, se détachait de la réalité extérieure. Un tel univers infini et dénudé évoque une dimension où, même marquée du sceau de la fragilité, tout est encore possible. Ce qui est conforté par les mots du *je* lyrique, comme dans ces extraits : « Je voyage l'aiguille de la boussole pointée vers ce qui tremble » (Brassard 2012, 66), « Encore un peu de fatigue, et la fenêtre débouchera peut-être sur une clairière où rendre les armes » (Brassard 2012, 69).

Conclusion

Pour conclure sans conclure, puisque cette œuvre surprenante offre de multiples pistes d'analyse, nous tenterons de répondre à l'interrogation émise en introduction : l'écriture dystopique remplace-t-elle le besoin de nouvelles utopies ? La lecture de *Choix d'apocalypses* et *Le livre clairière* nous permet de pénétrer un univers où l'écriture dysphorique dérive paradoxalement vers une écriture de l'espoir lucide et désenchanté. En fait, si les deux recueils portent à croire que l'univers poétique de Mario Brassard se nourrit d'une contre-utopie, cette impression se dissipe à la lecture de la dernière partie du *Livre clairière*. Ici, le temps des utopies et des dystopies est révolu. Ces *topoï* sont remplacés par un « lieu de présence », un immense « chantier de survivance » (Vattimo 1987, 164) où « la vie mord de partout, louve dans un corps de lune » (Brassard 2012, 67). Cette métaphore, filée grâce à deux images féminines, ne peut qu'annoncer, par la présence de la « lune », la transformation incessante et la renaissance et, par la figure de la « louve », l'esprit terrien et la fécondité. En fait, ce lieu de présence réfère à un endroit réel, peut-être précaire, mais dans lequel la fragilité humaine, la vulnérabilité de l'existence ainsi que sa force régénératrice constituent les seules chances de survie.

1   Hannah Arendt, *Zur Person*, entretien avec Günter Gaus, émission diffusée en 1964 à la télévision allemande (RFA), https://www.youtube.com/watch?v=dsoImQfVsO4 (consultation 10/06/2017). L'expression « fabrication de cadavres » est employée par Arendt dans *Le système totalitaire* (2005, 190). Il est essentiel de ne pas oublier l'influence de Heidegger et surtout de son ouvrage *Être et Temps* (publication originale 1927).

2   Ici l'intertexte est *légèrement* transformé par le biais d'une métonymie. On ne fabrique pas de cadavres (l'effet), mais on fabrique la mort (la cause).

3   Ici, il s'agit d'une méta-dédicace.

4   Je souligne.

5   Je souligne.

6   Il ne contient pas le syntagme « le livre des clairières », formé par un nom et son complément.

7   http://www.cnrtl.fr/definition/violacées (consultation 10/06/2017).

8   Je souligne.

9   Ces deux extraits rappellent une tendance propre à l'auteur, c'est-à-dire celle de détourner des clichés dans le propos de déstabiliser le lecteur, de brouiller son horizon d'attente. Je souligne.

10 http://www.linternaute.com/dictionnaire/fr/expression/blanc/3/ (consultation 10/06/2017).

11 http://www.linternaute.com/dictionnaire/fr/expression/blanc/3/ (consultation 10/06/2017).

Bibliographie

Arendt, Hannah : *Le système totalitaire*. Paris : Seuil, 2005.
Brassard, Mario : *Choix d'apocalypses*. Montréal : Les Herbes rouges, 2003.
Brassard, Mario : *La somme des vents contraires*. Montréal : Les Herbes rouges, 2006.
Brassard, Mario : *Le livre clairière*. Montréal : Les Herbes rouges, 2012.

Corriveau, Hugues : « Mario Brassard, corps à vif ». In : *Le Devoir* (02/03/2013), http://www.ledevoir.com/culture/livres/372267/poesie-mario-brassard-corps-a-vif (consultation 25/02/2017).

Miron, Gaston : *L'homme rapaillé*. Montréal : l'Hexagone, 1994.

Pessoa, Fernando : *Œuvres poétiques d'Álvaro de Campos*. Paris : Bourgois, 1988 [1944].

Vattimo, Gianni : *La fin de la modernité*. Paris : Seuil, 1987.

Nouveaux cadres éthiques
New Ethical Frameworks

Ana María FRAILE-MARCOS (Salamanca)

The Crisis of Love in Dionne Brand's *Love Enough*[1]

Résumé

Cet article soutient que le roman de Dionne Brand *Love Enough* (2014) apparaît comme une enquête sur l'éthique et la politique de l'amour. La représentation sombre d'une ville indifférente permet d'ouvrir l'espace urbain de Toronto à la sociabilité humaine et à la coopération à travers l'interaction des différents types d'amour : *agape, eros, philia,* et *storge.* En ce qui concerne l'analyse de l'amour comme outil affectif et politique qui combine le « romantisme rêvant » (Clarke 2012, 162 ; trad. A. Fraile-Marcos) avec l'éveil de la conscience politique, cet article est inspiré par les théories de Terry Eagleton, Sara Ahmed, Lauren Berlant, Slavoj Žižek, Michael Hardt, Rosi Braidotti, Frantz Fanon, George Elliott Clarke, et bell hooks.

Introduction

In his analysis of Dionne Brand's early work, George Elliott Clarke argues that it shows a paradoxical dynamic that drives all her œuvre, namely the "dialectic of romanticism dreaming and political consciousness awakening" (Clarke 2012, 162). In my reading of Brand's recent novel *Love Enough* (2014), I posit that the author continues the exploration of this dynamic through the reactivation of love as both an affective and political tool. Thus, Brand's engagement with affect balances competing versions of personal love against a renewed call to achieve social change through revolutionary love. Whereas personal love becomes a hindrance, a distraction for the revolutionary dreamer, it is also posited as the means through which to overcome the "futility and smallness" of existence (Brand 2014, 138). Through a series of linked vignettes conveying the social mesh of life in Toronto, *Love Enough* appears as a laboratory testing various kinds of love and their use in affecting social justice and personal change.

The Aristotelian and Christian traditions propose four different categories of love that fall within the definitions of the Ancient Greek terms *agape* (ἀγάπη), *eros* (ἔρως), *philia* (φιλία), and *storge* (στοργή) (cf. Lewis 1960). *Agape,* or char-ity, refers to the unconditional love of God for his children and of man for God, although Thomas Aquinas expanded its meaning to denote the practice of willing the good of another. Although *eros* is linked to intimate love and sexual passion for a person, in the *Symposium* Plato used it to refer to the appreciation of beauty within people through contemplation, and then he extended it to the appreciation of beauty itself, arguing that *eros* helps the soul recall knowledge of beauty, contributing to an understanding of spiritual truth. Therefore, even erotic desire may be seen as a search for truth and transcendence, aspiring to the non-corporeal, spiritual plane of existence. *Philia,* instead, involves the dispas-sionate virtuous love that includes loyalty to friends, family, and community. According to Aristotle's *Nicomachean Ethics,* this sort of brotherly love also in-volves the shared enjoyment of an activity. Finally, *storge* means the natural af-fection for community and family, but an affection that can become a hindrance to spiritual growth when these relations hold you down. In this case, love turns into mere acceptance or putting up with particular circumstances. Hence, the discussion about love is intertwined with theorizing about beauty (aesthetics), epistemology, and ethics.

This paper argues that, together with the dismal depiction of an indifferent city, Dionne Brand's *Love Enough* hints at the possibility of creating Toronto's urban space as the site for human sociability and cooperation directed at communal survival and self-fulfillment through the exploration of the interaction of the various kinds of love mentioned above. This city of outstanding racial and ethnic diversity, where almost half of the population is foreign-born, is often praised as the embodiment of the success of Canadian multiculturalism. Brand's Toronto, however, is peopled by vulnerable denizens whose fortuitous encounters in the decentered, rhizomatic space of the city reveal their struggle to come to terms with personal deracination and alienation, as well as with their own role as agents in the construction of a responsible glocal citizenry, that is, of a society that must learn to negotiate, *through love,* the differential effects of globalization on both the local community and the lives of individuals.[2]

Eros: Love of Beauty

> This ability to find one's own beauty, and to define beauty for one's self, is also politic. It is an act of resistance against all people who declare your community a slum, or who define you personally as ugly or ignorant, or on the margin.
>
> (Clarke in Compton 1998)

The novel's opening scene reminds the reader of the aesthetic component of an ethics of love that is conveyed through material beauty. If, according to Plato, it is the essence of beauty that draws us to love a person or object, the appreciation of beauty is already a form of love. Extremely sensitive to the sensorial, June is a black lesbian social activist in her forties who migrated to Toronto in her youth "from another country, another city" (Brand 2014, 91) and now works at the Women's History Archive. Her search for beauty amidst some of the grimmest enclaves in the city brings to the fore the relationship between love, ethics, and aesthetics. June's quest is anchored in the ancient philosophical thought that holds beauty to be an essential ingredient for the good life. Driving east along Toronto's derelict Dupont Street, the "car-wrecking shops, taxi dispatch sheds, rooming houses, hardware stores, desolate all-night diners and front yards eaten up by a hundred winters' salt" (Brand 2014, 1-2) resound with the precarious lives of the neighborhood's dwellers. Yet, June revels in the transient, breathtaking" (Brand 2014, 1) beauty of a summer sunset reflected in the side mirrors of her car and made ever more glorious by the contrast with the ugliness around. To June, beauty reaches the category of a radical political ethics, because it can trespass geographic and social class boundaries, appearing where it is most "[n]eeded" (Brand 2014, 2) – that is to say, in the inner-city streets. The unexpected "quotidian beauty" of the sunset provides her with a "counterintuitive" (Brand 2014, 1) insight: her connection to even the most marginalized and impoverished souls in the city, who can share, and find solace and spiritual balance, in the contemplation of the sunset. However, even though June relies on the senses to achieve the elation that takes her to reconnect with humanity at large, her commitment to beauty is more cerebral than affective. It is her reasoning about a sort of democratization of beauty that makes her happy (cf. Brand 2014, 2), rather than a solipsistic admiration. June's love, however, goes beyond aesthetic beauty and beyond the egotism of erotic love, and embraces *agape* or *caritas*, a kind of love for your neighbor that is political, active, and, hopefully, productive of a new social life (cf. Hardt 2009, 181).

June similarly defends the transformative power of love emanating from aesthetic beauty when she excitedly embraces the news that she has overheard on the radio about the mayor sending one hundred musicians to the Jane and Finch corridor to combat crime and violence in the neighborhood (cf. Brand 2014, 28-33).[3] This makes perfect sense to her, as she explains:

> The gunmen are children. They need music. They could use some bicycles, some painters, some soccer balls, some fucking trees. The place is pure postindustrial dreck. Who wouldn't want to murder somebody? A hundred trees, a hundred teachers, a hundred trips out there, a hundred anything – not a hundred policemen. (Brand 2014, 31)

June relies on the power of beauty – helped into being by the city authorities – to counteract social conflict and criminality.

However, when beauty is conceived as a sensuous property of objects that we are naturally predisposed to desire or consume, *eros* emerges as a self-centered kind of love that leaves both the lover and the object of his love unfulfilled and disconnected. The beautiful Mercede illustrates this situation in the novel. Mercede is a battered woman, and the mother of two other main characters of Italian descent, Lia and Germain aka Ghost, in this poly-vocal novel of intertwined lives, times, and spaces. When her partner abandons her and their two children to find his luck in Alberta, she begins taking to men who are drawn to her beauty as a means of achieving the socio-economic status that possessing a beautiful woman may provide: "The thing is, they expected wealth to come with beauty. When wealth didn't come along after Mercede, they asked why; if they had beauty why didn't they have wealth too? These were poor men and even though they thought beauty would be enough, it wasn't enough. Wealth did not follow beauty." (Brand 2014, 52) As a result, their love turns into violent hatred, for Mercede and for themselves: "All of Mercede's men punished her for being beautiful, in the end. And all of Mercede's men punished her in the end for choosing them." (Brand 2014, 52)

Equally harmful is Sybil's love of whiteness, which can be understood in the context of Frantz Fanon's theorizing about colonial love. Having absorbed Western standards of beauty, Sybil, a destitute and mentally disturbed black woman who visits June at the archive every other Wednesday, washes her face and hands in Clorox until they are bleached white. Consequently, the novel emphasizes how beauty, like love, is neither essentially ethical nor moral. The fact that the pollution in Lake Ontario may offer strikingly beautiful colors while being dangerously poisonous only reinforces this conclusion (cf. Brand 2014, 2-3). The polluted urbanscape matches the lives of the novel's characters, who have been accumulating layers of negative experiences and feelings that synthesize in what June sees as "[a] concentrated toxin" that can be only dissolved by love, "[b]ut it must be love enough" (Brand 2014, 5). Thus, the novel shifts between Sara Ahmed's refusal of the "assumption that love can provide the foundation for political action, or is a sign of good politics" and the recognition that political vision can be grounded in love: "But what would political vision mean if we did not love those visions?" (Ahmed 2004, 141) Yet, none of the characters in this novel thinks they are loved *enough* to be happy. Love is understood as lack of love: "Because, after all, isn't love absence? Like the absence of a limb makes you notice where it was and what it did." (Brand 2014, 68)

AGAPE: Love as a Political Tool

In contradistinction to personal love, *agape* emerges in the novel as an act of political love, the kind of love that any "true revolutionary" must embrace, as Che Guevara famously put it: "Our vanguard revolutionaries must idealize this love of the people, of the most sacred causes, and make it one and indivisible [...]. We must strive every day so that this love of living humanity is transformed into actual deeds, into acts that serve as examples, as a moving force." (Guevara 1965, 24-25) Yet, rather than highlighting the role of revolutionary, or socially transformative love, the novel explores the difficulties of balancing political and personal love.

June stands the closest to Guevara's revolutionary take on love, torn by the drama of combining "a passionate spirit with a cold intelligence, and mak[ing] painful decisions without flinching" (Guevara 1965, 24). Drawn by a sense of social justice that justifies revolution, she has a history of taking as lovers refugee revolutionaries escaping from Latin American and African countries: "She was, in this way, in terms of love, in terms of sex, indiscriminate." (Brand 2014, 61) However, her love for them is political, rather than erotic. Rather than loving them, she loves the idea of what they represent: "She loved the idea of people rising up against injustice and political terror [...]. This impersonal love, this political love was for June a deeper love, a more democratic love, the ethical love." (Brand 2014, 65) This understanding of love as "a political category," a "category of struggle" that enables solidarity (Žižek 2013), hinders, however, her ability to connect with and understand the other, and her lovers remain forever strangers (Brand 2014, 65). This is most apparent when her erstwhile Chilean lover Isador appears seventeen years later on her doorstep with a bouquet of roses to thank her for her help and invite her to join him and his Canadian family in their first trip to Santiago de Chile. June does not recognize him – "they were strangers" (Brand 2014, 65) – and refuses either to accompany him or to sympathize with the man. June is unable to see people but from a certain angle (cf. Brand 2014, 68), which prevents her from loving them in their wholeness: "Her love [...] was bigger than the love individuals have for each other. Not to put too fine a point on it, if she did love Isador, it was not Isador personally, but the revolution Isador represented that she loved." (Brand 2014, 65)

Doubly marked by the failure of her first romantic relationship and by her childhood discovery that her father had a double life and a second family, June refuses to reciprocate the love that she is given. She believes that "[h]er love was simply bigger than the personal" (Brand 2014, 65), and shows a higher regard for *agape*, or universal love for truth and humanity, than for *eros* or even *philia*. This hinders her relationship with Sidney, "June's first lover without a cause" (Brand 2014, 133). Sidney possesses a "zeal for life" (Brand 2014, 135) that renders her hopeful and optimistic, contrary to June, who reads her optimism as a form of "consumerism" (Brand 2014, 138). In her eyes, her lover Sidney and society in general – or late capitalist society in particular – seem trapped by a "cruel optimism" (Berlant 2011) that prevents them from realizing that "the world can no longer sustain one's organizing fantasies of the good life" (Berlant 2011, 4). Yet, it is this "rich vein of innocent ore [...], a spontaneous space in Sidney that had not yet been dragged by the world" (Brand 2014, 135) which draws June to Sidney: "Sidney acted as if you had to attack each day with all your desires," even if desire has also been commodified by this ultra-capitalist society and turned into "retail desires" (Brand 2014, 138). Sidney's attraction to June, on the other hand, "was ultimately carnal. June did not know that she was sensual. When she went on her rants she appeared sexually suggestive to Sydney, her political intensity physical" (Brand 2014, 139). Yet, Sydney's lack of social consciousness bothers June, even as she sometimes exchanges her revolutionary stance for more intimate strategies of social transformation in her attempts to awaken those closer to her and engage them in personal ways; for example, June rejects any expensive material gift on her birthday but asks Sydney instead for "an embrace each day and a kindness each week" (Brand 2014, 114). As it turns out, Sydney does not follow June's instructions, and June is hurt and resentful of her forgetfulness. As June accepts her failure to make Sydney see beyond the failed promises of capitalist consumerism, she concludes that "[l]ove is love. It wears off" (Brand 2014, 115), thus acknowledging the limits of love as a tool for social and personal transformation. Nevertheless, the last lines of the novel point at Sydney's political awakening, as it dawns on her that love "is hard if you really want to do it right" (Brand 2014, 180).

Philia and *Storge*: An Ethics of Transposition

If *agape* as revolutionary love fails to produce a large-scale social transformation in the novel, personal love becomes central to what Rosi Braidotti calls "a materialist, nomadic philosophy of becoming" (Braidotti 2006, 4). Underlining mutating hybrid subjectivities such as Lia's and Da'uud's, the novel contests normative identities while drawing attention to the importance of the spatial and temporal contextualization of the subject. In her study about nomadic ethics, Braidotti uses the notion of transposition, which she borrows from music and genetics, to focus on the possibilities for subject transformation when "a leap from one code, field or axis into another" occurs, bridging the gaps between, for example, "the omnipresence of a state of crisis on the one hand and the possibility of sustainable futures on the other" (Braidotti 2006, 7). In what follows I aim to illustrate how *philia* and *storge* facilitate transposition in Braidotti's terms, opening up spaces of hopeful transformation in the midst of the characters' ongoing crises, which, though experienced at the personal level, relate to larger socio-political crises connected, for instance, to current global mobility of people and capital.

The challenge to live by a love ethics that relies on *philia,* or the loyalty to family and friends, after having been transplanted to a social context whose rules differ from those learned before immigration to Canada, is exemplified by the ordeals of two interconnected families. On the one hand, Mercede's Italian immigrant parents could never breach the chasm between themselves and their Canadian daughter, which has serious consequences for the emotional health of the third generation, made up of Lia and Ghost. On the other hand, new immigrant families such as that of Bedri – Ghost's friend –, his sister, and their father Da'uud face similar problems to develop a subjectivity nurtured by filial love.

In Mercede's case, she believes all her troubles stem from her mother's lack of love: "Mercede said that Renata hated her, did not love her, did not love her enough." (Brand 2014, 49) Mercede's daughter Lia is convinced, too, that her grandmother's lack of love for Mercede made her "wild" (Brand 2014, 49) as an adolescent and turned her incapable of giving her own children the kind of love that would have provided them with a stable childhood, and not one in and out of foster homes and the Children's Aid Society. "*Perché non hai tenuto di più a Mercede?,*" Lia interrogates her grandmother, "*Why didn't you love Mercede better?*" (Brand 2014, 100) The question 'unpins' Renata (cf. Brand 2014, 103), unleashing a confession of her hidden love, admiration for, and jealousy of Mercede's free spirit: "If it was up to her, she would have run away too, lived a life of fierce self-will and self-destruction. A woman should have that right too." (Brand 2014, 102) In the brief spells in which the siblings have lived with Mercede, her love

> was exhausting because it needed love back constantly [...]. Mercede's love could not hold out against the panic of never being loved enough. And so she worried she did not love them enough without knowing how to love them enough according to that calculus. And feeling that she was failing, she would leave for days on end with someone who loved her. (Brand 2014, 50)

Whereas Germain suffers from "the same kind of unassuageable love hunger as Mercede had," which turns into "a war of love between them" (Brand 2014, 53),

Lia develops a kind of filial love for both her mother and brother that leads her to renounce to her own pleasure out of a sense of responsibility for them.

Encumbered by an ethics of care for her family that she is unable to reject, Lia's love for them tethers her to the city, to the detriment of her own interests. In her case, *storge* prevails over *eros*, becoming a hindrance to her self-fulfillment and spiritual growth. Yet, beauty returns in the novel as the means to make transposition possible, that is, to allow Lia to go beyond *storge* back to *eros* through the appreciation of beauty. As Lia rides Jasmeet's bicycle in the city, she applies the Heraclitean idea of in-flux-subjectivity to herself, and imagines that she can become someone else at each block, "some other part of who she might be" (Brand 2014, 21), in the midst of a world of shifting subjectivities and a city in continuous rapid transformation that erases any landmarks of her life there (cf. Brand 2014, 25). Only when she moves from Toronto to live on Ward's Island on the lake and thus fulfil one of Jasmeet's dreams, to live there, does she accept her friend's advice to "unlock the beautiful" (Brand 2014, 47). Lia wishes "beauty can come into her, metamorphose, suffuse her skin" (Brand 2014, 147), allow her to "unhook herself" (Brand 2014, 152) from her careless family. Eventually, Lia feels "untethered. As if she is connected to no one, and disconnected from everyone. She is only intent on this one thing now: beauty" (Brand 2014, 151), and the reader may envision that she will finally overcome her pain, and love herself.

Filial love is also explored in the relationships between Bedri and his Somali father, Da'uud; between Bedri and June, who adopts a motherly attitude toward him even though he behaves like a thug; and between Bedri and his friend Germain/Ghost. Da'uud's love for his alienated son Bedri manifests itself as he seeks to protect him from "[t]he lethal tensions in the city" (Brand 2014, 79). He knows that Bedri tends to get in trouble. As a kid he always got involved in fights at school, and at the beginning of the novel Bedri and his friend Ghost have just stolen a car and beaten its owner, perhaps to death. The kind of radical masculinity that Bedri and Ghost enact as carjackers seems the natural outcome for these youths who live on the margins of a city that "does not love them," as Brand (2014) puts it in a CBC radio interview, but neither lets them go, drawing them to it like a magnet. When they become aware of the magnitude of what they have done – "We are thugged out, man! Thugged out!" (Brand 2014, 12), Ghost tells Bedry – they decide they cannot sell the stolen car to their contact on the East coast of Canada, as it is going to be linked to a murder. Their complicity in crime seems to strengthen their filial love – "Bedri felt Ghost's hand on his shoulder, brotherly and loving" (Brand 2014, 12) – while they momentarily contemplate escaping to Montreal, which appears to their imagination as "another country" (Brand 2014, 39), with the promise of a clean-slate beginning. However, both boys are revealed to be very different. As they drive in circles in the city in their flight from the crime scene, and Ghost fails to convince Bedri to stop thinking about what had just happened – "Don't think too hard, thug. It's easy like that, man, easy like that. Fucker should have given it up" (Brand 2014, 14) –, he suggests they get dope and a beer to assuage their fear, anger, and bad conscience. However, filial love intervenes, stirring Bedri's ethical conscience and bringing to the surface the complex network of emotions within the family. In this moment of crisis and confusion, Bedri cannot take his father and family out of mind.

To a large extent, Bedri's ethical scruples are embedded in his father's problematic morality, which emerges as a set of contradictory dicta combining statements such as "*To be without a friend is to be poor indeed*" (Brand 2014, 43) with misogynist and terrorist apologies. Thus Da'uud declares that "[y]our woman should be in the house or in a grave" (Brand 2014, 43) and tells Bedri that he wishes he would be making jihad and becoming a suicide bomber rather than see him become a thug (cf. Brand 2014, 71), something which Da'uud immediately regrets: "He is not even a religious man. At times he is harsh with them [his children], he says things he doesn't mean. He cannot make that Bedri do anything." (Brand 2014, 72) Despite their current distance and contest of wills, Bedri feels accountable to his father – "How would he explain it to his father?" (Brand 2014, 43) – and keeps his loyalty and love for Da'uud. In his mind, "[h]is father loomed over him, grabbing his face, squeezing tears from his eyes. *I lose everything, for you to shame me*" (Brand 2014, 15). His influence leads him to tell Ghost he should not have joined him in this venture. For them this is an epiphanic moment after which "[t]heir friendship hung in the sweating air of the car, rough and harmful" (Brand 2014, 40), forecasting, perhaps, that they will follow different paths from then on, with Bedri refusing to be dragged further into delinquency. While both friends part, Bedri feels "left" (Brand 2014, 45).

At this point of utter alienation from family and friends, Bedri finds refuge in June's home, where she performs a sort of filial love for the kids in the neighborhood, providing support without judging them, and we can entertain the idea of Bedri's redemption. June's intervention is one of compassion, as she accepts her own responsibility to become an ameliorative factor in Bedri's life. In this sense her action is political, but it is problematized, as it lends itself to be interpreted as accepting the current conservative shift from the liberal state's responsibility for equal opportunities and social justice to the local action of *individual* compassion. Despite her overall progressive politics, June's move can arguably be read as an instance of what Lauren Berlant identifies as "compassionate conservatism," whereby compassionate action directed to alleviate social suffering "is seen as at best a local response put out by individuals and smaller institutions […]. The problem of social interdependence is no longer deemed structural but located in the faith that binds to itself a visible, lived-in community" (Berlant 2004, 3). The individual, rather than the socio-political institutions, is made responsible for his own welfare and that of the community.

Da'uud, an exiled economist who works as a night-shift taxi driver in Toronto, feels unmoored by the experience of migration. He is not just uprooted from his place of birth, but dislocated in terms of his field of work, his social status, and his position of patriarchal authority within the family, becoming someone with no voice: "[N]obody listens to him. Not his wife, not his daughter, not his son, nobody." (Brand 2014, 80) Yet, characteristically in this novel, utter desolation is shunned and a pinch of hope let in, as Da'uud corrects himself: "Well perhaps his wife, Amal. She listens." (Brand 2014, 80) Nevertheless, Da'uud's diasporic experience in a world ruled by the neoliberal market has led him to occupy a universal position, as Marx would put it, that dissolves all particular modes of life. As Slavoj Žižek (2013) explains,

> [i]t's not a universality with regard to others. Today I am an engineer, when I lose this work tomorrow I can be a taxi driver. Our particular field of work is experienced as something ultimately contingent, the same goes for market commodities. So universality is a way of life as it were, a mode of our immediate experience.

It is perhaps in an attempt to preserve his individuality that Da'uud clings to his past and the 'imaginary community' of his far-away nation. Da'uud's experience of translocation both across the global space of migration and in the space of the city he crosses back and forth as a taxi driver provides him with a sort of "nomadic philosophy of becoming," to use Braidotti's term (2006, 4), which meanders between the apparently antagonist systems of rationalism and irrationality. Da'uud decries the blind embrace of faith – faith in politics, religion, racial, or ethnic superiority, science, economics – that makes "people irrational and murderous" (Brand 2014, 79). All over the world, in Mogadishu, Addis Ababa, Rome, Oslo, and now in Toronto, he has witnessed "this same violence of faith" (Brand 2014, 80). His savvy as an economist only reinforces his night-shift taxi driver perception of the violent nature of humanity and definitely shatters the opposition between the West and the East, the 'First' and the 'Third' Worlds as, respectively, the repositories of either reason and peace or blind faith and disruption.

Yet, Da'uud thinks that positive transformation can be affected by travel. In this hope, he tries to get Bedri out of Toronto and sends him to Somalia on a trip that reverses the direction of his own migration from Somalia to Canada. Da'uud envisions this trip as a redemptive, cleansing rite of passage allowing Bedri to shed his previous identity progressively in the successive connecting airports, which function not only as Marc Augé's (1995) supermodern 'non-places,' but as heterotopian spaces (cf. Foucault 1967) that leave him suspended "in the middle of time" (Brand 2014, 83), preparing him to recreate himself anew: "Five airports from here to Somaliland. Da'uud told Bedri, you will pass through five airports. Each one a passageway to how life is supposed to be lived." (Brand 2014, 82) Bedri's movement across the global space should bring about the sort of transposition that would allow for a new beginning and a better self: "[H]ere is your new life. You know no one and no one knows you. You will make no mistakes here and all past mistakes are erased. You begin." (Brand 2014, 84) However, Da'uud's Heraclitean incantation – "When you return, if you return, you never return the same. And where you return to is not the same" (Brand 2014, 85) – is neutralized by the city upon Bedri's return to Toronto as, "after only a few months, the city seeped into him once more" (Brand 2014, 85). For Da'uud, the problem lies in his son's lack of imagination (cf. Brand 2014, 85), the sort of imagination that leads to transposition as the only way to survive in the postmodern era of crumbling illusions.

Conclusion

From this analysis, the city emerges as an ambivalent space of random but usually intense encounters that elicit insight into the nature of contemporary urban life in Canada for those on the margins of society. As a material locale, the city is the crossroads for the clash of dream against reality, "romanticism versus political realism, and wishful thinking versus the real-life contingencies of geography and history" (Clarke 2012, 154). The city may swallow you or give you the chart to navigate it, providing the space for engagement with the other and social and personal transformation. Yet, the city itself is in constant mutation and transformation, so the chart, like love, is always provisional. Today the place of love in the struggle against social inequality and injustice tends to encounter the cynicism of those who think that to believe in a love ethics as a transformative force is "for the naïve, the weak, the hopelessly romantic" (hooks 2000, xix). Yet, bell hooks reminds us that "all the great movements for social justice in our society have strongly emphasized a love ethic" (hooks 2000, xix). Pondering on the ethics and politics of love, and of beauty as its aesthetic branch, Brand seems to point at the defeat of revolutionary love in favor of personal transformation by means of individualistic acts of love. When the state fails, the individual steps in, forging affective affiliations that help sustain the individual, but can hardly transform the community. This, the novel seems to suggest, is mostly the task of institutional action, represented in the novel by the City's initiative to combat criminality in the Jane and Finch corridor by engaging kids in the study and love of music, an apt metaphor for communal harmony and collaboration. Installed in the postmodern moment of apocalyptic global and personal crises and generalized (un)awareness of failing illusions, Brand's novel retrieves the focus on love, and more precisely on the consequences of not feeling loved enough, to present the reader, not with easy or romantic solutions, but with the urgency of practicing love in everyday life, pointing out that even the fantasy of love can create new realities.

1   Research for this paper has taken place within the framework of the research project Narratives of Resilience: Intersectional Perspectives about Literature and Other Contemporary Cultural Representations (FFI2015-63895-C2-2-R), graciously funded by the Spanish Ministry of Economy and Competitiveness.

2   For more about the concept of the glocal in the context of the city and Canadian literature, cf. Fraile-Marcos' *Literature and the Glocal City* (2014).

3   Interestingly, this episode in the novel is inspired by real-life private initiatives, rather than institutional ones, although supported by the City of Toronto to fight violence and crime through music education programs for youth in the Jane and Finch corridor – one of the largest concentrations of criminal gangs of any area in Canada. Cf. *Listen to This* (Baquero 2010), about the city-funded music program in the Jane and Finch neighborhood, conceived by pianist/teacher Thompson Egbo-Egbo and backed by the City's Arts in the Hood program: https://www.youtube.com/watch?v=MLOetv6QZNc (accessed 27/04/2015); cf. also Adler (2014) and Brown (2011).

Bibliography

Adler, Jordan: "Jazz Project Gives Inner-City Kids a Chance." In: *CJN* (03/02/2014), http://www.cjnews.com/culture/arts/jazz-project-gives-inner-city-kids-chance (accessed 27/04/2015).

Ahmed, Sara: *The Cultural Politics of Emotion.* Edinburgh: Edinburgh University Press, 2004.

Augé, Marc: *Non-Places: Introduction to an Anthropology of Supermodernity.* Translated by John Howe. London: Verso, 1995.

Baquero, Juan: *Listen to This.* Proximity Films, 2010. DVD.

Berlant, Lauren (ed.): *Compassion: The Culture and Politics of an Emotion.* New York/London: Routledge, 2004.

Berlant, Lauren: *Cruel Optimism.* Durham: Duke University Press, 2011.

Braidotti, Rosi: *Transpositions: On Nomadic Ethics.* Cambridge: Polity, 2006.

Brand, Dionne: *Love Enough: A Novel.* Toronto: Knopf Canada, 2014.

Brand, Dionne: "CBC Books: Love Enough." In: *CBC Books.* CBC Radio Canada (30/09/2014), http://www.cbc.ca/books/2014/09/love-enough.html (accessed 10/10/2015).

Brown, Louise: "Violins or Violence? Kids of Jane and Finch Change Their Tune." In: *Toronto Star* (04/05/2011), https://www.thestar.com/news/world/2011/05/04/violins_or_violence_kids_of_jane_and_finch_change_their_tune.html (accessed 27/04/2015).

Clarke, George Elliott: "Locating the Early Dionne Brand: Landing a Voice." In: Clarke, George Elliott: *Directions Home: Approaches to African Canadian Literature.* Toronto: University of Toronto Press, 2012, 154-163.

Compton, Anne: "Standing Your Ground: George Elliott Clarke in Conversation." In: *SCL/ÉLC* 23,2 (1998), https://journals.lib.unb.ca/index.php/scl/article/view/12866/13916 (accessed 23/04/2016).

Eagleton, Terry: *The Ideology of the Aesthetic.* Oxford: Blackwell, 1990.

Fanon, Frantz: *Black Skin, White Mask.* New York: Grove Press, 1967.

Foucault, Michel: "Of Other Spaces (1967), Heterotopias." Translated by Jay Miskowiec, http://sgrattan361.qwriting.qc.cuny.edu/files/2010/09/of-other-spaces.pdf (accessed 16/04/2017).

Fraile-Marcos, Ana María (ed.): *Literature and the Glocal City: Reshaping the English Canadian Imaginary.* New York: Routledge, 2014.

Guevara, Ernesto Che: *Socialism and Man in Cuba.* New York: Ocean Press, 1965.

Hardt, Michael: "De Singularitate I: Of Love Possessed." In: Hardt, Michael / Negri, Antonio (eds): *Commonwealth.* Cambridge: The Belknap Press of Harvard University Press, 2009, 179-188.

hooks, bell: *All About Love: New Visions.* New York: Harper Perennial, 2000.

Lewis, C. S.: *The Four Loves.* New York: Harcourt Brace, 1960.

Žižek, Slavoj: "On Love as a Political Category." In: *Cinema Europa, 6th Subversive Festival* (16/05/2013), https://www.youtube.com/watch?v=b44IhiCuNw4 (accessed 10/10/2015).

Carmen MATA BARREIRO (Madrid)

Crises, politique et littérature au Québec : du silence à l'engagement (Wajdi Mouawad, Nicole Brossard, Louise Dupré)

Summary

This article proposes to study the central role of ethics (philosophical ethics, civic ethics, ethics of care – cf. Ricœur, Cortina, Bourgault/Perreault) in the work of Wajdi Mouawad, Nicole Brossard, and Louise Dupré. Using an interdisciplinary approach, it examines some formal and thematic characteristics (translation, memory, images of the urban space) and the ways in which these authors' literary work focuses on empathy, *reconnaissance* (cf. Ricœur 2004), and resistance.

Remarques préliminaires

Dans l'ouvrage collectif *L'urgence de penser* (2014) proposant une analyse critique de la Charte des valeurs québécoises, devenues des « valeurs de laïcité et de neutralité religieuse » (Livernois/Rivard 2014, 5), l'écrivain et éditeur Rodney Saint-Éloi souligne les limites de la politique – « la politique cesse d'être une éthique du vivre-ensemble pour devenir une mathématique de l'ennui » (Saint-Éloi 2014, 144) – et fait appel à la littérature : « L'humanité ici est en panne d'histoire, de pensée, de sens et de poésie. Le vrai combat prend son sens dans l'imaginaire. » (Saint-Éloi 2014, 145)

La réflexion sur les limites de la politique et sur les voix nécessaires des écrivains est devenue transnationale, dans des sociétés touchées par la propagation de l'onde de choc de la crise économique mondiale ou par des crises spécifiques. Dans des crises particulièrement graves telles que le génocide des Tutsi au Rwanda en 1994, des historiens tels que Stéphane Audoin-Rouzeau et Hélène Dumas avouent que « l'intelligibilité complète d'un tel phénomène reste pour l'instant hors de portée des sciences sociales » (Audoin-Rouzeau/Dumas 2014, 8). Le sociologue français Alain Touraine, dans son livre *La fin des sociétés* (2013), où il analyse les conséquences de la crise financière et sociale actuelle – dont l'avènement des « cultures communautaristes fondées sur l'homogénéité » (2013, 38), la montée de l'« individualisme consommateur, facteur de désocialisation et d'anomie » (2013, 38) et le déclin du social et des sociétés –, fait appel à « l'esprit de création » (2013, 17). Cette « capacité de création » devrait « nous permettre de triompher du pouvoir arbitraire et destructeur de l'argent comme du pouvoir politique absolu » (2013, 17).

Au Québec, d'important-e-s écrivain-e-s contemporain-e-s expriment leur foi en la littérature et en sa place incontournable dans la réflexion sur le monde et sur l'éthique, en rejoignant les nouvelles approches de théoriciens de la philosophie politique et morale comme Martha Nussbaum (2000, 2010), aux États-Unis, et Michel Dion (2013), au Québec. Ainsi, Nicole Brossard disait, dans une entrevue : « Je crois que toutes les littératures sont aujourd'hui aux prises avec un nouveau monde à comprendre et à reconfigurer dans l'espace imaginaire » (Mata 2012, 81).

Nous avons choisi comme objet d'analyse la façon dont l'œuvre récente de trois figures très reconnues de la littérature québécoise actuelle, Wajdi Mouawad, Nicole Brossard et Louise Dupré, exprime leur regard et leur posture face à ce monde, leur lucidité et leur agir mémoriel, l'éthique et l'engagement face à des crises sociales et face à des crises intimes. Nous visons à montrer les voies que ces trois écrivains empruntent pour réfléchir sur les problèmes de notre monde contemporain et pour construire un imaginaire où interagissent la résistance et l'espoir.

Nous adhérons à une définition et à une représentation de l'éthique nourries par l'œuvre de philosophes comme Paul Ricœur (2007, 2017), María Zambrano (2015) et Adela Cortina (2013), ainsi que par les théories féministes de l'éthique du *care* (Bourgault/Perreault 2015). Ricœur associe le terme d'‹ éthique › à la « visée d'une vie accomplie sous le signe des actions estimées bonnes » (2007, 311), et il définit la « visée éthique » par trois termes : « *visée de la vie bonne, avec et pour les autres, dans des institutions justes* »[1] (2007, 312). La responsabilité comme objet de l'éthique face à la technoscience et face à l'autrui vulnérable, l'éthique de la compassion et la question de l'engagement (cf. Ricœur 2017, 153, 167, 9 ; Cortina 2013, 130, 51, 121) se traduisent, dans l'œuvre des trois écrivains proposés, par leur lucidité et prise de conscience de « la responsabilité [...] de participer à la mise en œuvre des références de demain » (Mouawad in Côté 2005, 44, 113) ; on y trouve également une « inquiétude » et un « état constant de vigilance » (Brossard 2004, 117, 14) ainsi que l'empathie et une interrogation sur la responsabilité humaine envers le mal du monde (cf. Dupré).

Wajdi Mouawad : écriture de l'exil et de la guerre, la reconnaissance

Wajdi Mouawad, dramaturge, metteur en scène et romancier, qui s'auto-définit comme un « voyageur égaré » pour qui le théâtre est « la boussole » (Côté 2005, 14) avec laquelle il tente de s'orienter, a vécu la guerre du Liban et l'exil dans son enfance. La douleur inhérente à cette double violence traverse et transperce son œuvre.

La puissance tragique du théâtre de Mouawad est reconnue sur le plan international. La tétralogie intitulée *Le sang des promesses* dont font partie *Littoral, Incendies, Forêts* et *Ciels*, a été l'objet d'un long compte-rendu dans le numéro de la revue *Annales. Histoire, Sciences Sociales* consacré aux « Savoirs de la littérature ». Mélanie Traversier (2010, 551) y souligne qu'« [a]u-delà de l'audace, et de l'ambition déployées dans ses fresques théâtrales par le dramaturge, [...] son œuvre intéresse également les historiens par sa volonté têtue d'interroger sur scène les brutalités du monde contemporain ».

Seuls : « [m]ise en crise identitaire et mise en cadre »[2]

La pièce de théâtre ou plutôt le « spectacle de théâtre » (Mouawad 2008, 11) *Seuls*, créé en 2007 et ayant la forme du solo, ouvre un nouveau chantier, que *Sœurs* poursuit, en 2014, au cœur du cycle « domestique » (Mouawad 2015, quatrième de couverture), et qui sera complété par *Frères, Père* et *Mère*. La Grande Histoire et l'univers familial y convergent, et nous y retrouvons la mémoire, individuelle et collective, ainsi que la dimension éthique qui caractérise son œuvre.

Après l'écriture et la mise en scène de *Forêts*, Mouawad cherche une manière différente d'écrire. L'édition du texte de *Seuls*, sous-titrée « Chemin, texte et peintures », montre comment la volonté de « tuer le ‹ bavardage › qui jusqu'ici était le mien » (Mouawad 2008, 12) l'amène à une « polyphonie d'écriture » (2008, 12), où tout ce qui relève du langage scénique fait partie de l'écriture textuelle.

La première scène de *Seuls*, qui a comme titre « Conclusion », fait apparaître le personnage d'Harwan, qui soutient sa thèse de doctorat. Dans son discours, il explique qu'étant « [é]tudiant en sociologie de l'imaginaire, [il s]'interroge depuis [s]on mémoire de maîtrise sur la question de l'identité » (2008, 125) et qu'il a proposé à son directeur de thèse de travailler sur Robert Lepage, ce qui a abouti à « *Le cadre comme espace identitaire dans les solos de Robert Lepage* » (2008, 132-133).

L'intrigue se construit autour de la rencontre manquée d'Harwan avec Lepage, qui aurait dû avoir lieu à Saint-Pétersbourg, et autour de la lecture du tableau de Rembrandt *Le retour du fils prodigue*, qui se trouve au Musée de l'Ermitage. Associée à cette trame dynamique, apparaît ce que Dominique D. Fisher appelle « [m]ise en crise identitaire et mise en cadre » (2011-2012, 129). Le personnage d'Harwan est aux prises avec la question de son origine, de la mémoire de la guerre du Liban, de l'exil et de la perte de la langue maternelle, et ces préoccupations sont exposées dans des discours adressés à son père, qui est censé avoir eu un accident cérébro-vasculaire et être dans le coma. Mais le spectateur, qui est tenu dans cette illusion, découvre que celui qui est dans le coma est Harwan, victime d'un accident dans la cabine d'un photomaton. L'espace de ce cadre – de même que les autres cadres de la pièce tels que le mur écran et la toile de Rembrandt – devient l'espace qui visualise le rapport entre la crise identitaire, le traumatisme et la violence.

Dans la scène finale de *Seuls*, la projection vidéo du tableau de Rembrandt se juxtapose à la voix du directeur de thèse félicitant Harwan pour la qualité de la conclusion de sa thèse, retrouvée chez l'étudiant le matin de son accident, et dont il lui fait la lecture. Les didascalies signalent qu'Harwan « saisit le couteau[,] […] fissure la paroi[,] […] grimpe dans la peinture. […] Il est à jamais dans son cadre » (Mouawad 2008, 184). Harwan peut se fondre dans l'espace de la toile en vue de se substituer au fils prodigue et de retrouver la langue d'origine et le pays de son enfance. Les derniers énoncés de la conclusion de sa thèse, des questions transmises par la voix de son directeur, précèdent l'entrée d'Harwan dans le cadre du tableau : « Qu'est-ce qui, depuis si longtemps espère mon retour ? […] Qu'ai-je donc quitté sans même le comprendre ? Ai-je perdu toute mémoire ? Comment dit-on *mémoire* en arabe ? » (2008, 184)

Sœurs : écriture de la reconnaissance

Après *Seuls*, symbole du fils, *Sœurs*, créé en 2014, est le deuxième maillon du cycle « domestique » (Mouawad 2015, quatrième de couverture). C'est de nouveau un spectacle polyphonique et une pièce en solo, jouée par une seule interprète qui porte deux personnages et se démultiplie en plusieurs incarnations, grâce à divers matériaux : sons, images, objets, gestes.

En ce qui concerne la fable, une tempête de neige oblige une avocate et médiatrice interculturelle brillante, Geneviève Bergeron, à rester une nuit à Ottawa après une conférence. L'impossibilité d'avoir un service en français, sa langue maternelle, dans sa chambre interactive de l'hôtel se greffe sur la mémoire de la violence subie par sa mère dans son enfance au Manitoba, liée à l'assimilation linguistique et culturelle. La colère explose et aboutit au saccage de la chambre. La rencontre d'une experte en sinistre, Layla Bintwarda, d'origine libanaise, dans la chambre vandalisée, déterminera un rapport de sororité entre les deux femmes, qui ont le même âge, qui sont des sœurs aînées et qui doivent faire face à la problématique de la vulnérabilité de leurs parents âgés et au devoir de mémoire.

La dimension philosophique, éthique voire politique de cette pièce est particulièrement riche. Le texte liminaire, « En guise de prologue » (Mouawad 2015, 5-10), évoque le point de départ de sa genèse, comment le fait de regarder sa sœur en train de repasser a poussé Mouawad à « penser à la vie de cette femme[,] [aux] sacrifices qui avaient été les siens, ses rêves, ses espoirs, ses secrets, le peu d'intimité dont elle a pu jouir » (2015, 5). « *Sœurs* a peut-être surgi de cette compréhension, pour ne pas dire révélation, du rôle de ma sœur au cœur de la tragédie de ma famille, rôle qui consiste à effacer les plis et tenter de redéployer l'histoire. » (2015, 6) Ce regard de l'auteur actualise ainsi des acceptions philosophiques que Paul Ricœur a étudiées dans *Parcours de la reconnaissance* (2004), à savoir « la reconnaissance comme identification » (2004, 41-105) et « la reconnaissance mutuelle » (Mouawad 2015, 221-355), qui concerne une demande qui reste le plus souvent en attente et parfois en souffrance, et qui comporte une forme de gratitude. Le personnage de Layla Bintwarda, inspiré de Nayla Mouawad, explique comment, après la guerre du Liban, qui a déterminé la fin de son enfance, la fuite du pays, l'exil et le fait de devoir s'occuper de ses frères et de ses parents l'ont astreinte à « étrangle[r] [s]es rêves » (Mouawad 2015, 45).

Sœurs va au-delà du drame personnel et s'engage dans la reconnaissance de la douleur des victimes de la guerre (guerres du Liban et de Syrie), de la violence, de l'exil et du mépris, regardées « à travers le prisme de deux femmes qui n'auraient pas dû se rencontrer, mais les guerres et les exils et les injustices ont créé les conditions géopolitiques pour qu'elles se rencontrent » (Mouawad 2015, 8).

Nicole Brossard : l'imaginaire de la ville et la traduction, la résistance

« [J]'ai toujours voulu être de mon temps » (Brossard 2004, 53), écrit Nicole Brossard dans l'essai *L'horizon du fragment*. Cet énoncé, qui est l'un des traits constitutifs de son ethos et de sa posture d'écrivaine, traduit un regard, qui vise à comprendre, et un agir, ancré dans la notion de responsabilité :

> Être de mon temps, c'est-à-dire comprendre le monde qui m'entoure et celui qui nous traverse à travers les modes, les désirs collectifs, détecter le mensonge. [...] Depuis toujours, il me semble avoir associé l'idée d'être de son temps à une notion de responsabilité comme si chaque génération avait pour tâche de trier les archaïsmes, de résister aux chimères de la science marchande, de dénouer les peurs irrationnelles et les haines misogyne et raciste. (Brossard 2004, 53-54)

La responsabilité s'avère ainsi indissociable de la résistance, résistance à la société patriarcale et aux grands récits dominants dont celui du néolibéralisme, qui décide des valeurs des sociétés et des vies des êtres humains. Karim Larose et Rosalie Lessard, dans le texte de présentation du numéro de *Voix et Images* qui est consacré à l'œuvre de l'écrivaine en 2012, soulignent cet aspect : « [L]e poème brossardien n'a [...] qu'une constante : il demeure une forme critique, dialectique, le vase communiquant du connu et de l'inconnu, une séquence de la pensée qui serait acte de résistance. » (Larose/Lessard 2012, 9)

Nous allons explorer le regard de Nicole Brossard sur le monde, à travers deux prismes, qui sont aussi deux espaces d'analyse et de reconfiguration : l'imaginaire de la ville et la traduction. Nous nous intéresserons particulièrement à l'évolution de son regard, à l'émergence de l'inquiétude et de l'angoisse, à la présence de « mots intranquilles »[3].

L'imaginaire de la ville

« [D]epuis toujours je recommence mes villes » (Brossard 2010a, 9), écrit Nicole Brossard au début de l'épigraphe du recueil *Lointaines*. La ville constitue un topos axial dans son œuvre, dans ses romans (*French Kiss : étreinte/exploration*, *Picture Theory, Hier*), dans ses essais (*La lettre aérienne*), et dans sa poésie (*Je m'en vais à Trieste, Lointaines*), qu'elle approche comme « femme du présent », comme « exploratrice » et comme « insoumise », des traits de son « Autoportrait » dépeint dans son essai *L'horizon du fragment* (Brossard 2004, 127-128).

Dans la décennie 1970, dans le roman *French Kiss : étreinte/exploration* (1974), perçu comme une œuvre « visionnaire » (Simon 2008, 204), la conscience féministe métamorphosait la ville et déterminait la fusion voire la confusion entre ville et corps. Dans la décennie 1980, son concept d'« urbaines radicales » (Brossard 2009, 69) traduisait une attitude de subversion et d'exploration de l'interdit qui est le fruit du travail de la conscience féministe et de l'émotion lesbienne. Et, dans la décennie 2000, la lecture et l'écriture de la ville chez Brossard se modifient.

La comparaison entre deux recueils qui traduisent des paysages urbains, *Je m'en vais à Trieste* (2003) et *Lointaines* (2010a), est révélatrice. L'épigraphe de *Je m'en vais à Trieste* suggère la puissance du regard, des mots et du désir : « Tout ce qu'on a vu, compris et aimé / tous les jours ailleurs un tremblement / du désir et du futur. » (Brossard 2003, 7) Le titre de chaque poème évoque une ville ou un lieu de l'espace urbain : « Trinity College », « Athènes », « Key West », « Coyoacán », « Barcelone », « Vienne », « Venise ». Le plaisir des sensations gustatives, la beauté des couleurs, la caresse du silence, la fascination de l'art et des corps l'emportent. Les instantanés suscités par les villes de Beyrouth, de Jounieh et de Byblos, au Liban, nous invitent à regarder les « cicatrices » (2003, 137) de la guerre mais aussi la volonté de « guérison » (2003, 138), « une ardeur de femme » (2003, 135). Malgré la « menace » de la violence, particulièrement envers les femmes (cf. « Tucson », « Guadalajara », « Fort Collins »), la vie triomphe sur la mort : « les femmes redressent le passé » (2003, 89) à Anse à la Barque, à l'île de Guadeloupe. Et l'injonction de lutter contre « l'obscurité » fait face à la guerre : « [O]n prépare la guerre / ne laisse pas l'obscurité s'installer / seul le verbe vie décide. » (2003, 115)

Dans le recueil *Lointaines*, les poèmes sont introduits par des titres tels que « Villes avec un visage », « Villes avec leurs morts », « Villes avec ou sans la guerre » et « Villes avec leurs fous de dieu ». Le ton est particulièrement grave dans les poèmes qui évoquent la violence envers les femmes et la menace inhérente au fanatisme religieux qui déterminent des « villes sans recommencement de lumière » (Brossard 2010a, 36). Mais le dernier poème du recueil, « Villes avec mon visage qui revient », fait émerger de nouveau l'espoir : « villes avec espoir », et des « femmes lovées dans une joie d'errance et d'infini » (2010a, 45). En effet, le choix de la ville comme lieu de combat et comme déclencheur de réflexion chez Brossard, la revendication de la liberté dans la ville et de la préservation du désir comportent et réussissent l'équilibre entre la désespérance et l'espoir.

La traduction et sa dimension philosophique et politique

Chez Nicole Brossard, la « fascination pour la traduction », qui est une constante depuis les années 1980, est associée à la question de l'identité, à la question de l'autre et du « devenir autre » (Brossard 2010b, 143) et à « la question du sens et du processus qui permet de le valider et de le faire sien » (Brossard 2004, 98). L'*incipit* de son livre *Et me voici soudain en train de refaire le monde* (2015), où elle observe diverses approches en traduction, pose une question essentielle :

> Pourquoi la traduction n'est-elle pas un sujet comme un autre, je veux dire en quoi prédispose-t-elle à une authentique ferveur du sens, allant parfois jusqu'au débat, comme si en chaque mot se cachait un enjeu de vie, une vision du monde miniaturisée ? (Brossard 2015, 7)

Si *Le désert mauve* (1987) a attiré l'attention des traductologues comme Sherry Simon et Patricia Godbout, et est considéré comme une œuvre qui a joué un rôle indéniable dans la redéfinition du paradigme de la traduction dans la littérature québécoise (cf. Godbout 2010, 163-175), le roman *La capture du sombre* (2007) a une portée philosophique et politique considérable. Dès l'*incipit* de ce roman, le discours de la narratrice expose son projet d'« écrire lentement un livre dans une langue qui ne serait pas la mienne » (Brossard 2007, 5). Dans la genèse du projet, l'idée de fuir, de quitter la langue maternelle, de « m[ettre] de la distance entre ma langue maternelle et la réalité » (2007, 6) apparaît associée à une vision du monde sombre, à un « assombrissement » (2007, 7) face auquel elle a épuisé le vocabulaire dans sa langue maternelle : « Dans ma langue, j'ai épuisé le vocabulaire qui m'aurait permis de nommer ce noir intrigant qui approche : corbeau, rapace, félin, noir […] de soutane, de niqab, de tchador et de corps calciné. Il me faut maintenant d'autres mots pour tout ce sombre de nature et de civilisation qui vient. » (2007, 8) Le « 11 Septembre » 2001 apparaît comme l'un des facteurs de cet « assombrissement » et comme l'un des exemples de l'érosion de la langue maternelle, de la réduction de la polysémie potentielle.

La capture du sombre réfléchit parallèlement à la façon dont la vie invisible se révèle chez l'écrivain-e et lui permet de devenir autre, dans le cadre de la langue, ainsi qu'à la partie invisible de la langue et aux liens entre elle et le rapport à la langue chez l'écrivain-e. Dans l'article « OPAYSAGES : ou la partie invisible des mots », Nicole Brossard affirme : « [L]a partie invisible est peut-être ce qu'il y a de plus vivant en nous, [...] [n]otre intelligence du monde se cache dans la partie invisible de nos pensées [...]. C'est la partie désirante, rêveuse qui en chacun de nous alimente le potentiel de renouveau du contrat social. » (Brossard 2010b, 145) La clausule de *La capture du sombre* évoquant « la position de combat » (Brossard 2007, 140), témoigne de la foi en le pouvoir de transformation de la langue : « [J]e recommence à vouloir toucher la partie invisible en moi. [...] J'aimerais pouvoir donner un nom neuf à l'obscurité. » (2007, 140)

Louise Dupré : l'écriture de la vulnérabilité et de l'empathie

Louise Dupré est une écrivaine qui, ayant commencé à écrire dans les années 1980, fait partie de la « génération de l'intime » (Paterson 2009, 13), et c'est l'intime qui constitue l'objet de son engagement et de sa recherche et création : « [T]ravailler sur la subjectivité féminine, sur ses désirs inconscients, ses douleurs, est pour moi un motif d'engagement profond. » (Paterson 2009, 13) Le rapport entre mère et fille, la relation amoureuse, la blessure, l'abandon, la mort, constituent des thèmes présents dans son œuvre poétique, dans ses romans, ses nouvelles et son texte pour le théâtre *Tout comme elle*. La problématique de la mémoire, individuelle ou collective, voire de l'histoire, petite histoire ou Grande Histoire, prend une place importante ces dernières années : « [L]'écriture vient pour moi d'une nécessité de raviver la mémoire, sa propre mémoire, toujours liée à la mémoire collective. » (Paterson 2009, 23)

L'album multicolore (2014) est un récit de deuil entrepris quelques mois après la mort de sa mère. Des images correspondant à différents moments de la vie de sa mère dont des « instantanés » se succèdent, ainsi que le récit du travail d'intériorisation et de remémoration inhérent à ce que Freud a appelé le travail de deuil, à partir du choc qui déclenche un sentiment de « stupeur » (Dupré 2014, 15) jusqu'à la «[t]ristesse de n'être plus triste » (2014, 241) et le rétablissement.

L'*incipit* de l'ouvrage évoque le moment succédant au décès et la difficulté de faire face à l'un des événements les plus terribles chez un être humain : « Je la regarde dans son lit, blanche, aussi blanche que le drap. Elle vient de mourir, ma mère, et je ne le crois pas. » (2014, 11) Le silence de la chambre, qui fait partie d'une gamme de silences de l'après-décès, « désormais linceuls de la mort » (Corbin 2016, 177), devient un espace et un temps de sérénité, qui favorisent la réflexion : « Je peux enfin penser à ma mère, je peux penser à sa mort. [...] Après, qui est-on ? » (Dupré 2014, 13) Et les derniers paragraphes traduisent une grande sérénité. L'identification avec une posture de sa mère, « *Il ne faut pas se laisser aller* »[4] (2014, 101, 266), aboutit à un équilibre entre la tristesse et la joie : « La tristesse avec la joie dedans, est-ce que ce n'est pas aussi la mémoire avec l'oubli dedans, le bel oubli qui distrait un moment, allège, [...] permet de continuer la route malgré les fantômes autour ? » (2014, 268)

L'écrivaine doit faire face à des enjeux scripturaux d'ordre énonciatif et éthique. « L'écriture me résiste, jamais elle ne m'a autant résisté » (2014, 31), écrit-elle. Des questions sont posées : « [Q]u'est-ce que la vérité ? Je voudrais coller le plus possible aux faits, rendre intact son souvenir, la faire revivre dans ses moindres gestes, ses moindres paroles. [...]. Si je m'avouais la vérité, justement, j'admettrais que je tente l'impossible. » (2014, 20) Des doutes surgissent : « Et si je me leurrais ? Si mon récit était porté par le désir enfoui de défigurer mon enfance, d'en faire une histoire recevable [...] ? » (2014, 59) Et le respect détermine la volonté de s'astreindre, parfois, au « silence », « silence de tout ce qui a été [...] égaré dans la mémoire des générations. Silence du non-dit » (2014, 256). L'écriture de la vulnérabilité, le récit du déclin de la mère, l'analyse de ses énoncés, du déni, de la « dépossession de soi » (2014, 248), la constatation du fait que « [v]ieillir, c'est apprivoiser la violence » (2014, 89), convoque l'éthique féministe du *care* ou de la sollicitude (Bourgault/Perreault 2015) et nous invite à réfléchir sur notre fragilité : « Je suis entrée dans la conscience du temps qui fait lentement son œuvre. » (Dupré 2014, 260)

Plus haut que les flammes (2010), « La porte fermée » (2009) : l'empathie

Si, dans *L'album multicolore*, le travail de remémoration met en lumière des hommes et des femmes de plusieurs générations au Québec, qui ont vécu la Crise de 1929, le ‹ règne › de Duplessis, la Révolution tranquille, les périodes de Jean Lesage et René Lévesque, la nouvelle « La porte fermée » (2009) et deux longs poèmes, *Plus haut que les flammes* (2010) et « Dimanche » (2013), se focalisent sur des ‹ mémoires blessées ›, celles de la répression subie par les résistants au nazisme et de la Shoah, et celles de la traite négrière et de la répression de Duvalier en Haïti.

« La porte fermée » est, d'après l'écrivaine, « l'un des textes les plus autobiographiques qu'il m'ait été donné d'écrire » (Paterson 2009, 23), associé à un voyage en Allemagne, incluant la visite de Munich et de Dachau, qui lui a fait découvrir l'histoire des étudiants allemands animateurs du mouvement de résistance La Rose Blanche – dont Sophie Scholl –, victimes de la répression nazie. La nouvelle traduit la « [s]ensation de vertige » (Dupré 2009, 26) que l'auteure a ressentie dans des lieux de mémoire du nazisme, et sa réflexion sur l'idée qu'« [a]ucun peuple n'est à l'abri de l'horreur » (Paterson 2009, 23).

Dans le long poème *Plus haut que les flammes*, s'expriment parallèlement l'amour pour l'enfant qui est à côté de la poète-narratrice et le souvenir des enfants déportés et assassinés dans les camps d'extermination (cf. Dupré 2010, 14), l'évocation de leurs « minuscules vêtements » (2010, 16) et des « biberons cassés » (2010, 17). Un cri de douleur et une voix qui caresse s'y juxtaposent – une opposition entre la vie et la mort, entre le regard vers le passé, qui nous fait partager « ces récits / de sang et de couteaux » (2010, 26), et le regard engagé dans le présent et le futur, qui rappelle des raisons pour continuer à vivre et à lutter, pour entretenir et soigner « l'amour » (2010, 39) et « la consolation / pour la suite du monde » (2010, 39).

Dès le début du poème, la tension entre la mort et la vie se met en scène. La littérature, les mots, le poème, l'emportent sur la mort, sur « un enfer d'images / fouillant la poussière / des fourneaux » (2010, 13). L'énergie régénératrice de la nature (« les branches d'un érable / derrière la fenêtre / où une hirondelle veut faire / le printemps », 2010, 15) et les caresses de l'enfant deviennent alliées des mots : « les mots / susceptibles de redresser / la nuit » (2010, 45). Une caresse de l'enfant a le pouvoir de se transformer en baume capable de soulager la douleur, une douleur enracinée dans la douleur du monde (« elle est très vieille / ta douleur / elle vient du silence / des continents / noyés », 2010, 63) et nourrie par la lucidité (« l'histoire est laide / et tu le sais / l'histoire est rapace », 2010, 97).

« Dimanche » (2013) : passé de blessures et futur d'espérance

« Dimanche » est un long poème, créé dans le contexte des « Rencontres québécoises » en Haïti en 2013, et publié dans le collectif *Bonjour voisine*. Le poème invite le lecteur à un voyage qui le conduit du présent à la nature lumineuse au passé cruel de l'esclavage, « le passé / […] [et] ses cargaisons / humaines » (Dupré 2013, 198), et à celui des « martyrs de Duvalier » (2013, 200). De même que *Plus haut que les flammes*, il s'agit d'une écriture de l'empathie (cf. Gefen 2013) qui se met à la place d'autrui, pour en partager les émotions, la souffrance et « le courage » (2013, 197), et en comprendre la position. Mais parallèlement à cette approche esthético-éthique, Dupré réussit à construire un rythme où le mouvement vers le passé des blessures et vers le futur des « lendemains / qui dansent » (2013, 201) est un « rythme accordé / à l'énergie du soleil » (2013, 201).

Structuré en une série de mouvements, à l'instar d'une pièce de musique, le poème débute avec un premier mouvement qui fait apparaître simultanément des sensations porteuses de plaisir – « coulée de lumière / sur la peau / comme une pluie / parfumée / après l'orage » (2013, 195), qui déclenchent le sourire : « tu souris » (2013, 195). Mais la conjonction « pourtant » associée à une opération logico-sémantique de restriction ou d'opposition nous dévoile ce qui est caché sous la mer, et derrière ce présent lumineux fait irruption le passé lourd et sombre de la traite négrière : « [E]t pourtant / tu revois la mer / de tous les horizons / avec ses navires / sans merci / et les chants / désespérés / dans les cales. » (2013, 195-196) Et les larmes effacent le sourire : « [T]u as pleuré / de toutes tes larmes / devant la barbarie / tu pleures encore / devant les gémissements / des chaînes. » (2013, 196)

La conjonction ‹ mais › introduit un deuxième mouvement qui débute avec l'évocation de la lumière de l'aurore, qui comporte un imaginaire de recommencement, d'espoir et de courage : « Mais la grâce / du jour, ce matin / la lumière tiède / sur la peau / le réveil du coq / […] le courage / de continuer. » (2013, 196-197) Le courage, la volonté de faire face au soleil écrasant de la journée sont éclipsés par une nouvelle irruption du passé, précédée par la conjonction ‹ mais › : « [M]ais un coup de dés / jamais n'abolira / le passé / ni ses cargaisons / humaines / qu'on vendait / comme des bêtes / à des colons / prêts à tuer / pour de l'or. » (2013, 198) À la mémoire de l'esclavage de la colonie de Saint-Domingue se joint une autre mémoire, concernant une période plus récente, celle de la répression du dictateur Duvalier, des « martyrs de Duvalier / hommes, femmes / et enfants / massacrés / au hasard / de leur nom » (2013, 200).

Un nouveau recommencement, qui allie journée naissante et enfance, se met en scène dans le troisième mouvement, introduit par la conjonction ‹ mais › : « Mais la joie, les bambins / trottinant vers les écoles / […] / les livres aux odeurs / d'algues et de promesses. » (2013, 201) La représentation de l'enfance comme porteuse de promesses associées à l'éducation et aux bibliothèques permet d'envisager l'avenir avec plus de sérénité et invite à « rêver / de lendemains / qui dansent » (2013, 201). En vue d'exaucer ce rêve, des « *lwa* » (2013, 201), esprits, génies ou dieux vaudou, dont « les esprits vaudou / de la révolte » (2013, 202), sont évoqués voire convoqués.

Louise Dupré, s'approchant du peuple haïtien et de sa mémoire, appréhende ainsi un élément caractéristique de son imaginaire, « le merveilleux », que l'écrivain haïtien Jacques Stephen Alexis définissait en 1956 comme « l'imagerie dans laquelle un peuple enveloppe son expérience, reflète sa conception du monde et de la vie, sa foi, son espérance, sa confiance en l'homme, en une grande justice, et l'explication qu'il trouve aux forces antagonistes du progrès » (Dalembert/ Trouillot 2010, 62).

Un dernier mouvement, qui débute avec la conjonction ‹ mais ›, fait appel à la vie comme « ce terrible défi / lancé à la face / des tyrans » (Dupré 2013, 203) et comme « espérance » (2013, 203). La tension et les oppositions présentes dans les mouvements précédents s'amenuisent et font place aux vœux, à « l'espérance / que la ville / ne tremble plus / plus jamais » (2013, 203).

L'imaginaire que traduit chaque mouvement de ce long poème rejoint l'approche de la philosophe espagnole María Zambrano, qui a vécu les crises de l'exode espagnol républicain – la ‹ Retirada › – et celle des décennies 1930 et 1940 en Europe (cf. *L'agonie de l'Europe*, 1945), pour qui l'espérance a été une puissance créatrice et pour qui « la seule Aurore, serait la plus sûre garantie de l'être, de la vie et de la raison » (Zambrano 2015, 20).

Travail de mémoire et empathie constituent des traits essentiels de la réponse de Louise Dupré aux questions que l'écrivain et philosophe Michel Le Bris posait dans le collectif *Haïti parmi les vivants* (2010), écrit dans l'immédiateté du séisme qui a ravagé Haïti le 12 janvier 2010 :

> Qui dira l'incroyable dignité des gens, leur solidarité dans le malheur, leur calme ? Qui enfin dira comment cette île fut brisée, mise à genoux parce qu'elle avait osé se révolter ? Qui dira cette incroyable puissance de création qui l'habite ? (Le Bris 2010, 19)

Louise Dupré contribue ainsi à « dire Haïti, à la face du monde » (Le Bris 2010, 19). La ville de Port-au-Prince y est dépeinte comme un espace sur lequel les fléaux de la nature et de l'Histoire se sont abattus et dont la misère et « la privation » (Dupré 2013, 203) sont des traces, et comme une ville capable de résister, de faire face à son malheur, de développer une puissance de création : « Port-au-Prince / aux sept vies / chat noir, chat / capable de bondir / plus haut que les toits / des abris rouillés / qu'on ne peut nommer / *maisons.* » (2013, 199)

Émotion, éthique, empathie : des réponses et des postures face aux crises

Les trois auteurs étudiés traduisent, dans leur œuvre, leur sens de responsabilité face au présent, face aux exigences nouvelles de l'histoire, une responsabilité tournée également vers le futur. L'éthique constitue l'un des moteurs de leur lecture de l'histoire et de la mémoire ainsi que de la proposition et de l'élaboration des voies d'espoir.

L'œuvre, puissante, de Wajdi Mouawad, Nicole Brossard et Louise Dupré, acteurs et moteurs de la réflexion, de l'action et de l'émotion, exprimant et revendiquant la reconnaissance, la résistance et l'empathie, s'avère ainsi capable de nous faire avancer dans la prise de conscience et dans la lutte pour consolider la place de l'éthique dans nos sociétés et éradiquer l'indifférence et l'oubli.

Ils participent ainsi à une réflexion, transnationale et transdisciplinaire, sur les émotions, le travail de mémoire et l'éthique, réflexion qu'ils enrichissent. Ils partagent la foi en la puissance de transformation des émotions, revendiquée par des philosophes comme Georges Didi-Huberman (2016) ou des politologues comme Fernando Vallespín, qui, lors de la Leçon inaugurale de l'année académique 2015-2016 à l'Universidad Autónoma de Madrid, portant sur « Vieille et nouvelle politique »[5], a exposé comment la ‹ nouvelle politique › « se nourrit d'émotions positives comme l'indignation ou l'espérance »[6] – face au retour de la peur, l'émotion la plus négative.

Et ils rejoignent des acteurs d'autres domaines de création tels que le cinéma comme le réalisateur québécois Bernard Émond, qui aborde l'éthique comme l'un des axes majeurs de son œuvre, hantée par la crise des valeurs : « [L]'éthique demeure une affaire d'être humain. Et comment vivre sans elle ? » (Tremblay 2009, E1)

1   En italique dans le texte.
2   Fisher (2011-2012, 129).
3   « Ce livre des mots intranquilles » : dédicace d'un exemplaire d'*Après les mots*, le 5 décembre 2007.
4   En italique dans le texte.
5   « Vieja y nueva política ». Trad. C. Mata Barreiro.
6   Traduit de l'espagnol.

Bibliographie

Audoin-Rouzeau, Stéphane / Dumas, Hélène : « Le génocide des Tutsi rwandais vingt ans après : réflexions introductives ». In : *Vingtième Siècle. Revue d'histoire* 122 (2014), 3-16.

Bourgault, Sophie / Perreault, Julie (éds) : *Le care. Éthique féministe actuelle*. Montréal : Les Éditions du remue-ménage, 2015.

Brossard, Nicole : *Le désert mauve*. Montréal : l'Hexagone, 1987.

Brossard, Nicole : *Je m'en vais à Trieste*. Trois-Rivières/Luxembourg/Limoges : Écrits des Forges/Éditions Phi/Le bruit des autres, 2003.

Brossard, Nicole : *L'horizon du fragment*. Trois-Pistoles : Éditions Trois-Pistoles, 2004.

Brossard, Nicole : *La capture du sombre*. Montréal : Leméac, 2007.

Brossard, Nicole : *La lettre aérienne*. Montréal : Les Éditions du remue-ménage, 2009 [1985].

Brossard, Nicole : *Lointaines*. Paris : Éditions Caractères, 2010a.

Brossard, Nicole : « OPAYSAGES : ou la partie invisible des mots ». In : *Cahiers franco-canadiens de l'Ouest* 22,2 (2010b), 137-152.

Brossard, Nicole : *Et me voici soudain en train de refaire le monde.* Montréal : Mémoire d'encrier, 2015.

Corbin, Alain : *Histoire du silence. De la Renaissance à nos jours.* Paris : Éditions Albin Michel, 2016.

Cortina Orts, Adela : *¿Para qué sirve realmente la ética?* Madrid : Editorial Paidós, 2013.

Côté, Jean-François : *Architecture d'un marcheur. Entretiens avec Wajdi Mouawad.* Montréal : Leméac, 2005.

Dalembert, Louis-Philippe / Trouillot, Lyonel : *Haïti : une traversée littéraire.* Paris/Port-au-Prince : Culturesfrance/Éditions Philippe Rey/Presses nationales d'Haïti, 2010.

Didi-Huberman, Georges : *Peuples en larmes, peuples en armes. L'œil de l'histoire, 6.* Paris : Les Éditions de Minuit, 2016.

Dion, Michel : *Texte littéraire et réflexion éthique.* Québec : Éditions Liber, 2013.

Dupré, Louise : « La porte fermée ». In : *Voix et Images* 34,2 (2009), 25-27.

Dupré, Louise : *Plus haut que les flammes.* Montréal : Éditions du Noroît, 2010.

Dupré, Louise : « Dimanche ». In : Poitras, Marie Hélène (éd.) : *Bonjour voisine. Collectif Haïti-Québec.* Montréal : Mémoire d'encrier, 2013, 195-203.

Dupré, Louise : *L'album multicolore.* Montréal : Héliotrope, 2014.

Fisher, Dominique D. : « L'écriture du spectacle *Seuls* de Wajdi Mouawad : poétique et détours transculturels ». In : *L'Annuaire théâtral : revue québécoise d'études théâtrales* 50-51 (2011-2012), 125-139.

Gefen, Alexandre : « *D'autres vies que la mienne* : roman français contemporain, empathie et théorie du *care* ». In : Gefen, Alexandre / Vouilloux, Bernard (éds) : *Empathie et esthétique.* Paris : Hermann Éditeurs, 2013, 279-292.

Godbout, Patricia : « Le traducteur fictif dans la littérature québécoise : notes et réflexions ». In : *Cahiers franco-canadiens de l'Ouest* 22,2 (2010), 163-175.

Larose, Karim / Lessard, Rosalie : « Nicole Brossard : le genre premier ». In : *Voix et Images* 37,3 (2012), 7-12.

Le Bris, Michel : « Dire, au milieu des ruines, les hommes debout ». In : [s.i.] : *Haïti parmi les vivants.* Arles : Actes Sud, 2010, 13-19.

Mata Barreiro, Carmen : « L'Espagne chez Nicole Brossard. Entrevue avec Nicole Brossard ». In : Mata Barreiro, Carmen (éd.) : *Espagnes imaginaires du Québec.* Québec : Les Presses de l'Université Laval, 2012, 75-81.

Mata Barreiro, Carmen : « Nicole Brossard, ‹ rebelle-architecte › : la ville, espace d'insou-mission, horizon de réflexion ». In : Dufault, Roseanna / Ricouart, Janine (éds) : *Nicole Brossard. L'inédit des sens.* Montréal : Les Éditions du remue-ménage, 2013a, 139-158.

Mata Barreiro, Carmen : « L'écriture du corps dans l'œuvre de Louise Dupré : les mains, l'amour, la douleur ». In : *Revue des Lettres et de Traduction* 15 (2013b), 201-215.

Mouawad, Wajdi : *Seuls. Chemin, texte et peintures.* Montréal/Arles : Leméac/Actes Sud, 2008.

Mouawad, Wajdi : *Sœurs.* Montréal/Arles : Leméac/Actes Sud-Papiers, 2015.

Nussbaum, Martha C. : *Upheavals of Thought. The Intelligence of Emotions.* Cambridge : Cambridge University Press, 2001.

Nussbaum, Martha C. : *La connaissance de l'amour. Essais sur la philosophie et la littérature.* Paris : Éditions du Cerf, 2010.

Paterson, Janet M. : « Entretien avec Louise Dupré ». In : *Voix et Images* 34,2 (2009), 11-23.

Ricœur, Paul : *Parcours de la reconnaissance. Trois études.* Paris : Éditions Stock, 2004.

Ricœur, Paul : *Anthologie. Textes choisis et présentés par Michaël Fœssel et Fabien Lamouche.* Paris : Seuil, 2007 [1999].

Ricœur, Paul : *Philosophie, éthique et politique. Entretiens et dialogues.* Paris : Seuil, 2017 [1997].

Saint-Éloi, Rodney : « Aide-moi à comprendre la Charte ». In : Livernois, Jonathan / Rivard, Yvon (éds) : *L'urgence de penser. 27 questions à la Charte.* Montréal : Leméac, 2014, 143-147.

Simon, Sherry : *Traverser Montréal. Une histoire culturelle par la traduction.* Montréal : Éditions Fides, 2008 [2006].

Touraine, Alain : *La fin des sociétés.* Paris : Seuil, 2013.

Traversier, Mélanie : « Wajdi Mouawad, *Littoral, Incendies, Forêts, Ciels, Le sang des pro-messes. Puzzle, racines et rhizomes* ». In : *Annales. Histoire, Sciences Sociales* 2 (2010), 550-553.

Tremblay, Odile : « L'Abitibi comme métaphore ». In : *Le Devoir* (31/10/2009-01/11/2009), E1-E2.

Vallespín, Fernando : « Vieja y nueva política ». Leçon inaugurale, année académique 2015-2016, Universidad Autónoma de Madrid (10/09/2015).

Zambrano, María : *De l'aurore.* Paris : Éditions de l'éclat, 2015 [1987].

Émilie NOTARD (Berlin)

L'(in)quiétude du sens dans *Piano blanc* de Nicole Brossard

Summary

This article analyzes the concept of 'sense' as developed by Brossard in the context of Quebec's lesbian feminism of the 1980s. It is based on the sequences of the aerial perspective (1982) and on the rituals of writing (1988), which represent the heart of Brossard's theory of sense (cf. Rudy 2005). Sequences and rituals describe the transition from the patriarchal (non-)Sense to a new feminine sense, which evolves like a spiral that has to be renewed continuously so as not to close in on itself. In this paper, the Brossardian theory of sense will be applied to her poetry collection *White Piano* (2011): In this work, feminist sequences and rituals are transposed to the new ethical context of the end of the 20th century and the beginning of the 21st century so as to counter the new (non-)Sense of our (in)humanity. Our approach is divided into three parts which discuss the four rituals of writing – ritual with trembling, ritual with shock, ritual with sliding, and ritual with breath – which correspond to the rhythm of the white piano played by Brossard and the character of Emma. This will enable us to overcome anxiety so as to reach the tranquility of the renewed sense of life.

> l'art soulève la partie rebelle
> des mots grondés dans la tête d'Emma
> (Brossard 2011, 61)

Introduction

« [P]ourquoi suis-je si encombrée / d'ombre et d'humanité [...] » (Brossard 2011, 76), s'interroge Emma, le personnage lyrique de *Piano blanc* de Nicole Brossard, tout en « nou[ant] son foulard d'hiver et d'obscurité » (Brossard 2011, 76) comme pour signaler l'étouffement de sa voix, la suffocation de son souffle, l'étranglement de ses mots qui « part[ent] dans tous les sens » (Brossard 2011, 76) et qui composent une prose qu'elle compare à une « forme habillée de chagrin » (Brossard 2011, 76) – comme si Emma se décrivait elle-même.

Les nœuds formés dans la gorge et la prose d'Emma font écho à ce que Brossard écrivait en 1988 à propos du rituel avec tremblement dont la définition commençait ainsi : « Here it is the whole body that concentrates intensely in order to remember childhood and to untie the knots that have formed in its throat. » (Brossard 2005, 102) Plus de vingt ans avant la rédaction de *Piano blanc*, Brossard présentait une conférence intitulée « Rituels d'écriture : l'écriture comme trajectoire du désir et de la conscience ». Alice Parker en a réalisé deux traductions en anglais (1989 et 1992) dont une a été rééditée dans le recueil d'essais préparé par Susan Rudy : *Fluid Arguments* (2005). Les rituels d'écriture sont au nombre de quatre : rituel avec tremblement, rituel avec choc, rituel avec glissement, et rituel avec souffle. Ils correspondent aux six séquences de la vision aérienne schématisées par Brossard à la fin de « De radical à intégrales » (1982), essai publié en 1985 dans *La lettre aérienne*. Les quatre rituels d'écriture et les six séquences de la vision aérienne constituent le cœur de la théorie brossardienne du sens parce qu'ils décrivent la transition du Sens patriarcal vers un nouveau sens au féminin. Ils nous accompagneront dans notre étude de *Piano blanc*, où le personnage d'Emma amorce cette transition du Sens vers le sens et réalise le rituel avec tremblement.

En effet, en défaisant les nœuds qui se sont formés dans sa gorge, Emma exorcise sa peur et donne un sens à la voix qui croît en elle, ce qui correspond au résumé que fait Brossard du rituel avec tremblement : « [A] ritual that permits us at once to exorcise fear, to make the first stories burst forth, and make the body and thought available for new emotions. » (Brossard 2005, 103) En agissant ainsi, Emma fait apparaître un nouveau sens dans le Sens c'est-à-dire qu'elle fait émerger un contrordre au féminin (sens nouveau) dans l'ordre patriarcal (le Sens). Si Brossard situe le rituel avec tremblement et la séquence a de sa vision aérienne dans les écritures de Virginia Woolf et de Simone de Beauvoir, comment se fait-il qu'elle, qui n'a jamais associé ce rituel à son écriture, opère ce brusque retour en arrière avec le personnage d'Emma, fille du tournant du siècle, dans *Piano blanc* ?

Alors qu'en 1982 Brossard imaginait que son écriture en l'an 2000 se situerait au niveau du sens *inédit* et du sens *renouvelé* (cf. Brossard 1988, 103), elle n'avait pas prévu qu'à l'aube du 21e siècle le Sens patriarcal serait doublé d'une autre « grande noirceur » (Brossard 1988, 102) et ferait dévier le sens de son écriture. La trajectoire du sens nouveau planifiée dans les années 1980 n'étant plus d'actualité avec l'émergence d'un nouveau Sens (patriarcal), Brossard se voit dans l'obligation de transposer d'urgence les rituels d'écriture développés dans le contexte patriarcal du 20e siècle au contexte du 21e dont il est difficile de dénommer le fléau sinon peut-être en reprenant l'adjectif du titre de son dernier roman, à savoir le « sombre » (Brossard 2007b). Face à l'obscurité grandissante au 21e siècle, Brossard lève à nouveau le poing, reprend ses armes (les mots) et applique à nouveau ses stratégies féministes et lesbiennes qu'elle adapte à ses nouvelles préoccupations. Dès lors, la question éthique du féminisme s'élargit à l'humanité entière. C'est ce que Marie Carrière (2013, 121) a démontré en évoquant « l'état actuel d'infiltration et de déflexion des pensées féministes à travers [le] [...] cheminement d'écrivaine » de Brossard. Dans cet article, Carrière (2013, 121) rappelle les propos de notre auteure confrontée à « d'autres urgences, d'autres angoisses et révoltes qui [...] occupent désormais le devant de [ses] solidarités et de [sa] réflexion » en lesquelles Carrière voit l'expression d'un métaféminisme. Cette évolution du discours féministe brossardien a également été démontrée dans notre ouvrage intitulé *La traversée des sens* (2016), qui retrace la trajectoire féministe de Brossard sur trois décennies de 1977 à 2007. Mais si l'évolution et la transposition des stratégies féministes au contexte ‹ inhumaniste › du 21e siècle ont été observées pendant la première décennie du 21e siècle, qu'en est-il de cette première décennie passée ? L'écriture de Brossard s'articule-t-elle toujours autour de ce que nous appelons une « (in)quiétude (esth)éthique » (Notard 2016, 475-476), cette traversée nous faisant passer de l'inquiétude éthique à la quiétude esthétique à l'aide des rituels d'écriture féministes et lesbiens ? Cette trajectoire, qui était la seule possible en temps de crise entre 1996 et 2007, est-elle encore d'actualité en 2011 dans *Piano blanc* ? C'est le tempo du piano qui nous guidera pour répondre à cette question.

Émilie NOTARD

Agitato

piano coups de clavier dans les artères
(Brossard 2011, 48)

Le rituel avec tremblement est le point de départ de la théorie des rituels. Moment crucial de l'écriture, il est associé par certaines critiques, telles que Barbara Godard (1991, 11) et Alice Parker (1998, 176-177), à une crise. Parker divise le rituel avec tremblement en deux phases : d'une part l'aliénation en tant que crise identitaire du sujet féminin, et d'autre part une prise et crise de conscience. Le rituel avec tremblement permet de passer d'une phase à l'autre et de recouvrer une humanité perdue aussi bien dans le contexte patriarcal du 20ᵉ, comme dans *L'amèr*, que dans le contexte apocalyptique du 21ᵉ siècle, comme dans *Piano blanc*.

Le recueil s'ouvre sur le verbe « tressaillir » (Brossard 2011, 9)[1], ce qui n'est pas sans rappeler le tremblement du premier rituel d'écriture. Bien qu'écrit en majuscules, cet infinitif nous donne l'impression que les pronoms *je, tu, elle* et *on*, qui font imploser le sujet lyrique contemporain, n'osent pas conjuguer le verbe de peur que tout bascule dans l'horreur pressentie. Le calme de la première strophe est suspect : le tableau de sérénité ambiante qui y est dressé n'est qu'un trompe-l'œil. Tout suinte la peur face à un désastre à venir dont l'imminence est esquissée dès la seconde strophe : « on parle tout bas / de glisser vers l'abîme défiguré / loin de l'humanité » (11). À tout moment, les ténèbres mises en garde à vue peuvent être remises en liberté et accomplir l'apocalypse pressentie par le sujet lyrique qui, pour retarder l'heure fatidique, s'accroche au peu d'humanité qui l'entoure. Mais au lieu de s'en remettre à une énonciation purement lyrique, le *je* produit parallèlement une énonciation critique revisitant la notion traditionnelle de lyrisme, comme le souligne Evelyne Gagnon (2012, 69-70) en s'appuyant sur le concept de ‹ lyrisme critique › développé par Jean-Michel Maulpoix dans son ouvrage éponyme (2009). Le *je* fait donc appel à des paysages lyriques en évoquant le « règne animal » (12), la couleur « *azul* » (12) et la « nappe d'eau » (12) ; à son corps, terme répété deux fois (cf. 11, 13) et renforcé par la présence des « poignets » (11), de l'« œil » (12) et de la « cage thoracique » (13) ainsi que par le verbe « caresser » (12) ; ainsi qu'à la langue, terme répété deux fois dans la dernière strophe (cf. 13) et renforcé par la « première personne au pluriel » (12), par « les virgules » (12) et par « certaines phrases » (13). Néanmoins, cette langue semble lui échapper des mains au point d'en faire le deuil en évoquant les « langues mortes » (16), l'« absence de pronoms » (17), « la langue peine invivable » (17) ainsi qu'une « grammaire d'écho » (18) « sans ponctuation » (19). Endeuillé, le *je* lyrique croit cependant en une rédemption par la langue et réitère sa prière : « viens donc narration j'attends / tes questions indiscrètes tes idées de *fun vert* » (17). Cette attente de la délivrance par l'écriture correspond aux balbutiements du rituel avec tremblement : « The woman who writes, who wants to write, hears the voice, sees the inner landscape, knows the hour and the place of the event where something in her life began, stopped; but all this for the moment remains still unspeakable. » (Brossard 2005, 103) Franchir le cap du tremblement-tressaillement-balbutiement signifie se mettre soi-même au monde, « sortir de soi » (Brossard 2011, 14), ce qui « exige de filer doux / entre siècles et galaxies marelle céleste » (14) avec tout ce qu'ils ont d'inquiétant.

Plus en avant dans le recueil, le terme « tremblement » fait son apparition après une série de poèmes évoquant le dialogue et la lecture (46). Il a perdu la pesanteur qu'il avait trente ans auparavant et qu'il semblait avoir conservée au début de *Piano blanc*. Associé à la légèreté et à la malignité d'un petit singe, le tremblement fait le pitre avec son « alpha*bêt* trompeur » (46) et sa « tête renversée contraire à l'angoisse » (17). Il quitte son « manteau chaud » (48) et ses « intentions de mammifère » (48) pour mieux plonger dans la faille de l'histoire : « tremper dans l'histoire / tout bas / sombrer dans la suite et la soie lamée de l'horizon » (49). Or comment expliquer ce soudain revirement du tremblement ? D'un point de vue historique, le rituel avec tremblement est vieux de plus d'un siècle puisque Brossard le situe dans l'écriture des premières féministes qui ont pris la plume envers et contre tout. Une femme occidentale du 21e siècle comme Emma a moins de raison de trembler à l'idée de s'approprier un geste autrefois interdit aux femmes, à savoir celui d'écrire, que Woolf ou de Beauvoir. En revanche, elle a plus de raison de trembler que ces dernières en prenant conscience de l'« intensité troublante et troublée face aux bruits du temps » (Corriveau 2011). En effet, la première partie de *Piano blanc* est conçue comme une « mise en alerte » (Corriveau 2011), Emma y prenant conscience de la gravité de la situation et de la nécessité de réagir en écrivant ce qui pourrait refaire le monde, comme l'indique le titre du dernier essai de Brossard, *Et me voici soudain en train de refaire le monde* (2015). Elle a donc bien conscience de devoir défaire ces « nœuds de nuit dans la gorge » (Brossard 2011, 15) afin que les premiers récits d'un nouveau siècle puissent jaillir. Il n'est donc pas étonnant de trouver une page de prose intitulée « récit » dans ce recueil. Même si Emma n'a pas écrit le récit, la prose s'installe dans ses cahiers (cf. 77) et s'infiltre dans s/la poésie. Elle a bien conscience que, sans récit, elle n'aura pas voix au chapitre. Dans la partie intitulée « Piano prose », il est une série de poèmes intitulée « Sans récit », termes qui scandent 6 des 8 strophes pour mieux marteler ses poèmes d'avertissements en cas d'absence de récit. Sans récit, nous serions condamné-e-s à la répétition, à la peur, à l'opacité, à l'abîme et à l'amenuisement des continents. Si jusqu'ici il s'agissait de faire jaillir des récits dénonçant l'histoire patriarcale, quelle histoire les récits jaillis en ce début de 21e siècle doivent-ils annoncer ?

Forte

aussi je vais rapide
(Brossard 2011, 17)

Associé au combat féministe, le deuxième rituel dont parle Brossard, le rituel avec choc, a lieu dans un grand accès de colère dirigé contre le patriarcat au 20e siècle :

> When a woman invests a word with all her anger, energy, determination, this word crashes violently into the same word, the one invested with masculine experience. The shock that follows has the effect of making the word burst: certain words lose a letter, others see their letters reform in a different order. [...] Ritual with shock is the most violent and risky of the rituals, for the risk is great that one could wound oneself. In fact ritual with shock engenders necessarily a work of deconstruction. (Brossard 2005, 103, 104)

Parce qu'il engendre nécessairement une déconstruction, il est étroitement lié au rituel avec glissement qui poursuit le travail amorcé par le choc : « Ritual with sliding is a ritual that demands great concentration, for its function is to displace slightly but sufficiently the semantic aura of words in such a way that they produce an unforeseeable resonance without alteration in the signifier. » (Brossard 2005, 104) Au tournant du siècle, les œuvres de Brossard mettent en exergue moins la violence patriarcale que la violence de la civilisation où les souffrances infligées aux femmes se mêlent aux autres crimes contre l'humanité. Toujours dans le combat, Brossard a conservé un mode d'écriture déconstructionniste visible. Dans *Piano blanc*, la déconstruction de la langue passe par l'intrusion de mots en langues étrangères qu'elle prend soin de mettre en italique ; par des termes où la relation entre signifiant et signifié est brisée (cf. Guillemette/Cossette 2006) ; par une série de termes où un chiffre est collé au substantif qui le suit ; ainsi que par des jeux graphiques consistant à insérer des signes comme une partition folle de John Cage ou à presque effacer la typographie de certains mots voire vers.

Au 21ᵉ siècle, si Brossard conserve son écriture déconstructionniste, son discours de combat n'est plus le même. Dès lors, il ne s'agit plus de réinvestir le vocabulaire freudien ou lacanien, comme elle l'avait fait dans *L'amèr* (1977) ; il ne s'agit plus de décrire avec ironie voire sarcasme les désastres éthiques de notre siècle, comme elle l'avait fait depuis les événements du 11 septembre, en particulier dans *Après les mots* (2007a). Dans *Piano blanc*, Brossard dénonce « un confort de fin du monde » (Brossard 2011, 18), « le monde effacé les images d'adieu » (20) et nous confronte à « notre mythologie de nuit millénaire » (14) en évoquant « armes » (14), « peuples en fuite » (18), « dictature » (23), « caméras de surveillance » (25), « massacres » (26) et murs-frontières (cf. 31). Si Brossard semble banaliser ces désastres qu'elle fait apparaître – l'air de rien – au détour de ses vers, elle nous rend aveugles pour mieux nous rendre la vue, pour mieux nous ouvrir les yeux face aux « problèmes qui assaillent la planète (guerres, agressions militaires, menaces écologiques, frénésie marchande) » (Carrière 2013, 122). En effet, quand Brossard s'adresse à nous en ces termes : « vous rapide usagé en train de traverser / un siècle une catastrophe » (Brossard 2011, 83), elle nous montre du doigt, nous accuse, nous bouscule, nous secoue, comme jamais elle ne l'avait fait auparavant. Certes, elle réutilise le *leitmotiv* des ruines d'un présent dévasté – dont l'archéologie a commencé dès la fin des années 1980 dans *Le désert mauve* (1987) – comme on peut le voir dans cette strophe : « caméras de surveillance et bains tourbillons / l'Occident chancelle / dehors, un vent bleu / uniformes / chaises en plastique tournées vers le vide » (25). Certes, le paysage silencieusement apocalyptique décrit dans cette strophe n'est qu'un autre désert mauve du monde, qu'un autre déclin de notre civilisation, qu'une autre déchéance de notre humanité. Mais cette fois, il n'est même plus d'horizon pour espérer. Ce n'est pas un hasard que la strophe se termine sur le mot « vide » : ce vers réalise la prophétie du second poème-strophe de la première partie et nous entraîne inéluctablement dans sa chute vertigineuse vers le néant. Ce vers prouve que « la poésie sombre par moments dans ce ‹ trou noir sémiotique › qui aura caractérisé [...] le discours dominant de l'Amérique de l'après-11 Septembre » (Carrière 2013, 126).

Dévorée d'inquiétude, Brossard tente de nous rappeler nos « t/erreurs » (Brossard 2011, 42) du passé pour nous rappeler que l'humanité se retournera une fois de plus contre elle-même si nous ne restons pas vigilant-e-s. C'est en particulier le cas dans un poème berlinois (cf. 45) où elle nous rappelle dès la première strophe deux périodes dévastatrices de l'histoire berlinoise et allemande : d'une part, le national-socialisme en évoquant la topographie de la terreur, musée berlinois situé à côté du Musée Gropius et érigé là où se situait la police d'État secrète pendant le IIIe Reich et, d'autre part, les deux Allemagne et les deux Berlin en évoquant le mur. La chute dans le ‹ trou noir sémantique › sur laquelle s'ouvre le poème est renforcée par le mot « terreur » (45) dont le gris typographique nous plonge dans les brumes d'un passé qu'on semble avoir oublié au même titre que la leçon qu'on était censé en tirer. Puis, le poème bascule soudainement dans le passé qui occupe toute la strophe centrale. Brossard y fait référence à Himmler (« le petit homme à lunettes », 45), à l'insigne qui ornait les képis des SS (« crâne blanc sur sa casquette », 45) et aux victimes tombées pendant la Seconde Guerre mondiale (« 60 millions de visages », 45). Parce qu'elle est versatile, la vie réapparaît au sein de la dernière strophe en même temps que la couleur de l'encre et semble même porteuse de sens, comme en témoignent les adjectifs « fertile » et « crédible » (45), et du souffle (de vie), comme l'évoque le vers sur lequel se termine le poème.

Et comme dans un murmure d'échos, un mur en appelle un autre. Ainsi, Brossard commence sa série de poèmes intitulée « piano frontera » par cette strophe : « clôture on disait barbelée / mur ou murmure-moi / aussi une autre phrase / entre ici et au-delà la frontière / j'ai encore une tête sur les épaules » (31). Elle évoque ici le mur dressé entre les États-Unis et le Mexique et au-delà tous les murs qui se dressent de par le monde pour lutter contre la porosité des frontières. Le poème passe d'ailleurs par une lézarde du mur pour glisser vers une autre crise humaine : « de l'autre côté du rio le soleil lèche / un œil, parfait / traverser il le faudra / entre les croix et les clous / bouquets d'iris *no una de mas* [sic] » (31). Sans doute Brossard fait-elle référence dans cette strophe au mouvement féministe mexicain *Ni una más* fondé par la poète Susana Chávez assassinée en 2011 par les terroristes machistes qui œuvraient à Ciudad Juarez et contre lesquels elle se battait. Son mouvement luttait et lutte encore contre tout type de violences faites aux femmes, en particulier les féminicides, que Brossard évoque dans la seconde partie du recueil. Cette partie s'ouvre sur un poème dont l'épigraphe est constituée d'un horrible témoignage évoquant un cadavre : « les vautours avaient déjà mangé sa langue et ses yeux » (31). Dans ce contexte, on est obligé de se rappeler les mutilations de nombreux corps de Mexicaines telles que la décapitation. Parce qu'elle a « encore une tête sur les épaules » (31), Brossard se fait un devoir de rapporter ces meurtres qui se perpétuent contre les femmes au Mexique. La série de poèmes intitulés « Paupières » présente des variations à propos d'une tête de femme battue dont les parties – « bouche » et « lèvres », « œil » et « paupières », « tête » et « visage », « nuque » et « gorge », « ventres » et « organes vitaux », « cheveux » et « dents » (31-39) – semblent être filmées ou photographiées en gros plan, comme si l'objectif frôlait le rouge, lipstick et sang mêlés.

Bien après la citation d'Emily Dickinson qui fait office d'épitaphe, on apprend dans un poème (cf. 75) que la jeune photographe qu'est Emma vient d'exposer sur un mur une série de photos de femmes victimes de torture. On assiste là à une délocalisation du féminisme brossardien qui, au 20ᵉ siècle, était presque exclusivement occidental ainsi qu'à une ouverture du féminisme à d'autres problèmes éthiques que celui de la condition des femmes. La terrible inquiétude éthique qui en découle ne laisse pas Brossard et ses personnages indifférentes. Dans *Piano blanc*, Emma suffoque et le récit ne s'écrit pas parce que seule une prose trompe-l'œil s'impose, une prose qui « donnait l'impression de pouvoir soulager et donner du plaisir » (77). Il y a là des clôtures dans la respiration, pour reprendre le *leitmotiv* de *La capture du sombre*. Alors le tempo *forte* ralentit…

Piano

ne reste que nos vies lentes à devenir des vies
(Brossard 2011, 89)

Bien que « [l']eau entrait dans la bouche » (74) d'Emma, cette dernière parvient à articuler des « ultrasons » (91), pour reprendre le titre d'une sous-partie de « piano prose », des ultra-sons qui lui permettent de parler : « parler en prose parler dissipe les noyades d'origine » (92). Il s'agit « [d]es fuites de récit, comme on dit fuite d'eau, [qui] traversaient la présence, le moindre élan de poésie » (77, 78). Comme le souligne Evelyne Gagnon (2012, 82), le récit sert de prétexte au poème puisque le seul récit qui apparaît dans le recueil n'est autre qu'un poème en prose évoquant un récit promis qui n'a jamais été écrit à cause d'une interférence poétique. C'est donc à la poésie qu'Emma doit la sortie des obscures eaux vénitiennes – rappelant *Mort à Venise* de Thomas Mann –, et donc qu'elle doit la vie. Car c'est à l'aube que la poésie refait soudainement son apparition avec sa langue écorchée : « Puis un matin, la poésie a refait surface, s'accommodant un temps de la prose qui enrobait à peu près tous les détails auxquels je pensais. » (77) Emma refait également surface, sort ruisselante des eaux, « remorqu[ant] une aube de langage éventré / collée au grand tout concassé de l'histoire » (105). Et l'eau qu'elle régurgite n'est autre qu'« une seule gorgée de présent » (106). C'est à ce moment-là qu'elle décide de cesser de succomber aux appels des gouffres de l'histoire. Cette décision se fait d'ailleurs *leitmotiv* à variation dans les dernières pages du recueil : « laisse courir les incendies, l'essoufflement rebelle » (97), « je laisse tomber répéter » (105), « je laisse tomber mourir » (105, 109, 113). Le thème de la chute existentielle ressurgit et se prolonge. Il ne s'agit plus de sombrer dans le néant mais de le traverser pour mieux en sortir : « chute libre du soi vivant / par en-dessous du vide » (108). Car c'est là si proche de la mort que la vie reprend son souffle, comme elle le décrit dans le poème intitulé « Ombragée d'éphémère sans tutoiement » (107). Réanimée comme un cœur, la langue ravivée peut à nouveau insuffler de la vie autour d'elle. Elle recompose timidement un paysage d'eau et de vent, « entre racines et ravins » (108), ponts et canaux, plumes et écailles, pétales et épines, lierre et mousse. C'est un paysage timide, à peine esquissé, où arbres, fruits et épices surgissent surréalistes au détour d'un vers et deviennent ce que Brossard appelle des « petites survies » (24). C'est aussi un paysage intérieur, un paysage de souffle entre musique et silence, voix et murmure, prose et poésie, rythme et respiration. Le rituel avec souffle est à l'œuvre :

> Its most certain effect is to multiply energy by modulating it to the rhythm most appropriate to thought in the body. In this ritual the entire voice works very hard to find its just tonality. [...] There is music that we carry in us, music made of silences and harmony, privileged moments that only come upon us when our availability is total. The ritual with breath is practised [sic] in solitude with the sound of our respiration as its only companion. (105)

Si nous avons pu mesurer l'importance notable de ce rituel dans tous les recueils du tournant du siècle, il semble qu'il soit plus sensible dans *Piano blanc* de par la présence de cet instrument de musique qui règle la respiration du texte. Ainsi, pour retrouver son souffle, Emma s'installe au piano : « le pouvoir des questions / si tu t'installes au piano / au milieu de tourbillons conçus / pour notre disparition » (99). Dans ces quatre vers, la simple évocation du piano semble chasser les essaims de questions et de morts qui bourdonnent autour de nous. C'est seulement là, les doigts sur le clavier, que l'écriture peut commencer car de toute façon il fallait écrire au présent. Si la lumière peine à filtrer l'intense obscurité dans *Piano blanc*, Emma « fai[t] vœu de clarté si vive que l'iris vole en éclats » (56). Elle fait vœu de vie : « elle venait en silence / venir exister avec un cahier ou une caméra » (57). Ce profond désir de vie s'inscrit dans tout le recueil qui se termine d'ailleurs sur le mot « savoir-vie » (113). Au cœur de la langue se pose la question philosophique de l'existence : « qu'allons-nous faire exister / de très nu au-delà de respirer » (109). Afin de sortir de la tautologie, il faut d'abord que la langue se mette à l'œuvre : « vous voyez vivre ne sert qu'à vivre / il faut des dialogues c'est tout » (81). Il faut qu'Emma s'adresse à nous par le « vous » qui sert de titre au premier poème de la partie intitulée « Piano prose ». Dialoguer, il s'agit bien là d'un impératif (esth)ét*h*ique (cf. Carrière 2013, 130) auquel seule une poétique synesthésique peut répondre : « dans l'alphabet le sentiment tactile / de plusieurs fois la même voix » (Brossard 2011, 82) ; « oralité de poussière rose et sous-titres » (83) ; « déployez-vous jusqu'à fine soif et ruban de respiration » (84) ; « il fallait mélanger les goûts, langue, la soie le lin » (93). Ce sont des « preuves vivantes » (83), des mots qui (r)appellent (à) la vie, qui éveillent les cinq sens : « les cigales » (91) pour l'ouïe, le « pili-pili » (89) pour le goût, « un caillou » (85) pour le toucher, « les pupilles » (102) pour la vue et le « parfum » (72) pour l'odorat. Au moment de refermer le recueil qui se termine sur le mot « savoir-vie » (112), nous savons la vie, une vie que nous avons appris à (re)connaître aux côtés d'Emma qui du haut de ses vingt ans a dû traverser le sédiment patriarcal et inhumain d'innombrables siècles. Car si Emma a plongé dans les eaux sombres de notre histoire, « elle ne voulait pas être ce ruissellement / de répétition » (65). Comme une éponge, les pores de sa peau ont absorbé l'humidité des éternels recommencements non pas pour que ruissellent les horreurs de l'humanité mais pour que de la « clameur du clavier » (113) ruisselle la musique des « manuscrits d'éphémère »

(113) et leur « joie neuve » (113). En revisitant l'histoire derrière son écran et son objectif, Emma n'oublie jamais de respirer et de vivre au présent.

Conclusion

En guise de conclusion, nous pouvons affirmer que cette traversée – nous faisant passer de l'inquiétude éthique à la quiétude esthétique à l'aide des rituels d'écriture observés dans les écrits de Brossard entre 1996 et 2007 (cf. Notard 2016) – est toujours valable en 2011. La structure même du recueil *Piano blanc* en est la preuve. Elle porte en elle le mouvement allant du rituel avec tremblement avec la première partie intitulée « tressaillir » au rituel avec souffle avec la dernière partie intitulée « ruisseler » en passant par les rituels avec choc et glissement avec la partie centrale intitulée « paragraphes d'éternité ». Cette partie centrale est encadrée par deux intermèdes musicaux intitulés « piano blanc » et « piano prose », l'un permettant de retenir notre souffle avant de traverser les désastres de l'humanité captés par l'objectif d'Emma et l'autre permettant de reprendre notre souffle. *Piano blanc* s'inscrit donc dans la lignée des œuvres brossardiennes du tournant du siècle à la différence près qu'il semble mettre beaucoup plus l'accent sur le rituel avec souffle et sur le dialogue avec les lecteurs que ses autres œuvres de la même période. Mais bien qu'Emma parvienne à sortir vivante de là et à plaider pour la vie malgré tout, il est cependant un reste d'inquiétude : si le recueil se termine sur une petite ode à la joie, pourquoi a-t-elle lieu « *dans la nuit* de savoir-vie » (Brossard 2011, 113 ; je souligne) ?

1   Les citations renvoyant toutes à Brossard (2011), nous n'indiquerons, dans ce qui suit, que les pages respectives.

Bibliographie

Brossard, Nicole : *Le désert mauve.* Montréal : l'Hexagone, 1987.
Brossard, Nicole : *L'amèr ou Le chapitre effrité.* Montréal : l'Hexagone, 1988 [1977].

Brossard, Nicole : « Vision aérienne : des séquences de la SPIRALE en son énergie vers une culture au féminin ». In : Brossard, Nicole : *La lettre aérienne*. Montréal : Les Éditions du remue-ménage, 1988 [1985], 102-103.

Brossard, Nicole : *Baroque d'aube*. Montréal : l'Hexagone, 1995.

Brossard, Nicole : « Writing as a Trajectory of Desire and Consciousness ». Traduit par Alice Parker. In : Rudy, Susan (éd.) : *Fluid Arguments*. Toronto : The Mercury Press, 2005, 101-107.

Brossard, Nicole : *Après les mots*. Trois-Rivières/Esch-sur-Alzette : Écrits des Forges/Éditions Phi, 2007a.

Brossard, Nicole : *La capture du sombre*. Montréal : Leméac, 2007b.

Brossard, Nicole : *Piano blanc*. Montréal : l'Hexagone, 2011.

Brossard, Nicole : *Et me voici soudain en train de refaire le monde*. Montréal : Mémoire d'encrier, 2015.

Carrière, Marie : « L'écriture planétaire de Nicole Brossard ». In : Dufault, Roseanna / Ricouart, Janine (éds) : *L'inédit des sens*. Montréal : Les Éditions du remue-ménage, 2013, 119-135.

Corriveau, Hugues : « La musique de Nicole Brossard ». In : *Le Devoir* (02/07/2011), http://www.ledevoir.com/culture/livres/326567/poesie-la-musique-de-nicole-brossard (consultation 01/05/2016).

Gagnon, Evelyne : « Circulation lyrique et persistance critique : le passage au XXIe siècle chez Nicole Brossard ». In : *Voix et Images* 37,3 (2012), 69-83.

Godard, Barbara : « Performance/Transformance ». In : *Tessera* 11 (1991), 11-18.

Guillemette, Lucie / Cossette, Josiane : « Déconstruction et différance ». In : Hubert, Louis (éd.) : *Signo* (2006), http://www.signosemio.com/derrida/deconstruction-et-differance.asp (consultation 01/05/2016).

Maulpoix, Jean-Michel : *Pour un lyrisme critique*. Paris : José Corti, 2009.

Notard, Émilie : *La traversée des sens : trajectoire féministe dans l'œuvre de Nicole Brossard de 1977 à 2007*. Berlin/Münster/Wien/London : LIT Verlag, 2016.

Parker, Alice A. : *Liminal Visions of Nicole Brossard*. New York : Peter Lang, 1998.

Affronter/surmonter la crise

Facing/Overcoming Crisis

Piet DEFRAEYE (Edmonton)

Crisis in Michel Marc Bouchard: Re-Writing Melodrama

Résumé

Le théâtre de Michel Marc Bouchard continue à attirer un grand public. Son œuvre met en avant un assortiment éclectique de personnages en crise, et il le fait dans une langue stylisée et poétique. Tout en se référant à une vaste sélection de pièces de théâtre, dont *Les feluettes, Les muses orphelines* et *Les manuscrits du déluge*, l'auteur de cet article attire l'attention sur le mélodrame comme stratégie. Beaucoup des pièces de Bouchard révèlent des motifs et des structures de mélodrame comme l'hyperbole, l'imagination de l'enfant et le jeu. Ces éléments convergent dans le motif récurrent de la langue et de l'écriture même. Un grand nombre des personnages de Bouchard surmontent leur crise grâce à l'utilisation d'un langage imaginatif, inventant leur propre univers discursif comme stratégie de résistance. Ce sont précisément l'expressivité de ces personnages et leur excès qui deviennent une stratégie pour combattre et survivre aux structures répressives qui les entourent.

> [A]nd love had to disguise itself as many things
> to survive
> ("Rivalries" in Rio 2014)

Narrative, Conflict, and Melodrama

While the stage is typically a *lieu de conflit*, contemporary theatre has a divergent approach to how it presents its conflicts and crises. The role of narrative has lost part of its lustre in much of European contemporary theatre, epitomized in the practice of the postdramatic.[1] However, North American theatre, including Canada, continues to embrace a tradition that is firmly based in narrative structures. For many Quebec playwrights in particular, the play's fable is a prime mover in the structure of any dramatic development. Michel Tremblay's version of the *Volksstück* genre is no doubt the best example, with its urban settings, humorous hyperrealism, working-class characters, and use of *joual*. More recent epigones have moved away from this realist tradition. Jean-Pierre Ryngaert (2011-12) in "Figures du mélodrame dans les écritures d'aujourd'hui" gathers scattered evidence on a resurgence of melodramatic poetics and strategies in Quebec theatre, which in his view is primarily focused on a Manichean narrative torn between good and evil. Apart from Daniel Danis, he also lists Évelyne de la Chenelière, Wajdi Mouawad, and Michel Marc Bouchard as examples of playwrights whose stories feature a nuclear family, which becomes, in typical melodramatic fashion, "le lieu d'affrontements, de trahisons, de désespoirs, d'abandons, de séparations" (Ryngaert 2011-12, 174).

It is undoubtedly these strong emotions that pulled Michel Marc Bouchard towards the melodramatic genre. In an early interview, the playwright admits using melodrama as a strategy, "un moyen d'intéresser le spectateur en lui proposant une démarche émotive" (Dionne 1989, 13).[2] His œuvre marks a continuation of Tremblay's homegrown and popular tradition of theatre, sharing specific themes and motifs with Quebec's *dramaturge célèbre*, including a regular probing of issues on gender, but also, like Tremblay, a creative use of hyper-theatricality. Yet in contrast with Tremblay, Bouchard's plays certainly do not embrace the realist *Volksstück* genre; on the contrary, they consistently move away from the realistic mode. They incorporate innovative ways of presenting a complex dramatic world on stage, in which transformation, invariably theatrical or performative in nature, plays a crucial role and harkens back to the genre of melodrama.

The use of melodrama and the terminology associated with it as a referent in critical discourse is not without problems. When reviewers label Bouchard a "mélodramaturge" (Lévesque 1995) or his plays "moralistic melodrama" (Hayford 2001) they do so not in a complimentary way. It is certainly not my intention to define Bouchard's plays as melodrama. This analysis wants to expose some of the playwright's returning strategies in terms of plot, choice of characters, and emotional impact. While melodrama originally meant a specific historical genre of theatre that used musical background to underscore highly emotional moments, we have come to understand the term as denoting an extravagant drama with simple cliché-like characters, artificial plot contrivance, unexpected reversals, and sensational effects which are there to impress and move or emote an often middle or lower-middle class audience. Affect plays a crucial role. The mysterious world of melodrama is populated with non-conformist villains and heroes, whose crisis originates or culminates in aggression, revenge, betrayal, or (often frustrated) sexual desire. Bouchard explicitly aims his writing at a more popular reception, and for a long time did not eschew summer festival fare. Music often plays an important role in his plays, heightening the emotional exchange. His characters speak in a lyrical language and his discourse is often described in musical terms. Referring to *Down Dangerous Passes Road*, for instance, Sylvie Bérard defines his style as "un souffle pratiquement lyrique," and uses terms such as "rondeau" and "l'art de la fugue" to evoke it (1998, 40).

With the possible exception of *L'histoire de l'oie* (1991), most of his biggest successes use a melodramatic arrangement as their central strategy. This is most evident in plays like *Le voyage du couronnement* (1995), *Les muses orphelines* (1989), and *Les feluettes* (1988). We can also see this approach in more recent plays like *Les manuscrits du déluge* (2003) and *Tom à la ferme* (2011). Perhaps most tellingly, his 2015 exploration of Sarah Bernhardt in *The Divine: A Play for Sarah Bernhardt*, which premiered in English, lends further argument to Bouchard's predilection for the melodramatic with the play's spotlight on the celebrated thespian who brought melodrama to Canada with her repeated visits between 1880 and 1918.[3] This play marks a full circle with his breakthrough play *Les feluettes* written almost 30 years earlier, which Bouchard's subtitle defines as a rehearsal of a melodrama: *La répétition d'un drame romantique*.

Melodramatic Imagination

Michael Kirby succinctly summarizes the good and the bad that surround melodrama in his "Melodrama Manifesto of Structuralism." It certainly has a bad rap, as it "is thought to be obvious, exaggerated and trite. Its characters are considered one-dimensional, its plot contrived" (Kirby 1980). It "is not the way people behave; things do not happen like that." (Kirby 1980) On the other hand, melodrama provides a dynamic structure; it often creates "psychic traps – snares laid in childhood and adolescence – that are waiting to be sprung. [...] Instantaneous, direct, and powerful [...][,] there is no defense against them, even for the intelligent and the informed" (Kirby 1980).

Melodrama on stage has gradually fallen into disuse, not so much because of a radical change in taste, but perhaps because television does it so much better than the stage.[4] Theatre scholars and critics have suggested important corrections to the bad reputation of melodrama. Eric Bentley calls melodrama "drama in its elemental form; it is the quintessence of drama" (1972, 216). The excessiveness of the melodramatic imagination is, in other words, not necessarily contrived or bothersome. What strikes us as important in the genre – and for Bouchard's approach – is the fact that this imagination is possible, is lived and celebrated, and becomes a central strategy for the dramaturgical conflict. Peter Brooks, in his 1976 study of *The Melodramatic Imagination*, calls imagination the most essential characteristic of melodrama, and William Sharp adds that imagination is the necessary instrument that leads to change. The melodramatic world, says Sharp, is generally a simple world, but one in which "change of either the protagonist or the society he must struggle with is possible" (1992, 272). This potential for change – for better or worse – is borne out of a powerful force of imagination which intervenes in the perception of reality. While realist theatre documents reality, melodrama theatricalizes it, imaginatively.

In Michel Marc Bouchard's plays there is clearly a melodramatic imagination at work, which brings about a remarkable theatrical world of taboo and transgression, of limitation and possibility, of prosaic ordinariness and extravagance. His characters acquire melodramatic dimensions as they set themselves apart by profound hyperbole, and stage their crises histrionically and often in convoluted ways. So much so that, like in melodrama, these characters often inhabit clichés, like the lesbian soldier Martine in *The Orphan Muses*, or the repressed homosexual priest Saint-Michel in *Lilies*, or the jock brother Victor in *Down Dangerous Passes Road*. In line with this use of clichés – a better term might be primary psychic roles – the playwright's plots are often deceptively simple in protagonist and antagonist structures. Take, for instance, *Lilies*, which was adapted in 1995 by John Greyson into a screen film, a masterpiece of adaptation, which exploits the theatrics of melodrama within its own *mise en abyme*.[5] The play offers a variation on the old story of boy meets girl. Simon, just released from prison, confronts Bilodeau, an aging bishop, with a reconstruction – a *répétition* or rehearsal as the original French title suggests – of events that happened over 30 years ago in Roberval, when both were adolescent boys in the remote community of Lac Saint-Jean. *Lilies* brings together an eccentric collection of hysterical inhabitants, the most exotic of which are the impoverished Countess Marie-Laure de Tilly and her son Vallier, both of them derided by many in the town. Vallier falls in love with the handsome Simon, but the love affair is thwarted, not only by the leather whip of Simon's homophobic father, but also by a passionately jealous and sexually frustrated young Bilodeau on his way to the priesthood; it ends in the tragic death of Vallier. Just about all of the characters perform a larger self, in which passion plays a crucial role. Similarly, *The Orphan Muses* looks back at a re-play of the frustrated passions of three sisters and a brother. Their mother Jacqueline left the family home in Saint-Ludger-de-Milot – another insular village in the Lac Saint-Jean area – to pursue her fiery love affair with a Spanish dancer, but we learn how she never got further than the sewing sweatshops of Quebec City. The four children are eccentric survivors, manifestly marking their territory in a hostile world through imaginative and transgressive interventions.

Bouchard's themes are typically those of other Quebec plays including conflicts of love, sexuality, and sexual identity, and often focus on individuals opposed by a hostile society or family. While the machinations of memory and history contribute to a complex texture, it is the characters' imagination that gives them a strategy to cope with their individual predicament and to conquer obstacles, or at least come to terms with the snags and hardship of life.

However, the motif and power of imagination go beyond the thematic. Imagination is thematized within the play's dramatic presentation, and finds its way into the poetry of the language itself, which is a strategy that was fervent-ly embraced by writers of melodrama. This dramatic language is not only the discourse of the playwright, which for Michel Marc Bouchard often translates into a meta-theatrical dramaturgy, but it is also the language of the characters, evident in hyperbole, emotionality, and over-the-top *simili*. For this kind of theatricality to work for the audience, it requires a sophisticated physicalisation on the stage by the actors. The Countess in *Lilies* is not just an eccentric lady who is hurt by her past, and she is certainly not just a crazy neurotic woman, as a purely realist reading of the play would yield. It is her theatrical embrace of her predicament that develops her expansive character. She *plays* her life, and uses her imagination as a well of resources to transcend the unbearable limitations of her life, which allows her to live, or, in her own words, to "play the part" (Bouchard 1990, 64). It is her imagination that animates her and gener-ates that unforgettable metamorphosis of Lac Saint-Jean into the Mediterranean

Sea, where she imagines her son guiding the tourist-fishermen like "a buccaneer" (Bouchard 1990, 45) on the *Méditerranée*. Indeed, within the many dramatic levels of the theatrical *mise en abyme*, she herself constitutes a crucial level, or, more appropriately, stage of play, that connects, inspires, and rationalizes the imaginative performances of other characters.[6] The fact that Bouchard wants her – as well as the other female characters – to be played by a male actor not only foregrounds gender as a major motif, it also initiates a chain of playing, performativity, and make-belief that informs the entire population of *Lilies'* dramatic world. Each of them assumes a role in the drama that unfolds, and does so demonstratively. Vallier and Simon, for example, the two boys at the heart of the story, are constantly playing, trying, and rehearsing their roles of lovers, with varying degrees of success. Bouchard even has them use a historic melodrama; Gabriele D'Annunzio's *The Martyrdom of Saint Sebastien* (1911) gives them a text with which to explore and express – and *play* – their love for each other. Timothée, Simon's father, plays the Countess' valet and thus conspires in her performance. Even a character like the ballooning Lydie-Anne seeks refuge in playful imagination as a survival strategy with her incessant lying, another melodramatic feature.

Similarly, in *The Orphan Muses*, Luc Tanguay has not stopped imagining a life for his mother Jacqueline, who abandoned her four children 20 years ago to pursue a passionate love affair with a Spanish toreador. The book that Luc is writing imagines her as "a Queen of Spain" writing letters "to her Beloved Son" (Bouchard 1995, 43), as he puts it in the title of his *magnum opus*. Meanwhile, the elder sister Catherine has been hoarding her mother's short notes, which she received together with the bit of cash Jacqueline scraped together to help pay for clothing and the education of the younger siblings. "Cold, practical letters" (Bouchard 1995, 59), Martine appraises them, in contrast to the burning desire that consumed her mother's abortive flight. She wrote these letters, not from the imaginary and exotic Spain to which she allegedly travelled in pursuit of Federico, but from Quebec City where she got stuck trying to make ends meet while working in a sweatshop in the *Basse-Ville*, "making corsets for the ladies in Upper Town" (Bouchard 1995, 53). Isabelle's resurrection at the end of the play is also a sign of the power of imagination at play. While she was initially the retarded younger sister, now she steps forward as a pregnant woman who has enough courage to tap into her imagination and follow her mother's example to leave the stifling home and village. This time, however, Isabelle hopes that the odds of the real world won't be stacked against her, and imagination will triumph. The siblings meet each other in their parental home in small town Saint-Ludger under the pretext of a funeral. The Easter weekend allows them to revisit their past and, by re-playing their roles, to engender a resurrection of sorts which allows them to unshackle themselves of their *angst*, frustrations, and spite.

Strategies of Survival

The theme of imagination in Bouchard's dramatic world creates an obvious link with the genre of melodrama, but it also becomes a strategic choice for his characters to deal with and overcome crisis. The playwright finds recourse in the structures of melodrama in order to thematize his subject in a specific format and language. Melodrama is an effective choice, as the genre is indulgent in its use of imagination, sometimes excessively, sometimes bordering on the fantastic. Indeed, it is this excessiveness of his characters which may lead to dramaturgical missteps in the *mise en scène* lest they be represented on stage as freaks or crazies, as has been the case in a couple of productions.[7] Luc Tanguay is certainly eccentric, and while some of the Saint-Ludger villagers may want to see him locked up, for the spectator he is a lucid revealer of truth within an imagined reality.

Peter Brooks locates the origin of what he calls "the melodramatic imagination" in "the infantile dreamworld," in which there is a kind of "self-dramatization" (Brooks 1976, 35) of inner conflicts and crisis. Eric Bentley concurs and sees melodrama as belonging to the magical phase of the child, "the phase when thoughts seem omnipotent, when the distinction between *I want to* and *I can* is not clearly made, in short when the larger reality has not been given diplomatic recognition" (1972, 217). This can be turned around, however, and herein lies a recurrent Bouchard strategy, when the playwright has the larger objective reality stealthily invade the constructed reality of the dramatic world. We see this clearly in Bouchard's recent play *Tom at the Farm*. Tom, the main character, visits his in-laws after the sudden death of his lover. Throughout the play the dialogue with his macho in-law brother and his pondering in-law mother is constantly invaded with an imaginary dialogue with his deceased lover. The playwright thus sets up not one, but two imaginary worlds. In a scenic crossing of these two performative worlds, for instance, Tom dresses in his lover's clothes, and becomes, as it were, the deceased son for the grieving mother. The imaginative realities of these two worlds feed each other as a coping strategy of presence for both mother as well as surviving partner.

Bentley's observation that the melodramatic vision corresponds to the magical world of the child and of the adult dream world is certainly relevant for Michel Marc Bouchard's use of the melodramatic. His characters need not apologize for their excessiveness or their histrionic freakishness. Their imaginative oddity defines them not only as individuals, but also characterizes their ambitions and their struggles. The Countess' carrying on in *Lilies* about her "valet" and "chambermaid," her "fox-hunting," and the "South Wing" of the shed she lives in – her "manor house" – is nothing less than a non-compliant imagination at work. Luc Tanguay's parading around in his mother's outrageous Spanish dress in *The Orphan Muses* is never put into question. The dress, in fact, defines him; it determines who he is as a character. Similarly, the wing-wearing Danny in *Written on Water* is presented as matter-of-fact, as naturally belonging to the fauna of the play.

All these odd characters, however, are indicators of deep crisis. The troubles that are associated with Luc Tanguay wearing the dress and his impulsiveness expose the rigid social and gender structures and roles that are prevalent in the small village where the *The Orphan Muses* is set. In the first act of the play, after his visit with Madame Tessier of the Post Office, Luc is escorted home by a police sergeant; "real gentlemen, those policemen," Luc adds with an ironic wink (Bouchard 1995, 19). At the end of the play, Luc enters "in men's clothes. His head is bandaged, his arm in a sling. He has trouble walking" (Bouchard 1995, 60). He was obviously assaulted by homophobes as he walked into the church to sing at the Easter vigil dressed in his Spanish skirt, but Catherine, his older and austere sister, rescued him:

> He was sitting in a pool of blood on the church steps. Tessier's twins jumped on him the minute they saw him walk into the church. Luc didn't even have time to go up to the organ loft. In no time at all, there were four or five of them on top of him. Then they threw him out on the steps. Barbarians... (Bouchard 1995, 61)

As in most melodramas, the crises and conflicts that are described in Bouchard's plays are violent, bloody, and unforgiving. Yet, his characters manage to endure their stifling environments, albeit sometimes at tremendous cost. They survive by means of creative interactions of self-assertion. With the help of his former prison buddies, Simon in *Lilies* convokes Bishop Bilodeau for his staged confrontation with the past, which becomes the outer frame of the play. The encounter won't give him back his boyfriend Vallier, but it will still the passion of revenge and sweeten the memory of his great love. Similarly, immediately after Luc's thrashing by two of the village thugs in *The Orphan Muses*, a frustrated and until then inflexible Catherine, like her brother, decides on her own impetuousness:

> I had to get into the church to get Dr. Lemieux. When I found him, I realized I was right in the middle of the centre aisle. I don't know why but I stared at them all and began humming. […] The harder Dr. Lemieux tugged on my coat to get me to leave, the louder I sang. I walked out of the church singing at the top of my lungs, and the pianist started to play along with me. (Bouchard 1995, 61)

She goes on to describe how good her revenge on the conservative oppressiveness of the village felt as she "had nothing left to hide" (Bouchard 1995, 62).

It is an obviously melodramatic moment in the play: the three siblings gathered together, bandaging each other's literal and figurative wounds, waiting for the announced arrival/resurrection of their mother. There is even more melodrama with the *deus ex machina* resolution, when Isabelle, the youngest, steps forward on this Easter Sunday morning and impersonates the resurrected mother, thus setting herself free from the confines of her family. While playing her mother, she talks about herself in the third person to her siblings, thus commenting on her family: "She's going to have twelve kids, just to show you that children are beautiful. Twelve who will leave home... The most beautiful thing about a family is knowing how to leave it!" (Bouchard 1995, 63-64)

While the moment is melodramatic and the impersonation adds a humorous tone, as is common in Bouchard's theatre, the sentiment conveyed is chillingly serious. Throughout Bouchard's dealings with the notion of family, there is an echo of Florence Nightingale, perhaps one of the most un-melodramatic of writers. Writing in 1852, smack in the Victorian era that gave birth to melodrama, she formulates in her essay *Cassandra* the fiercest condemnation of family as a unit of protective (but also stifling) intimacy:

> The family? It is too narrow a field for the development of an immortal spirit, be that spirit male or female. The chances are a thousand to one that, in that small sphere, the task for which that immortal spirit is destined by the qualities and the gifts which its Creator has placed within it, will not be found. (Nightingale 2008, 567)

The family in Bouchard's œuvre is almost invariably part of strict community structures that have an incapacitating and censoring effect on its members, while retaining the seductively harboring qualities of both family and community. Remarkably, the agency that often transcends this stifling environment is the mother figure. Bouchard's mother characters function as if they were a response to Nightingale's denunciation of the prototypical mother: "The mother at home! There is no desert of the heart so oppressive as that of the mother at home in England in the nineteenth century." (Nightingale 2008, 450) The transference to twentieth-century rural Quebec foregrounds mothers who, in their isolation and conventional obliviousness, are psychically harmed. The Countess in *Lilies*, or Agatha in *Tom at the Farm*, or the absent Jacqueline in *The Orphan Muses* – each experience these pitfalls. They emerge, however, as clairvoyant protagonists with an oracular function.

Triumph, Despair, Protest

Bouchard's dramaturgy sticks closely to structures of melodrama, and it does so in a creative way. As James Smith points out in his brief examination of the genre: "[M]elodrama presses its own extreme conflicts to extreme conclusions." (1973, 8) These resolutions can reveal emotions of triumph, despair, or protest. Smith suggests that "in melodrama these emotions are savoured singly and in isolation, divorced from anything which might qualify, contradict or otherwise diminish [...] the prevailing 'monopathic tone'" (Smith 1973, 10).[8] Bouchard's plays definitely harbor emotions of defeat, triumph, and protest, but they do not constitute a monopathic tone. *Lilies*, which the critic André Ducharme labels as "ce mélodrame flamboyant" (1995, 91) contains a melodrama of defeat in the tragic undoing of the passionate love affair between Simon and Vallier, but it also holds a melodrama of triumph in Simon's efficacious confrontation of Bishop Bilodeau. *Lilies* is, of course, also a melodrama of protest; it addresses a gross bias and injustice as a result of homophobia and stifling conservative structures. In doing so, the play serves as a polemic within the present-day socio-political debate on relationships and sexuality and has become the epitome of Quebec theatre's gay cannon. One critic, Lorraine Camerlain, even reads the gay setting of the play, rather preposterously, as a grand metaphor "du modèle socio-démographique des Québécois francophones, qui sont en train de se faire hara-kiri en renonçant à se reproduire" (Camerlain in Lévesque 1988, 179).

Triumph, defeat, and protest are present simultaneously and complement each other, sometimes even in a single scene. When the Countess stages her own death in the sixth episode of *Lilies*, it is undoubtedly the most melodramatic moment in the play and perhaps in Bouchard's entire œuvre. It is an implausible scene, and yet ridden with prime emotions: a son accommodating his mother's death by burying her alive and choking her; a mother making room for her son "so the sunlight can reach the young saplings" (Bouchard 1990, 64). Her death is a ritual protest against the tyranny of life. It is her response to the blow of the hard-headed, down-to-earth mentality of a hostile environment that has revealed the great lie of the beloved husband she was waiting for. It is also an intense moment of triumph. Countess Marie-Laure de Tilly's imagination is so powerful that she can stage her own death, releasing herself from an insufferable crisis and allowing this mother to return to her Mother Earth.

A Theatre of Affirmation

As we look closer at these scenes, it becomes evident how Bouchard exploits fairly traditional notions of melodrama. Reviewers have often called his dramaturgy "overwrought" (Hayford 2001) and "overburdened" (Donnelly 1995), smacking "heavily of artifice" (Richards 1993) and also "baroque" and somewhat "overloaded" with "brawling estheticism" (Conlogue 1995, C2). He certainly does not avoid the excessiveness of the melodramatic imagination but, instead, uses it to give his characters opportunities to establish and maintain their integrity.

Melodrama, in other words, acquires a subversive quality in Bouchard's plays and offers opportunities for resourceful opposition for his protagonists in a hostile and deadening world. As such, his use of melodrama offers a way to explore the challenging historical and spatial transitions his characters are confronted with. Melodrama, in Bouchard's approach, becomes an aesthetic choice with political implications. His play with melodrama is part of an intricate dramaturgy that tries to represent the simultaneity of different realities and different levels of consciousness and imagination on the stage. Finding a strategy in order to produce a possible answer to their predicament is at least half of the work his characters are confronted with. Isabelle in *The Orphan Muses* anxiously notes down any new word that comes her way in her little notebook. This hilarious obsession allows her, at the end of the play, after literally gathering a language, to express herself and embark on a new voyage in her mother's steps, whom she never knew and never understood. She not only lacked the knowledge of what her mother was all about, but also the language to give voice to any such knowledge. As such, Isabelle brings about in language what her mother could not attain in the hard world of historical reality. At the end of his study, Peter Brooks draws attention to the connection between psycho-analysis and melodrama, a practice and a genre that, he stresses, emerged at the same time. Both are concerned with "the drama of a recognition," and "cure and resolution in both cases come as a result of articulation which is clarification" (Brooks 1976, 202). Isabelle's systemic repression finds resolution in her discursive acquisition to express it.

No surprise then that the foregrounding of language is a major motif in Bouchard's œuvre. Melodrama is a genre thoroughly steeped in a discursive world. The world of melodrama, with its unbridled imagination of the infant, is clearly a linguistically constructed realm. Its imaginative constructions of conflict and crisis belong not in the newspaper, where facts are reported, but in a fundamentally literary world. Many of Bouchard's characters live a profoundly diegetic life, where the narrative construction and re-construction of that life allows them to endure it. *Down Dangerous Passes Road* brings together three estranged brothers who intersect with each other through the memory of their deceased father's poetry; it allows them to unwrap their own individual pain and yearning. Victor, the eldest, observes: "We are prisoners of his poetry" (Bouchard 2000, 78), like the play script's characters themselves who are prisoners of Bouchard's diegetic composition, and through it, free themselves in a discursive world. Indeed melodrama in its desire for articulation gives its characters a *natural* license to "saying what is 'in real life' unsayable" (Brooks 1976, 41).

This preoccupation with the power of language, it turns out, is very much the central focus of *Written on Water*, undoubtedly Bouchard's most enigmatic play. The central crisis in the play is the experience of aging. Here we have a group of people trying to hold on to their own writing of the past, facing a future that doesn't seem to belong to them. William, one of the members of the writing circle, says it succinctly: "Being old is all I do, full-time now. I spit old age, I cough old age, I burp old age, I fart old age. Old age is coming out of every part of my body, at least, all the parts that are still working." (Bouchard 2004, 60) Like most of his plays, this one, too, is situated in the Saguenay-Lac-Saint-Jean region of Quebec, where Michel Marc Bouchard grew up, and is inspired by the historical memory of devastating floods. Several people died and over 16,000 were evacuated due to a series of mudslides and weak dams during the heavy torrential rains of July 1996. In his play, Bouchard constructs a community that is profoundly impacted by these events, but he chooses to focus on the cultural devastation: the deluge has scattered the collected writings of a seniors' group. In a desperate attempt to hold on to the past, Samuel, the elderly leader, tries to coerce the others to assemble the fragments and re-write the lost manuscripts. In their struggle to re-write, the individuals recognize the near impossibility of recreating the past without being influenced by their current state of being. Ironically, the tragic flood comes to represent a cleansing experience, where the seniors release the shackles of the past and free themselves into the future.

The exercise of (re-)writing is not a salvaging act of cultural archeology, but rather an affirmative intervention of renewal. As the original title *Les manuscrits du déluge* signposts, the play does not focus on the 1996 catastrophic tragedy itself. As such, it is a great example of Peter Brooks' suggestion that "melodrama succeeds tragedy" (Brooks 1976, 81) as a "response to the loss of the tragic vision" (Brooks 1976, 15). While the play radiates a profound melancholy, as the genre of melodrama often does, its focus is not on death versus survival, but on writing. As in all melodrama, it simulates tragedy rather than create it; its focus is on externalization. The characters in the play create a *mise en abyme* of possibilities of play. *Written on Water* is Bouchard's clearest attempt at writing a poetics of his own practice, which seems to echo Jean Starobinski's aphorism "Écrire, c'est transformer l'impossibilité de vivre en possibilité de dire" (1963, 422). The characters' survival certainly requires their physical endurance, but equally important is their unstymied discursive play with what was and what is still to come.

Clearly, the motif of play is a crucial aspect in Bouchard's theatre. As melodrama is quintessentially about playing, it is no coincidence that the genre often becomes an actual motif in his plays. Father Saint-Michel in *Lilies*, yet another character associated with the theatre, is obviously enamored of melodrama, even though he rejects the genre because of its allure to popular audiences (cf. Bouchard 1990, 16-17). His valiant defense of theatre sounds like a solid recipe for melodrama and reads as a creed for Bouchard's own dramaturgy:

> [T]heatre should reach everyone. One can do anything in the theatre, you know. One can reinvent life. One can be in love, jealous, insane, tyrannical or possessed. One can even lie and cheat. One can kill without feeling the slightest remorse. One can die of love, of hate, of passion ... (Bouchard 1990, 17)

Theatre, in other words, makes things possible; it allows imagination to live and allows life to be imaginative. This theatrical quality of Bouchard's world amplifies the role of writing itself. While his worlds are clearly operating on a literary level, it is also the literariness, their discursive (re-)formulation, which allows the characters to deal with the crises that develop in this literary world. This yearning for expression, "melodramatic rhetoric," as Brooks (1976, 41) calls it, "represents a victory over repression," whether that repression is psychic, social, or political. Just like the Countess in *Les feluettes*, who creates her imaginary world around Lac Saint-Jean purely in words – a world of aristocrats around the *Méditerranée* –, so do the siblings in *The Orphan Muses* use writing and words as a means to deal with their frustrations and to harbor their hopes, a struggle most clearly exemplified in Isabelle's tenacious compilation of words. The characters in *Written on Water* push this even further: they live their lives through their reconstructed writing. It is an ineffable kind of life. "Why can't we become metaphors? Why can't we be allegories or figures of speech? [...] I wish I could enter my writing" (Bouchard 2004, 78), says Danny, the flighty character with wings, whose remaining presence in the inundated village is, as it were, its surest guarantee for a firm link between past and future. He adds, for good measure: "If we could become what we write, it would be extraordinary." (Bouchard 2004, 78) While "metaphors are figures of speech that mask lies" (Bouchard 2004, 94) in Martha's words, they are at the same time expansive strategies to transcend what is possible, to overcome a continuous sense of crisis – whether it is aging, betrayal, abuse, hatred, homophobia, dysfunctional family, jealousy, sacrifice, or just plain old disillusionment, lying, or disguise. As for any protagonist in the genre of melodrama, the power of writing, or words and language in general, are for Bouchard's characters a strategy which, in the simplest of terms, enables them to live a life.[9]

1   Cf. Lehmann (2006, 68-71).

2   In a 2002 conversation with the playwright in his Montreal home, he seemed somewhat surprised and reluctant to be critically associated with the genre of melodrama. Since then, many of the subsequent plays have but supported this critical appreciation on my part.

3   For a comprehensive overview of Sarah Bernhardt's visits to Canada, cf. Hare/Hathorn (1981). For her visits to Western Canada, also cf. my radio interview (Defraeye 2007).

4   Cf., among others, Ien Ang (2007), Jonathan Goldberg (2016), Michael Stewart (2014). Linda Williams's study (2014) of the television serial *The Wire* exemplifies superbly how television pursues the melodramatic genre.

5   Peter Brooks (1976, 49) observes that "melodrama finds one possible outcome in grand opera." No surprise that Bouchard's *Lilies* was also adapted into opera, with music by the Australian composer Kevin March in 2016, under the same title. Arthur Kaptainis (2016) opens his review of the Opéra de Montréal premiere by calling it an "all-male melodrama."

6   For a more in-depth analysis of the dramaturgical structure and the multiple *personnages* in *Lilies*, cf. Defraeye/MacDonald (1997).

7   The scope of this analysis does not allow to go further into different productions of Bouchard's plays, though actors and directors who have approached his scripts in a straightforward realist mode have had trouble conveying the necessary affect the plays ask for. Mary Vingoe's 1998 production of *The Orphan Muses* for the Eastern Front Theatre in Halifax, to cite just one example, adopted a folksy realist mode and, according to reviewer Ron F. MacDonald (1998), stumbled and failed "to engage the gears of theatricality," necessary for the "playful expressionism that merges melodrama with dreamy romanticism."

8   James Smith credits Robert Bechtold Heilman (1960) as the source for "monopathic tone".

9   Thanks to Heather Fitzsimmons-Frey who was a superbly organized graduate research assistant helping me out with archival research on Bouchard productions. Thanks to Nathan Bartlett for his scrupulous proof-reading and Cristian Badiu for last-minute help in bibliographic checking.

Bibliography

Ang, Ien: "Television Fictions Around the World: Melodrama and Irony in Global Perspective." In: *Critical Studies in Television: Scholarly Studies in Small Screen Fictions* 2,2 (2007), 18-30.

Bentley, Eric: *The Life of the Drama*. New York: Atheneum, 1972.

Bérard, Sylvie: "La mort dans l'âme." In: *Lettres Québécoises* 92 (1998), 39-40.

Bouchard, Michel Marc: *Les feluettes ou La répétition d'un drame romantique*. Montreal: Leméac, 1987.

Bouchard, Michel Marc: *Lilies*. Translated by Linda Gaboriau. Toronto: Coach House Press, 1990.

Bouchard, Michel Marc: *The Orphan Muses*. Translated by Linda Gaboriau. Winnipeg: Scirocco, 1995.

Bouchard, Michel Marc: *Down Dangerous Passes Road*. Translated by Linda Gaboriau. Vancouver: Talonbooks, 2000.

Bouchard, Michel Marc: *Written on Water*. Translated by Linda Gaboriau. Vancouver: Talonbooks, 2004.

Brooks, Peter: *The Melodramatic Imagination: Balzac, Henry James, Melodrama, and the Mode of Excess*. New Haven: Yale University Press, 1976.

Conlogue, Ray: "Quebec Theatre's Bright New Hope." In: *The Globe and Mail* (07/10/1995), C1-2.

Defraeye, Piet / MacDonald, Marylea: "*Les feluettes*, un drame de répétition." In: *Dalhousie French Studies* 41 (1997), 129-137. Also published in: Bednarski, Betty / Oore, Irène (eds): *Nouveaux regards sur le théâtre québécois*. Montreal: XYZ, 1997, 129-137.

Defraeye, Piet: "La visite d'une légende: Sarah Bernhardt." In: CBC-RDI (08/10/2007) (radio interview by Danièle Petit).

Dionne, André: "Interview: Michel Marc Bouchard. Tout plein d'émotions." In: *Lettres Québécoises* 53 (1989), 10-13.

Donnelly, Pat: "*Voyage* is an Overburdened Vessel Buoyed up by Good Performances." In: *The Gazette* (Montreal) (23/09/1995), D7.

Ducharme, André: "Théâtre pour deux." In: *L'Actualité* (15/09/1995), 88-92.

Goldberg, Jonathan: *Melodrama: An Aesthetics of Impossibility.* Durham: Duke University Press, 2016.

Hare, John / Hathorn, Ramon: "Sarah Bernhardt's Visits to Canada: Dates and Repertory." In: *Theatre Research in Canada* 2,2 (1981), https://journals.lib.unb.ca/index.php/tric/article/view/7510/8569 (accessed 14/05/2016).

Hayford, Justin: "Lilies or the Revival of a Romantic Drama." In: *The Chicago Reader* (26/04/2001), http://www.chicagoreader.com/chicago/lilies-or-the-revival-of-a-romantic-drama/Content?oid=905241 (accessed 22/05/2017).

Heilman, Robert Bechtold: "Tragedy and Melodrama: Speculations on Generic Form." In: *Texas Quarterly* 3 (1960), 36-50.

Kaptainis, Arthur: "New Opera *Les feluettes* Works on Many Levels." In: *Montreal Gazette* (23/05/2016), http://montrealgazette.com/entertainment/music/review-new-opera-les-feluettes-works-on-many-levels (accessed 11/06/2017).

Kirby, Michael: "Melodrama Manifesto of Structuralism." In: Gerould, Daniel (ed.): *Melodrama.* New York: New York Literary Forum, 1980, xiv.

Lehmann, Hans-Thies: *Postdramatic Theatre.* Translated by Karen Jürs-Munby. London: Routledge, 2006.

Lévesque, Robert: "Un bateau que Dieu sait qui... ." In: *Le Devoir* (26/09/1995), B8.

Lévesque, Solange: "À propos des ‹ Feluettes › : questions et hypothèses." In: *Jeu* 49 (1988), 174-179.

MacDonald, Ron F.: "Uninspired Production Mars *Orphan Muses.*" In: *The Daily News* (Halifax) (10/10/1998), 31.

Nightingale, Florence: *Suggestions for Thought.* Edited by Lynn McDonald. Waterloo: Wilfrid Laurier University Press, 2008.

Richards, David: "Theater in Review." In: *The New York Times* (09/12/1993), C18.

Rio, Nela: "Rivalries." Translated by Sophie M. Lavoie and Hugh Hazelton. In: *Numéro Cinq* 5,8 (2014), http://numerocinqmagazine.com/2014/07/31/vertical-labyrinth-poems-in-translation-nela-rio/ (accessed 19/05/2017).

Ryngaert, Jean-Pierre: "Figures du mélodrame dans les écritures d'aujourd'hui." In: *L'Annuaire théâtral* 50-51 (2011-12), 171-180.

Sharp, William: "Structure of Melodrama." In: Redmond, James (ed.): *Melodrama.* Cambridge: Cambridge University Press, 1992, 269-280.

Smith, James: *Melodrama.* London: Methuen, 1973.

Starobinski, Jean: "L'encre de la mélancolie." In: *La Nouvelle Revue Française* 123 (1963), 410-423.

Stewart, Michael (ed.): *Melodrama in Contemporary Film and Television.* Basingstoke: Palgrave Macmillan, 2014.

Williams, Linda: *On* The Wire. Durham: Duke University Press, 2014.

Véronique PORRA (Mayence)

Corps hors cadre dans le ‹ jeune › cinéma québécois

Summary

In recent years a new generation of film directors has emerged in Quebec. Among them are Xavier Dolan (*Laurence Anyways, Mommy*), Anne Émond (*Nuit#1*), and Chloé Robichaud (*Sarah préfère la course*), whose principal characters are facing existential crisis expressed through a specific representation of the body. Transformed, mistreated, even (auto)mutilated, the body becomes a problematic interface with the world around. The aesthetic performance created by the directors through the significant practice of framing reveals the renewal of filmic discourse, highlighting a new, hopeless, and narcissistic relationship to present 'hypermodernity' (Lipovetzky 1984).

Remarques préliminaires

De nombreuses voix ont, ces dernières années, attiré l'attention sur le fait que le cinéma québécois connaîtrait un important renouveau. Plusieurs dossiers spéciaux ont été publiés sur le sujet, au Québec puis à l'étranger, dans des revues spécialisées (*Cinébulles, 24 images, Les Cahiers du cinéma*, etc.), puis dans la presse généraliste, par exemple dans *L'Express*. En fonction des approches, on retient divers critères, diverses phases chronologiques, diverses désignations aussi : l'on parle tantôt d'un ‹ nouveau cinéma québécois ›, l'on va parfois jusqu'à identifier une ‹ nouvelle nouvelle vague ›[1], ou l'on évoque le ‹ jeune cinéma québécois ›, la dernière appellation faisant doublement référence à la jeunesse, celle du phénomène et celle des réalisateurs. Mais on constate là aussi que la jeunesse n'est pas toujours définie de la même manière.[2]

    L'identification de cette dernière catégorie s'est surtout cristallisée autour du personnage et de l'œuvre de Xavier Dolan, comme si celui-ci avait fait, dans le paysage artistique québécois, office de révélateur d'une tendance qui l'avait partiellement précédé. Bien que les critiques du jeune réalisateur ne soient pas toujours dithyrambiques, force est néanmoins de constater que son émergence a eu un effet structurant dans la perception du champ cinématographique contemporain. Ayant bouleversé les codes et les discours du long-métrage avec *J'ai tué ma mère* (2009), dont il a écrit le scénario à seulement 16 ans, Dolan a désormais acquis une reconnaissance internationale. Catalyseur de l'attention portée au phénomène voire accélérateur de la dynamique, il en cache parfois aussi l'ampleur. En effet, pour en être l'élément le plus visible, le plus médiatisé, le plus spectaculaire peut-être par son esthétique débordante et son hyperactivité militante, Dolan n'est pas l'unique représentant d'une tendance qui se dessine, loin s'en faut.[3]

La production cinématographique québécoise contemporaine n'est assurément pas monolithique. Les productions sont hétérogènes, les esthétiques et les appartenances génériques ou sous-génériques très diverses, ce qui rend toute typologie complexe, d'autant plus que l'on n'a pas encore suffisamment de distance critique pour aborder le phénomène sereinement, c'est-à-dire hors des pressions immédiates du champ artistique. On reconnaît néanmoins des lignes communes à certaines de ces œuvres, notamment parmi les metteurs en scène nés dans les années 1980. Faut-il pour autant, à l'instar de certains critiques, y voir une tendance à la reproduction d'esthétiques calibrées, pré-formatées ? Certes, le fait que ces jeunes voire très jeunes réalisateurs soient issus d'un même milieu intellectuel et artistique montréalais, soient passés parfois par les mêmes écoles ou les mêmes collectifs[4], contribue à générer des points communs, des passages obligés qui deviennent des *topoï* soit au niveau discursif, soit au niveau de la réalisation esthétique. Mais au-delà, il semble bien que se dégage un discours filmique de la crise tout à fait spécifique. Or à l'évidence, cette crise se cristallise autour de la représentation des corps[5], en particulier dans leur rapport au cadrage. Ces corps en crise sortent du cadre normatif social, mais font aussi l'objet d'un jeu de cadrage signifiant et très développé. Quatre films tournés par de très jeunes réalisateurs/réalisatrices serviront ici de corpus d'étude : *Laurence Anyways* (2012) et *Mommy* (2014) de Xavier Dolan (né en 1989), *Nuit#1* (2011) d'Anne Émond (née en 1982) et *Sarah préfère la course* (2013) de Chloé Robichaud (née en 1988).

Personnages en crise

Les films qui constituent le corpus de cette étude ont tous en commun de retracer un moment de crise plus ou moins étalé dans le temps d'un personnage central. Cette extrême focalisation de l'histoire individuelle est spectaculairement soutenue par le jeu de la caméra (gros plans, personnages isolés, entourage flou, personnages qui se disent soit en voix off soit dans de longs monologues).

Dans *Laurence Anyways*, Laurence Alia, qui semble mener une vie d'homme accompli, heureux dans le couple très fusionnel qu'il forme avec sa compagne Fred, apparemment épanoui dans sa vie d'enseignant de littérature dans un CÉGEP, décide de devenir une femme. Le film est donc le récit rétrospectif de sa vie, que Laurence, devenu femme et écrivaine, livre dix ans plus tard à une journaliste qui l'interroge sur son œuvre littéraire. L'essentiel de la narration retrace en premier lieu le long chemin que constitue la marche vers la transsexualité, et ce que cela implique, pour Laurence, mais aussi pour sa compagne Fred. La voix off de Laurence répondant à la journaliste, qui ouvre le film avant l'apparition de la première image, pose immédiatement la question de la lecture normative du monde et donc des êtres :

> [J]e recherche une personne qui comprenne ma langue, et qui la parle, même. Une personne qui sans être un paria, ne s'interroge pas simplement sur les droits et l'utilité des marginaux, mais sur les droits et l'utilité de ceux qui se targuent d'être normaux. (00:00:43 – 00:01:00)

Si l'on peut considérer que Laurence a atteint son but, le film retrace à de nombreuses reprises la violence à laquelle Laurence a été exposé mais aussi celle qu'il a fait subir aux autres.

Mommy retrace la relation violente et fusionnelle entre une mère instable, Diane, et son fils, Steve, adolescent hyperactif et violent, brutalement exclu de l'institution dans laquelle il était pris en charge. Sans aucun soutien institutionnel, Diane devra faire face aux crises cyclothymiques de Steve tout en gérant une situation professionnelle et financière précaire. L'aide viendra partiellement d'une jeune voisine bègue et introvertie, Kyla, qui, un temps, réussira à canaliser les délires violents du jeune homme. Porteuse elle aussi d'un traumatisme elle en est, par son comportement introverti, en quelque sorte le négatif. Construit selon la structure de la tragédie, *Mommy* est sans aucun doute le film qui joue le plus spectaculairement avec le cadrage comme élément signifiant. L'image carrée qui domine crée une impression d'étouffement mais aussi de déséquilibre lorsque les corps des personnages en sortent. Elle est remplacée à trois reprises par une image rectangulaire classique, notamment au milieu du film dans une scène emblématique : après de nombreuses crises de violence, Steve semble trouver un semblant d'apaisement ; alors que les trois protagonistes se promènent ensemble dans la rue – Kyla et Diane à vélo, Steve sur son skateboard – Steve arrive plein champ face caméra et, dans une interaction entre fiction et réalisation, ouvre le cadre de ses propres mains. Il transforme ainsi l'image carrée fragmentée et instable en un panorama élargi et harmonieux, faisant place à une perspective globale annonciatrice d'espoir (01:13:50 – 01:13:58, ill. 1 et 2). Cette fragile stabilité sera éphémère, tout comme le recours à l'image rectangulaire, puisque peu de temps après, Steve sera interné en psychiatrie à la demande de sa mère, épuisée par ses accès de violence. La fin du film, montrant Steve qui a réussi à se libérer de sa camisole courant dans le couloir de l'hôpital, place le spectateur devant la certitude de la défenestration à venir et donc de l'issue fatale.

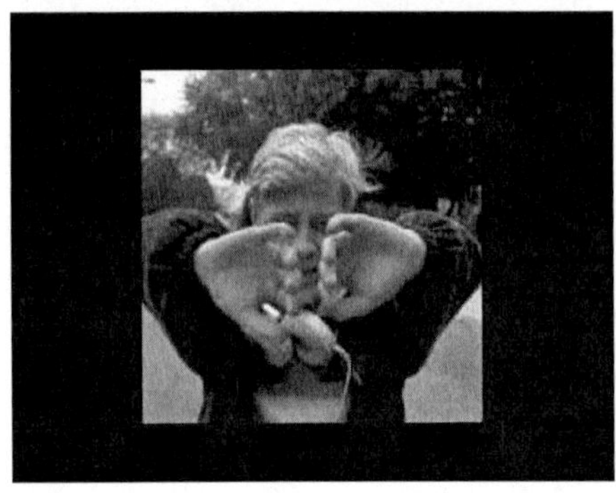

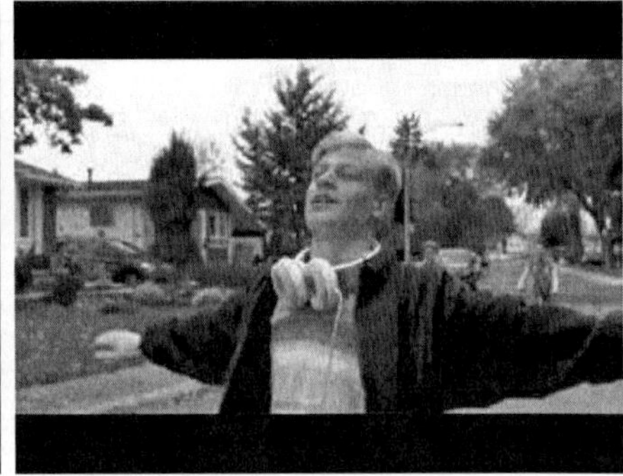

Ill. 1. Xavier Dolan : *Mommy* (01:13:51) Ill. 2. Xavier Dolan : *Mommy* (01:13:57)

Nuit#1 d'Anne Émond retrace la nuit des deux seuls protagonistes, Clara et Nicolaï. Présents dans la même boîte de nuit, ces deux jeunes adultes, qui ne se connaissent pas, entament une relation sexuelle torride dans l'appartement du jeune homme, relation non aboutie qui évolue rapidement vers une double verbalisation de leur mal-être existentiel. La suite de la nuit sera en effet rythmée par les tentatives de départ avortées de Clara et de longues confessions, dans lesquelles les deux protagonistes se racontent mutuellement leur mal de vivre, longs passages qui ressortissent plus du monologue. Les deux personnages, perdus intérieurement, termineront la nuit sur le toit de l'immeuble où ils finissent par trouver un apaisement relatif. Clara est clairement attirée par le vide, mais les dernières images nous la montrent retournée à sa vie plus ou moins rangée d'enseignante, écoutant des enfants d'une dizaine d'années réciter machinalement des textes poétiques appris par cœur et dont la succession marque un *crescendo* dans le motif de l'errance existentielle.[6]

Dans *Sarah préfère la course*, nous suivons une jeune femme de la banlieue de Québec, qui pour poursuivre sa passion doit rejoindre le centre d'entraînement de l'Université McGill à Montréal. Très vite se pose la question du financement de ce projet d'études. Elle conclut dès lors un accord avec son ami Antoine, qu'elle n'épousera que parce que le mariage permet d'avoir accès aux programmes de bourses. Arrivée à Montréal et après quelques succès et surtout quelques heurts dans le monde impitoyable du sport de haut niveau, Sarah apprend qu'elle souffre d'une insuffisance cardiaque. Ne voulant perdre son seul centre d'intérêt dans la vie, elle décide, au mépris de sa vie, de dissimuler son état. Le film se termine sur une course à laquelle elle participe. On voit nettement qu'elle ressent une douleur au thorax, elle décide alors d'accélérer. Là non plus, l'issue n'est pas mise en image, seulement suggérée, mais le spectateur sort avec la certitude que Sarah va perdre la vie pour avoir refusé de renoncer à cette fragile raison de vivre.

Corps étrangers dans le corps social

D'une manière générale, ces jeunes réalisateurs mettent donc en scène de jeunes protagonistes de 16 à 35 (voire 45) ans en totale rupture avec les attentes de la société (qui leur font aussi parfois écho, ou tout au moins sont définis comme autant d'échos générationnels par la critique). Les personnages vivent enfermés dans leur individualisme – folie, introversion, obsessions, double personnalité, trouble de l'hyperactivité (TDAH), etc. – et ne trouvent pas leur place dans un monde dénué de repères, soumis à des valeurs qui leur sont totalement étrangères, qu'ils ne veulent ni ne peuvent assimiler. Ils sont dès lors étrangers aux autres mais surtout étrangers à eux-mêmes en tant qu'éléments du corps social.

Dans l'introduction à un volume collectif publié en 2014 intitulé *La violence du quotidien*, Florence Thérond tente de dégager les traits principaux de ce qu'elle appelle les « influences sociétales sur la création contemporaine ». S'appuyant sur *L'ère du vide* de Gilles Lipovetzky, elle souligne les éléments suivants :

> 1) le repli sur le quotidien et l'obsession du proche : le déclin des idéaux et des valeurs publiques conduit à une valorisation de l'ego [...]. Mais dans l'espace de la famille, les proches deviennent des figures monstrueuses [...]. Le regard des proches, qui scrute ou tue, hante les personnages et la paranoïa dit la crainte de la dissolution du moi. Les identités vacillent, les corps pourrissent, les personnages font l'expérience de l'inquiétante étrangeté du moi après celle de l'étrangeté des êtres proches [...] ; 2) toute la barbarie de l'humanité semble s'inscrire dans le corps individuel et son intimité. L'entrelacement de l'intime et du collectif, de l'individuel et du social est partout présent. Les discours sociaux « ventriloquent l'individu » [Viart/Rubino 2013, 8] façonné par la société de consommation et soumis à la valeur travail et au conformisme bourgeois ; 3) [...] la violence est coupée de toute perspective utopique : beaucoup de ces œuvres ne proposent aucun modèle, aucun message pour transformer le monde. (Thérond 2014, 16-17)

L'on pourrait ajouter à ceci que les réalisateurs et bon nombre de leurs protagonistes sont les enfants de cette ‹ ère du vide › diagnostiquée au début des années 1980. Ce qu'ils en présentent peut être interprété comme un paroxysme de l'évidement du sens existentiel aggravé par les crises du tournant du siècle. L'on songe ici aux diagnostics que font les sociologues poursuivant au début des années 2000 les réflexions de Krzysztof Pomian sur la « crise de l'avenir » (1980) : Pierre-André Taguieff soulignant la disparition de la notion de progrès dans *L'effacement de l'avenir* (2000) ou Zaki Laïdi lorsqu'il évoque, dans *Le sacre du présent* (2000), un présentisme ayant acté la mort des derniers idéaux.

Dans le corpus préalablement défini, ce malaise existentiel est illustré par diverses techniques, voire *leitmotivs* scéniques, que l'on retrouve chez chacun de ces réalisateurs. Le présentisme par manque de perspective préalablement évoqué, cette incapacité à concevoir l'idée d'avenir, se traduit effectivement par la multiplication des plans rapprochés, des ralentis, mais aussi des plans coupés que des plans larges viennent contredire. L'un des exemples les plus marquants est sans aucun doute la scène de *Mommy* dans laquelle Steve, qui vient d'être interné, appelle sa mère pour s'excuser. Le contraste avec la scène précédente, celle de son ‹ arrestation › par des infirmiers psychiatriques sur un parking désert où sa mère l'a conduit à son insu, qui avait alors généré une terrible scène de violence verbale et physique, est saisissant. Steve est désormais calme, sous l'emprise d'une camisole chimique qui le rend partiellement euphorique. Le message qu'il laisse sur le répondeur est plutôt conciliant. Cet épisode se déroule en trois phases : une première partie dans laquelle il plaisante sur les effets des médicaments, une seconde dans laquelle il présente des excuses très formelles sans aucun affect, et enfin une dernière partie où il laisse libre cours à ses émotions et fait part de l'amour qu'il éprouve pour sa mère. Ces passages discursifs sont chacun soutenus par un travail sur le cadrage : ou pour être plus précise, nous voyons des parties de son corps, de son visage, qui nous laissent dans un premier temps penser que Steve appelle de sa propre initiative et qu'un apaisement est possible. Mais l'élargissement du plan nous dit tout autre chose que ce corps découpé par la caméra : il nous révèle que le téléphone est en fait tenu par un employé de l'hôpital, que Steve est retenu par une camisole de force, que le discours lui a été imposé par l'autorité psychiatrique qui a assurément exercé une forme de violence à son égard (ill. 3 et 4). L'hypothèse d'une issue cathartique voire même d'un quelconque avenir est d'autant plus définitivement anéantie que ce message n'atteint pas Diane. Vaquant à d'autres occupations dans la pièce attenante, elle n'entend pas le téléphone sonner. C'est donc le répondeur qui recueille ce moment capital, enfermant Steve un peu plus, cette fois dans une camisole affective (01:57:22 – 01:59:21).

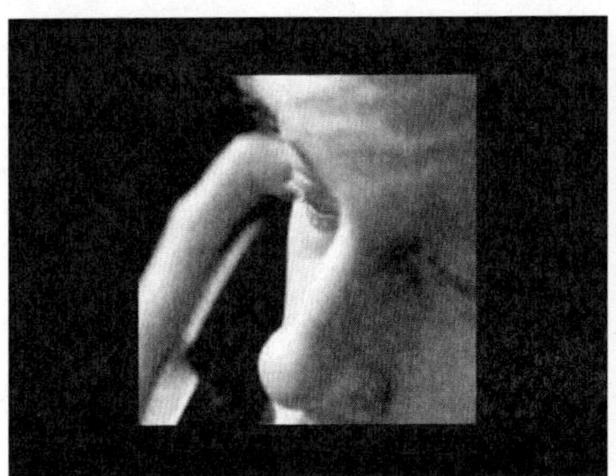

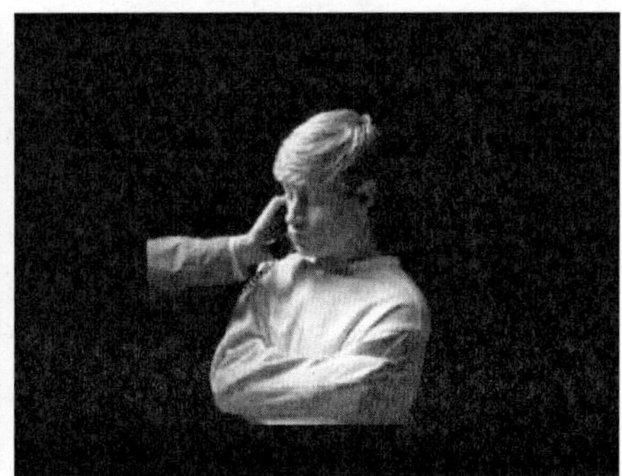

Ill. 3. Xavier Dolan : *Mommy* (01:57:25)   Ill. 4. Xavier Dolan : *Mommy* (01:58:08)

En matière de *leitmotiv*, on peut ici mentionner la récurrence d'un plan analogue soulignant l'enfermement des protagonistes principaux dans une dynamique linéaire sans issue chez les trois réalisateurs. Tous trois nous présentent en effet l'image du personnage principal filmé de dos, avançant dans des topographies étroites et souvent sans issue identifiable : tunnels, cages d'escaliers, ruelles, couloirs du métro. En voici quelques exemples : 1) le début de *Laurence Anyways*, où un personnage qui nous est encore inconnu mais que l'on identifie par son tailleur-jupe comme un personnage féminin, filmé de dos, sort de chez lui et marche droit devant lui, suivi par les regards interloqués des passants et des habitants qui actualisent l'aspect anormal de cette présence corporelle (00:01:39 – 00:03:30). Filmée exclusivement de dos, la silhouette finit par se perdre dans la brume (ill. 5) ;

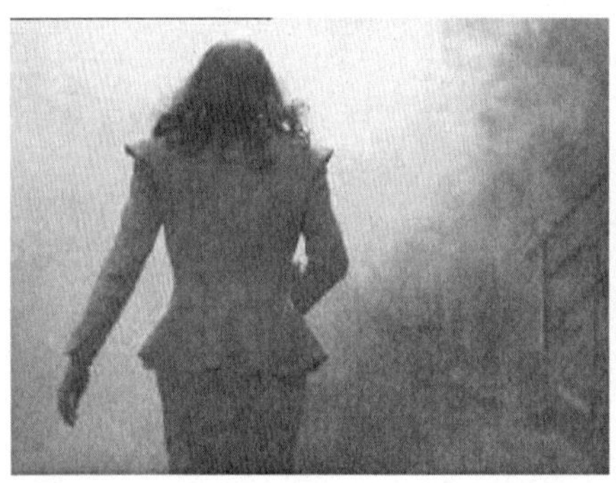

Ill. 5. Xavier Dolan :
Laurence Anyways (00:03:23)

Ill. 6. Xavier Dolan :
Mommy (02:08:35)

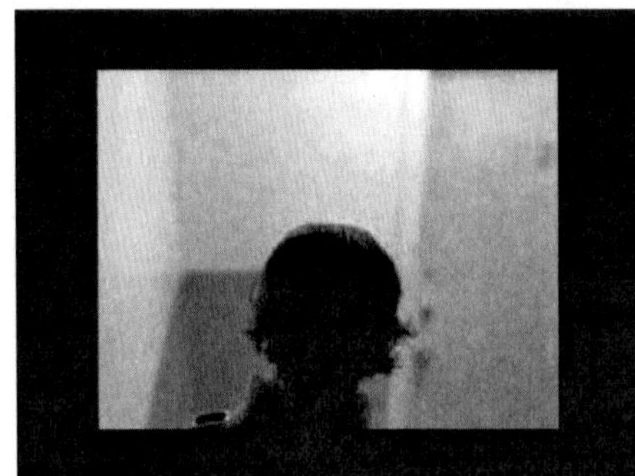

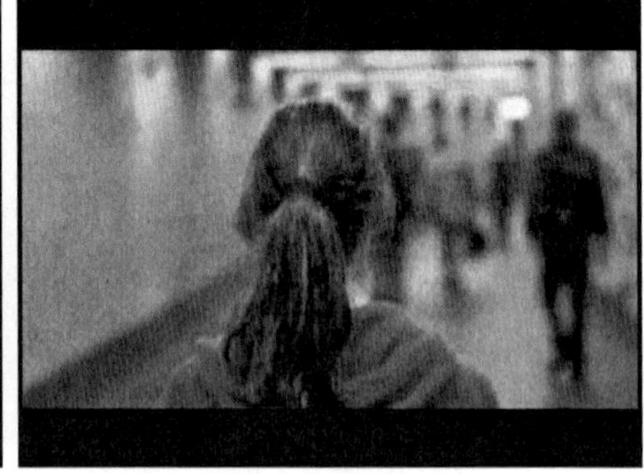

Ill. 7. Anne Émond :
Nuit#1 (00:38:02)

Ill. 8. Chloé Robichaud :
Sarah préfère la course (00:39:36)

2) la scène finale de *Mommy* précédemment évoquée, annonciatrice de la défenestration imminente, qui utilise le même procédé, avec gros plans et ralentis (ill. 6) ; 3) la deuxième tentative de départ de Clara dans *Nuit#1* d'Anne Émond, lorsque la protagoniste est filmée de dos alors qu'elle descend dans une hideuse cage d'escalier puis débouche dans une rue sombre (00:37:58 – 00:38:20, ill. 7) où elle est prise dans une averse ; 4) enfin la scène où l'on nous montre Sarah, peu de temps après son mariage arrangé avec Antoine, qui prend le métro alors que la bande son diffuse une conversation téléphonique au cours de laquelle elle refuse d'accéder à la demande d'Antoine de révéler leur relation (00:39:30 – 00:39:52, ill. 8). Ces scènes durent à chaque fois plusieurs minutes. Les personnages sont alors sans visage, pris dans un tunnel physique et symbolique, un carcan que le mouvement de la caméra met en évidence. Placée dans le dos de l'acteur, il s'agit d'une fausse caméra subjective, qui permet de montrer les impressions visuelles souvent angoissantes du personnage, mais aussi de montrer au premier plan un personnage vidé d'identité dans un contexte hostile, dans une perspective de voie tracée, sans attrait, sans fin, sans aboutissement.

Corps perdus dans l'espace identitaire collectif

Tous ces films mettent aussi en évidence une position de porte à faux des personnages par rapport aux repères identitaires collectifs. La première insécurité est une insécurité du genre, celle par exemple qui s'insinue dans la vie et le comportement de Laurence au début de *Laurence Anyways*, avant que le doute ne laisse place à l'évidence et à un projet dont plus rien ne le détournera.

Mais le spectre du refus de l'appartenance collective ou plus exactement le constat que les personnages font de vivre en surface, sans aucune attache identitaire, est beaucoup plus large. Ainsi Sarah, interrogée par un étudiant qui rédige un article pour le journal de l'Association des étudiants sur ses motivations profondes ou ses sphères d'intérêt, n'a-t-elle absolument rien à répondre, sinon qu'elle aime courir et qu'elle serait fière de remporter des victoires pour le Canada. Lorsque le journaliste lui fait remarquer que sa réflexion montre qu'elle « ne [se] considère pas vraiment comme souverainiste », son silence souligne son incompréhension, mais aussi son indifférence à l'égard du fait politique (00:37:00 – 00:38:34). Nous touchons là à un autre point commun à ces films.

Tous incluent un discours ou métadiscours sur la québécité, exhibée dans les films notamment au travers de la langue. En la matière, les films de Dolan sont particulièrement ‹ territorialisés › et même si le rôle-titre de *Laurence Anyways* est tenu par l'acteur français Melvil Poupaud, les dialogues sont très marqués par les québécismes et l'argot montréalais ; les images véhiculent par ailleurs un imaginaire de la nordicité parfois très identifiable (étendues enneigées, glace, feuilles d'érable, luminosité, etc.).

Mais le cas de *Nuit#1*, qui inclut le motif de l'appartenance à une identité québécoise au sein même de la problématique de la crise identitaire de l'individu, mérite ici particulièrement d'être relevé. La question de l'appartenance à une identité collective culturelle, politique, historique québécoise est doublement conjuguée dans ce film. Ce thème apparaît par exemple tout d'abord dans la confession de Nicolaï : issu d'une famille de Néo-québécois originaires d'Ukraine, il souligne dans sa longue confession sa non-appartenance à la culture québécoise et canadienne. Totalement indifférent, il n'en connaît pas les références de base ; mais il souligne en parallèle sa non-appartenance à la culture ukrainienne, à laquelle il n'est finalement rattaché que par le fait qu'il parle russe avec ses parents et par une envie régulière de manger des raviolis ukrainiens (*varenyky*). Le motif de l'appartenance identitaire trouve cependant sa pleine expression avec le personnage de Clara. Face au mal-être de Nicolaï, elle se réfugie dans une allégeance culturelle ouvertement déclarée, en faisant référence à *Prochain épisode* d'Hubert Aquin, « plus grand écrivain québécois de tous les temps » selon elle, et dont elle cite un long passage qui fait à l'évidence écho à la violence suscitée par son propre malaise :

> Pendant des années, j'ai vécu aplati avec fureur, j'ai habitué mes amis à un voltage intenable, à un gaspillage d'étincelles et de courts circuits. Cracher le feu, tromper la mort, ressusciter cent fois, courir le mile en moins de quatre minutes, introduire le lance-flamme en dialectique et la conduite suicide en politique, voilà comment j'ai établi mon style. (00:33:39 – 00:34:07)

Voyant dans Aquin un reflet de ce qu'elle ressent (« dans ce livre, il y a tous mes secrets »), elle semble donc s'inscrire, tout au moins dans le premier tiers du film, dans la lignée d'une idée de l'identité québécoise qui a fait des grands auteurs de la Révolution tranquille un repère fondateur (00:33:37 – 00:34:50). Elle souligne alors la beauté de ce passage, qui contraste fondamentalement avec l'histoire qu'elle est en train de vivre : « Enlacés éblouis dans un pays en détresse, nous avons roulé en un seul baiser, d'un bout à l'autre de notre lit enneigé. »[7] Mais arrivée à sa propre confession, elle invalide définitivement ce dernier repère :

> J'crois à rien, j'pense sincèrement que j'ai pas d'idéaux, c'est trop impliquant [...]. On dirait qu'j'suis pas capable d'appartenir au monde, d'en faire partie réellement. C'est que j'cite des passages d'un livre que j'comprends pas. J'ai aucune idée de c'que j'peux faire pour mon pays en détresse. J'pense même qu'au fond j'men câlice. (01:16:15 – 01:17:01)

Tous ces protagonistes sont donc voués à une solitude absolue, dans un monde dont ils refusent tous les repères et auquel ils sont totalement étrangers, solitude qui n'est même plus narcissique puisqu'elle porte en elle leur propre anéantissement.[8]

Le corps comme interface problématique – corps modifiés, mutilés et dérives narcissiques

Il n'est donc pas surprenant que le discours et la représentation dévient vers une hyperreprésentation du corps, désormais incarnation de l'insécurité existentielle, et de son utilisation. La sexualité est devenue stigmate de la dérive sociale. *Nuit#1*, par son côté métadiscursif très poussé, livre assurément quelques clefs d'interprétation. Comme nous avons déjà eu l'occasion de l'évoquer, Nicolaï raconte son dégoût de la vie, son manque de perspective, son ennui, ses échecs, son comportement socialement suicidaire. Mais c'est surtout Clara qui verbalise ce lien pathologique au corps, cette nécessité de baiser, de se droguer, de boire jusqu'au malaise pour tromper son mal-être. La scène de la confession intime de Clara est très révélatrice. Tandis que le plan large inclut Nicolaï assis près de la baignoire, la plupart des plans rapprochés nous montrent Clara nue, recroquevillée dans la baignoire, tentant de verbaliser son malaise existentiel et les dérives auxquelles il la conduit. À l'évidence, Émond reproduit la posture de la confession psychanalytique[9], mais dénude intégralement son personnage, mettant en évidence la dimension d'un corps crispé sur un froid intérieur et extérieur, dans le cadre aseptisé et glacial d'une baignoire (ill. 9). Clara se livre donc sans aucune retenue, expliquant toutes ses dérives sexuelles, de la nymphomanie en passant par des pratiques d'ordre masochiste, faisant sans cesse le lien avec son impossibilité d'appréhender sa vie et le monde qui l'entoure. En somme, elle livre tout à la fois le récit et l'interprétation somatique et psychanalytique de cet abus permanent du corps : « J'ai un corps, mais y a rien qui habite ce corps. J'suis une surface… une enveloppe corporelle vide… je sais pas si tu comprends … » (01:08:20 – 01:08:32)

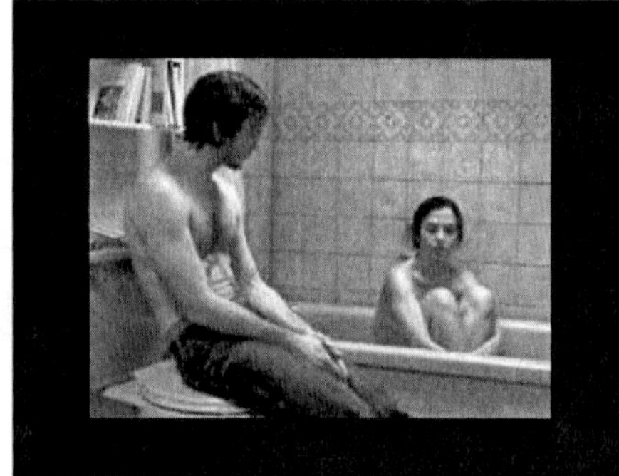

Ill. 9. Anne Émond :
Nuit#1 (01:07:40)

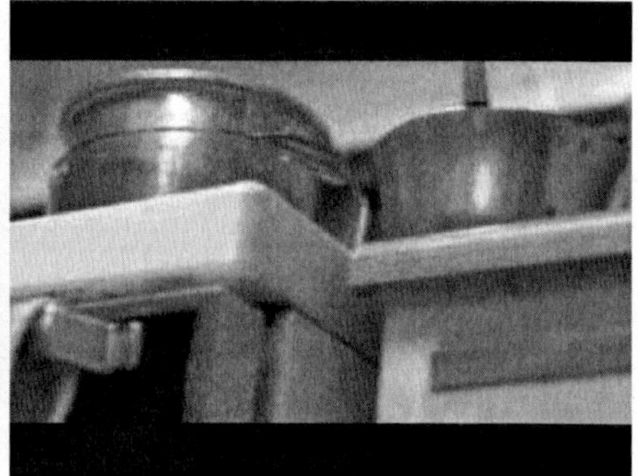

Ill. 10. Chloé Robichaud :
Sarah préfère la course (01:09:01)

Le corps est donc bien cette interface entre un moi que l'on n'arrive pas à définir, qui s'affirme par la vacuité – et l'on retrouve cette notion d'« ère du vide » (Lipovetzky 1984), mais ayant cette fois envahi l'individu au plus profond de lui-même – et un monde extérieur que l'on est dans l'impossibilité totale d'appréhender. Il ne s'agit même plus d'un refus révolutionnaire des normes, mais tout simplement d'une incompréhension totale, d'un dépassement absolu, d'un absurde de l'hypermodernité. On retrouve le même phénomène de la relation perturbée au corps dans *Sarah préfère la course*. Elle prend ici la forme de la compensation de la vacuité par la brutalisation du corps dans le sport de compétition, jusqu'à la mort programmée.

La relation de couple, qui elle aussi implique le corps, montre une sexualité marquée par les stigmates de la dérive sociale. L'on pense ici bien sûr à la sexualité extrême de *Nuit#1*, vécue comme un défoulement, une recherche de la perception de soi dans des dérives proches de l'automutilation (Clara dit aimer la sodomie, le sexe de groupe, avoir mal, vomir, etc.). Mais on pense bien sûr aussi aux dérives narcissiques de toutes ces relations.

Nicolaï est pour Clara un moyen de s'anesthésier ; Antoine reste pour Sarah une donnée technique dans son projet d'optimisation budgétaire ; et l'acte sexuel consenti par Sarah juste après le diagnostic de sa maladie cardiaque est une sorte de passage obligé, de taxe à payer, qui ne suscite que de l'absence : Sarah couchée sur le dos attend que ça se fasse en regardant le plafond. Son indifférence est telle qu'elle pousse presque Antoine à l'impuissance. Le corps passif de la protagoniste couchée sur le dos, tout d'abord filmé dans son intégralité, se fragmente : la caméra fait un gros plan sur le flanc partiellement dénudé de Sarah. Puis le corps sort de l'écran, marquant ainsi un changement de perspective : nous passons à une caméra subjective puisque nous ne voyons plus dès lors que ce que Sarah perçoit : des images saccadées des étagères de la cuisine remplies de casseroles et du plafond (ill. 10). L'acte est donc totalement privé de toute connotation érotique et totalement désincarné voire mécanique (01:06:20 – 01:09:05).

Bref, les corps s'enchevêtrent mais n'exultent pas. Clara et Nicolaï se jettent l'un sur l'autre mais leurs désirs sont décalés. Soit Nicolaï perd ses moyens quand Clara le désire, soit Clara n'a plus envie lorsque Nicolaï retrouve ses moyens. Là aussi, le corps est une interface impuissante à régler les problèmes de l'intime et à plus forte raison ceux de la relation à l'autre et au monde. Il n'est dès lors qu'une surface problématique de plus.

Seuls Laurence et Fred vivent, tout au moins au début de leur histoire, une vie amoureuse et sexuelle épanouie. Mais de légers indices signalent le lent effritement de l'identité genrée de Laurence. Sa quête va prendre des allures de dérive narcissique, et la transformation du corps de Laurence se fera au prix du sacrifice de Fred. Le paroxysme est atteint lorsque Laurence et Fred, après une longue séparation, se retrouvent à l'Île au Noir qui avait, dans leurs jeunes années, nourri leur fantasme de bonheur absolu. Cette scène, qui est l'une des plus connues du film, illustre parfaitement cet effet de miroir, au travers de l'imitation de la démarche, de la silhouette vestimentaire, mais aussi de la physionomie, de Laurence qui devient Fred. Mais il y a avant tout dans cette scène quelque chose de désaccordé, en porte à faux : tandis qu'une pluie de linge, *leitmotiv* soulignant le bonheur intime, rappelle les moments heureux[10], la bande son diffuse la musique dissonante de *A New Error* de Moderat (2009)

(02:01:22 – 02:03:05). Fred croit retrouver Laurence tel qu'elle l'a aimé. Mais Laurence est déjà une autre, celle qui dans Fred ne cherche plus que sa propre image, un reflet de sa propre identité, une surface de projection. En fait, il ne s'agit pas d'un voyage de retrouvailles mais de la poursuite implacable de la quête de Laurence, prêt(e) à tout, qui emmène Fred voir un transsexuel qui a été opéré, « un homme qui avait été femme » (02:02:57). Fred, qui depuis s'était mariée et avait eu un enfant, a quitté son nouvel équilibre familial pour une perspective d'avenir qui n'est définitivement plus la sienne, détruisant ainsi sa vie pour une illusion que Laurence lui a donnée.

Conclusion

Dans *L'ère du vide*, Lipovetzky parlait longuement des conséquences des évolutions de l'hypermodernité sur la psychologisation des corps. Le malaise de l'individualisme dans une société où les repères s'abolissent, de l'émergence du présentisme, dans les années 1980, amenait déjà des formes de narcissisme qui n'étaient cependant pas en rupture avec les codes mais ressortaient plutôt, pour reprendre l'expression de Lipovetzky (1984, 91), comme « un hyperinvestissement de codes et fonctionn[aient] comme type inédit de contrôle social sur les âmes et les corps » . Dans les productions que nous avons étudiées, à l'évidence, le corps s'oppose aux codes et aux contrôles ; et l'importance du jeu sur le cadrage des corps met l'accent sur l'aspect essentiel de cet élément. La relation au narcissisme a été modifiée. Le corps n'est plus que cette surface qui fait écran entre un malaise intérieur indéfini et un monde étranger. Comme le disait Clara, il est une surface qui « réfléchit la lumière » (01:07:56), qui se blesse. En tant qu'interface, il est investi de nouvelles charges symboliques. Mais dans un rapport au monde pathologique, il est avant tout refusé, modifié, mutilé puis effacé. Il est hors cadre dans tous les sens du terme, sans pour autant que cela soit synonyme de libération. Il devient alors acteur et victime de l'aliénation, seul écran à opposer encore à l'immense angoisse du vide lorsque le monde échappe à toute narration.

1   Cette appellation apparaît à partir de 2009 et désigne dans un premier temps la génération de Denis Côté, Denis Villeneuve, Stéphane Lafleur, Maxime Giroux et Rafaël Ouellet, ensemble auquel on intègre rapidement Xavier Dolan. Cf. également la relativisation et la critique des diverses catégorisations dans Privet (2011).

2   Cf. Dequen/Gajan (2011) ; Faradji (2009) ; Lavallée (2010) ; Sirois-Trahan (2010).

3   Xavier Dolan connaît désormais une consécration internationale, entretenue institutionnellement entre autres par la sélection récurrente de ses films dans de grands festivals, dont le festival de Cannes. À l'instar du cinéma de Denis Villeneuve, son cinéma, lui aussi, s'internationalise et ce pas seulement en termes de production et distribution. Très marqué par sa territorialisation québécoise jusqu'à très récemment, Dolan, avec son film *Juste la fin du monde* sorti en 2016, marque une nouvelle étape dans cette évolution. Bien que Dolan ait été peu perçu en France au début de sa jeune carrière, *Mommy* va avoir l'effet d'un déclencheur de succès. Le film, très médiatisé et présenté à Cannes où il reçoit le prix du jury, va révéler le jeune réalisateur au grand public français au point qu'au moment de la sortie en salles de *Mommy* à Paris, les cinémas parisiens présenteront simultanément l'ensemble de ses films, lui conférant ainsi une hypervisibilité.

4   C'est la raison pour laquelle Sirois-Trahan (2010, 76) parle à ce propos de « mouvée » . Il évoque notamment le collectif Kino qui, fondé à Montréal en 1999 avant de s'internationaliser, a vu passer bon nombre de jeunes metteurs en scène. Alors jeunes vidéastes, ceux-ci se sont essayés au court-métrage dans le cadre de ce forum d'échanges, avant de se consacrer au long-métrage (cf. Sirois-Trahan 2010, 76).

5   Le complexe liant la notion de crise à la représentation (cinématographique) du corps a déjà fait l'objet de recherches spécifiques : cf. entre autres l'ouvrage de Davina Quinlivan, *Filming the Body in Crisis* (2015). S'appuyant entre autres sur les études de Steven Shaviro, Laura U. Marks et Vivian Sobchack, Quinlivan s'interroge, à partir des théories de Mélanie Klein, sur la puissance cathartique de la représentation cinématographique.

6   Les jeunes enfants récitent successivement les paroles des chansons « La langue de chez nous » d'Yves Duteil, « Tu te lèveras tôt » de Félix Leclerc, « Pour un instant » d'Harmonium pour atteindre un paroxysme avec la récitation hésitante de « Demain seulement » d'Alain Grandbois par une petite Juliette, qui renvoie au malaise de Clara. Si les deux premiers titres peuvent encore présenter des motifs d'attachement identitaires, aussi mélancoliques soient-ils, les deux derniers évoquent la dépersonnalisation (« j'ai

oublié mon nom ») et la familiarité de la mort (« car la mort n'est qu'une petite chose glacée »).

7 Notons que le personnage de Clara n'est pas sans rappeler celui de *Putain* de Nelly Arcan : on y retrouve la même sexualisation désenchantée, l'utilisation du corps comme interface et surface de projection du mal-être existentiel mais aussi la double vie de la protagoniste et le lien à la littérature, puisque la protagoniste de *Putain* est étudiante en littérature. Anne Émond, qui a elle aussi suivi des études de littérature avant de se tourner vers le cinéma ne fait d'ailleurs pas mystère de la fascination qu'elle éprouve pour Nelly Arcan. Présenté en 2016, son dernier film, *Nelly*, est librement inspiré de la vie et de l'œuvre de Nelly Arcan.

8 L'impossibilité à surmonter un mal-être inscrit au plus profond de soi, un état dépressif qui se développe en dépit de l'entourage dans la plus grande solitude, constitue l'essentiel de la trame narrative du deuxième long-métrage d'Anne Émond : *Les êtres chers* (2015).

9 On notera qu'Anne Émond reprend une partie des paroles prononcées par Clara dans cette scène pour les inclure à une scène de psychanalyse dans *Nelly*.

10 Cf. l'interprétation que Gabriel Laverdière (2012) donne de cette scène. Il souligne notamment l'analogie entre l'image de la pluie de linge multicolore et le tableau de Magritte intitulé *Golconde*, interprétation intéressante si l'on considère le rôle majeur que joue l'interpicturalité dans *Laurence Anyways*.

Bibliographie

Dequen, Bruno / Gajan, Philippe (éds) : « Renouveau du cinéma québécois ». In : *24 images* 152 (2011), 4-34.

Faradji, Helen : « Nouvelle vague 2.0 ». In : *24 images* (blogue Premiers plans 26/02/2009), http://www.revue24images.com/articles.php?article=713/ (consultation 01/12/2015).

Laïdi, Zaki : *Le sacre du présent*. Paris : Flammarion, 2000.

Lavallée, Sylvain : « Sur le renouveau du cinéma québécois ». In : *Séquences* (12/11/2010), http://ducinematographe.com/2010/11/sur-le-renouveau-du-cinema-quebecois/ (consultation 01/12/2015).

Laverdière, Gabriel : « L'esthétique rock queer, de C.R.A.Z.Y à Xavier Dolan ». In : *Nouvelles vues : revue sur les pratiques et les théories du cinéma au Québec* 13 (2012), http://

www.nouvellesvues.ulaval.ca/fileadmin/nouvelles_vues/fichiers/Numero16icono/ Nouvelles_vues_-_L_esthetique_rock_queer__de_C.R.A.Z.Y._a_Xavier_Dolan.pdf (consultation 01/12/2015).

Lipovetzky, Gilles : *L'ère du vide. Essais sur l'individualisme contemporain.* Paris : Gallimard, 1984.

Macherey, Pierre : *Le sujet des normes.* Paris : Éditions Amsterdam, 2014.

Pomian, Krzysztof : « La crise de l'avenir ». In : *Le Débat* 7 (1980), 5-17.

Privet, Georges : « La théorie du grand tout ou la quête éternelle d'une nouvelle ‹ nouvelle vague › ». In : *La jetée* (18/11/2011), http://archive.wikiwix.com/cache/?url= http%3A%2F%2Fwww.la-jetee.com%2F2011%2F11%2Fla-theorie-du-grand-tout-ou-la-quete.html (consultation 01/12/2015).

Quinlivan, Davina : *Filming the Body in Crisis. Trauma, Healing, and Hopefulness.* Londres : Palgrave Macmillan, 2015.

Sirois-Trahan, Jean-Pierre : « La mouvée et son dehors : renouveau du cinéma québécois ». In : *Les Cahiers du Cinéma* 660 (2010), 76-78.

Taguieff, Pierre-André : *L'effacement de l'avenir.* Paris : Éditions Galilée, 2000.

Thérond, Florence (éd.) : *La violence du quotidien. Formes et figures contemporaines de la violence au théâtre et au cinéma.* Lavérune : Éditions l'Entretemps, 2014.

Viart, Dominique / Rubino, Gianfranco (éds) : *Écrire le présent.* Paris : Armand Colin, 2013.

Filmographie

Dolan, Xavier : *Laurence Anyways.* Alliance Vivafilm, 2012. DVD.

Dolan, Xavier : *Mommy.* Séville International, 2014. DVD.

Émond, Anne : *Nuit#1.* K-Films Amérique, 2011. DVD.

Émond, Anne : *Les êtres chers.* Les Films Séville/Metafilms, 2015. DVD.

Émond, Anne : *Nelly.* Les Films Séville/Go Films, 2016. DVD.

Robichaud, Chloé : *Sarah préfère la course.* Les Films Séville, 2013. DVD.

Mémoire, vérité et histoire
Memory, Truth, and History

Marion KÜHN (Québec)

Passé envahisseur, oubli ravageur.
Figures problématiques de la mémoire et de l'oubli dans le roman québécois contemporain (Saucier, Caron, Leblanc)[1]

Summary

The present article deals with the representation of a problematic access to the past in three contemporary Quebec novels: *Il pleuvait des oiseaux* (2011) by Jocelyne Saucier, *Rose Brouillard, le film* (2012) by Jean-François Caron, and *Artéfact* (2012) by Carl Leblanc. While the novels differ considerably with regard to historical references, their similar plots invite for a comparison, since in each instance a young artist/writer tries to bring to light the life story of one or several elderly women. Based on the distinction of three types of "abuses of memory – and of forgetting" (Ricœur 2004, xv) established by Paul Ricœur in *Memory, History, Forgetting* (2004), the article discusses the implicit and explicit reflections on individual and collective memory and its transmission raised in the context of a quest for historical truth. In doing so, it particularly focalizes on the presence of an extradiegetic narrator in the three texts, whose unrealistic authority (and omniscience) contrasts with the investigators' futile attempts to find the truth and underlines the narrative dimension of the three fictional crises of memory.

Introduction

Dans l'introduction à *La mémoire, l'histoire, l'oubli*, Paul Ricœur semble constater une crise dans le rapport au passé lorsqu'il déplore « l'inquiétant spectacle que donnent trop de mémoire ici, trop d'oubli ailleurs, pour ne rien dire de l'influence des commémorations et des abus de mémoire – et d'oubli » (Ricœur 2000, I). Se distanciant du « moment-mémoire » (Nora 1992, 1006) de notre époque, Ricœur attribue la publication de cet ouvrage – unissant une phénoménologie de la mémoire, une épistémologie de l'histoire ainsi qu'une herméneutique de la condition historique – entre autres à son souci d'une « politique de la juste mémoire » (Ricœur 2000, I). Or, cette idée d'une juste mémoire semble trouver un écho particulièrement riche dans la littérature québécoise contemporaine, Pierre Nepveu (1999, 214) ayant déjà placé l'écrivain québécois « sous le signe d'une éthique de la mémoire et de la présence aux formes, et d'une herméneutique jamais achevée ». La quête d'un passé insaisissable ou l'emprise d'un passé traumatisant constituent, de fait, des sujets de choix du roman québécois actuel et sont traitées de diverses manières, comme l'ont, entre autres, relevé Marie Parent (2013), Karine Cellard et Martine-Emmanuelle Lapointe (2011) ainsi que Robert Dion (2015). Ce dernier souligne « le caractère très élaboré du cadre contemporain où prend place la quête, ou plutôt l'enquête historique » (Dion 2015, 76) dans de tels romans, qui s'inscrivent d'ailleurs dans un courant international qu'Emmanuel Bouju (2013, 52) appelle « le ‹ roman de l'historien › (au sens où le narrateur imite une figure possible de l'historien en une fiction d'enquête indiciaire attachée à la remontée des traces, à l'écho des voix perdues, à l'archéologie du présent) ». Grâce à leur position rétrospective, ces romans soulèvent diverses questions sur la culture et la politique mémorielles contemporaines qui encadrent la quête indiciaire[2].

Au Québec, *Il pleuvait des oiseaux* de Jocelyne Saucier, *Rose Brouillard, le film* de Jean-François Caron et *Artéfact* de Carl Leblanc se démarquent dans ce courant par la mise en contraste des processus de remémoration et de transmission de la mémoire. Ce faisant, ces trois romans illustrent l'actualité des enjeux des trois types « d'abus de la mémoire naturelle » distingués par Paul Ricœur, soit la « mémoire *empêchée* », la « mémoire *manipulée* » et la « mémoire *obligée* » (2000, 83). Pour ce faire, ils ont recours à un flou onomastique et à une voix narrative extradiégétique qui chapeaute le récit. Si la première stratégie renvoie à la fragilité de l'identité et de la mémoire, la deuxième donne, dans les trois cas, l'impression d'une autorité narrative irréaliste. De fait, pour parler avec Nicolas Xanthos (2011, 116), « la position [...] d'un narrateur en parfaite maîtrise de sa parole et de son récit [est une] [...] figure mythique en ce double sens qu'elle renverrait à une sorte d'âge d'or narratif et qu'elle apparaît, aujourd'hui et dans ces romans d'enquête, comme chimérique ». Sensible à ces enjeux, Francis Langevin (2015) étudie la transmission problématique de la mémoire dans les deux romans situés en région[3], soit *Il pleuvait des oiseaux* et *Rose Brouillard, le film*, en soulignant « l'omniscience dubitative » (Langevin 2015, 87) des instances narratives respectives. Sur la base de ces observations, il s'agira, dans ce qui suit, de proposer une systématisation de la mise en scène des formes de la crise de la mémoire dans le roman québécois contemporain en analysant successivement les trois manifestations de l'abus de mémoire proposées par Ricœur. Dans ce contexte, l'ajout d'*Artéfact* de Carl Leblanc, l'une des moins fréquentes excursions de la littérature québécoise dans la mémoire de la Seconde Guerre mondiale,[4] permettra d'illustrer la variété des figures problématiques de la mémoire et de l'oubli dans le roman québécois actuel.

La mémoire empêchée et la mémoire qui empêche de vivre

La première forme des « abus de la mémoire », la *mémoire empêchée*, se situe, selon Ricœur (2000, 82), sur le « niveau pathologique-thérapeutique ». Puisant dans deux études de Freud[5], il résume sous cette rubrique le mécanisme de refoulement d'un événement traumatique. Celui-ci s'exprime souvent par une « compulsion de répétition » (Ricœur 2000, 84), c'est-à-dire par des actions sans lien apparent au souvenir qui correspondent au « phénomène de hantise » (Ricœur 2000, 84). Ricœur insiste sur l'importance d'un véritable « travail de remémoration » (Ricœur 2000, 85) qui représente la seule solution afin de prendre conscience de l'événement traumatisant et de concilier le sujet traumatisé avec ce qu'il a refoulé, c'est-à-dire la seule solution afin d'arriver indemne à une « issue positive » (Ricœur 2000, 89).

Le cas de figure d'un passé qui envahit le présent est illustré à l'exemple de deux personnages dans *Il pleuvait des oiseaux* de Jocelyne Saucier : la mémoire empêchée d'un survivant des « Grands Feux qui ont ravagé le nord de l'Ontario au début du XXe siècle » (Saucier 2011, quatrième de couverture) et la mémoire des autres qui empêche une jeune photographe de vivre sa propre vie.

Le premier, le taciturne Boychuck, a choisi de s'exiler dans les bois avec deux camarades afin d'y vivre (et d'y mourir) librement, c'est-à-dire en dehors de la société et de ses contraintes. Qualifié de « blessure ouverte » (Saucier 2011, 63) par des gens de la région, Boychuck affronte finalement les événements refoulés lors de son exil. Son moyen d'expression de ce que Ricœur (2000, 83) appelle une « mémoire *blessée*, voire *malade* » est la peinture. Ses tableaux, qui donnent « l'impression d'étouffer dans un monde en dissolution » (Saucier 2011, 47) à ses deux compagnons, semblent toutefois plus relever d'une « compulsion de répétition » (Ricœur 2000, 84) que d'un vrai « travail de remémoration » (Ricœur 2000, 85) qui le libérerait de l'emprise du passé. Les centaines de peintures de l'œuvre secrète de Boychuck qui témoignent de son retour obsessionnel au passé traumatisant semblent être créées au rythme des bribes de souvenirs douloureux qui surgissent et le hantent.

C'est du moins l'hypothèse d'une jeune photographe qui arrive au campement peu après la mort de Boychuck. Fascinée autant par le regard que par le récit d'une rescapée des Grands Feux qu'elle avait rencontrée à Toronto, la photographe retrace l'histoire d'autres survivants afin de monter une exposition de leurs portraits. Intriguée par les deux ermites, son enquête perd toutefois de son urgence, lorsque les deux vieillards accueillent une nouvelle arrivée dans leur communauté. Il s'agit d'une vieille dame qui avait été internée dans un hôpital psychiatrique depuis sa jeunesse. La photographe s'attache à cette nouvelle venue fragile, qui l'appelle Ange-Aimée en souvenir d'une ancienne codétenue et qui choisit pour sa nouvelle vie à elle le prénom Marie-Desneige, s'inventant ainsi une nouvelle identité (cf. Langevin 2015, 86).

Marie-Desneige, dont le long séjour en institution psychiatrique a « aiguisé les sens » (Saucier 2011, 113), s'avère capable de décoder les tableaux de Boychuck, ce qui relance la quête de la photographe. Langevin (2015, 87) a relevé « le romanesque » de l'intrigue, au cours de laquelle la photographe isole une série de tableaux racontant une histoire d'amour tragique qui serait au cœur de l'œuvre de réminiscence de Boychuck.

Après sa découverte, la photographe sépare sa vie entre la préparation d'une exposition d'une sélection de tableaux avec ses photos et des visites à ses « vieux amis des bois » (Saucier 2011, 13, 16), ce qui provoque chez eux la question : « T'as pas de vie à toi pour t'intéresser autant aux autres ? » (Saucier 2011, 146) Sur le plan de la narration, un flou onomastique met en accent cette vie par procuration. En effet, le personnage est d'abord désigné par sa fonction, c'est-à-dire « la photographe » ou « la visiteuse », avant d'être temporairement affublé du nom d'une autre, Ange-Aimée, un rôle qu'elle accepte « par compassion, par amitié » (Saucier 2011, 27). Le fait qu'elle se soucie du bien-être de la vieille dame indique par ailleurs qu'elle ne tombe pas dans le piège d'une « exonération du souci présent par la mémoire du passé » (Todorov 1995, 55) qui caractérise, selon Todorov (que Ricœur cite aussi), le « nouveau culte de la mémoire » (Todorov 1995, 53). À partir du moment où l'enquête redémarre grâce à Marie-Desneige, elle redevient « la photographe ». Ce jeu de rôles qui se détecte dans l'onomastique traduit sa fuite dans la vie des autres. Ce sont finalement ses vieux amis qui l'obligent à suivre leur exemple et à affronter sa propre vie dans l'ici et maintenant, lorsqu'ils disparaissent sans laisser de traces. Supposant leur mort, la photographe essaie de retrouver l'instigatrice de sa quête à Toronto, mais rencontre, à sa place, un homme auquel elle confie son vrai nom, ce qui semble indiquer la fin de sa fuite identitaire.

C'est grâce au narrateur omniscient aux allures de conteur qu'à la différence de l'enquêteuse le lecteur connaît le destin de la communauté des bois qui réserve une fin heureuse pour deux des trois personnages âgés. En effet, le récit se partage entre deux niveaux de narration. Une voix de conteur introduit le récit et l'interrompt régulièrement en insérant des mises en situation parfois proleptiques avant de céder la parole à d'autres narrateurs qui développent l'histoire. La voix qui chapeaute le récit dès le début a aussi le dernier mot, livrant, selon Jacques Pelletier (2011, 12), une « finale qui réunit les contraires dans une nouvelle, et supérieure, harmonie et qui s'apparente en cela au conte merveilleux ». Ce faisant, le récit du roman *Il pleuvait des oiseaux* ne semble se distinguer qu'en apparence de l'exposition juxtaposant les tableaux de Boychuck et les portraits de survivants, qui résulte d'un important travail de sélection, de configuration et d'interprétation de l'expression de la mémoire blessée de Boychuck. Cette mise en scène qu'effectue la photographe lors de la préparation de son exposition touche la deuxième forme des « abus de mémoire » relevés par Ricœur.

La mémoire manipulée – le passé au musée

Située sur le « niveau pratique » (Ricœur 2000, 97) de la mémoire collective, la *mémoire manipulée* concerne principalement des « expressions publiques de la mémoire » (Ricœur 2000, 99) qui servent à légitimer l'autorité des détenteurs du pouvoir. La possibilité d'une telle manipulation de la mémoire est due à sa fragilité. Celle-ci résulte de la « proximité entre imagination et mémoire » (Ricœur 2000, 98) ainsi que du rôle qu'elle joue lors « de la quête, de la requête et de la revendication de l'identité » (Ricœur 2000, 98), dont Ricœur souligne « le caractère purement présumé » (Ricœur 2000, 98). En effet, le « rapport difficile au temps » (Ricœur 2000, 98) de l'identité occasionne « le recours [...] à la mémoire, en tant que composante temporelle de l'identité, en conjonction avec l'évaluation du présent et la projection du futur » (Ricœur 2000, 98). Dans ce contexte, Ricœur attire l'attention sur le rôle du récit dans la constitution d'une identité et explique le potentiel de manipulation qu'offrent la configuration et la sélection des éléments.

Une telle manipulation se détecte dans *Il pleuvait des oiseaux*, où le passé envahisseur cristallisé en images qui empêche Boychuck de vivre se transforme en une histoire à dénouement positif exposée au musée. En effet, la photographe choisit et agence les tableaux, leur donne des titres et rédige des cartons explicatifs de sorte que l'exposition conjointe des toiles de Boychuck et des photos des survivants correspond aux « thèmes chers au cœur de jeunes artistes qui aiment que la vie racle les bas-fonds avant d'atteindre la lumière » (Saucier 2011, 173). C'est « ce romanesque », comme le souligne Langevin (2015, 87), qui « va rendre possible la transmission de[s] [...] tableaux », mais non de la mémoire douloureuse.

Tandis que la photographe effectue une quête indiciaire afin d'étayer sa version par des preuves, la mise en scène de la mémoire dans *Rose Brouillard, le film* de Jean-François Caron a recours à un passé imaginaire. Une crise économique menaçant le petit village (fictif) de Sainte-Marie, un comité de villageois a décidé de réinventer Sainte-Marie, dorénavant nommé Sainte-Marée de l'Incantation et de doter la municipalité d'« une histoire pas comme les autres » (Caron 2012, 174) afin d'attirer des touristes. Un auteur dénommé Caron comme l'auteur du roman est chargé de réécrire l'histoire du village rebaptisé et de lui forger, par là même, une nouvelle identité. Parmi les « expressions publiques de la mémoire » (Ricœur 2000, 99) inventée se trouvent des maisons pittoresques transplantées d'ailleurs et le rituel d'une danse d'incantation des femmes de pêcheurs. Dans ce contexte – et sans d'abord connaître l'ampleur de la mise en scène –, une jeune cinéaste est engagée par une société de développement avec la tâche de retracer l'histoire de vie de la mystérieuse Rose Brouillard, qui aurait vécu, enfant, sur une île au large du village. Ayant trouvé la vieille dame à Montréal, la cinéaste, dont le lecteur ne connaîtra pas le vrai nom, découvre que Rose est atteinte d'Alzheimer, mais réussit toutefois à filmer son retour sur l'île, le tout dans le but d'ajouter une touche d'émotions à la visite touristique des lieux.

L'histoire de ce retour aux origines est véhiculée par un récit pseudopolyphonique qui dépasse largement l'enquête. En effet, dans un bref prologue, une voix anonyme évoque l'image de l'archipel pour décrire son récit : « Je serai tout : leurs voix, je les assumerai toutes. Je suis un archipel. » (Caron 2012, 9) Ensuite, ce *je* prête sa voix à divers personnages vivants et morts. Se chevauchant à travers les époques, leurs paroles miment un récit polyphonique qui couvre de manière anachronique, voire achronique[6], des épisodes entre la jeunesse d'Onile, le (supposé) père de Rose, qui fut assistant d'un veilleur de phare avant la Seconde Guerre mondiale, et le retour sur l'île de Rose au début du 21e siècle. De courtes mises en situation allusives et proleptiques précèdent chaque prise de parole telles des didascalies.

Ainsi, le *je* narrateur anonyme se glisse explicitement dans la peau des personnages afin de présenter au lecteur une multitude d'impressions et de confessions, d'anecdotes et d'images, dont se dégage un imaginaire collectif de Sainte-Marie devenu Sainte-Marée de l'Incantation. Selon Langevin (2015, 87), « cet aménagement multiphonique des voix imite le désordre supposé du souvenir qui n'a pas encore été organisé en récit [...], ce qui accentue encore la dialogique entre le naturel et le factice, entre l'expérience et sa traduction ». Qui plus est, il illustre que le village de Sainte-Marie n'existe plus que par les paroles éclatées réunies par une voix qui s'affiche ouvertement comme fictive. Placé au-dessus de la mêlée, le lecteur est amené à faire le travail du biographe, voire de l'historien, c'est-à-dire à construire le « pont entre les îles » (Caron 2012, 217) du récit foisonnant et fragmentaire, pour reprendre l'image qu'évoque Rose elle-même : « Les îles sont des mots échappés, qui dépassent la pensée. Des chapitres comme des éclaboussures. [...]. S'il y avait un pont entre les îles, mes souvenirs se rejoindraient. » (Caron 2012, 217)

En plus de souligner l'interprétatif et le construit de tout récit d'histoire et de vie visant à établir une identité (cf. Ricœur 2000, 98), le roman révèle un mécanisme pareil dans l'attribution de noms propres, ce qui suscite des réflexions sur la fragilité de l'identité, qui se détecte, selon Ricœur, particulièrement lors de la « confrontation avec autrui » (2000, 99). Attribués d'un nom auquel ils ne s'identifient pas, plusieurs personnages, tels la cinéaste (cf. Caron 2012, 87) et Onile (cf. Caron 2012, 106), sont en effet conscients de l'écart qui sépare leur perception de soi de celle que les autres ont d'eux. Rose, pour sa part, ne reçoit son nom – qui n'est, pour elle, « pas tout à fait le [s]ien » (Caron 2012, 41) – qu'après avoir été emmenée au village suite au décès d'Onile. Confrontée à l'autre et obligée de vivre en société, elle finit par s'apercevoir comme « un être humain qu'[elle] n'étai[t] pas avant de rejoindre la côte » (Caron 2012, 111). Ayant ainsi acquis une nouvelle conscience de soi, Rose voit au présent son identité menacée par la maladie d'Alzheimer, qui lui fait perdre les points de repère que procure « cette ligne du temps qui devrait ordonner les événements et les choses » (Ricœur 2000, 47).

De retour sur l'île, c'est le contact physique avec les éléments de la nature qui semble faire ressurgir sa mémoire, comme le souligne Langevin (2015, 88). Se remémorant – ou s'imaginant – la mort de sa mère, Rose fournit à la fin du récit un élément clé de son histoire que le lecteur tente de restituer avec (voire à la place de) celle qui est consciente de l'effritement de sa mémoire et, qui plus est, de son identité. Rose finit toutefois par accepter cet état identitaire vacillant qu'elle décrit comme une « existence à choix multiples » (Caron 2012, 45). Dans le dernier segment du texte, elle renonce à suivre l'exemple de sa mère désespérée, c'est-à-dire à sauter de la falaise, et s'ancre avec confiance dans le présent en affirmant que « [t]out va bien. Tout ira bien » (Caron 2012, 239). Lorsqu'elle se reconnaît, dans ce contexte, dans le village pourtant « méconnaissable, perdu dans ses souvenirs. Un village qui se conte tout croche, qui [lui] ressemble » (Caron 2012, 23), elle semble faire allusion à la tentative du village d'affronter le présent et l'avenir par la mise en scène d'une mémoire inventée. En même temps, elle compare les ravages de la maladie d'Alzheimer aux effets dévastateurs de la manipulation de la mémoire collective.

Ce danger inhérent à la « muséification de la mémoire » (Langevin 2015, 89) constitue aussi un enjeu dans *Artéfact*, qui raconte l'enquête d'un journaliste sur un objet extraordinaire exposé au Centre commémoratif de l'Holocauste de Montréal : « le cœur d'Auschwitz », un carnet de vœux en forme de cœur que des travailleuses d'une usine d'armement d'Auschwitz avaient clandestinement confectionné pour célébrer les 20 ans d'une des leurs. La présentation strictement factuelle de cet objet cache, en effet, son histoire tragique (fictive) mise en scène dans le roman de Carl Leblanc. La double enquête que mène François Bélanger, le protagoniste d'*Artéfact*, sur des aspects de la Seconde Guerre mondiale, évolue dans le contexte problématique d'une « mémoire obligée » (Ricœur 2000, 105) de la Shoah.

La mémoire obligée – de la face cachée du passé

Sous la dénomination de la *mémoire obligée*, qu'il situe au niveau « éthico-politique », Ricœur traite de la notion du devoir de mémoire qu'il relie à un sentiment de dette et de reconnaissance envers les victimes et qu'il paraphrase comme « le devoir de rendre justice, par le souvenir, à un autre que soi » (Ricœur 2000, 108). La « mémoire abusivement commandée » (Ricœur 2000, 82) se manifeste le plus souvent sous la forme d'une « frénésie de la commémoration » (Ricœur 2000, 109) qui est régie par la hantise et non par le devoir de justice. Publié vingt ans après le constat d'une « tyrannie de la mémoire » de Pierre Nora (1992, 1012), *Artéfact* suscite des réflexions sur ses conséquences.

Le protagoniste d'*Artéfact* doutant fortement de l'intérêt du public pour un « énième récit sur la Shoah » (Leblanc 2012, 26), le devoir de mémoire qu'accomplit celui qui couvre d'habitude les guerres de motards et les scandales de la mafia relève d'abord purement du devoir professionnel. Le roman part ainsi du constat que l'injonction de se souvenir a entraîné une impression générale de sursaturation à l'égard de la mémoire de la Seconde Guerre mondiale. L'impression de distance par rapport aux événements historiques, surtout à Montréal, une ville qui a décidé de « laisser l'Histoire aux autres » (Leblanc 2012, 35) selon le narrateur hétérodiégétique, s'ajoute, en effet, à un sentiment d'« overdose de Shoah » (Leblanc 2012, 20) dû à la désapprobation de la stratégie militaire contemporaine d'Israël.

Dans ce contexte d'un sentiment de « trop de mémoire » de la Shoah souligné à plusieurs reprises par le narrateur (cf. Leblanc 2012, 35, 49, 125), François, qui est affecté à couvrir « l'affaire Krylenko » pour son journal, s'étonne de la « mémoire fervente » (Leblanc 2012, 22) de jeunes juifs qui manifestent devant la maison montréalaise du supposé criminel de guerre ukrainien Alexandre Krylenko. Lors d'une réception au Centre commémoratif de l'Holocauste qu'il visite dans le cadre de ses recherches, il soulève la fragilité de la mémoire de la Shoah, qui « se tendrait et s'amincirait peu à peu jusqu'à devenir un fil tenu » (Leblanc 2012, 122), et compare sa transmission par le truchement de commémorations à un résultat du « dressage » (Leblanc 2012, 123) des jeunes générations, soit un exercice artificiel vidé de sa dimension identitaire, qui doit, de plus, rivaliser avec toutes les distractions du présent (cf. Leblanc 2012, 42).

Écrit en temps de crise de la mémoire, son article sur Krylenko affirme l'impossibilité de connaître le fond des accusations contre cet ancien membre de la police auxiliaire ukrainienne qui prétend avoir sauvé un juif. L'histoire de ce « lâche » (Leblanc 2012, 82), dont François apprend après-coup qu'il avait effectivement sauvé un juif, mais seulement après avoir abandonné sa femme également juive, introduit le *leitmotiv* de l'ambiguïté. Tel un fil rouge, celui-ci sous-tend aussi l'enquête principale sur l'artéfact éponyme. Fasciné par le « cœur d'Auschwitz », le journaliste essaie de restituer l'histoire de ce carnet, qui symbolise pour lui la survie du courage et de l'empathie dans un univers qui s'efforçait à déshumaniser les humains, un artéfact qui représente donc, selon lui, « une belle histoire » (Leblanc 2012, 147, 155).

Lors de ses recherches, il doit faire face à la disparition, à la douleur et à l'oubli, mais aussi à des sentiments ambivalents inexpliqués des témoins qui le touchent profondément et suscitent un sentiment d'urgence : « Il s'agissait d'une histoire si ancienne. Mais le temps pressait. » (Leblanc 2012, 101) L'impression d'un non-dit finit par s'installer lorsqu'il découvre que le treizième texte du carnet a été ajouté plus tard, en 1945, par Dana, la fondatrice du musée de l'Holocauste de Montréal, auquel elle avait légué le carnet plus tard. À la différence du lecteur, il ne semble toutefois pas être en mesure de dévoiler l'énigme du carnet.

En effet, les chapitres dans lesquels le narrateur hétérodiégétique relate les enquêtes de François alternent avec des chapitres non numérotés, mais datés qui interrompent le cours de l'enquête. Plongeant dans le passé, ils racontent au présent des scènes de la vie des signataires à différentes époques. Le premier de ces douze brefs instantanés est situé à la veille du 20e anniversaire de Klara, la destinataire du carnet, à Auschwitz. Sont rapportées, ensuite, plusieurs scènes de vie du passé des signataires liées de près ou de loin au carnet. Le dernier de ces chapitres rejoint le présent, car la fille de Dana y trouve le journal intime de sa mère qui rapporte les circonstances du décès de Klara. Battue brutalement en essayant de sortir le carnet d'Auschwitz, elle avait dicté le treizième texte à Dana juste avant sa mort. Le journal de Dana souligne les regrets des signataires qui se sentent responsables d'avoir fabriqué un « *objet maudit* » (Leblanc 2012, 152), dont la seule valeur est dorénavant de contenir le « *testament* » (Leblanc 2012, 152) de Klara.

Un commentaire du narrateur omniscient qui indique dans le dernier chapitre du livre que François prend une tache rouge dans le carnet pour de l'encre,

« ne pouvant imaginer qu'il s'agissait du sang de Klara qui avait saisi la main de Dana » (Leblanc 2012, 155), confirme l'ambivalence du « cœur d'Auschwitz » –, symbole d'une victoire des valeurs humaines dans un endroit déshumanisant pour les visiteurs du musée et symbole d'une « insouciance » (Leblanc 2012, 152) tragique pour les signataires.

C'est par le *leitmotiv* de l'ambiguïté que le récit d'*Artéfact* s'oppose ainsi aux « discours convenus » (Leblanc 2012, 60) et au « récit mille fois répété et désormais dévalué de l'horreur auschwitzienne » (Leblanc 2012, 61). Qui plus est, à l'aide de retours au passé fictionnalisés, le récit redonne une personnalité aux noms que François déchiffre laborieusement sur le carnet. Le roman semble vouloir surmonter la crise de la sursaturation et de l'indifférence à l'égard de la Shoah par la mise en scène de destins tragiques individuels et de dilemmes existentiels aussi concrets qu'insaisissables, qui pointent vers la complexité cachée par le terme abstrait du « devoir de mémoire ».

Conclusion

L'analyse successive de la mise en scène des trois formes d'abus de la mémoire distinguées par Ricœur a révélé l'omniprésence d'éléments d'une « mémoire manipulée », qui renvoie à la dimension médiatique de la mémoire transmise. En effet, l'exposition organisée par la photographe dans *Il pleuvait des oiseaux* illustre la manipulation inhérente à toute représentation médiatique du passé, une problématique que *Rose Brouillard, le film* attaque dans sa variante consciente, tandis qu'*Artéfact* met en évidence la sélectivité de la mémoire matérialisée. L'omission du rôle qu'a joué le carnet de vœux dans la mort de Klara dans sa présentation au musée relève, de fait, aussi d'une forme de manipulation de la mémoire.

Ayant suscité des réflexions sur l'impossibilité de raconter ‹ la vérité › historique, les trois romans font le choix ouvert de la fiction. En effet, le dispositif narratif des trois romans diverge de la configuration d'un « roman de l'historien » telle que décrite par Bouju (2013, 52) en ce que, chaque fois, le lecteur dispose de plus d'informations que le personnage-enquêteur grâce à une voix narrative extradiégétique qui régit le récit de manière ostentatoire. De la sorte, la posture énonciative d'un conteur dans le cas d'*Il pleuvait des oiseaux* permet, d'une part, d'évoquer explicitement la crise identitaire de la photographe et, de l'autre, de mettre en évidence que la mémoire transmise par l'exposition ne rend pas justice à la mémoire vécue.

Dans le cas des deux autres romans, le narrateur complète même l'enquête avec les moyens de la fiction, prenant donc la relève là où le personnage échoue d'aller au fond de la ‹ vérité ›. Caron, pour sa part, oppose le foisonnement de la parole mémorielle à la rigidité du récit historiographique, car le récit pseudo-polyphonique et fragmentaire de *Rose Brouillard, le film* démontre que tout récit de mémoire visant à établir une identité est sélectif, construit, voire souvent inventé. Mettant en scène la « proximité entre imagination et mémoire » (Ricœur 2000, 98), le roman illustre ainsi la citation du cinéaste Pierre Perrault mise en exergue : « Les pays prennent naissance dans la mémoire, et la mémoire ne manque pas d'imagination ». Chez Leblanc, le double récit rappelle l'individualité des victimes de la Shoah souvent masquée par la notion abstraite du « devoir de mémoire ». Dans ces deux romans, le recours à la fiction semble aller au-delà d'une recherche de la vérité historique afin de proposer des éléments de ce que Ricœur appelle une « politique de la juste mémoire » (2000, I).

1   Cette recherche a été financée par le Conseil de recherche en sciences humaines (CRSH) du Canada.

2   Au sujet du « paradigme indiciaire », cf. Ginzburg (1989). Ginzburg y démontre de quelle manière la connaissance à partir d'indices qui caractérise, entre autres, les enquêtes policières, est devenue un modèle épistémologique en sciences humaines.

3   Au sujet d'une « régionalité » du roman québécois actuel, cf. par exemple Langevin (2010 et 2013).

4   Cf. à ce sujet Viau (2002) et le dossier « La guerre dans la littérature québécoise » de la revue *Voix et Images* (2012), dirigé par Michel Biron et Olivier Parenteau.

5   Il s'agit de « Erinnern, Wiederholen und Durcharbeiten » et « Trauer und Melancholie », publiés dans Sigmund Freud, *Gesammelte Werke*, vol. 10, Frankfurt am Main, S. Fischer Verlag, 1946, 126-136 et 428-446 respectivement.

6   Il est, par exemple, impossible de situer dans l'ordre du récit le segment attribué à une « villageoise sans nom » (Caron 2012, 172), qui révèle à la cinéaste la raison de la réinvention de Sainte-Marie et l'ampleur des travaux effectués tout en la sommant de garder le secret.

Bibliographie

Bouju, Emmanuel : « Force diagonale et compression du présent. Six propositions sur le roman ‹ istorique › contemporain ». In : *Écrire l'histoire* 11 (2013), 51-60.

Caron, Jean-François : *Rose Brouillard, le film*. Chicoutimi : La Peuplade, 2012.

Cellard, Karine / Lapointe, Martine-Emmanuelle (éds) : *Transmission et héritages de la littérature québécoise*. Montréal : Presses de l'Université de Montréal, 2011.

Dion, Robert : « Le roman québécois contemporain et l'histoire ». In : *Québec français* 175 (2015), 76-78.

Ginzburg, Carlo : *Mythes, emblèmes, traces. Morphologie et histoire*. Traduit de l'italien par Monique Aymard. Paris : Flammarion, 1989.

Langevin, Francis : « Un nouveau régionalisme ? De Sainte-Souffrance à Notre-Dame-du-Cachalot, en passant par Rivière-aux-Oies (Éric Dupont, Sébastien Chabot et Christine Eddie) ». In : *Voix et Images* 36,1 (2010), 59-77.

Langevin, Francis : « La régionalité dans les fictions québécoises d'aujourd'hui. L'exemple de *Sur la 132* de Gabriel Anctil ». In : *temps zéro* 6 (2013), http://tempszero.contemporain.info/document936 (consultation 04/02/2017).

Langevin, Francis : « Raconter la mémoire ». In : *Québec français* 175 (2015), 85-89.

Leblanc, Carl : *Artéfact*. Montréal : XYZ, 2012.

Nepveu, Pierre : *L'écologie du réel. Mort et naissance de la littérature québécoise contemporaine*. Montréal : Boréal, 1999 [1988].

Nora, Pierre : *Les lieux de mémoire*. Vol. III.3 : *De l'archive à l'emblème*. Paris : Gallimard, 1992.

Parent, Marie : « La revanche du roman historique ». In : *Liberté* 301 (2013), http://revueliberte.ca/content/la-revanche-du-roman-historique (consultation 04/02/2017).

Pelletier, Jacques : « Feu ! Feu ! Joli feu ? ». In : *Nuit blanche, magazine littéraire* 123 (2011), 10-12.

Ricœur, Paul : *La mémoire, l'histoire, l'oubli*. Paris : Seuil, 2000.

Ricœur, Paul : *Memory, History, Forgetting*. Traduit par Kathleen Blamey et David Pellauer. Chicago : The University of Chicago Press, 2004.

Saucier, Jocelyne : *Il pleuvait des oiseaux*. Montréal : XYZ, 2011.

Todorov, Tzvetan : *Les abus de mémoire*. Paris : Arléa, 1995.

Viau, Robert : *Le mal d'Europe : la littérature québécoise et la Seconde Guerre mondiale*. Beauport : Publications MNH, 2002.

Marion KÜHN

Xanthos, Nicolas : « Raconter dans le crépuscule du héros. Fragilités narratives dans le roman d'enquête contemporain ». In : Fortier, Frances / Mercier, Andrée (éds) : *La transmission narrative. Modalités du pacte romanesque contemporain.* Québec : Nota bene, 2011, 111-125.

Danielle DUMONTET (Mayence)

Postmémoires traumatiques dans *Forêts* de Wajdi Mouawad et *Le ciel de Bay City* de Catherine Mavrikakis

Summary

In the 1980s, we have witnessed an important shift from history to memory in literary texts. This shift has led to a so-called war or even saturation of memory (Régine Robin). At the same time, some historians deplore the fact that the boundaries between literature and history have become blurred. As the end of the era of testimony approaches due to the fact that the witnesses of the major catastrophes of the twentieth century are disappearing, we can now observe a 'passage de témoin,' as Catherine Coquio notes in *Le mal de vérité*. Coquio relies on the work of Marianne Hirsch and the concept of 'postmemory,' which designates the writings of the 'génération d'après' ('generation after'). For Hirsch, the relationship between postmemory and the past is not ensured any more by means of memories or recollections but mediated by imaginative involvements, creations, and projections. In numerous texts written after the turn of the millennium, Coquio sees an actualization of the past through the means of fiction – of an imaginary space where witnesses and those who write in the aftermath (vertical and horizontal memory) collide. This essay analyzes the phenomenon of transgenerational transmission through a close look at two characters depicted as heirs of memory: Loup in the play *Forêts* by Wajdi Mouawad and Amy in the novel *Le ciel de Bay City* by Catherine Mavrikakis.

Le passage de témoin

Les violences des guerres, des génocides et des conflits religieux ont marqué le vingtième siècle, et il semblerait que le vingt-et-unième siècle ne soit pas non plus épargné avec les actes de terrorisme qui frappent la population un peu partout dans le monde. La représentation des expériences traumatisantes des guerres et des actes de violence constituant un des thèmes centraux des littératures françaises et francophones contemporaines, un grand nombre d'études ont paru ces dernières années interrogeant les relations entre Histoire et littérature. Dans le chapitre intitulé « Écrire l'histoire » du volume *La littérature française au présent*, paru en 2005, Dominique Viart avait déjà constaté, à partir du milieu des années 70 du siècle dernier, un retour de l'écriture historiographique. Depuis, les textes littéraires mettant en scène les violences dues aux guerres se sont multipliés avec l'émergence d'écritures hors genre, de genres hybrides, ni véritablement fictionnels, ni vraiment historiques. Débats et textes critiques s'intéressant tout particulièrement aux relations Histoire/littérature accompagnent désormais ces nouvelles écritures – d'autant que l'ère du témoin venant à sa fin, du moins pour la Shoah, « le jeu de la fiction testimoniale s'est institué à la faveur du relais des témoins aux ‹ héritiers › », comme le constatait Catherine Coquio dans son introduction aux actes du colloque « Littérature et histoire en débats » de 2013.[1]

Coquio est revenue dans *Le mal de vérité ou l'utopie de la mémoire* sur ce qu'elle appelait en 2013 le « régime de l'après », et ce qu'elle dénomme aujourd'hui le « passage de témoin » :

> Du ‹ devoir de mémoire › au ‹ passage de témoin ›, le volontarisme de la transmission se poursuit, tentant de compenser la perte d'une ‹ tradition › commune […]. Le ‹ passage de témoin › est sans doute la pointe extrême d'une formation symbolique qui hérite d'éléments religieux plus ou moins rationalisés ou assumés, et qu'on voit se réinvestir là où la mémoire devient du témoignage. (Coquio 2015, 147)

Elle s'appuie sur les travaux de Marianne Hirsch et le concept de ‹ postmemory › développé par cette dernière et repris dans la deuxième édition de son essai *Family Frames. Photography Narrative and Postmemory* de 2012, dans lequel elle explique comment elle en était venue à proposer le terme, consciente du fait que le post pourrait induire en erreur et laisser croire que nous nous trouverions en deçà de la mémoire. Mais ce terme lui semblait justement adéquat pour les enfants des survivants de la Shoah comme elle-même qui ne connaissaient pas les événements si ce n'est par relations interposées :

> In my reading, postmemory is distinguished from memory by generational distance and from history by deep personal connection. Postmemory is a powerful and very particular form of memory precisely because its

connection to its object of source is mediated not through recollection but through an imaginative investment and creation. [...] Postmemory characterizes the experience of those who grow up dominated by narratives that preceded their birth, whose own belated stories are evacuated by the stories of the previous generation shaped by traumatic events that can be neither understood nor recreated. I have developed this notion in relation to children of Holocaust survivors, but I believe it may usefully describe other second-generation memories of cultural or traumatic events and experiences. (Hirsch 2012a, 22)

Pour Coquio, nous assistons dans ces récits de filiation à une actualisation du passé par la fiction

[qui] est le lieu imaginaire où se croisent les témoins et ceux qui écrivent ‹ après ›, la mémoire verticale et horizontale. Mais ce croisement peut s'effectuer de deux manières différentes : en faisant le deuil d'un mode de transmission (testimonial) pour en élaborer un autre (culturel), ou en cherchant à éterniser le témoignage *dans* le processus culturel lui-même, en transformant l'héritier en témoin. (Coquio 2015, 149)

C'est justement cette phrase de Coquio qui nous interpelle tout particulièrement, et qui nous amènera à analyser les modes de transmission de la mémoire à travers la figure de l'héritier ou de l'héritier-témoin dans la littérature contemporaine écrite au Québec.

Deux figures d'héritières dans *Forêts* de Wajdi Mouawad et *Le ciel de Bay City* de Catherine Mavrikakis

Dans la pièce *Forêts* de Wajdi Mouawad, créée en 2006, troisième partie du quatuor intitulé *Le sang des promesses*, Loup, jeune fille en colère, reproche à sa mère Aimée décédée de lui avoir légué la douleur en héritage. Le fardeau qui pèse sur les épaules de la jeune adolescente québécoise est trop lourd pour elle. Elle est condamnée à vivre avec la responsabilité de la mort de sa mère, décédée parce que, atteinte d'une tumeur au cerveau, elle refuse au dernier moment de sacrifier la vie de son enfant. La veille du jour prévu pour son avortement, le 6 décembre 1989, a lieu la tragédie de l'école polytechnique à Montréal dans laquelle mourront quatorze jeunes femmes. Aimée déclare alors : « [J]e n'en tuerai pas une quinzième » (Mouawad 2006, 37), faisant le choix fatidique de donner la vie, tout en signant sa propre condamnation à mort. Après son décès, les scientifiques vont s'emparer de son cerveau, dans lequel se trouvait une anomalie, dont ils espèrent pouvoir percer les mystères : au centre de la tumeur se trouvait un os. Et c'est cet os qui sera à l'origine de la recherche d'un paléontologue, Douglas Dupontel, qui imposera à Loup la nécessité de fouiller dans son passé, de remonter le fil chronologique d'une histoire dont elle ne veut pas. Douglas Dupontel : « Vous ne voulez pas savoir ? Vous ne voulez vraiment pas savoir, Loup ? Un passé mystérieux nous hurle des réponses. L'entendez-vous ? » (Mouawad 2006, 59)

Dans *Le ciel de Bay City*, roman de Catherine Mavrikakis paru en 2008 à Montréal et en 2009 à Paris, la jeune protagoniste, Amy, est elle aussi en colère, contre sa famille ou ce qui lui reste de famille, sa mère Denise qui idolâtre sa fille aînée mort-née, et qui la considère comme une attardée, et sa tante devenue une grenouille de bénitier :

> Ces deux-là tentent d'oublier ce à quoi elles ont échappé, leur conversion au catholicisme, les multiples cachettes pendant la guerre, les secrets bien gardés dans une bigoterie minutieusement authentiquement chrétienne ou dans la fierté républicaine. Loin des furies de l'Europe, des années après la terreur, l'horreur, le ciel de Bay City charrie encore quelques cadavres. Pour ces deux femmes, il reste gros d'un passé terrifiant, archaïque, cruel. Dans les mots de ma tante et de ma mère, l'Europe éclate tous les jours de son histoire insensée. Dans les mots des deux sœurs, mille secrets sont celés et la mort de leurs parents, partis en fumée, est inscrite. (Mavrikakis 2008b, 36-37)

Amy se voit condamnée à vivre une vie sans âme dans une banlieue américaine impavide sous un ciel chargé de pollution, à la couleur mauve, voire violacée. Les habitants de la maison de tôle de Bay City avaient espéré se débarrasser des scories maléfiques de leur passé en s'insérant sur le nouveau continent. Mais le passé de l'Europe ne peut pas être éradiqué, il reste inscrit dans les corps des deux sœurs malgré leurs efforts pour oublier tout ce qui pourrait les relier à leur histoire douloureuse. Elles avaient pourtant mis tous leurs espoirs en ce Nouveau Monde, qu'elles imaginaient vierge d'une histoire douloureuse, mais leurs morts sont inscrits à jamais en elles. Elles ont transmis malgré elles un héritage familial qu'elles croyaient avoir enterré dans le silence, et Amy, pour se débarrasser de la douleur qui l'habite, mettra le feu à la maison de Bay City dans la nuit du 4 au 5 juillet 1979. Toute la famille meurt brûlée dans l'incendie, sauf Amy, du moins c'est ce qu'affirme la narratrice dans l'ouverture du roman. À partir de cette confession, la narratrice essaiera de reconstituer les journées qui ont précédé cette terrible nuit, du dimanche 1er juillet 1979 à son départ de Bay City le 1er janvier 1980, interrogeant les faits qui ont fait d'elle une meurtrière qui anéantit le passé et toute trace de l'histoire familiale.

Deux personnages féminins condamnés par leurs auteurs à enquêter, à combler les vides de leur histoire, à comprendre leurs traumas respectifs, à re-tisser les fils douloureux d'une généalogie interrompue par l'Histoire en folie, mais aussi deux personnages du Nouveau Monde, l'une, jeune Québécoise « une adolescente boutonneuse, vulgaire, grossière, et sans aucune tenue vestimentaire digne de ce nom » (Mouawad 2006, 54-55), bien installée dans un présent sans histoire, l'autre jeune punk d'une banlieue nord-américaine, confrontés au fait que l'Histoire traverse aussi les océans. Deux personnages vivant dans le Nouveau Monde, deux héritières condamnées par leurs auteurs à s'enfoncer dans les méandres des catastrophes de l'Histoire du vingtième siècle qui se sont abattues sur le vieux continent, une Histoire qu'ils n'ont pas vécue et dont ils ne sont que les témoins des témoins. Deux personnages créés par des auteurs, qui, même si l'histoire littéraire a tendance à les présenter comme des auteurs néo-québécois, se veulent avant tout écrivains sans frontières, réécrivant dans ces deux textes les catastrophes du vieux continent en esquissant une écriture du désastre.

Wajdi Mouawad explique dans *Le sang des promesses* combien la réalisation de la pièce *Forêts* s'est imposée à lui comme une suite logique à ses deux pre-mières pièces, *Littoral* et *Incendies*, dans lesquelles les protagonistes, confrontés à un héritage familial lourd de secrets empêtré dans les violences de l'Histoire, sont forcés de combler les blancs de leur propre histoire. La découverte de l'Histoire de son pays d'origine, le Liban, de la guerre civile dans laquelle celui-ci s'enli-sera, conduit Mouawad à s'interroger sur les images manquantes[2] de la guerre du Liban qui amena sa famille à s'exiler. Après avoir thématisé dans ses premières pièces les situations conflictuelles au Moyen-Orient, il souhaitera aller plus avant et explorer cette haine qui peut opposer des peuples fraternels, qu'il lui semblera plus facile d'imaginer avec le passé, « car le passé se rattache à l'imaginaire, tandis que le présent, surtout celui qui est sanglant, annule le mythe, la fiction et oblige presque au documentaire » (Mouawad 2009, 60). Habité qu'il est par les tragédies grecques et par les tragédies du monde moderne, soucieux d'interroger les haines ancestrales entre les peuples, Mouawad va se pencher sur l'Histoire de l'Europe qui apparaît pour la première fois dans son œuvre. Il comprend alors que, si la guerre de 14 est la première catastrophe du vingtième siècle, l'explication de la haine entre Français et Allemands a son origine dans la guerre de 1870, et qu'il lui faudra rendre compte de la filiation entre 1870, 1914 et 1945. Dans *Forêts*, il va donc remonter le temps jusqu'en 1870, mettant en scène ces trois guerres de 1870, 1914 et 1945, qui sont à l'origine des catastrophes qui se sont abattues sur l'Europe du vingtième siècle et qui ont précipité le monde dans une haine et une remise en question de l'humanité sans commune mesure. L'Histoire européenne est donc esquissée sur un temps long, de 1870 à 2006, avec les trois guerres, la Shoah, et la chute du mur de Berlin. À ces événements dramatiques s'ajoute la tragédie de Polytechnique à Montréal qui n'intéresse pas le monde, comme le fait remarquer un des personnages de *Forêts*, Baptiste, le père de Loup et le mari d'Aimée. Il s'agit pour l'auteur d'explorer les conséquences des catastrophes subies par les acteurs ou témoins de ces mêmes catastrophes. C'est ainsi que les jeunes protagonistes innocents des trois premières pièces du quatuor *Le sang des promesses* de Wajdi Mouawad, Loup dans *Forêts*, Wilfrid dans *Littoral*, Jeanne et Simon dans *Incendies*, vont devoir faire un voyage dans le passé de leurs familles, enquêter, rechercher pour arriver à combler les vides de l'héritage familial et constater que les traumas voyagent et traversent les océans.

Catherine Mavrikakis, avant la parution de *Le ciel de Bay City* en 2008, avait déjà publié, outre de nombreux essais, trois romans dont nous retiendrons ici deux titres pour notre propos, *Fleurs de crachat* (2005) et *Deuils cannibales et mélancoliques* (2000). Dans *Fleurs de crachat*, la narratrice Flore Forget veut absolument comprendre la souffrance qu'elle ressent depuis toujours ; grâce aux séances psychanalytiques, elle arrivera à situer les origines de cette souffrance dans la nuit de l'enfance et son passé familial, ayant pris sur elle la maladie de sa mère, malade de la Seconde Guerre mondiale. La séance de cure psychanalytique permet à la narratrice d'interroger le passé familial lié à l'Histoire du vieux continent et de mettre à nu toutes les strates du passé : « [J]e vous raconte ma vie et puis celle des autres, la bouche toute remplie des morceaux du passé. » (Mavrikakis 2005, 46-47) Nous avons retenu aussi pour notre propos *Deuils cannibales et mélancoliques* pour la mort omniprésente dans ce texte et la nécessité de trouver des modalités de faire le deuil, afin qu'il y ait transmission et non pas cannibalisation de l'être par la mort : « Il faut face aux morts avoir grand-faim, il faut être cannibale et les bouffer tout rond ou les déchirer de nos dents avides. Il faut avaler nos morts ou c'est eux qui nous bouffent. Il n'y a rien à faire, c'est la loi de la jungle et du deuil. » (Mavrikakis 2000, 124) L'auteure tisse des liens intertextuels entre ces trois textes. Flore s'identifie tout comme Amy avec les victimes de la Seconde Guerre mondiale, mais si Flore se rêvait déjà en Anne Frank, Amy, la jeune Américaine, est devenue une Anne Frank guerrière et rebelle qui tuera par le feu tous les membres de sa famille.

Ces deux textes, le roman de Mavrikakis tout comme la pièce de Mouawad, interrogent les effets de l'Histoire sur les témoins des grandes catastrophes de la modernité mais avant tout sur leurs descendants, sur les héritiers, redessinant la cartographie de l'Histoire, de la mémoire et de l'oubli. Nous ne sommes plus à l'ère du témoin, mais sommes dans l'ère du passage de témoin et nous sommes confrontés ici à deux modalités de la transmission de la mémoire, une transmission interrompue dans le cas de Loup et une transmission traumatique dans le cas d'Amy.

La transmission interrompue

Loup est étouffée par une souffrance et une colère auxquelles elle ne comprend rien : elle est en ce sens une sœur de Wilfrid ou de Simon qui ne veulent pas entreprendre le voyage dans le passé du père pour l'un ou de la mère pour l'autre. Mais, ce voyage dans l'espace et le temps s'impose à eux, s'ils veulent remplir les cases vides d'une généalogie familiale défectueuse. Son passé mystérieux lui hurle des réponses ou des amorces de réponse. C'est ce qui est affirmé par le paléontologue Dupontel, s'adressant à Loup ; l'os qui se trouve dans le cerveau de sa mère est l'os manquant du crâne « probablement concassé à coups de marteau » (Mouawad 2006, 57) d'une jeune femme d'une vingtaine d'années, et retrouvé dans les sols des camps de concentration, recherché désespérément par le père de celle-ci. Les parents imposent leur histoire à leurs descendants au-delà de leur mort, suicide pour le père Dupontel, mort par maladie pour Aimée, la mère de Loup. Douglas Dupontel le fils et Loup la fille doivent remonter le fil du temps. Dupontel a pour lui la science, la paléontologie et les analyses scientifiques que son père lui a laissées ; Loup, elle, ne possède rien, sa mère ayant été adoptée, la transmission étant interrompue. À la recherche d'indices sur l'histoire de sa mère, Loup apprendra que sa vraie grand-mère, Luce, a été adoptée elle aussi, qu'elle est arrivée en 1943 au Québec avec un aviateur qui la confie à ses propres parents, disant que sa mère viendra la chercher un jour. Effectivement, Luce recevra la visite d'une jeune femme, Sarah Cohen, qui lui dévoilera l'identité de sa mère, lui montrant une photo sur laquelle se trouvent son père Samuel, mort assassiné, sa mère Ludivine qui mourra dans le camp de concentration de Treblinka en 1944, et elle-même Sarah, tous membres d'un réseau de la Résistance, le réseau Cigogne.

Pour Luce qui n'a pas connu sa mère, le couteau de l'enfance restera à jamais planté dans sa gorge et cette douleur se transmettra à Aimée qui la transmettra à Loup. Car qui est cette Ludivine, cette mère disparue, assassinée pendant la Seconde Guerre mondiale ?

> Luce. Comme si nous étions, toutes les quatre, liées à quelqu'un d'autre, quelqu'un qui tente de nous appeler non pas du passé mais des ténèbres et son cri, pour attirer notre attention, a pris des formes terrifiantes : le crâne de Ludivine, ma mâchoire arrachée, et le cerveau de ta mère. Aujourd'hui il s'adresse à toi et tu n'as pas le choix : tu dois casser le fil de nos enfances concassées ou il te fracassera le cœur. (Mouawad 2006, 81)

Les pièces du puzzle sont réparties dans une forêt de plus en plus impénétrable, les voies qui mènent à la lumière constituent, tel un labyrinthe, un parcours initiatique qui après les épreuves apporte la renaissance. Mouawad abolit les notions de lieux et de temps, les scènes sont jouées simultanément, les acteurs se glissent aussi dans plusieurs personnages, ce qui donne l'impression au spectateur d'être en présence de toutes les guerres. Cependant, Dupontel et Loup ajoutant une pierre après l'autre reconstituent la généalogie de Loup, fille d'Aimée (adoptée), fille de Luce (adoptée), fille de Ludivine (adoptée), fille de Léonie Keller et de Lucien Blondel (soldat déserteur de la Première Guerre mondiale, assassin de son propre frère), elle-même fille d'Hélène Keller, fille d'Odette Keller, épouse d'Albert Keller et maîtresse du père de ce dernier, Alexandre Keller, dont elle aura les jumeaux, Hélène et Edgard. La famille Keller est à l'origine de la tragédie qui débute en 1871 avec la trahison fondamentale de l'industriel Alexandre Keller qui décide de passer à l'ennemi avec ses usines de fer, ses machines à vapeur et surtout ses rails de chemin de fer sur lesquels est inscrit le nom de Keller. Cette première trahison sera à l'origine de toutes les autres trahisons, des abandons, des silences, des non-dits qui provoqueront les autres drames ou crimes comme celui de l'inceste, le tout sur fond de guerre. Les violences causées par les guerres initiées par l'homme, les haines qui en résultent, génèrent le crime le plus monstrueux, l'inceste entre père et fille et entre sœur et frère. Mouawad dira à propos de *Forêts* :

> *Forêts*, en ce sens, raconte une histoire, celle d'une jeune fille d'aujourd'hui qui, bien qu'elle ne le veuille pas au début, sera forcée tout de même d'aller voir où se trouve cet instant qui refuse de mourir et qui, depuis, déchire la trame de sa vie. La quête est d'autant plus douloureuse que cette seconde se situe quelque part, non pas dans le temps de sa propre existence, mais plutôt dans le passé de ses parents. Comment faire alors pour remonter le temps ? (Mouawad 2009, 71)

Il faut trouver la pièce manquante, celle qui permet de remettre tous les morceaux du puzzle en place : d'après les recherches effectuées par Douglas Dupontel, Ludivine, stérile, n'a jamais eu d'enfant, alors qui est donc la mère de Luce ? Ludivine a échangé son identité avec Sarah pour la sauver des camps de la mort. Et si Sarah Cohen n'a pu avouer à Luce qu'elle était sa mère, c'est que cette dernière vouait un véritable culte à Ludivine et qu'elle n'a pas voulu la déstabiliser encore davantage. Le sacrifice de Ludivine a réparé la faute originelle de la famille Keller. La forêt a livré son secret et permis à Loup d'enterrer sa mère ; sa filiation a pu être établie, une généalogie avec laquelle elle peut vivre, reconstituée. Cette filiation assumée lui permettra peut-être de se construire un jour une identité féminine et de transmettre sa mémoire à celle qui viendra après elle pour lui dire : « Je ne t'abandonnerai jamais. Je ne t'abandonnerai jamais. » (Mouawad 2006, 162)

La transmission de l'héritage familial rendue impossible dans le cas de Loup a généré l'oubli et avec celui-ci la répétition de la catastrophe. Ricœur s'appuyant sur *Deuil et mélancolie* (1915) de Freud pour aborder les problématiques de l'oubli, précise que « l'oubli est l'œuvre de la compulsion de répétition, laquelle empêche la prise de conscience de l'événement traumatique » (Ricœur 2000, 576). Mais Mouawad, habité qu'il est par les tragédies grecques comme nous l'avons dit plus haut, développe l'idée d'un travail cathartique et offre la rédemption à Loup, grâce à la vérité retrouvée et rétablie qui détient alors une valeur purificatrice.

La transmission traumatique

Amy est hantée par la mort dans le ciel mauve de Bay City, dans lequel elle voit flotter des cadavres, dans lequel elle imagine sa mort et celle de sa famille. Elle est habitée par les morts, tous les morts, les morts de sa famille comme les morts du territoire sur lequel est plantée une banlieue qui se voudrait sans visage et surtout sans histoire :

> Je ne vis les choses que par procuration. Je suis hantée par une histoire que je n'ai pas tout à fait vécue. Et les âmes des Juifs morts se mêlent dans mon esprit à celles des Indiens d'Amérique exterminés ici et là sur cette terre. Ils sont tous là présents en moi, parce que l'Amérique, du Michigan au Nouveau-Mexique, c'est cela. Un territoire hanté par les morts d'ici ou d'ailleurs, venus de partout, un territoire encore troué comme une passoire, même après le 11 septembre, les barricades et les fortifications frontalières. (Mavrikakis 2008b, 53)

Sa mère et sa tante n'ont jamais pu faire le deuil de leurs morts. Leur histoire individuelle étant intimement imbriquée dans l'Histoire collective, elles ont choisi le silence voulant enterrer à jamais un passé trop horrible. Pour ces deux femmes, Denise et Babette, la transmission de l'héritage familial a été brisée, leurs parents juifs les ayant confiées à une famille catholique de Normandie pour leur éviter une mort certaine. Même si elles changent donc de nom, de religion, d'histoire, le passé reste toutefois à jamais incrusté en elles et dans la réalité européenne. C'est pourquoi les sœurs Duchesnay voulant se débarrasser d'une histoire familiale lourde et partiellement inconnue, s'installent au Nouveau Monde où le présent s'étire et se dilate au détriment du passé. Elles se réinventent, l'une choisissant l'athéisme, l'autre la bigoterie, mais le passé ne les quitte pas. En cachette de sa sœur, Babette a décidé de collecter les informations sur sa famille disparue et reconstitue un arbre généalogique de sa famille, les familles Rozenzweig et Rosenberg dont 48 membres sont morts dans l'enfer des camps de concentration. La rapide présentation de ses reliques à laquelle procède Babette permet à Amy d'avoir accès à ses ancêtres, mais Babette qui reconstitue, reconstruit, ne fait pas le deuil de ses morts. Elle a été dévorée par la guerre : elle possède des documents qui lui donnent l'impression de régner sur un royaume des morts dans lequel s'agitent des ombres. Ricœur insiste sur l'importance du geste de sépulture, sur l'importance des rites sociaux : « [S]on trajet est celui même du deuil qui transforme en présence intérieure l'absence physique de l'objet perdu. » (Ricœur 2000, 476) Babette collectionne des faits du passé de sa famille, mais pour elle sa véritable naissance a eu lieu lors de sa conversion au catholicisme. Depuis, elle vit au rythme de sa nostalgie d'une France désuète et déréalisée, mais surtout dans une bigoterie grâce à laquelle elle a pu se réinventer. Elle impose aussi à sa maison des nettoyages qui tel un baptême purificateur la délivrent de toutes traces du passé. C'est au cours d'une telle phase de nettoyage, alors qu'une machine se détracte et se transforme en monstre, qu'Amy découvre dans le cagibi du *basement* « sur une paillasse sale, une femme très, très âgée, assise à côté d'un vieillard grabataire » (Mavrikakis 2008b, 80). Les regardant dans le faisceau d'une lampe de poche, elle se rend compte que ce sont des vieillards prématurés. « Voici Elsa Rozenzweig et voici son mari, Georges Rosenberg, tes grands-parents » (Mavrikakis 2008b, 83), hurle alors Babette rattrapée par son passé et qui a vu un jour dans son *basement* les spectres de ses parents morts à Auschwitz :

> C'est là qu'ils disparurent après avoir laissé leurs deux filles dans cette famille catholique de Normandie. C'est là qu'ils s'envolèrent en fumée. Oui, j'ai les lettres, les témoignages, j'ai tout, caché dans le placard de ma chambre. [...] Elsa et Georges Rosenberg que tu vois ici sont morts à Auschwitz. Elle, maman, le 18 décembre 1943, dans une chambre à gaz. Lui, papa, au mois de mai 1944, quelque temps avant la Libération. (Mavrikakis 2008b, 84)

Babette lave et récure pour ne pas étouffer sous les cendres des siens, « pour ne pas avoir les poumons obstrués par les fumées grises et funèbres » (Mavrikakis 2008b,

85). Alors que sa sœur Denise ne veut plus rien savoir du passé et lui interdit même de l'évoquer devant elle, Babette est habitée par ce passé qui l'obsède malgré elle. Les spectres[3] de ses parents sont revenus la hanter pour qu'elle puisse leur montrer la voie vers la délivrance de leur condition de juif errant, et les libérer de cette religion maudite en les convertissant au catholicisme. Pour Amy, ils sont l'incarnation du mal, de la douleur et des souffrances que l'homme peut imposer à l'homme. Elle va donc s'occuper de ses grands-parents, les prendre dans ses bras, les coucher dans son lit, les emmener faire une promenade en voiture décapotable pour qu'ils puissent voir le ciel. Mais ses grands-parents ont vu dans son regard la souffrance qu'Amy porte en elle. Alors qu'Amy prend son grand-père Georges dans ses bras, elle entend pour la première fois sa voix qui lui souffle de mettre le feu à tout cela. Sa décision est prise, elle va mettre fin à sa souffrance et à celle de toute sa famille par le feu. Le feu embrasera le ciel pour la dernière fois.

Laurent Demanze qui a travaillé sur le récit de filiation à partir des romans de Pierre Bergounioux et de Pierre Michon entre autres, a constaté que ces récits peinent à pactiser avec le deuil et la perte, « disent au contraire les dérèglements d'un deuil impossible à faire, d'une transmission brisée, sans doute parce que cette perte n'est pas la leur. Comme si ces héritiers avaient reçu en partage un deuil et prenaient à leur compte la douleur d'un autre » (Demanze 2009, 15). Il s'appuie dans sa démonstration sur l'article de Freud, *Deuil et mélancolie* (auquel se réfère aussi le titre du roman de Catherine Mavrikakis, *Deuils cannibales et mélancoliques*), et sur les travaux de Nicolas Abraham et de Maria Torok, qui ont analysé le phénomène du fantôme qui prend possession de l'héritier. Pour ces derniers, ce ne sont pas les trépassés qui viennent hanter, mais les lacunes laissées par les secrets des autres. Si ces revenants ne sont qu'une invention des vivants, cette prise de possession a partie liée à l'anthropophagie et au cannibalisme, comme nous avons pu le constater avec l'apparition d'un os d'un être humain dans le cerveau d'Aimée dans *Forêts*. Ils peuvent aussi imposer à l'héritier des actes insolites, lorsqu'il est confronté au désastre d'un parcours familial ou aux ébranlements d'un désastre historique et le forcer à répéter les catastrophes puisque l'héritier a quasiment dévoré les fantômes du passé. C'est l'acte de cannibalisation réalisé par Amy qui prend la décision de faire disparaître sa famille par le feu : « Il me faut incendier le ciel violet et foutre le feu à ce qu'il reste d'Auschwitz. » (Mavrikakis 2008b, 193) Mais cet acte ne l'a pas libérée : mère à son tour d'une fille devenue adulte, Heaven, elle devra constater que les spectres la hantent, elle aussi.

Catherine Coquio dans *Le mal de vérité ou l'utopie de la mémoire*, s'appuyant sur les recherches de Hirsch, se demande quelle est la signification de ce besoin frustré de savoir qui pousse les enfants à se livrer aux souffrances des parents ou grands-parents. Nous avons ici quelques éléments de réponses à ses questions.

Amy a repris à son compte un double trauma, celui de la génération des témoins, ses grands-parents, celui des deux sœurs qui, elles, ont refoulé ce passé indicible – et ce d'autant plus que la transmission ne fonctionne pas, la relation mère-fille étant impossible et la relation mère de substitution-fille étant hautement traumatique. Le diagnostic est clair, Amy souffre d'un syndrome post-traumatique intergénérationnel auquel vient se greffer sa culpabilité de survivante. La catastrophe de la Seconde Guerre mondiale a provoqué dans le cas de l'héritière Amy la rupture de la filiation de sa mère et de sa tante, la dislocation d'un système culturel avec des religions concurrentielles, une obsession de deuil pour sa tante et un interdit de deuil pour sa mère.

Conclusion : deux textes, deux voies et deux voix

À travers ces deux textes de Catherine Mavrikakis et de Wajdi Mouawad, nous avons pu analyser comment les héritiers des catastrophes du vingtième siècle sont confrontés aux temps antérieurs de leurs familles respectives, même si celles-ci ont décidé de rompre avec le passé et de commencer une vie nouvelle dans un monde qui se serait débarrassé des scories du passé pour se tourner vers un futur innocent. En cela, ils s'inscrivent tous les deux dans une écriture de la postmémoire comme l'a analysée Marianne Hirsch dans *Family Frames* en donnant la parole aux héritiers. Laurent Demanze avait fait dans son article la constatation suivante : « L'héritier est à la fois *dépossédé* de son inscription généalogique et *possédé* par ces vies antérieures de l'ascendance » (Demanze 2009, 12), car si les familles ont enfoui leurs secrets, la mémoire familiale s'inscrit malgré tout dans les interstices du corps des descendants et l'habite, qu'ils le veuillent ou non.

Cependant, il est intéressant de constater que les réponses de ces deux auteurs divergent fondamentalement ; les histoires familiales se répètent chez Mouawad, du moins dans son quatuor *Le sang des promesses,* la transmission étant à chaque fois interrompue ou rendue impossible. Pour l'auteur, il faut trouver le moment de rédemption, c'est pourquoi la quête est au cœur de sa création pour cerner les lacunes, recoller les morceaux et retrouver les racines ou les rhizomes. Et c'est justement cette quête douloureuse qui permet d'accéder à la catharsis et de rompre avec le cercle infernal des répétitions douloureuses. Chez Mavrikakis, par contre, nous avons, dans le cas d'Amy, la protagoniste de *Le ciel de Bay City*, à faire à une transmission de traumatismes intergénérationnels qui provoquent en elle de telles souffrances qu'elle ne peut y échapper que par le meurtre de toute sa famille par le feu. Il n'y aura pas dans son cas d'effet cathartique, car les spectres continuent d'habiter sa propre fille.

Nous avons ici deux textes, deux voix et deux voies qui montrent combien le passé habite le présent et le poids qui pèse sur les héritiers.

1   Le colloque eut lieu en 2012 et fut publié sur le site de Fabula en 2013.

2   Nous faisons allusion ici au titre du documentaire de Rithy Panh, *L'image manquante*, réalisé en 2013 et sorti en salles en 2015, dans lequel l'écrivain et cinéaste franco-cambodgien interroge les trous et les creux de l'Histoire de la machine de guerre khmère rouge en reconstituant à partir de figurines de glaise l'extermination systématique de sa famille.

3   Les spectres sont très présents dans les textes de Catherine Mavrikakis : dans l'oratorio *Omaha Beach*, les soldats enterrés dans le cimetière américain de Coleville-sur-Mer en Normandie viennent faire la fête chaque nuit. Indépendamment de leur nationalité, Allemands, Canadiens, Américains dansent ensemble. Dans *La ballade d'Ali Baba*, c'est le spectre du père de la narratrice qui revient la hanter.

Bibliographie

Abraham, Nicolas / Torok, Maria : *L'écorce et le noyau*. Paris : Flammarion, 1987 [1978].

Asholt, Wolfgang / Bähler, Ursula (éds) : *Le savoir historique du roman contemporain* (= Revue des Sciences humaines, 321). Lille : Presses Universitaires du Septentrion, 2016.

Coquio, Catherine : « Le territoire des ogres ». In : *Fabula/Les colloques* (06/10/2013), http://www.fabula.org/colloques/document2150.php (consultation 20/02/2017).

Coquio, Catherine : *Le mal de vérité ou l'utopie de la mémoire*. Paris : Armand Colin, 2015.

Demanze, Laurent : « Les possédés et les dépossédés ». In : *Études françaises* 45,3 (2009), 11-23.

Dumontet, Danielle : « *Fleurs de crachat* de Catherine Mavrikakis ». In : Dupuis, Gilles / Ertler, Klaus-Dieter (éds) : *À la carte. Le roman québécois (2000-2005)*. Frankfurt am Main : Peter Lang, 2007, 263-282.

Hirsch, Marianne : *Family Frames. Photography Narrative and Postmemory*. Cambridge : Harvard University Press, 2012a [1997].

Hirsch, Marianne : *The Generation of Postmemory. Writing and Visual Culture After the Holocaust*. New York : Columbia Press University, 2012b.

Mavrikakis, Catherine : *Deuils cannibales et mélancoliques*. Montréal : Trois, 2000.

Mavrikakis, Catherine : *Fleurs de crachat*. Montréal : Leméac, 2005.

Mavrikakis, Catherine : *Omaha Beach*. Montréal : Héliotrope, 2008a.

Mavrikakis, Catherine : *Le ciel de Bay City*. Montréal : Héliotrope, 2008b.

Mavrikakis, Catherine : *La ballade d'Ali Baba*. Montréal/Paris : Héliotrope/Sabine Wespieser Éditeur, 2014.

Mouawad, Wajdi : *Littoral. Le sang des promesses / 1*. Montréal : Leméac, 1999.

Mouawad, Wajdi : *Incendies. Le sang des promesses / 2*. Montréal : Leméac, 2003.

Mouawad, Wajdi : *Forêts. Le sang des promesses / 3*. Montréal : Leméac, 2006.

Mouawad, Wajdi : *Le sang des promesses. Puzzle, racines et rhizomes*. Montréal : Leméac, 2009.

Ricœur, Paul : *La mémoire, l'histoire, l'oubli*. Paris : Seuil, 2000.

Viart, Dominique / Vercier, Bruno : *La littérature française au présent*. Paris : Bordas, 2005.

Daniel POITRAS (Toronto)

Crise du présentisme et voyage dans le temps à bord du *Volkswagen Blues* de Jacques Poulin

Summary

Jacques Poulin's novel *Volkswagen Blues* has mainly been studied as a road trip throughout America. The adventures of Jack and Pitsémine would symbolize Quebec's openness toward its American situation, and almost the beginning of a new era characterized by a multicultural world of hybridity. Rather than emphasizing the questions of identity or *américanité*, I propose to focus on the semantics of historical times at work in the novel, and more precisely on the temporal crisis during which it was written: 'présentisme.' As they travel, the two protagonists are confronted with a folkloric or touristic present time which can be overcome only through the channeling of history. Books, museums, sites, people, and roads deepen their experience of time and, through the transformative process of the road trip, generate their metamorphosis. But to what end, if neither History nor an open future exist anymore?

> *Quel temps / résiste / au temps présent*
> *quelle voix / recycle / en feu / cette image de souffre*
> *plus vive / que l'écran / des ressources / et des drames*
> *inusités / issus / du continent*
> (Beausoleil 2012, 28)

Remarques préliminaires

« Quel temps / résiste / au temps présent » ? L'enchaînement, à première vue, témoigne bien d'une crise du temps. Mais le verbe, au centre, est en quelque sorte décalé ; il semble contenir un appel, celui de « résiste[r] », afin d'échapper au présent tyrannique. Cette crise et cet appel, je crois les retrouver dans le roman *Volkswagen Blues* (1984) de Jacques Poulin, qui traite pourtant avant tout, du moins en apparence, de spatialité. J'adopterai le regard de l'historien en faisant l'hypothèse que ce roman, en plus de porter sur la traversée de l'espace américain, témoigne d'une crise de l'historicité, souvent associée à la nébuleuse postmodernité, mais que j'aborderai ici avec le concept, beaucoup plus opératoire lorsqu'il s'agit de temporalité, du présentisme. Avec ce concept, François Hartog (2003) cherchait à décrire le passage du régime d'historicité moderne – où le futur est l'horizon clef – à celui du présentisme, où futur et passé sont en quelque sorte siphonnés vers le présent, ce qui interdit les projections dans un temps long et engendre un rapport au temps dominé par l'immédiateté et la courte vue.

J'éviterai de m'appuyer sur le cadre post-référendaire ou sur la montée du multiculturalisme, souvent utilisés pour situer *Volkswagen Blues* dans son temps. Si Poulin lui-même admettait rechercher, à travers ce roman, la « part de l'âme québécoise qui est américaine » (Poulin dans Vasseur/Roy 1984, 50), c'était sans aborder de front la question nationale. Par ailleurs, si plusieurs des enjeux, tropes et mythes de ce roman se retrouvent dans d'autres ouvrages de l'auteur, je fais le pari qu'on peut repérer, grâce à la sémantique des temporalités historiques (cf. Koselleck 1990), des articulations du passé, du présent et du futur (diégétiques et extra-diégétiques) qui permettent de situer le roman dans le régime d'historicité du présentisme. S'il est vrai, comme le mentionnait Guri Ellen Barstad, que « *Volkswagen Blues* est un voyage à travers l'Histoire » (2016, 115), je montrerai plus précisément que dans la description du *road trip*, plusieurs thématiques, portraits et enchaînements s'éclairent particulièrement bien lorsqu'on les envisage en fonction d'un passé et d'un futur expérimentés comme largement inaccessibles.

Sur la route, Jack et Pitsémine, les héros d'infortune de cette crise de l'historicité, doivent surmonter une série d'illusions et de nostalgies, mais sans perdre de vue le passé. Narrateurs opiniâtres et historiens patentés, ils carburent moins à l'espace qu'à la temporalité : sans elle, le *road trip* s'atrophierait dans un présent plat, violent ou kitsch. Par la vertu transformatrice du parcours, ils semblent parfois rouvrir ce futur bouché et résorber l'impasse du présentisme. Mais n'est-ce pas au prix des aspirations collectives qui, sacrifiées pour aller de l'avant, résonnent tout au long du roman, à la fois appels et tentations ? C'est bien l'un des paradoxes du présentisme que le roman met en scène : si le futur est démagnétisé, il y a tout de même des itinéraires qui, désenclavés des grands récits, mènent tant bien que mal vers un futur inédit.

Savoir livresque et narrativité

Le roman s'ouvre sur une énigmatique carte postale écrite par le frère de Jack montrant un paysage de Gaspésie, une écriture illisible – qui s'avérera être celle de Jacques Cartier – et une signature : *Ton frère Théo*. Devinant un appel à l'aide, Jack part à la recherche de son frère qu'il n'a pas vu depuis 20 ans et qui est vraisemblablement perdu quelque part aux États-Unis. Il équipe en conséquence son vieux *Volkswagen*, qui devient une véritable maison mobile, ultime ancrage autour duquel s'aggloméreront les rencontres, les souvenirs, les cartes et les livres. Sur la route qui le mènera de Gaspé à San Francisco, il rencontrera une auto-stoppeuse marchant pieds nus, Pitsémine, qui se prendra au jeu de l'enquête et deviendra sa complice.

D'emblée, on est frappé par l'importance accordée au savoir livresque par Poulin, qui a lui-même expérimenté, pour écrire ce roman, le *road trip* vers l'ouest avec carnets, livres et appareil photo à la main (cf. Poulin dans Vasseur/Roy 1984, 52). En tout, l'auteur aura consacré six années à ce livre, dont une dédiée à la recherche. Les références littéraires, historiques et musicales abondent, mais n'ont en fait rien de décoratif et ne sont surtout pas opposées à une expérience plus sensible, plus ‹ vraie ›. À cet égard, parmi les caractéristiques mentionnées par Jean Morency (1994, 9) pour décrire le mythe américain (sentiment de l'espace, thématique de l'errance, volonté de rupture avec le groupe, méfiance à l'égard de la culture, attrait ressenti pour la nature, entrecroisement des rêves prométhéen et dyonisien), Poulin ne sacrifie pas la culture, même si celle-ci, pour être énoncée, nécessite le recours au passé ou à la mémoire. Les livres, les musées, les bibliothèques, les cartes et les plaques sont en fait tous chargés de contes et de récits ; ils donnent une profondeur historique au périple, qui est constamment dédoublé : l'exploration de l'espace et l'accès à l'histoire forment une dialectique.

Parmi les scènes qui illustrent l'importance donnée aux supports narratifs (diégétiques) dans le roman, celle de l'excursion touristique sur le Mississippi est révélatrice. Jack est d'abord récalcitrant devant l'initiative de Pitsémine ; il constate que le bateau à vapeur des années 1820 utilisé pour l'occasion, le Natchez, est un faux, « une réplique construite à l'intention des touristes » (Poulin 1998, 143). On y sert, notamment, des *hot-dogs*. Mais la situation est renversée lorsqu'il découvre que le capitaine, érudit, a la capacité de faire revivre l'histoire, par exemple en parlant de l'importance de la ville de Saint-Louis, plaque tournante pour les explorateurs et les pionniers aux siècles passés.

En général, c'est Pitsémine qui tient éveillé Jack en lui racontant des histoires. En direction de Chicago, elle décide d'aller se reposer et Jack ouvre la radio, qui crache les nouvelles du jour : augmentation du chômage, inondation en Louisiane, sécheresse en Égypte, bombardement du Liban, etc. Il s'agit de l'une des rares entrées de l'actualité qui permet de dater un peu plus précisément le roman. Mais l'irruption ne dure pas. Irrité, le conducteur tourne le bouton et tombe sur une « chanson française, lointaine et comme perdue dans une mer de paroles anglaises – une vieille chanson » (Poulin 1998, 109). La musique supplée à l'absence de la narration de Pitsémine et, parce que la chanson est *vieille* et qu'elle rappelle des souvenirs à Jack, elle colmate la présence du passé momentanément ébréchée par l'actualité brute, par le présent implacable. Mieux encore, *française*, la chanson vient conforter une autre quête qui s'approfondira au fur et à mesure du parcours : celle des vestiges de la présence française en Amérique.

Le rôle de Pitsémine est déterminant à cet égard. Métisse (d'une mère inuit et d'un père québécois), femme-enfant, androgyne, mécanicienne, c'est elle qui répare le *Volks*, qui défriche le chemin et qui pousse Jack, écrivain timide, inquiet et mélancolique, à foncer. Mais elle est également une avide lectrice. Tout comme plusieurs autres personnages féminins des romans de Poulin, la « lectrice est une sage-femme qui aide l'écrivain à venir au monde » (Bernier 1998, 96). Pitsémine s'irrite lorsqu'on dit qu'une image vaut mille mots ; dans le *Volks*, elle écrit plutôt : « UN MOT VAUT MILLE IMAGES. » (Poulin 1984, 185) L'inscription en recoupe d'ailleurs une autre, que Jack avait découverte après l'achat du *Volks*, originaire d'Allemagne, et qui se lisait ainsi : « Die Sprache ist das Haus des Seins. » (‹ Le langage est la maison de l'être › ; Poulin 1998, 92)

Mais les deux inscriptions révèlent aussi une certaine urgence. Sous ses airs bon enfant, le *road trip* est une course contre la montre, ou plus précisément une course contre la perte de mémoire. C'est à ce propos, à mon avis, que le régime d'historicité du présentisme, qui émerge justement au tournant des années 1980, est pertinent pour comprendre *Volkswagen Blues*. Le roman est à l'opposé, sur le plan temporel, de *On the Road* de Jack Kerouac, roman publié en 1957 en plein régime d'historicité moderne, et qui mettait en scène des personnages frondeurs pour qui l'espace était ouvert à toutes les aventures et à tous les recommencements.

Les héros d'antan

Si Poulin confiait avoir peu de goût pour le roman à idées, *Volkswagen Blues* constituait néanmoins une vive critique des ambitions et des dérives des conquérants et des apprentis sorciers de tout acabit. La recherche de Théo, personnage prométhéen par excellence, devient le truchement pour parcourir à rebours les attentes et les figures du passé. « [M]on frère Théo, comme les pionniers, était absolument *convaincu qu'il était capable de faire tout ce qu'il voulait.* » (Poulin 1998, 149) En lui on « pouvait reconnaître Maurice Richard, Ernest Hemingway, Jim Clark, Louis Riel, Burt Lancaster, Van Gogh » (Poulin 1998, 240). Le joueur de hockey, l'écrivain chasseur de lions, le rebelle, le général, le peintre ; autant de figures d'intrépidité et de volontarisme. C'est à leur chute que le lecteur assistera tout au long du roman pour que puisse (re)naître l'écrivain.

Jack tient pourtant à ces figures, afin de préserver l'image qu'il se fait de son frère et aussi, de manière plus diffuse, de s'accrocher à un idéaltype de plus en plus décalé avec son propre horizon d'attente. Au début du parcours, en passant devant les panneaux de verre saupoudrés d'or de la Royal Bank Plaza de Toronto, il ne peut « s'empêcher de penser à l'or des Incas et à la légende de l'Eldorado. C'était comme si tous les rêves étaient encore possibles. Et pour Jack, dans le plus grand secret de son cœur, c'était comme si tous les héros du passé étaient encore des héros » (Poulin 1998, 85). Cette caractérisation s'applique bien sûr à l'écrivain idéal, confiant, arrogant, implacable, qui n'hésite pas à aller jusqu'au bord du gouffre et de l'épuisement pour arriver à son but ; bref, « il écrit comme un fou, comme un maniaque » (Poulin 1998, 51). Si ces contrastes (et le malaise lancinant qu'ils nourrissent) sont l'un des points de départ de *Volkswagen Blues*, la découverte du caractère anachronique de l'idéaltype prométhéen invite en retour à réinvestir le passé. À cet égard, le *road trip* suscitera une métamorphose non pas tant du caractère de Jack, mais plutôt de sa représentation du temps.

Une des façons utilisées par Poulin pour morceler et discréditer ce prométhéisme est de superposer les plans temporels et de réactiver le passé sous forme d'anticipation rétrospective, c'est-à-dire en invitant les protagonistes à retrouver certains horizons passés – comme celui, on le verra, des pionniers – afin de renouveler leur lecture du passé et du présent. La dimension ‹ enquête › du roman se prête particulièrement bien à cette réactivation. Au musée de Gaspé, le couple est ému par deux cartes géographiques, l'une de l'Amérique française et l'autre de l'Amérique précoloniale. Ces deux cartes, qui occuperont les pensées de Jack et de Pitsémine, permettent déjà de « distinguer très clairement le passé qui les isole du présent qui les unit » (L'Hérault 1989, 31). Cet isolement se résorbera partiellement à mesure qu'ils recréeront, à partir d'une géographie projetée, les horizons alternatifs (une Amérique française *et* une Amérique des Premières Nations en harmonie) dont les deux cartes sont porteuses.

S'il est facile d'écarter de la main les généraux sanguinaires et les cowboys racistes, il est plus difficile, pour Jack, de faire face aux héros ambigus, parmi lesquels il doit vite ranger son propre frère. Parmi ceux-ci, on retrouve le célèbre coureur des bois Étienne Brûlé. L'un des premiers blancs à explorer le continent et à se métisser avec les Amérindiens, est-il un symbole d'ouverture ou plutôt un *bum*, un débauché, et pis encore un traître – il aurait aidé les frères Kirke dans leur assaut de la ville de Québec en 1629 ? Le suspens accable Jack qui découvre peu après, au poste de police de Toronto, une fiche sur Théo où sont répertoriés ses effets personnels, entre autres un revolver, *On the Road* et un autre livre intitulé *The Oregon Trail Revisited*, de Gregory M. Franzwa. L'hypothèse d'un homme en cavale se confirme et le couple découvre bientôt que Théo aurait ici volé une carte, et là assommé un gardien de sécurité. Il aurait même participé, soupçonne Jack, au Front de libération du Québec.

Cette dernière hypothèse, comme en passant, tend à rapprocher les dérives de la violence individuelle et collective tout en insérant l'histoire québécoise dans une trame plus large en lui faisant partager cette part plus sombre de l'aventure américaine. Après tout, c'est Théo lui-même qui avait suggéré à son frère le pseudonyme de Jack Waterman, en l'honneur de Kerouac sans doute, mais aussi, peut-être, en faisant allusion aux Weathermen, groupe révolutionnaire états-unien de la fin des années 1960 qui, comme le FLQ, ne reculait pas devant la violence.

Sur le plan mémoriel, les souvenirs de Jack et le montage narratif héroïsant son frère sont de plus en plus flous. Bientôt, il admettra que Théo est « à moitié vrai et à moitié inventé » (Poulin 1998, 148), avant de conclure : « Tout cela ne tenait pas le coup. » (Poulin 1998, 240) Sur la piste de son frère, Jack découvrira bientôt une photographie datée de 1977 où Théo apparaît en compagnie d'Allen Ginsberg, de Lawrence Ferlinghetti et de quelques autres grandes figures de la contre-culture de San Francisco. Mais il est le seul, sur la photo, à ne pas être identifié. « Un homme sans identité, c'est un peu comme s'il disait un ‹ homme sans importance ›, non ? » (Poulin 1998, 293) De fait, lorsqu'il le retrouve enfin, à la toute fin du parcours, au coin des rues Market et Powell à San Francisco, Théo est en chaise roulante ; paralysé, il ne reconnaît plus son cadet et semble avoir oublié jusqu'à sa langue d'origine. Contrairement au capitaine Achab, héros melvillien qui meurt de façon grandiose en poursuivant son monstre marin, Théo dépérit, aliéné, dans l'anonymat.

Il s'agira de l'ultime leçon à l'égard des dangers de la nostalgie au sujet d'une certaine Amérique. Pitsémine l'expérimentera elle aussi lorsqu'elle passera la nuit couchée à côté de la tombe du chef Mohawk Thayendanegea en espérant communier avec ses propres racines. Au matin, elle admettra : « Il ne s'est rien passé du tout. Échec total. » (Poulin 1998, 93-94) Un court chapitre au titre évocateur (« Mourir avec ses rêves ») viendra marquer la transition. Il met en scène Jack et Pitsémine qui fredonnent la chanson « Hobo Bill's Last Ride » de Jimmy Rodgers racontant l'histoire d'un itinérant qui finit par mourir dans un train (cf. Poulin 1998, 193). Le titre du chapitre peut être lu de deux façons : ou bien mourir sans avoir accompli ses rêves (comme Théo), ou bien mourir à certains rêves et, peut-être, s'éveiller à d'autres (comme Jack et Pitsémine). D'une façon ou d'une autre, il n'y a plus de retour possible.

Sur la route des pionniers

> *Parfois, en traversant l'Amérique, les voyageurs retrouvaient des parcelles du vieux rêve qui avaient été éparpillées ici et là.* (Poulin 1998, 110)

En cours de route, Jack et Pitsémine sont particulièrement marqués par le Museum of Westward Expansion à Saint-Louis, consacré à la conquête de l'Ouest. C'est désormais sur la piste de l'Oregon que le couple va s'acheminer. Ce choix consacre l'itinéraire déjà parcouru, puisque c'est également par le Saint-Laurent, le Mississippi et par la suite la piste de l'Oregon que les explorateurs et les pionniers s'étaient engouffrés dans les siècles passés. Pour marquer le caractère initiatique de leur parcours, Poulin souligne bien qu'en route, même à bord du vieux *Volks*, Jack et Pitsémine « parlaient à voix basse, comme dans une église, un cimetière, un lieu sacré » (Poulin 1998, 219). Le choix de ces trois lieux n'est pas anodin : il semble indiquer, autour du thème de la possibilité de *croire* en autre chose (ou en un autre futur), une oscillation entre le passé enterré du présentisme (un cimetière) et celui qui, coûte que coûte, survit (un lieu sacré, une église).

Mais la sacralisation à mots couverts du parcours n'indique pas un retour à l'origine. Comme l'écrivait Morency, le mythe américain symbolise moins la quête de l'éden perdu que celle de la « réitération du processus de métamorphose » (1994, 215). Ce processus, dans le roman, prend d'abord la forme d'une transformation du quotidien ; c'est lui, avec l'aide du savoir livresque, qui est susceptible de réactiver un certain passé potentiel. « On a beaucoup de choses à faire, dit la fille. – C'est vrai, dit-il. Il faut [...] apprendre des choses sur la conquête de l'Ouest. Apprendre à vivre. » (Poulin 1998, 175) Le quotidien dont ils veulent désormais s'inspirer n'est plus celui des héros, mais celui des gens ordinaires.

Significativement, lorsqu'il évoque ces derniers, Poulin ne fait plus intervenir les nombreuses références américaines et utilise plutôt comme support narratif (et comme guide de vie quotidienne) un livre d'histoire, *The Oregon Trail Revisited*, comme si « la fiction ne pouvait rendre justice à l'histoire ni accréditer adéquatement le courage de ces héros anonymes » (Lapointe 1989, 23). Avec le souci du réalisme et du détail qui le caractérise, Poulin multiplie les descriptions des véhicules, de la nourriture, de l'organisation des expéditions et des épreuves rencontrées sur les routes inhospitalières. Un dessin est particulièrement révélateur : celui d'un charriot du 19e siècle qui fait penser, comme le remarque d'ailleurs Jack, à « un bonnet de femme » (Poulin 1998, 218). L'association réaffirme comme en passant la valorisation du pôle ‹ féminin › du parcours vers l'ouest en resserrant l'intrigue autour de ces maisons roulantes qui, à l'instar du *Volks*, ont pour fonction de conserver une mémoire – notamment à travers les objets et les meubles transportés –, mais aussi de mener ailleurs et, ainsi, d'opérer la métamorphose.

À un moment du périple, pour s'assurer que le vieux *Volks* gravisse une colline particulièrement abrupte, Jack pense à sacrifier quelques-uns des nombreux livres qui l'alourdissent. Après tout, les pionniers sacrifiaient au besoin leurs meubles afin de poursuivre leur route. Le lecteur anticipe ce geste qui confirmerait l'émancipation de Jack du passé et enclencherait une phase de ‹ collage › à un réel plus brute, moins médié par la culture. Mais le dépouillement n'aura pas lieu. Lori Saint-Martin remarquait que dans l'œuvre de Poulin, si « les livres rapprochent de la vie », « ils empêchent [cependant] de la connaître de première main » (1999, 552). Mais cette acquisition directe, dans *Volkswagen Blues* et en plein présentisme, ne peut renvoyer à un présent en soi régénérateur. C'est une autre façon de réitérer que tout le bagage culturel du *Volks* est essentiel au périple ; sans la mise en récit du passé, qu'il s'agisse d'échanges ludiques, d'anticipations rétrospectives, d'apparitions soudaines ou de recherches plus érudites, le *road trip* tombe à plat.

Afin d'éprouver eux-mêmes le parcours cahoteux et, ainsi, charger l'espace de temps, Jack et Pitsémine se lisent à haute voix les péripéties des pionniers. Poulin brouille volontiers les repères temporels en multipliant, sans en avertir le lecteur, les transitions entre les actions passées et présentes. Déjà, cette superposition s'était produite au début du roman, où Jack était invité, et le lecteur avec lui, à se mettre à la place de Théo afin d'anticiper rétrospectivement son parcours (c'est-à-dire en fonction d'un autre horizon d'attente) pour trouver une piste afin d'amorcer l'enquête. Passé et présent s'étaient également brouillés lorsque Jack avait appris que le coureur des bois Étienne Brûlé était non pas un héros mais un *bum*, nouvelle qui l'avait assommé « comme un homme qui vient de recevoir une mauvaise nouvelle concernant un de ses proches » (Poulin 1998, 82). Avec les pionniers, il ne s'agit plus d'entrer dans la tête d'un (anti)héros, mais bien plutôt de recréer une situation où l'utopie n'était pas encore entachée par l'aventurisme violent ou par le progrès saccageur.

Mais la lecture à voix haute implique davantage que la réitération de l'histoire passée ; grâce à l'anticipation rétrospective, Jack et Pitsémine recréent le suspens (et l'horizon ouvert) expérimenté par les pionniers. Il y a bien « confusion entre le passé et le présent » (Pardiñas 1992, 60) ou plutôt, pour être plus précis, entremêlement. Ils débattent par exemple à propos du choix d'un guide : « Comme ça, vous avez un guide ? », demande Pitsémine. « Bien sûr, dit Jack [...], [o]n a choisi un francophone pour qu'il soit capable de s'entendre avec les Indiens. » (Poulin 1998, 195) Le candidat n'est pas francophone par hasard ; un peu moins compromis dans les crimes commis à l'égard des Amérindiens, il s'oppose au cowboy ou au général américain. Il permet de rêver tout haut à une histoire alternative qui serait la contrepartie de la trame violente, sanglante ou intolérante de l'histoire advenue.

Significativement, Jack choisit de baptiser ce nouveau guide Théo, comme s'il cherchait à absoudre momentanément son frère en mettant l'audace et la volonté de celui-ci au service d'un autre récit. Les indices trouvés précédemment sur Théo peuvent alors être interprétés autrement. Après tout, dans la liste des effets de Théo à Toronto, on retrouvait certes le très nietzschéen *On the Road,* mais également… *The Oregon Trail Revisited*. Qui plus est, lors de l'incident du musée, Théo a sans doute assommé un gardien, mais c'était pour mettre la main sur une carte de 1840 dessinée par un jésuite d'origine française et de la rapatrier au Québec. Geste culturel ou action criminelle ? Et puis, avant de devenir *bum* et d'y perdre son identité francophone, Théo n'avait-il pas fait des études en histoire, cette matière même qui aurait pu le sauver de sa chute présentiste et, qui sait, de son aliénation dans l'Amérique anglophone ? En d'autres mots, les crimes du frère de Jack, qui l'incriminent au présent, se relativisent si on les aborde à la lumière des fragments d'histoire et de mémoire qu'il nous a lui-même laissés comme une invitation à trouver une autre fin à son parcours.

Déracinement et futur à tâtons

Si la piste de Théo menait à l'horizon révolu du prométhéisme, celle de l'Oregon est conditionnée par le présentisme. L'accent mis par Poulin sur les détails quotidiens – plutôt que sur les finalités – du parcours des pionniers révélait déjà une des limites de l'itinéraire suivi par Jack et Pitsémine, qui avancent à tâtons sans pouvoir s'appuyer sur une grande quête fondatrice (comme la conquête de l'Ouest) ou sur une révolution quelconque à venir. Les deux protagonistes ne parviennent pas à « une vision plus équilibrée des choses qui leur permet de marier passé et avenir » (Barstad 2016, 116), puisqu'un tel équilibre entre les horizons du temps appartient plutôt au régime moderne d'historicité. Sur le plan narratif, cette avancée dans le brouillard est l'inverse de celle que scandait l'écrivain idéal de Jack au début du roman, qui tirait les ficelles d'une main de fer grâce à laquelle « les personnages savent très bien où ils vont » (Poulin 1998, 51).

La rencontre par le couple de Saul Bellow indique bien les contraintes et les possibilités de cette navigation à vue. Si l'écrivain américain, qui comprend bien le français, les encourage à poursuivre vers l'ouest, le vrai sens de la rencontre apparaît au moment où Jack, en feuilletant le roman *Les aventures d'Augie March* (1976) de Bellow, tombe sur ce passage : « *Je suis une sorte de Colomb pour tous ceux qui sont à portée de main et je crois fermement qu'on peut les rejoindre dans cette* terra incognita *immédiate qui s'étend devant chaque regard.* » (Poulin 1998, 121) Ce Colomb nouveau genre ne travaille plus pour les rois ou les visionnaires ; il est là pour ceux qui vivent « *à portée de main* », c'est-à-dire ceux qui, n'ayant plus le luxe du temps long, s'acheminent vers cette *terra incognita* immédiate. L'oxymore est emblématique du présentisme pour une autre raison aussi : puisque cette *terra incognita* s'étend devant chaque regard, elle n'a plus la teneur collective des utopies passées et risque de s'effilocher dans le postmodernisme.

La station finale du roman, à San Francisco, met en évidence cette limite. Dès leur arrivée, Jack et Pitsémine se rendent au coin de Haight et Ashbury, haut lieu de la contre-culture des années 1960. Ils espèrent y retrouver les « traces du mouvement, quelques indices qui auraient rappelé que des milliers de jeunes et de moins jeunes, venus de tous les coins du pays, avaient essayé de mettre en pratique dans ce secteur une nouvelle conception de la vie et des rapports entre les gens » (Poulin 1998, 306). Bref, de retrouver l'une des incarnations, à l'époque contemporaine, de l'utopie nourrie par les pionniers. Mais ils déchantent vite et constatent que les commerces et les touristes ont remplacé les rêves de jadis. Pitsémine, de son côté, expérimente la même déconvenue lorsqu'elle constate, après avoir rendu hommage aux autochtones qui ont occupé, entre 1969 et 1971, l'île d'Alcatraz, au nord de San Francisco, que les Premières Nations semblent vouées à subir des défaites.

La mise en parallèle du constat d'échec de la contre-culture – qui a pourtant contribué à émanciper les sociétés occidentales –, et de l'occupation d'Alcatraz – qui a pourtant fait avancer la cause des Amérindiens –, incite moins à évaluer la pertinence factuelle du bilan historique du roman qu'à identifier le rapport à l'historicité dont il témoigne. S'il est vrai, en général, que dans l'œuvre de Poulin « le bonheur collectif est irréalisable » (Lapointe 1989, 20), il est particulièrement délicat ou pénible, au tournant des années 1980, de parler des rêves émancipatoires des années 1960. La possibilité d'un avenir autre que maintenait la tension temporelle propre à la modernité s'étiole.

Pitsémine elle-même, qui remplace *de facto* les guides, autochtones ou européens, que les pionniers engageaient au 19ᵉ siècle, n'a pas de plan fixe : elle ne sait jamais d'avance où elle ira. Poulin reconduit ici, sans doute, le cliché de l'‹ Indien errant ›, mais l'hybridité de la Métisse – qui participe aussi à l'aventure des Blancs – lui permet de mettre en scène une déliquescence généralisée des aspirations collectives. Le contraste est en fait évident entre la caractérisation de la Métisse selon les traits typiquement attribués à la figure de l'Amérindien (proximité avec la nature, liberté sexuelle, guide spirituel, etc.) et son impossibilité à vivre au sein d'une culture amérindienne. Ce décalage permet à Poulin d'exploiter des stéréotypes afin de subvertir des attitudes eurocentriques (cf. Vautier 1994), mais il amène également la Métisse à privilégier une identité hybride à son identité amérindienne. C'est une autre façon de mettre en scène l'impossible retour en arrière : ni dans le prométhéisme, ni dans les coutumes.

On a écrit à propos de *Volkswagen Blues* que Jacques Poulin « réconcilie l'homme québécois avec sa destinée continentale » (Morency 1994, 213). Le mythe de l'enfance perdue, qui anime la littérature américaine et toute l'œuvre de Poulin, cèderait ici à celui de la renaissance à travers la rencontre. Mais il s'agit pourtant, dans ce cas-ci, d'une réconciliation partielle, particulièrement au plan temporel. L'acte sexuel raté entre Pitsémine et Jack sur le bord de la route indique les limites du rapprochement entre les deux protagonistes. Vraisemblablement, malgré un parcours transformateur, Jack ne peut assimiler cette autre américanité – et presque cette nature – que représente Pitsémine. Extirpé de la nostalgie à l'égard de Théo, Jack a troqué un horizon anachronique pour un horizon embrouillé. Et pourtant, il repartira de San Francisco plus ou moins transformé vers le Québec, Pitsémine préférant, de son côté, rester quelque temps à San Francisco, cette ville mosaïque où les repères identitaires lui semblent floués.

La métamorphose partielle de Jack, libéré de l'horizon prométhéen, et le déracinement de Pitsémine ne mènent pourtant pas à la consécration d'un multiculturalisme de cohabitation. Si la Métisse aboutit à San Francisco – « elle pensait que cette ville, où les races semblaient vivre en harmonie, était un bon endroit » (Poulin 1998, 318) –, Poulin ne promeut pas nécessairement une assimilation de l'identité autochtone de son héroïne dans la mosaïque multiculturelle. S'il est vrai que Poulin tend à faire de Pitsémine le symbole d'une « hybridité générique », il n'est pas sûr qu'il lui enlève toute agentivité en tant qu'Autochtone (Macfarlane 2009, 15 ; trad. D. Poitras). Après tout, malgré le parcours mémoriel cahoteux qui a mené Jack et son amie de la Gaspésie à la Californie, San Francisco n'est qu'une halte pour l'un et pour l'autre. Pitsémine n'y dissout pas ses origines dans un magma d'hybridité qui mettrait sur un pied d'égalité les revendications territoriales des nations autochtones et celles des autres minorités (cf. Macfarlane 2009, 15). Poulin donne plutôt un dernier ressort au *road trip* en confiant le *Volks* à Pitsémine, condamnée à une quête qui ne peut s'accomplir à San Francisco, et en faisant dire à Jack que son amie est « quelque chose de neuf, quelque chose qui commence. Vous êtes quelque chose qui ne s'est encore jamais vu » (Poulin 1998, 247).

Conclusion

Les personnages que Poulin met en scène, s'ils doivent avancer à tâtons vers un inconnu qui n'a plus rien d'une terre promise, font tout au moins éclater les grands récits. À l'image des pérégrinations des pionniers, ces itinéraires s'effectuent au jour le jour, mais contrairement à elles, ils ne sont plus magnétisés par une utopie mobilisatrice comme celle de la conquête de l'Ouest. À la fin d'une entrevue, le magazine *Nuit blanche* mentionnait à Poulin le contraste entre l'espace serré du *Volks* et la vastitude de l'Amérique. L'auteur répondit : « [J]e peux seulement ajouter que ça me semble exprimer ou évoquer, sur le plan symbolique, la situation du Québec en Amérique, dont on parlait au début. Et j'espère que cette situation débouchera elle aussi sur une sorte d'ouverture... » (Vasseur/Roy 1984, 52) Le *Volks*, métonymie d'un Québec qui cherche sa place ? Mais de quelle place peut-il s'agir si l'ouverture est laissée à elle-même ? Pitsémine incarnait les mêmes questions à propos des nations autochtones. À coup sûr, la crise d'historicité mise en scène dans *Volkswagen Blues* prévaut encore largement à notre époque.

Bibliographie

Barstad, Guri Ellen : « Quelque chose qui commence ? Une lecture de deux romans québécois ». In : Hjelde, Arnstein / Kvam, Sigmund et al. (éds) : *Language and Nations. Crossroads and Connections.* Münster : Waxmann, 2016, 105-124.

Beausoleil, Claude : *Ficelle n°110 Amérikerouac.* Montréal : Rougier, 2012.

Bernier, France : *Du paratexte au texte : lire l'Amérique dans* Volkswagen Blues *de Jacques Poulin.* Mémoire de maîtrise. Université Laval, 1998.

Hartog, François : *Régimes d'historicité. Présentisme et expériences du temps.* Paris : Seuil, 2003.

Lapointe, Jean-Pierre : « Sur la piste américaine : le statut des références littéraires dans l'œuvre de Jacques Poulin ». In : *Voix et Images* 15,1 (1989), 15-27.

L'Hérault, Pierre : « *Volkswagen Blues* : traverser les identités ». In : *Voix et Images* 15,1 (1989), 28-42.

Koselleck, Reinhart : *Le futur passé. Contribution à la sémantique des temps historiques.* Paris : EHESS, 1990 [1982].

Macfarlane, Heather : « *Volkswagen Blues* Twenty-Five Years Later : Revisiting Poulin's Pitsémine ». In : *Studies in Canadian Literature/Études en littérature canadienne* 34,2 (2009), 5-21.

Morency, Jean : *Le mythe américain dans les fictions d'Amérique : de Washington à Jacques Poulin.* Québec : Nuit Blanche, 1994.

Pardiñas, Blanc Navarro : « Phénoménologie de l'acte de lecture : l'exemple de *Volkswagen Blues* de Jacques Poulin ». In : *Tangence* 36 (1992), 52-62.

Poulin, Jacques : *Volkswagen Blues.* Montréal : Babel, 1998 [1984].

Saint-Martin, Lori : « L'androgynie, la peur de l'autre et les impasses de l'amour : *La tournée d'automne* de Jacques Poulin ». In : *Voix et Images* 24,3 (1999), 541-557.

Vasseur, François / Roy, Michelle : « Voyage à travers l'Amérique ». In : *Nuit blanche* 14 (1984), 50-52.

Vautier, Marie : « Postmodern Myth, Post-European History, and the Figure of the Amerindian : François Barcelo, George Bowering, and Jacques Poulin ». In : *Canadian Literature* 141 (1994), 15-33.

Conflits culturels
Cultural Conflicts

Hans-Jürgen LÜSEBRINK (Saarbrücken)

Écrire la crise du multiculturalisme – fictions et positionnements dans la littérature québécoise contemporaine (Monique LaRue, Abla Farhoud, Larry Tremblay)

Summary

Divided into four main sections, this contribution first points out the issues and challenges of the rise of fundamentalist movements since the beginning of the new century. In a second step it analyzes, as a paradigmatic example of the literary reflection of conflicts related to the more and more culturally diverse Canadian society, the essay *L'arpenteur et le navigateur* (1996) by the Quebec writer Monique LaRue and the novel *Le sourire de la petite juive* (2011) by Abla Farhoud, who was born in Lebanon before emigrating to Canada. A very contemporary image of terrorism – and especially of very young terrorists – is examined in the third section which concerns the novel *L'orangeraie* (2013) by the Quebec novelist Larry Tremblay whose plot is situated in Palestine and then in Quebec. The fourth and final part examines Monique LaRue's most recent essay *La leçon de Jérusalem* (2015) which, from a Quebec point of view, focuses on the Holocaust as it is reflected by Margarete von Trotta's documentary movie on Hannah Arendt and her reports on the Auschwitz trial in the early 1960s. LaRue's *Lesson of Jerusalem* perceives the reflection on the Holocaust with its radical and its fatal denial of otherness and diversity as a platform to rethink and reevaluate multiculturalism and interculturalism in the Canadian and Quebec contexts.

Enjeux et défis – promesses et transformations du multiculturalisme

Le multiculturalisme a constitué – et continue à représenter dans une certaine mesure –, à la fois une réalité sociale, de plus en plus importante dans toutes les sociétés occidentales, et une sorte d'utopie de convivialité harmonieuse possible entre des communautés provenant d'horizons culturels très divers. Né en 1941, d'abord avec l'adjectif « multiculturel » employé par la journaliste Iris Barry dans un article du *New York Herald Tribune Books*[1], le terme désigne une « société cosmopolite, pluriraciale, multilingue, composée d'individus transnationaux » pour qui « le vieux nationalisme d'antan n'avait plus la moindre signification » (Lacorne 1997, 20). Lié, aux États-Unis, au mouvement des droits civiques des années 1960 et à l'égalité politique obtenue par les Noirs américains, le terme de multiculturalisme se réfère en même temps à la « réalité sociale des grandes métropoles du Canada, comme Montréal et Toronto, depuis la fin des années 1950 » (Lacorne 1997, 20). Si le multiculturalisme au sens sociologique, comme co-existence de communautés ethno-culturelles diverses au sein d'une société donnée, a pris de nouvelles dimensions au cours de ces dernières décennies, la connotation conviviale et harmonieuse qui lui avait été associée, notamment dans le cadre canadien, depuis les années 1970, s'est trouvée remise en cause par trois nouveaux éléments.

Premièrement, la renaissance des nationalismes – en Europe, mais aussi, dans une moindre mesure, en Amérique du Nord, depuis le début des années 1990, et au Québec par exemple autour du référendum de 1995 –, a contribué à remettre en question le modèle de la société multiculturelle et à faire renaître des schémas anciens de ressentiments, voire de xénophobie et de haine.

En second lieu, et en liaison avec les deux évolutions mentionnées ci-dessus, le multiculturalisme comme modèle de convivialité entre différentes communautés ethno-culturelles au sein d'une société donnée, est devenu de plus en plus problématique à transposer dans la réalité ; il a généré de plus en plus de conflits et semble être devenu pour beaucoup un modèle devenu désormais difficile, voire impossible à gérer. Lacorne (1997, 20-21) souligne, en effet, que la « fragmentation sociale de l'Amérique des années 1960, aggravée par la révolte des étudiants contre la guerre du Viêtnam et les émeutes des ghettos noirs », était à la source des « passions multiculturelles » des années 1980-1990, suivies d'une crise du multiculturalisme liée à l'essor du communautarisme ethno-culturel depuis les années 1990. Le romancier Neil Bissoondath, professeur à l'Université Laval à Québec, avance les raisons suivantes pour la crise et les contradictions du multiculturalisme, qu'il diagnostique dans son livre *Le marché aux illusions. La méprise du multiculturalisme* :

> Parce que nous avons renoncé à établir les limites de la diversité, parce que nous avons accepté avec beaucoup d'insouciance la mentalité de la division, nous perdons pied devant la confusion des valeurs qui règne. Nous sommes devenus craintifs et hésitants au nom du multiculturalisme alors qu'il nous aurait fallu fixer la frontière de ce qui est acceptable ; nous confondons l'imposition de limites avec le manque de respect et nous courons le danger d'être entraînés dans un chaos éthique. Nous disons non à l'infibulation volontaire, mais nous croyons pouvoir dire oui à la ségrégation raciale volontaire [...]. Excision, système judiciaire parallèle, ségrégation raciale, confusion. Il semble que je dresse ici le catalogue des aspects les plus noirs du multiculturalisme. Sans doute. (Bissoondath 1995, 155)

L'instauration de la Commission Bouchard-Taylor au Québec en 2007 et la genèse des termes et des concepts d'interculturalisme et d'accommodements raisonnables semblent être à la fois des indicateurs et des conséquences de cette mise en cause du multiculturalisme canadien, au-delà même du Québec. Le modèle multiculturel, créé pour réaliser une société conviviale et harmonieuse, est devenu de plus en plus conflictuel ; il met l'accent, d'après l'écrivain canadien Neil Bissoondath d'origine trinidadienne, sur ce qui « différencie » et « divise » (1995, 233), et non pas sur ce qui rend semblable et unit les différentes cultures au sein d'une société. « La société multiculturelle », souligne encore Bissoondath,

> a eu tendance à réduire le rôle et l'autonomie de l'individu en cherchant à confiner les individus à l'intérieur de limites précises et fortement tributaires des stéréotypes. Le rôle positif que l'ethnicité – les antécédents ethniques, culturels et historiques – pourrait jouer dans la création de la totalité du moi en est devenu confus. (1995, 222)

On pourrait ajouter à ces constats de Bissoondath qui datent du milieu des années 1990 que ce rôle de l'ethnicité est devenu surtout beaucoup plus controversé et conflictuel avec les deux évolutions esquissées : celle de la renaissance nationaliste et celle de la percée des courants ethno-religieux radicalisés, qui ont eu un impact de tout premier plan sur la politique multiculturelle et la gestion quotidienne de la diversité, mais aussi sur la perception sociale et la gestion au quotidien des processus de migration.

En troisième lieu, les flux de migrations des dernières décennies – qui n'ont pas été beaucoup plus importants quantitativement que ceux des décennies antérieures – ont néanmoins entraîné des dimensions conflictuelles beaucoup plus fortes et importantes. Ces conflits que l'on pourrait qualifier d'interculturels, sont certes dûs, en partie, à la renaissance mentionnée des nationalismes ; mais surtout, et en premier lieu, à l'essor de nouveaux modèles identitaires, souvent anti-modernistes, anti-occidentaux et liés à des courants politico-religieux radicalisés. Leur essor est d'abord lié à la Révolution Iranienne en 1978 et à la vague de radicalisation qu'elle a entraînée ; mais ces nouveaux modèles ne concernent pas seulement l'islamisme radical. Il touche aussi des courants radicaux liés à d'autres religions, comme l'orthodoxie juive et les mouvements évangélistes occidentaux ; et il est lié, au moins indirectement, aux aspects les plus sombres de l'histoire contemporaine, se manifestant dans les phénomènes du terrorisme et des attentats-suicide.

Clivages et auto-ghettoisation

La renaissance du nationalisme, et de certains schémas de ressentiments et de xénophobie, observable à chaud dans le contexte du référendum de 1995 au Québec et liée en partie à la personnalité du chef du Parti Québécois à l'époque, Jacques Parizeau, se trouve notamment au centre d'un essai de Monique LaRue, *L'arpenteur et le navigateur*, issu d'une conférence donnée à l'Université de Montréal en 1996 qui avait soulevé un très vif débat. Celui-ci fut prolongé en 2009 par l'auteure sous forme d'une fiction romanesque, dans le roman *L'œil de Marquise* (2009) qui est situé dans le Québec de l'époque du référendum sur l'indépendance de 1995, mais dont l'action se déroule aussi dans d'autres cultures, notamment aux États-Unis et au Japon. Ce roman met en parallèle deux frères pourvus de caractères très différents et choisissant des options tout à fait opposées face au phénomène du nationalisme et du multiculturalisme : tandis que l'un des frères, un médecin, est un indépendantiste et un défenseur convaincu de la langue française, l'autre, « un architecte connu à travers le monde pour ‹ ses archipels de jardins et ses métissages de paysages › est fasciné par les déplacements et les voyages » (Gauvin 2014, 130). Ces deux personnages incarnent ainsi des figures contemporaines du couple antagoniste et emblématique de l'arpenteur et du navigateur que l'auteure avait étudié de manière plutôt théorique dans son essai du même nom. Considérant l'écrivain comme « le barde, le coryphe de sa tribu » (1996, 13)[2], et en même temps comme un « être de mémoire » qui « reconnaît la profondeur du passé » (1996, 13), Monique LaRue fait référence, dans son essai, aux formes de repli identitaire, mais aussi de xénophobie et de ressentiment qui avaient ressurgi dans le contexte du référendum de 1995, et les oppose aux formes d'ouverture multiculturelle qui seraient caractéristiques pour la société et la culture québécoises contemporaines. Elle distingue, dans cette perspective, deux types d'écrivains au sein de la littérature québécoise : la figure de l'arpenteur, créée au 19e siècle, qui trace des frontières, transmet les valeurs traditionnelles d'une communauté nationale, et qui semble incarnée par des écrivains comme Lionel Groulx, l'auteur notamment du roman nationaliste *L'appel de la race* (1922), et Félix-Antoine Savard, l'auteur de *Menaud, maître-draveur* (1937), roman de la terre par excellence. La figure de l'arpenteur renvoie ainsi à une conception ethnique de la littérature et de la culture, basée sur un « sentiment d'appartenance lié à l'ascendance et à la descendance » et définie par une langue, une religion et des « origines nationales » communes (LaRue 1996, 13).

À l'opposé, la figure du navigateur, incarnée par excellence par les écrivains migrants, illustre une littérature transgressant les frontières, sans lieu d'ancrage fixe, reflétant le « besoin de s'arracher à la terre natale, à sa famille, à la dimension ethnique de la langue et à toute attache pour naviguer vers l'ailleurs, vers le nouveau, vers l'inconnu » (LaRue 1996, 19). Il « rompt les amarres, largue son passé, mais transporte avec lui sa mémoire » (LaRue 1996, 26). Même si Monique LaRue s'identifie personnellement avec la seconde figure, celle du navigateur, considérant que « toute œuvre d'art, toute création authentique » commencent plutôt « par un arrachement que par un enracinement » (LaRue 1996, 19), elle met néanmoins en lumière la co-présence des deux modèles au sein de la littérature et de la culture québécoises contemporaines. Et elle souligne que des concepts transgressant la nation et le cadre de la culture nationale, comme celui de « transculture », ne reflèteraient pas encore, tout au moins dans le Québec des années 1990, une réalité socio-culturelle profonde, mais plutôt une idée intellectuelle. « La transculture », écrit-elle, « est une noble idée, mais dans la réalité, même chez les esthètes, c'est plutôt et encore le sentiment ethnique qui prime. » (LaRue 1996, 9) Elle ajoute, à propos de la persistance

de la conception d'une littérature nationale héritée au Québec du milieu du
19ᵉ siècle qu'elle voit en pleine transformation, suivant l'évolution de la société
elle-même :

> Notre littérature a jusqu'à maintenant été l'expression d'un monde com-
> mun, d'une expérience commune et relativement homogène, et nous ne
> nous sommes pas souvent demandés ce qu'était un écrivain québécois.
> [...] La diversité des perspectives forme-t-elle encore « une » littérature,
> une littérature spécifique parmi d'autres littératures distinctes, ou aurons-
> nous bientôt autant de littératures que de groupes ethniques ? (LaRue
> 1996, 11)

Cet essai n'a pas manqué de soulever une très vive polémique, qui débuta par
un article de la journaliste Ghila B. Sroka dans le journal *La Tribune juive*[3],
lui reprochant des positions xénophobes et des propos anti-migrants – que
Monique LaRue ne faisait, en fait, que rapporter.[4] *L'arpenteur et le navigateur* a eu
le mérite de cristalliser, de manière très dense, le double défi posé par l'importance
croissante d'un repli ethno-culturel aussi bien du côté des mouvements nationalistes occidentaux qu'au sein de certains groupes et communautés d'immigrés.
La figure du « navigateur », incarnée pour Monique LaRue aux États-Unis par
Joseph Brodsky et au Québec par des écrivains comme Sergio Kokis, Ying Cheng
et David Homel qui expriment « la diversité du français en Amérique » (LaRue
1996, 28), représente pour elle un modèle d'identification, susceptible d'aider à
dépasser la crise actuelle du multiculturalisme. L'essai de Monique LaRue, écrit
dans le sillage du référendum de 1995 et certes un des essais les plus contro-
versés et les plus intensément discutés de l'histoire intellectuelle du Québec de
ces dernières décennies, garde toute son actualité dans le contexte multiculturel
contemporain qui est à la fois semblable et profondément différent. « Quoiqu'il
en soit », nota Danielle Laurin dix ans plus tard dans un article paru dans le quotidien montréalais *Le Devoir*, « à l'heure où les Québécois s'interrogent sur leur
degré de racisme, sur la notion d'accommodement raisonnable, et sur le sens du
mot nation, il fait bon relire *L'arpenteur et le navigateur* » (2007).

    La romancière québécoise Abla Farhoud, d'origine libanaise, met en
lumière, avec les moyens de la fiction narrative, la seconde évolution esquissée
dans les remarques introductives de cette contribution, celle des défis que repré-

sentent l'importance croissante des revendications ethno-culturelles de certaines communautés d'immigrants, notamment musulmanes, sikhs et juifs-orthodoxes, avec les formes d'exclusion (et d'auto-ghettoisation) qui en découlent. Son roman *Le sourire de la petite juive* (2011) est composé d'une multitude de fragments-portraits tissés autour de personnages vivant dans un milieu éminemment inter-culturel de Montréal, celui de la rue Hutchinson située entre les quartiers de Mile End et d'Outremont. Parmi ces personnages que le lecteur voit surgir, tels des éclairs, à travers de brefs récits très intenses, on voit ainsi apparaître des fi-gures comme Antonella Rosetti, d'origine italienne, et sa famille ; la Togolaise Nzimbou, étudiante en informatique qui habite chez une infirmière québécoise à la retraite, Madeleine Desrochers, à qui elle apprend à se servir de l'ordinateur pour découvrir le monde de l'internet ; le jeune juif hassidique Srully, habitant New York et en visite chez ses parents à Montréal, qui rêve de consacrer sa vie à l'étude de la Torah ; Jean-Hugues Briançon, un Français immigré au Québec ; ou encore le couple et la famille mixte formés par le Tunisien Chawki, la Québécoise Isabelle et leurs trois enfants. Deux personnages reçoivent une attention particu-lière parmi ces figures souvent hautes en couleur dont le lecteur saisit chaque fois, dans chacun des fragments narratifs, des bribes de biographie donnant une vision de l'intérieur de leur vécu : l'écrivaine Françoise Camirand qui désire écrire, à l'instar de l'auteure du livre dont elle constitue un reflet autobiographique, un roman sur la rue Hutchinson et ses habitants ; et Hinda Rochel, une jeune juive hassidique, qui tient un journal intime publié par fragments dans le roman d'Abla Farhoud, qui est une élève brillante, aimant la lecture et l'écriture, et refusant de plus en plus le rôle de future épouse et mère obéissante, repliée sur son foyer et sa communauté, que veulent lui imposer sa famille et son entourage.

Ce roman d'Abla Farhoud est ponctué de dialogues interculturels dont deux semblent particulièrement intéressants : celui, d'une part, entre le Tunisien Chawki et son épouse québécoise Isabelle qui souhaite que leurs enfants bénéfi-cient d'une éducation biculturelle et bilingue, que leur père, qui a fui la Tunisie à cause des violences claniques dont sa famille a été victime, a longtemps refusée[5] (cf. Farhoud 2011, 132). Chawki va changer cependant d'attitude à partir des événements du 11 septembre 2001 qui ont accru considérablement, dans son environnement immédiat, les préjugés à l'égard des Arabes et des immigrés ori-ginaires du Moyen-Orient et du Maghreb, et modifié ainsi sa perception de son propre passé et de sa propre identité :

> Chawki s'était mis à raconter aux enfants sa jeunesse vécue en Tunisie
> et la vie de leurs grands-parents dont ils n'avaient jamais entendu parler.
> Il cherchait aussi une manière de leur enseigner l'arabe. Sans trop savoir
> comment ni par où commencer, il a fait le tour de quelques librairies de
> ville Saint-Laurent, puis il a trouvé, à deux pas de chez lui, à la biblio-
> thèque de Mile End, un rayon plein de livres en arabe pour enfants, des
> CD d'apprentissage, de la musique arabe, enfin tout ce qu'il fallait pour
> entreprendre sa tâche. (Farhoud 2011, 133)

D'autre part, le dialogue – potentiel – entre les habitants d'origines culturelles très diverses et les membres de la communauté hassidique dont le nombre a constamment augmenté pendant les 30 dernières années, est décrit par Abla Farhoud comme étant largement marqué par le refus et le silence. « Depuis vingt-cinq années », fait-elle dire à un de ses personnages, Willa Coleridge, « qu'elle habitait la rue Hutchinson, elle avait réussi à arracher quelques sourires à de très jeunes enfants pas encore endoctrinés. Mais Willa gardait l'espoir qu'un jour un homme ou une femme hassidique lui sourirait ou du moins répondrait à son sourire. » (Farhoud 2011, 29) Et au sujet de ce dialogue interculturel à la fois dési-ré et avorté, rendu impossible par le refus obstiné de communication par l'Autre, même au niveau non-verbal le plus élémentaire, celui du sourire, la narratrice évoque comme suit les pensées suivantes de son protagoniste, Willa Coleridge :

> À l'égard des juifs de sa rue, ce n'était pas de l'intolérance qu'elle éprouvait,
> mais de la peine. Elle aurait aimé les connaître, elle sentait qu'ils pouvaient
> lui apporter des réponses aux questions qu'elle se posait. Elle les savait très
> croyants, comme elle. Apprendre d'eux, c'est tout ce qu'elle voulait. […]
> Willa voulait connaître, apprendre, elle était toujours prête à ouvrir ses
> yeux et son cœur, mais elle ne savait pas comment arriver à percer ce mur
> que les hassidim portaient par-devers eux. (Farhoud 2011, 29)

Le roman se termine sur une lueur d'espoir, lorsque la jeune juive Hinda Rochel se tourne, avec « un sourire réservé, mais beau » (Farhoud 2011, 209), vers l'autre personnage important du livre, l'écrivaine Françoise Camirand. Mais dès le début du roman, qui thématise l'extrême difficulté, voire l'impossibilité et en définitive l'échec du dialogue interculturel avec la communauté hassidique, le lecteur entre dans un dialogue fictif avec cette communauté grâce au journal intime, certes imaginaire mais tout à fait plausible, de la jeune juive Hinda Rochel. Celui-ci est évoqué, par fragments, tout au long du roman. La lecture de ces fragments de journal intime qui se substitue, en quelque sorte, au dialogue interculturel inexistant entre la communauté hassidique et son environnement immédiat, donne à voir une vision de l'intérieur de cette communauté : de ses valeurs, de ses rituels, de ses figures d'identification et de ses symboles, de ses traditions très contraignantes, et de son rapport spécifique à la foi et à l'Écriture Sainte. À travers ce journal intime fictionnel, et le prisme des réflexions de cette jeune fille juive qui commence à prendre secrètement ses distances par rapport à sa communauté et à s'interroger sur le destin qui lui est réservé, le lecteur perçoit des clivages internes, des germes de contestation et de révolte, et l'esquisse d'une évolution de l'Autre rendant, peut-être, possible à l'avenir un dialogue interculturel jusque-là toujours refusé.

Abla Farhoud, en thématisant l'auto-ghettoisation de certaines communautés ethniques, tente de représenter ainsi, avec les moyens de la fiction littéraire, un aspect refoulé du dialogue interculturel. Par leurs récits, par des voix et des images radicalement discordantes et dérangeantes – et pour certains critiques même politiquement incorrectes –, ses personnages montrent l'envers du tableau parfois idéalisé de la société multiculturelle canadienne et québécoise. Érigé souvent en modèle sur le plan international, le multiculturalisme canadien, de même que sa variante québécoise, incarnés par l'ouverture à la diversité et la conception des accommodements raisonnables[6], sont habités tous deux par la vision idéale d'un dialogue interculturel enrichissant, harmonieux et équilibré. Une des fonctions importantes de la fiction littéraire et cinématographique contemporaine, au Québec et au Canada comme dans d'autres sociétés et cultures, est de montrer les enjeux et les failles de cette vision, ainsi que toutes les illusions dont elle est porteuse.

Imaginer et écrire le terrorisme en situation multiculturelle (Larry Tremblay)

Le roman *L'orangeraie* de l'écrivain et dramaturge Larry Tremblay, paru en 2013, renoue avec le troisième défi esquissé, celui lié à l'essor de courants ethno-religieux radicalisés qui ont fait émerger, notamment depuis le milieu des années 1990, différentes formes de terrorisme. Il plonge le lecteur, d'une manière extrêmement dense et prenante, en 168 pages, d'abord dans l'univers d'un couple de paysans – qui possèdent notamment des orangeraies – au Moyen-Orient, Zohal et Tamara, ayant deux fils-jumeaux, Amed et Aziz, dont les grands-parents (en l'occurrence les parents de Zohal, leur père) viennent d'être tués par une bombe ennemie. Représentant probablement des Palestiniens victimes de bombardements israéliens, cette famille se voit rapidement placée devant l'exigence formulée par la communauté d'une vengeance, sous la forme d'un attentat-suicide devant être commis par un des deux fils-jumeaux. Le récit se noue par la suite autour du choix du père qui s'est porté sur Aziz, tandis que la mère veut sacrifier Amed atteint d'une maladie musculaire incurable. Tamara, la mère des jumeaux, finit par convaincre Amed de se substituer à son frère et de porter la ceinture avec des explosifs que leur avait remis un leader politique prônant le terrorisme, du nom de Soulayed, très respecté mais en même temps fortemement craint par la communauté. La mère n'arrive toutefois à s'imposer que temporairement face au paternalisme masculin et à sa violence : Aziz ne parvient pas à garder son secret, traumatisé par la mort-suicide de son frère, poursuivi par des cauchemars et se sentant coupable. Sa mère subit alors par la suite des sévices violents de la part de son mari, furieux d'avoir été trompé, et Aziz lui-même, devenu la honte de la famille et de la communauté, prisonnier d'un système de valeurs implacable, est forcé à l'exil : d'abord chez des parents loin du village, et ensuite au Canada où il rejoint la sœur répudiée de sa mère, Dalil, qui avait été obligée de quitter le pays parce qu'elle s'était mariée avec un Israélien.

La dernière partie du roman se passe au Québec et relie ainsi l'univers d'abord très lointain, presque irréel, de la violence terroriste du Moyen-Orient avec l'univers plus proche de Montréal et de ses communautés immigrées. Situé huit ans après les événements tragiques racontés dans la première partie du roman, le récit montre Aziz étudiant le théâtre à Montréal, qui refuse de jouer dans la pièce portant sur la guerre écrite par son professeur québécois de théâtre ; il y devait incarner le rôle d'un enfant qui, après avoir vu ses parents assassinés devant ses yeux par un soldat ennemi, est tué à son tour par ce même soldat. La raison de ce refus est double : d'une part il met en cause le droit – et en même temps la capacité – de son professeur de mettre en scène des réalités qu'il n'a jamais connues lui-même personnellement et qui lui sont transmises seulement à travers des représentations médiatiques manipulées ; et, d'autre part, il se voit confronté, à travers ce rôle qu'il doit jouer, avec un retour du refoulé extrêmement puissant, faisant ressurgir les traumatismes et les violences de son enfance, et aussi l'absurdité barbare du sacrifice de son frère jumeau. Aziz avait, en effet, appris plus tard que celui-ci, croyant entraîner avec son suicide des soldats ennemis dans la mort, avait en réalité tué des enfants de son âge, car Soulayed l'avait emmené à son insu avec sa ceinture explosive dans l'immédiate proximité d'une école.

Téléscopant ainsi les dimensions violentes d'un multiculturalisme lointain, celui du Moyen-Orient, de la Palestine, du Liban et d'Israël, et celles, beaucoup moins violentes, mais aussi conflictuelles, du multiculturalisme au Canada et au Québec, Larry Tremblay met en lumière, dans un récit dense qui restera sans doute un des grands romans québécois et canadiens de notre époque, les tenants et aboutissements actuels de la crise des sociétés multiculturelles contemporaines : telle l'emprise, extrêmement problématique, de formes radicalisées de la pensée religieuse sur la vie politique, et par extension sur l'ensemble des comportements quotidiens ; telle l'invention de l'ennemi et la transmission de la haine de l'Autre, qui est désigné par les membres de la famille d'Aziz et de son entourage à travers des métaphores animalières, notamment les expressions de ‹ chiens › et de ‹ rats › ; et tels aussi les rouages et les conséquences de la manipulation d'individus et de la fanatisation de masses, rendues possibles à cause de l'absence d'une société civile ouverte permettant la liberté d'information et la circulation de visions, de valeurs et d'opinions diverses et plurielles. Le fait que ce roman place en son centre le sort d'enfants entraînés dans la guerre et dans le suicide par la volonté de leurs parents et d'autres adultes, rend ce récit particulièrement poignant ; mais la destinée du personnage d'Aziz ayant réussi à sortir de son milieu et à émigrer, apporte en même temps une lueur d'optimisme et l'espoir de pouvoir dépasser la crise conflictuelle profonde, trop souvent violente, que traversent les sociétés multiculturelles contemporaines bouleversées par les nouveaux défis à la fois du terrorisme et de l'islamophobie. La position de l'auteur de ce roman, à la fois distanciée et marquée par une indéniable empathie interculturelle pour ses personnages, s'explique en grande partie par son propre parcours biographique ayant suscité son intérêt intense pour des cultures différentes – comme celles du Moyen-Orient ou de l'Inde – et le situant parmi les écrivains québécois les plus ouverts vers le transculturel et ses défis contemporains.

Hans-Jürgen LÜSEBRINK

Les ombres et défis de l'Holocauste face à la diversité ethno-culturelle (Monique LaRue)

Dans un ouvrage récent intitulé *La leçon de Jérusalem*, paru en 2015, Monique LaRue reprend la discussion soulevée par son essai *L'arpenteur et le navigateur* presque vingt ans auparavant en la plaçant dans un contexte totalement différent : celui du débat autour du film de Margarete von Trotta sur Hannah Arendt qui pose d'emblée la question de la mémoire de l'Holocauste dans les sociétés multiculturelles contemporaines. L'accusation adressée à Hannah Arendt, après ses reportages sur le procès Eichmann à Jérusalem, d'être une ‹ nazie › puisqu'elle aurait – aux yeux de ses critiques – trop de complaisance avec l'accusé, l'un des principaux acteurs de l'Holocauste, soulève, dans l'optique de Monique LaRue, une double problématique, d'une actualité immédiate pour le débat autour du nationalisme et de la société multiculturelle au Québec : celle, d'une part, de la puissance manipulatrice des ‹ mots-valise › (comme ‹ nation › et ‹ raciste ›) dans le contexte médiatique ; et celle, d'autre part, de la genèse des formes de perception racistes et xénophobes, de la construction négative de la figure de l'Autre. La perception d'Adolf Eichmann comme homme ordinaire – et non pas comme monstre singulier – que les critiques de Hannah Arendt lui avaient reprochée en 1961, focalise, en effet, l'attention sur l'ancrage social et socio-culturel du racisme et de ses soubassements mentaux ; ceux-ci se situeraient, dans l'Allemagne des années 1930 comme au Québec des années 1990, non pas en marge, mais au cœur et dans les points les plus névralgiques d'une société, là où se cristallisent les conflits refoulés et les clivages non-apparents. Le ressentiment xénophobe et son paroxysme, la volonté d'exterminer l'Autre, seraient ainsi nés de la banalité du quotidien. Des personnages comme Eichmann ne seraient ainsi pas, à première vue, des monstres hors du commun, mais représenteraient, tout en les transformant, des structures mentales et des modes de perception sociale, comme l'obéissance inconditionnelle à l'autorité, la xénophobie, le ressentiment, l'antisémitisme et la haine de l'Autre, partagés par une partie non négligeable de la population. Le débat controversé autour de son essai *L'arpenteur et le navigateur* aurait abouti, selon Monique LaRue, à « faire taire le racisme banal, le racisme automatique, le racisme de la bêtise et du préjugé dans le microcosme littéraire » (2015, 99). Même si le film de von Trotta ne place pas en son centre, comme le fait l'essai de Monique LaRue, le multiculturalisme (contemporain) et concerne, avec le Troisième Reich, une société fondamentalement différente, le détour réflexif à travers ‹ l'affaire Hannah Arendt › retracée dans le film lui a fait prendre conscience de la « fragilité du dialogue social et de la puissance des mots » (LaRue 2015, 99) même dans une société à première vue tolérante comme la société multiculturelle canadienne.

Conclusion

Les œuvres romanesques et essayistiques de Monique LaRue, de Larry Tremblay et d'Abla Farhoud montrent, à travers la crise du multiculturalisme qu'ils traitent avec le biais de la fiction et de la pensée réflexive (caractérisant le genre de l'essai) les liens sous-jacents qui relient les approches multiculturelle et nationaliste de la vie en société. Les deux positions sont, en effet, susceptibles d'intégrer des positions ethniques, xénophobes et nationalistes, formulées et défendues au nom de la protection des valeurs et des traditions propres à une communauté nationale ou ethno-culturelle. Ces positions peuvent générer ce que Monique LaRue appelle, toujours inspirée par Arendt, le « racisme banal », « le racisme automatique » ou encore le « racisme de la bêtise et du préjugé » (LaRue 2015, 99) dans des comportements quotidiens, mettant l'Autre à distance en le considérant non seulement comme différent, mais aussi comme mécréant ou non-intégrable.

Les œuvres analysées montrent en même temps la « fragilité du dialogue social » (LaRue 2015, 99) qui est à la base de la société multiculturelle canadienne et de sa conception de la diversité sociale et culturelle qui implique, dans ses principes, le respect mutuel, la tolérance, mais aussi une volonté de dialogue et de convivialité. Ces valeurs sont mises en cause et menacées, telle est la vision transmise par les fictions romanesques de Larry Tremblay et d'Abla Farhoud et les essais de Monique LaRue, par des pratiques sociales et des modes de perception nationaux et communautaires, ou tout au moins rendues beaucoup plus difficiles à réaliser qu'il y a encore une ou deux décennies. La « puissance des mots » (LaRue 2015, 99) – comme ‹ nation ›, ‹ ethnie ›, ‹ valeurs religieuses ›, ‹ valeurs communes ›, ‹ racisme › – pour lesquels les médias, de la presse à internet, constituent une plateforme majeure de diffusion, a, tel est le constat notamment de Monique LaRue, une responsabilité importante dans cette évolution.

Les auteurs québécois contemporains comme ceux évoqués dans cette contribution, se focalisent moins sur la situation québécoise en particulier, marquée depuis les années 1970 par une prise de distance politique générale par rapport au multiculturalisme et ses implications idéologiques, débouchant notamment sur l'élaboration du concept alternatif d'interculturalisme (Bouchard 2011, 2012 ; Cardin 2016). Ils se concentrent plutôt sur des situations multi-culturelles spécifiques dans le cadre canadien, marquées par la co-présence et en même temps par la convivialité – harmonieuse ou conflictuelle – de personnes et de groupes appartenant à des cultures différentes. La fiction, qu'elle soit roma-nesque ou essayistique, aurait-elle, dans ce contexte, la lourde tâche de mettre en lumière ces nouveaux défis, de leur prêter une voix et de leur donner, avec les récits qu'ils développent et les personnages qu'ils mettent en place, une force à la fois réflexive et émotionnelle d'autant plus nécessaire aujourd'hui ?

1   Barry (1941) ; il s'agit, en effet, d'un compte-rendu du roman de Haskell par Iris Barry.

2   Monique LaRue (1996, 13) ajoute : « L'écriture est locale dans sa langue, langue et nation sont intimement liées. »

3   Sroka (1997). Cf., pour l'ensemble du dossier des polémiques autour du livre de Monique LaRue : http://vigile.quebec/archives/ds-societe/docs3/srokapoubelle.html (consultation 07/05/2017).

4   Cf., pour cette polémique, Dumont (2003) et la bibliographie établie par Raymond (2003, 120-121), ainsi que, pour la polémique elle-même, notamment les articles de 1997 de Sroka, De Sève, Lévesque, Nepveu, Klang, Jasmin, Demers et Bissonnette.

5   « Je suis musulman par mes parents et par mon éducation, je l'ai été pendant mes vingt-cinq premières années de vie. Paix et prières à ceux qui le sont encore, et je ne le suis plus. Je suis non religieux. Vous, mes enfants, vous n'êtes pour l'instant ni catho-liques ni musulmans. Vous choisirez quand vous serez en âge de choisir, si vous avez envie de choisir. Laissez aux autres les dissensions, les disputes et la haine. » (Farhoud 2011, 132)

6   Cf. sur cette problématique entre autres Bouchard/Taylor (2008) ; Geadah (2007) ; Potvin (2008) ; Fuchs (2008).

Bibliographie

Barry, Iris : « Melodrama, Tract, Good Story » [review of Edward F. Haskell's *Lance*]. In : *New York Herald Tribune Books* (12/07/1941), 3.

Bissonnette, Lise : « Un cauchemar ». In : *Le Devoir* (03/07/1997), 9.

Bissoondath, Neil : *Le marché aux illusions. La méprise du multiculturalisme.* Traduit de l'anglais par Jean Papineau. Montréal : Boréal, 1995.

Bouchard, Gérard : *L'interculturalisme. Un point de vue québécois.* Montréal : Boréal, 2012.

Bouchard, Gérard et al. (éds) : *L'interculturalisme. Dialogue Québec-Europe.* Actes du symposium international sur l'interculturalisme, Montréal 25-27 mai 2011, http://www.symposium-interculturalisme.com/pdf/livre_complet_FINAL_hyperliens.pdf (consultation 07/05/2017).

Bouchard, Gérard / Taylor, Charles : *Fonder l'avenir. Le temps de la conciliation.* Québec : Gouvernement du Québec, 2008.

Cardin, Judith : *Politique de l'immigration choisie au Canada. Traité d'indignation d'une Afro-Canadienne.* Paris : L'Harmattan, 2016.

De Sève, Micheline : « Malaise au pluriel. L'auteur Monique LaRue a échoué à conjurer les démons de l'identité ». In : *Le Devoir* (05/05/1997), A7.

Demers, Jeanne : « Une lecture erronée et destructrice ». In : *Le Devoir* (17-18/05/1997), A7.

Dumont, François : « *L'arpenteur et le navigateur* : les ambiguïtés d'un essai romanesque ». In : *Voix et Images* 28,2 (2003), 98-108.

Farhoud, Abla : *Le sourire de la petite juive.* Montréal : VLB, 2011.

Fuchs, Max : « Risse im Paradies ? Integrationsprobleme in Kanada und eine politische Antwort ». In : *inter\kultur* (*Politik & Kultur*) 1 (2008), 3, https://www.kulturrat.de/wp-content/uploads/2016/07/interkultur-1.pdf (consultation 07/05/2017).

Gauvin, Lise : *Aventuriers et sédentaires. Parcours du roman québécois.* Montréal : Typo, 2014.

Geadah, Yolande : *Accommodements raisonnables. Droit à la différence et non-différence des droits.* Montréal : VLB, 2007.

Jasmin, Claude : « La bonne foi et la défiance. À qui le Québec fait-il peur ? ». In : *Le Devoir* (15/07/1997), A7.

Klang, Gary : « Trop, c'est trop. Peut-on chanter ce pays accueillant sans sortir les grandes orgues du nationalisme ? ». In : *Le Devoir* (03/07/1997), 4.

Lacorne, Dénis : *La crise de l'identité américaine. Du melting-pot au multiculturalisme.* Paris : Fayard, 1997.

LaRue, Monique : *L'arpenteur et le navigateur.* Montréal : Éditions Fides, 1996.

LaRue, Monique : *L'œil de Marquise.* Montréal : Boréal, 2009.

LaRue, Monique : *La leçon de Jérusalem.* Montréal : Boréal, 2015.

Laurin, Danielle : « Le malentendu. Monique LaRue, une écrivaine qui n'a pas peur de déranger ». In : *Le Devoir* (20-21/01/2007), F3.

Lévesque, Claude : « À propos du ‹ Québec xénophobe › ». In : *Le Devoir* (03/07/1997), 9.

Nepveu, Pierre : « Recension de *L'arpenteur et le navigateur* dans *Tribune juive.* Lire à l'envers : Ghila Sroka a fait une lecture aberrante et grossière de l'ouvrage de Monique LaRue ». In : *Le Devoir* (26/04/1997), A11.

Potvin, Maryse : *Crise des accommodements raisonnables. Une fiction médiatique ?* Outremont : Athéna, 2008.

Raymond, Richard : « Bibliographie critique de Monique LaRue ». In : *Voix et Images* 28,2 (2003), 109-122.

Sroka, Ghila B. : « De LaRue à la poubelle ». In : *La Tribune juive* 4,3 (1997), 4-5, http://vigile.quebec/archives/ds-societe/docs3/srokapoubelle.html (consultation 07/05/2017).

Tremblay, Larry : *L'orangeraie.* Québec : Éditions Alto, 2013.

Srilata RAVI (Edmonton)

Ethnographic Practices, Good Intentions, and Writing the Indigenous Other in Gérard Bouchard's *Uashat*

Résumé

Gérard Bouchard, sociologue et historien québécois de grande renommée, déclare que son roman *Uashat* (2009) est né du fait que l'histoire « d'un déracinement brutal et une rupture tragique » vécue par les Innus du nord du Québec serait inévitablement perdue dans la langue des sciences sociales (Bouchard in Ravi/Couture 2015, 224). *Uashat* est un récit fictif inspiré par ses expériences ethnographiques chez les Innus qui, dans les années 1950 et encore aujourd'hui, sont victimes de l'exploitation de Rio Tinto, compagnie minière internationale. Serait-il possible de démarquer d'une manière si nette les limites entre l'objectivité de l'investigation scientifique et l'identification empathique dans la création romanesque, comme le suggère l'auteur d'*Uashat* ? Cet essai s'interrogera sur les liens complexes entre les bonnes intentions, l'autoréflexivité et les relations de pouvoir qui caractérisent la représentation des peuples autochtones dans le roman de Bouchard.

Introduction

As we watch several thousand migrants from the comfort of our living rooms making their way across unfriendly borders, we represent the other in heart-breaking images, we pose our benevolent regard on this mass movement of misery, or we speak for the abject other without, for the most part, reflecting on our privileged positions or having to listen to the represented other. As bell hooks (1990, 151) has so aptly noted, when talking about the other, "[i]t is not just important what we speak about, but how and why we speak," otherwise we run the risk of conflating the other with a position of weakness and victimhood, where we can feel responsible for 'them' without having to listen to anyone but ourselves. I believe that in Canada today, the Syrian refugee crisis has transformed our homes and work spaces into problematic sites of confrontation with alterity, not only because we seem to participate so uncritically in the globalization of compassion for the 'distant' other, but our 'compassionate' representation of the migrant crisis tends to relegate to the sidelines our own problematic settler constructions of Indigenous societies in Canada.

Audra Simpson (2014) and several other Indigenous scholars have argued that modern anthropology remains complicit with imperial ideologies. They have blamed Euro-American prejudicial biases for the negative portrayal of Indigenous societies. It cannot be denied that while professing to represent the specific interests of the other, Western scholars have been more concerned that the other fit into dominant mainstream society. Such representations, Edward Hedican argues, have served as a conduit through which "selected facets of Native American life have been funneled into the mythmaking machine of North American society" (2014, 93).

That being said, James Clifford and George Marcus (1986) in their groundbreaking work *Writing Culture: The Poetics and Politics of Ethnography* brought a fresh self-consciousness to the social sciences by claiming that even in disciplines, like ethnography and anthropology that consider the scientific study of the other, textual representation and authoritative assumptions need to be interrogated. The book introduced new directions in North American anthropology. At the same time in the last thirty years or so there has been a steady growth of Indigenous voices in a diverse range of discourses. The Indigenous peoples' opposition to the hydroelectric projects in James Bay in the 1970s and in the 1980s, the Oka crisis in 1990, the rising number of land rights claims that have appeared before federal and provincial courts, and the more recent *Idle No More* movement bear testimony to the increasing political activism of Indigenous populations in Canada voicing their rights to be heard. These factors have contributed not only to a significant rise in "l'autoreprésentation des réalités amérindiennes longtemps oblitérées par le discours et les représentations de l'Autre" (Destrempes/Lüsebrink 2007, 7; cf. also Gatti 2004; 2006) but also the aspiration on the part of settler writers to produce more sympathetic representations of Indigenous societies. Tracing these changes in fictional representations, literary critic Jean Morency claims that in comparison to earlier depictions in literature from Quebec, Louis Hamelin and Daniel Poliquin, respectively in *Cowboy* and in *L'Obomsawin*, have offered "une conception plus juste de la réalité autochtone" (Morency 2007, 97). Yet how nuanced, really, are these attempts that seek to detach the portrayal of the 'Amérindiens' from conventions that reinforce binary schemas when describing cultures in literary and non-literary works?

Thomas King in *The Inconvenient Indian: A Curious Account of Native People in North America* notes that Indigenous realities are complex undertakings and cannot be defined by easy binarisms:

> So, let's agree that Indians are not special. We're not ... mystical. I'm fine with that. Yes, a great many Native people have a long-standing relationship with the natural world. But that relationship is equally available to non-Natives, should they choose to embrace it. The fact of Native existence is that we live modern lives informed by traditional values and contemporary realities and that we wish to live those lives on our terms. (King 2012, 266)

King is responding to persisting and dominant modes of representation, which despite increasing awareness of Indigenous issues in artistic, academic, and public domains, continue to marginalize the Indigenous people through conscious and unconscious cultural practices. Celia Haig-Brown in her article on Indigenous thought and non-Aboriginal people notes that

> [i]nteracting with Aboriginal people for whom persisting deeply held beliefs and knowledge structures continue to shape their discourse, non-Aboriginal people may begin the process of learning what for them are secondary discourses, even eventually finding their fundamental world view affected. Over time, a secondary world view may be unconsciously acquired sometimes leaving the primary one fundamentally and irreversibly altered, even alienated (Haig-Brown 2010, 937).

Are practices of writing by settler scholars about Indigenous societies, whether in fictional accounts or in ethnographic texts, becoming more self-reflexive and self-critical as the author quoted above suggests? Even as Haig-Brown observes the potential of "deep learning" during Indigenous/settler interactions (Haig-Brown 2010, 927, fn 6), she also warns us in the same article that "shallow learning" (as opposed to "deep learning") can lead "most well-intentioned persons to violations of cultural protocol and demonstrations of cultural insensitivity" (Haig-Brown 2010, 927, fn 6). This relation between good intention, self-reflexivity, and power relations is what I wish to explore in my reading of Gérard Bouchard's 2009 novel *Uashat*, a fictional account of an ethnographic experience inspired by the exploitation of Innu First Nation communities by Rio Tinto in the 1950s.

Uashat: Fictionalizing an Ethnographic Exercise

Gérard Bouchard, historian and sociologist, is the celebrated author of *Genèse des nations et cultures du Nouveau Monde* (2000) and the co-author of the much debated Bouchard-Taylor report on reasonable accommodation in Quebec. What many people may not know is that he has also written three novels, *Mistouk* (2002), *Pikauba* (2005), and *Uashat* (2009). In a recent publication dedicated to a critical discussion of his scholarly contributions he writes: "Ils [ses romans] sont nés, tous les trois d'un même problème, à savoir la difficulté des sciences sociales à faire écho aux émotions et au vécu des acteurs." (Bouchard in Ravi/Couture 2015, 223) As he reflects on the complex question of representation in the social sciences, he regrets that his scholarly publications like *Quelques arpents d'Amérique* (1996) could never do justice to "tout le capital d'invention et d'expression lié à la parole" (Ravi/Couture 2015, 223). In many ways, his self-criticism underlines the problems that frame the ethnographic project mentioned above. Gérard Bouchard, in a lecture given at the University of Alberta in Edmonton in September 2015, explained that the source for his novel, *Uashat*, was a series of interviews that he had conducted as part of a research project with the inhabitants on the Innu reserves, many of them Elders, who communicated the stories of their ancestors to him. His semi-autobiographical novel, he declares, was born when he realized that the emotional narrative of "un déracinement brutal et une rupture tragique" (Ravi/Couture 2015, 224) of the Innu people of Northern Quebec would be inevitably lost in the scientific language of the social sciences. The sincerity of his project notwithstanding, can the lines between authenticity of scientific enquiry and empathetic identification in creative writing be so clear-cut?

Gérard Bouchard's novel *Uashat* is set in 1954 at the time when the Federal Government wanted to move the Innus of Uashat to a newly constructed reserve in Malioténam in order to make room for the development of Ville de Sept-Îles which was living the IOC boom at the time. The novel's protagonist, Florent Moisan, originally from a working class background in Lévis in Northern Quebec, is a student of sociology who is doing research for his university professor, M. Larocque. His task is to listen to and record testimonies of the Innu families on the reserve of Uashat and to draw family histories. Despite being successful in receiving testimonies from most inhabitants on the reserve, the young Quebecker is distraught by his own helplessness in the face of the forced eviction of the inhabitants of the Uashat reserve. Disappointed on the one hand by the rejection of his affection by a young Indigenous woman named Sara, and on the other, traumatized by the unexpected deaths of two members of the reserve, the suicide of Grand Père, who had hosted him, and the passing of Gabrielle, Sara's grandmother ("une vieille dame, toute ridée, mais très digne," 46), who had been very compassionate towards him, Florent abandons the research project and university studies and eventually severs all contact with his family and friends in Lévis. *Uashat* is an interesting combination of creative writing (by way of its novelistic form) and ethnographic writing (by way of its diegetic premise), and as such allows us to critique the frontiers of scientific objectivity and narrative authenticity. On the one hand, according to James Clifford, ethnographic practices as a form of writing culture define practices where "experiential, interpretive, dialogical and polyphonic processes" are at work and any attempt for coherent presentation supposes "a controlling mode of authority" (Clifford 1983, 142). On the other, by definition, the conventional realist novel presents an ordered, stable, and an inherently meaningful world based on authorial assumptions. Can the structural form of the realist novel (*Uashat*) which fictionalizes an ethnographic exercise (Florent's research) fully represent the "experiential, interpretive, dialogical and polyphonic processes" which are at work in an ethnographic practice? Will it not end up reducing such a space to a discrete other world created by a controlling voice?

Narrative Control, Power Structures, and Good Intentions

Gérard Bouchard defines his creative writing project as an affective and compassionate response to the words of the Innu people, words that overwhelmed him, words that he feared would be "impoverished" in social science discourse:

> [J]'ai été tellement impressionné par la parole de ces vieux chasseurs, désormais expulsés de leur histoire, qu'elle se serait inévitablement appauvrie dans la langue des sciences sociales. Le projet de monographie a donc cédé la place au roman *Uashat*. (Bouchard in Ravi/Couture 2015, 224)

Despite being well-intentioned on the part of the author, can imaginative writing (as opposed to scientific writing in the social sciences) in the form of a realist novel erase the power structures that figure in ethnography and offer a self-critical text?

Florent's journal, which serves as the fictional frame of *Uashat*, contains his entries from May to October of the year 1954. The novel does not contain the testimonials of the Uashat inhabitants *per se*, but details Florent's experiences of recording the testimonials of the various inhabitants of the reserve, his encounters with the lived realities of the Innus, as well as Florent's complicated relationship with Sara ("[e]lle a quelque chose d'impénétrable, qui vous tient à distance," 57). The journal in turn is embedded within the framing narratives of Florent's professor. A preface by professor Larocque introduces the context of the journal ("le tragique été de 1954," 12) while a "postface" which informs the reader that the professor received the journal from Florent's mother reveals the fate of his student. Feeling morally responsible for Florent's mental state and failure to pursue his higher education, the professor writes that he felt compelled to publish his student's journal in its original form ("tel quel, avec ses maladresses, ses lacunes, ses redites," 12) in the hope that it would reach the missing young man ("un dernier appel lancé au disparu," 322). Even if the reader never learns whether the objectives of the publication of Florent's journal are met, have Bouchard's intentions been fulfilled? Does the novel, as a fictional enterprise, relate the "vécu des acteurs" with greater fidelity and authenticity as the author intended? Furthermore, does it help to reflect on and critique the role of the settler scholar interacting with Indigenous communities?

If the central plot in *Uashat* is driven by a university professor's research interest in Indigenous histories, the narrative of Florent's sojourn on the reserve is propelled by his own fatal and flawed attraction to Sara, the young Innu woman. Florent is unable to comprehend her refusal of his offer of a 'better' life and her unwillingness to tread a healthier path away from drugs and sex. Florent's own underprivileged working class background in Lévis (182-193; 266-267) parallels to some extent the poverty and the squalor of the reserve dwellings on Uashat. The young ethnographer's observations of poverty, racism, and the ill-treatment suffered by the Innus on the reserve are punctuated by his memories of his mother's devotion to her boys in her role as a single parent. The narrative's geographical frame Uashat/Ville de Sept-Îles structures the fictional space, while the to-ing and fro-ing between the narrative's present set in 1954 and a colonial and pre-colonial past in the testimonies of the Innu families structures the text's temporal axis. Florent's uncontrollable and inexplicable desire for the 'elusive other,' represented by a sexually promiscuous Sara in the novel, is rendered all the more potent because of his own frail health while Sara's inscrutability parallels the mystic ramblings of Grand Père whose hospitality renders Florent's presence a reality on the reserve. As the tragic events of the forced evacuation of the inhabitants of Uashat in 1954 unfold before him, Florent becomes more and more conscious of his naivety and his own contradictory and superficial commentaries (cf. 317) on the residents of the reserve, even as he acknowledges in despair that things will only get worse: "Les choses vont se gâter, c'est sûr." (314)

Quebec scholars (Létourneau 1989; Vincent 1986; Vincent/Arcand 1979) have drawn our attention to how struggles of Francophones against Anglophone infringement have historically sidelined Indigenous rights and entitlements. Gérard Bouchard's narrative of Florent's self-doubts, anxieties, and emotional involvement with the marginalized situation of the Indigenous people of Uashat, who are helpless against both the political and economic pressures from outside the reserve, is without any doubt sympathetic to the cause of the crisis lived by the Innu people in 1954. In fact, one could say that Bouchard uses his own authority as an acclaimed scholar to raise awareness of Indigenous rights in Quebec. Through Florent's entries the reader learns about the day to day struggles of the Innu people and the unpardonable oppression exercised on the community. The journal exposes the reprehensible measures taken to force the members of the community to relocate to Malioténam in the name of urban development and narrates how Indigenous peoples battled to "live modern lives informed by traditional values and contemporary realities and [...] wish[ed] to live those lives on [their] terms" (King's word quoted earlier). The narrative also dispels the possibility of any paternalistic gesture through Florent's acceptance of his own marginalized/outsider situation vis-à-vis both the community and Sara. Such also has been the general understanding of the novel in the press:

> *Uashat*, le dernier roman de Gérard Bouchard, qui paraît ces jours-ci chez Boréal, a le mérite de mettre sous les projecteurs un aspect méconnu de l'histoire du Québec [...]. *Uashat*, pour sa part, se déroule au milieu des années 50, à une époque où la réserve est secouée par une crise. Cette période était intéressante, pour l'historien qu'est Gérard Bouchard, notamment parce qu'elle donne la mesure de certains excès perpétrés par les Blancs à l'encontre des Amérindiens. (Montpetit 2009)

One could argue that the central premise of collecting oral histories values the oral traditions of Indigenous cultures, and places those traditions, rather than colonial ones, at the center. However, in Bouchard's novel – where ethnographic writing practice progresses through a series of journal entries that relate the fieldwork practice of collecting stories – the main speaking voice that emerges is that of the apprentice scholar, Florent. While the journal provides the reader with the intimate subjectivity of the observer/participant, the embeddedness of the journal within a framing explanatory report by the professor/principal narrator removes the reader away from the "vécu des acteurs" thus undermining the impact of the story of the "déracinement brutal" (Ravi/Couture 2015, 224) of the Indigenous populations from their lands. In effect, the novel's double framing creates a double distancing: on the one hand through the violence of settler colonialism, and on the other, through the narrative's authorial authority. Even while giving the appearance of *not* speaking *for* the other, the novel ends up doing just that.

Ramaswami Harindranath notes that even though acts of testimony are acts of identity formation demonstrating the multiplicity of the struggles of the marginalized, the marginalization or subalternization of the indigene persists in the use of these testimonies (what Bouchard calls "le vécu des acteurs") in development discourse (cf. Harindranath 2006, 126). We see this happening in Bouchard's novel where Florent's presence in Uashat is linked to a grant received by professor Larocque to research Indigenous ways of knowing ("leurs modes de vie, leurs perceptions, leurs croyances," 21). Despite the evocation of sex, drugs, and violence as the fallout of the industrial development of the region, the central frame of the novel remains entrenched in a progressive narrative of development relayed through the apologetic intervention of the professor. As such the precious polyphonic testimonies which are lost in the embedded journal are not mediated between politically conscious individuals (the ethnographer and the residents on the reserve) but become consigned to an act of ordering by "a controlling mode of authority" (Clifford 1983, 142), in this case, professor Larocque.

Narrative Framing and the Doubly Marginalized Indigenous Woman

Let us go back to Bouchard's claim that while the social sciences may not have the language to represent lived experiences, fiction can capitalize on the creativity and expressivity of the spoken word. In *Uashat*, the historian and sociologist transposes his disciplinary practice onto a fictionalized interface. Is he successful in envisaging the possibility of decolonizing ethnographic practices? By changing disciplines does he succeed in presenting a non-hierarchical site for dialogue? In Bouchard's story, Sara, as the obsessive focus of the ethnographer, becomes the primary site of Indigenous/settler interaction. Yet, Sara's voice does not come through in the novel's embedded journal. Sara does not speak, as she rarely expresses an opinion. She is spoken for by her family (the Napish), by the men who possess her sexually, and mostly by Florent who cannot possess her body nor her spirit. When Florent goes to see Sara for the last time (318-319), and when she returns Florent's gaze even as she is voluntarily abandoning her body to her male Indigenous friends, it would seem then that she is finally providing him with her testimony on her own terms. Florent moves away, mystified by the inexplicability of Sara's reaction and the violence of her act. The creative and affirmative voice/ *parole* that Bouchard wishes to be heard and the lived experience that he feels needs to be transmitted get extinguished because Sara does not end up looking at us (the reader) – her return gaze is deflected and redirected away by the novel's embedded narration. Gérard Bouchard's novel most certainly questions stereotypical representations of the Aboriginal other, but the novel's double framing ironically erases Indigenous agency by effacing Sara's resistance. In the end, the narrative frame places Florent's marginalization (represented in the novel by his working class origins, his helplessness as a settler scholar, and his physical frailty) as the underprivileged Quebecker within the same affective frame as Sara's subalternity, that of the doubly marginalized, female and Indigenous, other. By doing so, Bouchard equates the subjugated position of the working class male descendant of the white colonial settler with the doubly colonized position of the Indigenous woman. Despite good authorial intentions on the part of Bouchard, *Uashat* reinforces through its narrative structuring "how early events have set up gendered colonial structures that continue to dominate and enact violence at both the interpersonal and state level on Native peoples" (Goeman 2013, 19).

John Byrd and Michael Rothberg (2011) in "Between Subalternity and Indigeneity. Critical Categories for Postcolonial Studies" draw our attention to the risks that inhere in the particular forms of mishearing that take place even and especially in the state's recognition of Indigenous rights. They argue that in legal discourse the court simultaneously acknowledges and disavows indigeneity in the same sentence because the perspective of the Indigenous people that it takes into account is in effect framed in terms recognizable to the Canadian legal and constitutional structure (cf. Byrd/Rothberg 2011, 6). "What we have is a situation in which the two parties to a case do not share a common language in which to articulate the wrong that is at stake." (Byrd/Rothberg 2011, 7) This question of incommensurability, the authors argue following Jean-François Lyotard, is the "differend," the predicament "in which the state repeatedly places indigenous communities" (Byrd/Rothberg 2011, 7). In my reading of *Uashat*, I see the double narrative enclosure in the novel as a kind of literary *differend*: it identifies Indigenous difference but does not have the language to translate it. An Indigenous perspective can only be translated into a language commensurable with the dominant discourse (in this case the generic norms of the novel). However, as my reading shows, such a translation can occur only through the disenfranchisement of fundamental Indigenous claims (in Bouchard's translation, Sara's powerful silence is deflected away from the reader). In fact, I would go further to argue that at another level it could be said that Sara, through her final return gaze, refuses to give content to Indigenous difference, what Audra Simpson would argue as the "refusal" of the ploy of state recognition (Simpson 2007, 73; cf. also Simpson 2008). Such a refusal forces us to review our own ethical position with regard to the pain of subalternized or disenfranchised people. Should we be allowed to witness their pain if this witnessing only serves to affirm our humanity and our capacity to care? Should we like Bouchard's naïve protagonist be resigned to say: "Je pense que c'est trop compliqué pour moi; j'aurais dû me mêler de mes propres affaires" (317)?

As Joan Sangster aptly argues: "Privilege is not negated simply by inclusion of other voices." (Sangster 1994, 14) Gérard Bouchard's intention to include the disenfranchised voices that had overwhelmed him in a fictional narrative of Indigenous/settler interactions results in a problematic narrative of universal solidarity with Indigenous communities in Quebec. The focus in *Uashat* remains on the protagonist, Florent, who is fundamentally altered and alienated from himself because of his experiences on the reserve and as such the novel reasserts the hetero-normative structures of patriarchal and colonialist discourses, the author's conscious good intention to tell other stories notwithstanding.

Conclusion

In this essay, I have tried to show that Bouchard's wish to relate the force of the unspoken silence of the marginalized Innus gets embedded and lost in the Eurocentric language of the novel, only to reinforce the very power relations that his humanist intervention seeks to abolish. *Uashat* narrates the colonial story of the Innus' expulsion from their land; it gives form and shape to their pain of dispossession, without actually reflecting on the experiential, spiritual, political, and geographical nature of related land claims. In his sincere bid to give voice to the marginalized, could it be said that Bouchard has appropriated the pain of the Innus? On this point, Haig-Brown reminds us that "[t]he word in language is half someone else's" (Wertsch in Haig-Brown 2010, 946) and that "one must never lose sight of the half of the word that will always remain someone else's" (Haig-Brown 2010, 946).

Reading Bouchard's novel in light of his objective to fill a gap in social science research reminds us that exhibiting well-intentioned compassion without interrogating our assumptions can lead to awkward formulations. Good intentions often become a way of tempering dominant interests behind the "veil of humanitarianism" while "failing to empower Aboriginal people" in their struggle for social justice (Blackstock 2006, 67). Furthermore, Bouchard's creative writing project based on his autobiographical experience of collecting stories also raises pertinent questions about how we listen to Indigenous stories. Eva M. Garroutte and Kathleen D. Westcott (2013) in their essay in the collection *Centering Anishinaabeg Studies: Understanding the World Through Stories* suggest an oral history approach to listening which is not based on "representational assumptions" (Garroutte/Westcott 2013, 75). Bouchard's novel, in its Eurocentric approach to understanding stories, is based on "representational assumptions" and as such "it does not lead its hearers to conclude that they can move beyond empathic awareness to become of one mind with other beings" (Garroutte/Westcott 2013, 75). It is important to remember this when we participate consciously or unconsciously in practices of globalized compassion.

Bibliography

Blackstock, Michael D.: "Trust Us: A Case Study in Colonial Social Relations Based on Documents Prepared by the Aborigines Protection Society, 1836-1912." In: Haig-Brown, Celia / Nock, David (eds): *With Good Intentions: Euro-Canadian and Aboriginal Relations in Colonial Canada.* Vancouver: University of British Columbia Press, 2006, 51-71.

Bouchard, Gérard: *Quelques arpents d'Amérique. Population, économie, famille au Saguenay 1838-1971.* Montreal: Boréal, 1996.

Bouchard, Gérard: *Genèse des nations et cultures du Nouveau Monde. Essai d'histoire comparée.* Montreal: Boréal, 2000.

Bouchard, Gérard: *Mistouk.* Montreal: Boréal, 2002.

Bouchard, Gérard: *Pikauba.* Montreal: Boréal, 2005.

Bouchard, Gérard: *Uashat.* Montreal: Boréal, 2009.

Byrd, John / Rothberg, Michael: "Between Subalternity and Indigeneity. Critical Categories for Postcolonial Studies." In: *Interventions: International Journal of Postcolonial Studies* 13,1 (2011), 1-12.

Clifford, James: "On Ethnographic Authority." In: *Representations* 2 (1983), 118-146.

Clifford, James / Marcus, George: *Writing Culture: The Poetics and Politics of Ethnography.* Berkeley/Los Angeles: University of California Press, 1986.

Destrempes, Hélène / Lüsebrink, Hans-Jürgen: "Liminaire. Images de l'Amérindien au Canada francophone: littérature et image." In: *Tangence* 85 (2007), 5-11.

Garroutte, Eva Marie / Westcott, Kathleen Delores: "The Story Is a Living Being: Companionship with Stories in Anishinaabeg Studies." In: Doerfler, Jill / Sinclair, Niigaanwewidam James / Stark, Heidi Kiiwetinepinesiik (eds): *Centering Anishinaabeg Studies: Understanding the World Through Stories.* East Lansing/Winnipeg: Michigan State University Press/University of Manitoba Press, 2013, 61-79.

Gatti, Maurizio: *Littérature amérindienne du Québec: écrits de langue française.* Montreal: Hurtubise, 2004.

Gatti, Maurizio: *Être écrivain amérindien au Québec. Indianité et création littéraire.* Montreal: Hurtubise, 2009 [2006].

Goeman, Mishuana: *Mark My Words: Native Women Mapping Our Nations.* Minneapolis: University of Minnesota Press, 2013.

Haig-Brown, Celia: "Indigenous Thought, Appropriation, and Non-Aboriginal People." In: *Canadian Journal of Education* 33,4 (2010), 925-950.

Harindranath, Ramaswami: *Perspectives on Global Cultures.* Berkshire/New York: Open University Press, 2006.

Hedican, Edward. J.: "Eurocentrism in Aboriginal Studies: A Review of Issues and Conceptual Problems." In: *The Canadian Journal of Native Studies* 34,1 (2014), 87-109.

hooks, bell: *Yearning: Race, Gender, and Cultural Politics.* Boston: South End Press, 1990.

King, Thomas: *The Inconvenient Indian: A Curious Account of Native People in North America.* Toronto: Doubleday Canada, 2012.

Lee, Damien: "In Conversation with *Centering Anishinaabeg Studies*: A Review." In: *Decolonization: Indigeneity, Education & Society* 2,2 (2013), 132-144.

Létourneau, Jocelyn: "The Unthinkable History of Québec." In: *Oral History Review* 17,1 (1989), 89-115.

Montpetit, Caroline: "Faire revivre la mémoire des Territoires." In: *Le Devoir* (06/06/2009), http://www.ledevoir.com/culture/livres/253601/faire-revivre-la-memoire-des-territoires (accessed 11/08/2016).

Morency, Jean: "Images de l'Amérindien dans le roman québécois depuis 1945." In: *Tangence* 85 (2007), 85-98.

Ravi, Srilata / Couture, Claude: *Autour de l'œuvre de Gérard Bouchard. Histoire sociale, sociologie historique, imaginaires collectifs et politiques publiques.* Quebec: Presses de l'Université Laval, 2015.

Sangster, Joan: "Telling Our Stories: Feminist Debates and the Use of Oral History." In: *Women's History Review* 3,1 (1994), 5-28.

Simpson, Audra: "On Ethnographic Refusal: Indigeneity, Voice, and Colonial Citizenship." In: *Junctures* 9 (2007), 67-80.

Simpson, Audra: "Subjects of Sovereignty: Indigeneity, The Revenue Rule, and Juridics of Failed Consent." In: *Law and Contemporary Problems* 71 (2008), 191–216.

Simpson, Audra: *Mohawk Interruptus: Political Life Across the Borders of Settler States.* Durham: Duke University Press, 2014.

Simpson, Audra / Smith, Andrea (eds): *Theorizing Native Studies.* Durham: Duke University Press, 2014.

Vincent, Sylvie: "De la nécessité des clôtures: réflexion libre sur la marginalisation des Amérindiens." In: *Anthropologie et Société* 10,2 (1986), 75-83.

Vincent, Sylvie / Arcand, Bernard: *L'image de l'Amérindien dans les manuels scolaires du Québec ou Comment les Québécois ne sont pas des sauvages.* Montreal: Hurtubise, 1979.

Marion Christina ROHRLEITNER (El Paso)

El Otro Norte: The Rise of *Latinocanadá*. Latina/o Canadian Literature in the Wake of Anti-Immigrant Crises in the United States

Résumé

Se concentrant sur deux écrivains de l'Amérique latine, qui vivent et travaillent au Canada depuis des décennies, et sur un groupe de théâtre pan-latino qui existe à Vancouver depuis les années 1990, mon essai illustre comment le Canada joue un rôle de plus en plus important, quoique peu (re)connu, dans la production littéraire et théâtrale *latina*. Alors que la littérature *latina* écrite au Canada a longtemps été considérée comme une littérature d'exil, les écrivains latinos nés au Canada se perçoivent comme des Canadiens bien plus que, par exemple, les Chiliens exilés ; leurs voix sont devenues plus fortes depuis les années 1990. Mon essai met en valeur l'influence de la littérature *latina* états-unienne sur la littérature d'exil d'Amérique latine au Canada ; d'autre part, il montre que la littérature *latina* canadienne diffère de celle des États-Unis en ce qu'elle offre une perspective divergente à la xénophobie croissante aux États-Unis, qui cible, outre les musulmans, les émigrés et les migrants provenant du Mexique et de l'Amérique centrale. Ces œuvres littéraires de Canadiens latinos proposent une alternative à la crise d'immigration aux États-Unis, de même qu'elles partagent une perspective commune sur la littérature *latina* en tant que littérature intrinsèquement transnationale et multilingue.

Immigrant Genealogies of *Latinidad* in Canada and the US

President Barack Obama's 2008 presidential campaign coincided with the beginning of the worst economic crisis in the United States since the Great Depression as a result of the implosion of the fraudulent subprime mortgage market. Candidate Obama's campaign slogans, "Change We Can Believe In" and "Hope," offered a positive counterpoint to pervasive feelings of fear and despair in the United States, and inspired faith not only in repairing the national economy, but also the damaged international reputation of the United States in the aftermath of the George W. Bush and Dick Cheney administration. In spite of a remarkable economic recovery, the passing of the Affordable Care Act, and the adoption of legislation that ensures full civil rights for members of the LGBTQ community, President Obama's second term in particular was also characterized by growing racialized tensions, Islamophobia, and the criminalization of immigrants. In 2015 and 2016 alone, the United States witnessed dozens of killings of unarmed black men and women at the hands of the police, school shootings, and bombings of Black churches, and the bewildering rise of a presidential candidate who criminalizes all Mexican immigrants as "rapists" and "thugs," and confidently asserts that a border wall will not only be built, but also funded by the Mexican government. In the early stages of the presidential election cycle, a Canadian-born presidential hopeful called for a border wall between the United States and Canada in an effort to ward off the media-created specter of 'illegal' immigrants and Islamist extremists from north of the border. This discursive conflation of Islamist terrorists with Mexican immigrants is a remarkable low point in the rhetoric of a largely imaginary perpetual crisis that threatens an equally imaginary uniform way of US-American life and values.

It is in this odd political climate, and from my specific subject position in the El Paso/Ciudad Juárez border region that I read the work of Latina/o authors not only in the borderlands of the Southwest, but also in Canada, where Latina/o literature still occupies a somewhat marginal position. As Michelle Habell-Pallán, one of the few US-American scholars working on Latina/o Canadian literature and performance arts, asserts in the epilogue to *Loca Motion: The Travels of Chicana and Latina Popular Culture*, "when we think about the culture of *Las Américas, con acento*, Canada rarely comes to mind" (2005, 210). Rachel Adams (2008, 314), Winfried Siemerling, and Sarah Phillips Casteel (2010, 7-8) have pointed out that Canadian literature has often been overlooked in debates on Latina/o literature in the Americas in spite of the hemispheric turn in American studies in the first decade of the 21st century. This marginalization of Canadian voices in hemispheric American Studies is surprising and frustrating, given the rich creative work produced by Latina/o Canadian writers as well as their substantial investment in raising awareness for immigrant rights and social justice in Canada and in their countries of origin.

Furthermore, the lack of attention to Latina/o Canadian artistic production not only ignores the historical relevance and continuity of a US-Latina/o literary tradition in Canada and obscures the reality of transnational *latinidades* in all of North America; it also deprives us of the opportunity to learn about constructions of Latina/o identities outside of the often limiting and prescriptive and increasingly polarizing framework of the United States.[1]

In the past decade, Latina/os, especially recent immigrants from Mexico and Central America, have been experiencing renewed hostility in the United States. The three major manifestations of crisis in the United States in the second decade of the twenty-first century – economic insecurity, racial tensions, and anti-immigrant sentiments – are intimately intertwined with the tensions between the state and the demands of a disenfranchised working class, a significant part of whom belong to a historically racialized minority. A close second to the institutionalized violence against African Americans is the criminalization and vilification of Latina/os in the United States. This vilification manifests not only in the prominent usage of the dehumanizing term 'illegal alien' and in openly xenophobic rhetoric in the media, but also in the passing of laws such as Arizona SB 1070, which outlawed the successful Mexican American Studies Program in the Tucson Independent School District, and Arizona HB 2281, which effectively legalized racial profiling in the spring of 2010. The debt crisis in Puerto Rico, exacerbated by the island's colonial status within the union, is another example of the legal discrimination of Latina/os in the United States.

This focus on crisis culminated in the emergence of a Republican candidate and now President of the United States, who promises to "make America great again," presumably by returning to a fictitious state of heteronormative and white supremacist national bliss. Given this hysterical construction of threat, which is most often geared at Mexican immigrants to the United States, Canada is now again becoming an increasingly attractive location for Latina/o writers and artists. This is true especially since the adjuration of Justin Trudeau as Prime Minister on November 4, 2015, whose youthful image, progressive ideas, investment in valuing diversity and difference, and message of hope and change mirror, in many ways, the early phase of the Obama presidency.

The current anti-immigrant crisis in the United States stands in contrast to Canadian policies that have historically been mostly welcoming to refugees and immigrants from Latin America. Since the Spanish Civil War, and with particular force since the *coups d'états* in Chile and Argentina in the 1970s, the different immigration and asylum policies in Canada and the United States have been among the major factors for the rise of what Hugh Hazelton has called "Latinocanadá" – the evolution of a rich literary tradition by predominantly Spanish speaking Latin American immigrants and their Canada-born descendants (Hazelton 2007, 1). This emerging Latina/o Canadian literary tradition is formally and thematically in rich conversation with US-Latina/o literature, and draws on predominantly Chicana/o, Nuyorican, and Dominican American models. Latina/o Canadian literature continues US-Latina/o traditions, but also promotes a pan-Latina/o identity that moves beyond Latina/o identities that remain grounded in a national origin, such as literatures that identify specifically as Puerto Rican, Cuban American, or Mexican American. Latina/o Canadian literature, and especially Latina/o Canadian theatre, thus embraces and promotes a transnational, pan-Latina/o identity.

Canadian scholars such as Natalie Alvarez, Rachel Adams, Maria Feliciano, Sarah Phillips Casteel, Hugh Hazelton, Luis Molina Lora, Naín Nómez, Luis Torres, and Julio Torres-Recinos, among others, have been studying key aspects of Latina/o Canadian literature since its inception. Luis Molina Lora (2013, 16), for example, has emphasized the origins of Latina/o Canadian literature in first Spanish and later South and Central American literatures of exile; Natalie Alvarez has drawn attention to the importance of theatre in Latina/o Canadian cultural production; Mayte Gómez (1995) and Pablo Ramirez (2010) have studied the work of Argentinian-Canadian playwright Guillermo Verdecchia and his impact on Canadian audiences, and Hugh Hazelton has introduced Latina/o Canadian literature in Spanish to an English-speaking audience via translation.

In this context it is important to note that the criminalization of immigrants, especially in times of economic and political crisis, is not limited to the United States. For example, "in July of 2009 Citizenship, Immigration, and Multiculturalism Minister Jason Kennedy […] announced a visa requirement for all Mexican nationals traveling to Canada" (Alvarez 2013, 3). This decision was made on the heels of record number of refugee claims made by Mexican citizens in 2005 (cf. Alvarez 2013, 3). Canada is, thus, not immune to populist anxieties that blame immigrants and refugees for economic and criminal crises. However, Justin Trudeau's leadership, and Canada's self-understanding as a country built by Indigenous Peoples, First Nations, and immigrants, has thus far prevented as comprehensive anti-immigrant legislation as in the United States to take hold, and Latina/o Canadian writers are significant voices highlighting the accomplishments of Canadians of Latina/o American descent.

Constructions of *Latinidad* in Canada vs the United States

According to the 2011 census[2], most of the roughly 545.000 Canadians of Latin American descent hail from Mexico, Colombia, and El Salvador. However, a significant 387.000 of Latina/o Canadians are Canadian citizens by birth, which proves that there is a growing number of young, Canada-born Latina/os who are demanding their place in the proverbial Canadian mosaic. Toronto, Montreal, and Vancouver are the cities with the most significant numbers of Canadians of Latin American descent. The Olympic Peninsula has also become a hub of immigration from Latin America and a perhaps unlikely location of increased border control reminiscent of the highly policed and militarized US-Mexico border.

The main differences between the construction of *latinidad*[3] in Canada and in the United States consist in the varying geographical distance from the country of origin, a radically different historical relationship between the nations of the Southern hemisphere to the United States and Canada, the main impetus for emigration, and the chosen language(s) of publication. While there is no such border to contend with in the Canadian context, the US-Mexico border is often falsely invoked as a well-established natural and cultural division by promoters of an entirely fictitious singular, Eurocentric, Anglophone, Protestant US-American identity; in reality, the drawing of this border only dates back to 1848 and was not systematically enforced until the misleadingly labeled "Repatriation" program of the 1930s. The militarization of the US-Mexico border is even more recent, and started only with Operation Gatekeeper, passed under the Clinton administration in September 1994.

The dominant impetus for migration and immigration to the United States from Mexico also differs in significant ways from reasons for immigration to Canada. First, a significant part of the Mexican American presence in the American Southwest is not even the result of migration, but of expansionist warfare, which led to the incorporation of over 50% of former Mexican territory into the United States in the Treaty of Guadalupe Hidalgo. As Rodolfo Acuña stated in his spearheading study of Mexican Americans, *Occupied America,* "the border moved South" (2007, 14). Second, Mexican immigration to the United States is the result of both economic crisis and of civil strife, from the Mexican Revolution to the cartel wars of 2008 to 2012; however, economic crisis often occurred in the United States rather than in Mexico, for example when the US entry into World War II in December 1941 led to the establishment of the Bracero program in 1942.

In stark contrast, "the cultural production made by Latin Americans in Canada has been framed by the notion of exile" (Habell-Pallán 2005, 208). This emphasis on exile applies, in particular, to writers who fled state-sponsored terror in Chile and Argentina during the 1970s, and civil wars in El Salvador, Nicaragua, and Guatemala in the 1980s. Canadian publications on Latina/o Canadian literature from this time period therefore tellingly focus on a nation-based concept, as Naín Nómez's 1982 anthology *Chilean Literature in Canada/Literatura chilena en Canadá* shows. Given the overt and covert involvement of the United States in the *coup d'état* against Salvador Allende in 1973, US-American support of contras in Central America in the 1980s, and a restrictive policy for Latin Americans seeking political asylum in the United States as a result of this foreign policy, many Latin American refugees turned to Canada for asylum. The earliest phase of Latina/o Canadian literature is thus dominated by Chilean, Argentinian, and Salvadoran exilic writers such as Carmen Aguirre, Carmen Rodríguez, Nela Rio, and Alfonso Quijada Urías.

Latinidad and Language Choice

Racist language policies in the US-American public school systems, especially in Texas, California, and the American Southwest, have fostered a privileging of the English language; as a result of these policies, and because of the ongoing dominance of English in the US-American publishing market, the vast majority of US-Latina/o authors write in English rather than in Spanish or an indigenous language. As early as 1987 Gloria Anzaldúa calls this policy "linguistic terrorism" (²1999, 80) in *Borderlands – La Frontera: The New Mestiza.* Established Latina/o authors such as the Dominican American novelist Julia Alvarez have repeatedly asserted that their literary language is English, not Spanish, which is not only the result of white privilege, but also of educational and class status. In her essay "Doña Aída, with Your Permission," Alvarez famously defends her choice to write in English rather than in Spanish as follows:

> I am not a Dominican writer. I have no business writing in a language that I can speak but have not studied deeply enough to craft. I can't ride its wild horses. Just the subjunctive would throw me off. I know the tender mouth of English, just how to work its reins…And though I have read Pablo Neruda and Cesar Vallejo and Julia de Burgos and Ana Lydia Vega and Aída Cartagena Portalatín, I can only admire what they do in Spanish. I cannot emulate their wonderful mastery of that language. (Alvarez 1998, 172)

The Chicana veteran poet Lorna Dee Cervantes expresses a similar sentiment in "Refugee Ship," one of her earliest poems published in her National Book Award-winning collection *Emplumada*: "Mama raised me without language / I am orphaned from my Spanish name / The words are foreign, stumbling / on my tongue." (Cervantes 1981, 38)

In contrast, most Latina/o Canadian authors continue to write in Spanish, or engage English and French in bilingual publications, such as the Chilean Canadian poet Carmen Rodríguez. Canada's language policies have a vastly different history due to the influence of the French majority in Québec and other provinces with large French-speaking populations. Even though Hugh Hazelton has emphasized that "Latin America has come to Canada and it is through translation that it is making its mark" (Molina Lora/Torres-Recinos 2013, 303), Jorge Etcheverry and others have argued that the Canadian publishing system and its reading public are arguably more open to literature published in languages other than English, as the creation and success of Ediciones Cordillera in Ottawa in the late 1970s has shown (cf. Molina Lora/Torres-Recinos 2013, 7).

Even though the notion of exile has indeed dominated Latina/o literature produced in Canada in the 1970s and 1980s (cf. Gutierrez 2001; Molina Lora 2013; Torres 2001) a growing number of Canada-born Latina/o writers promise a shift in the focus of literary and artistic production away from a desire to return and towards negotiations on how to stay and become an intrinsic part of the fabric of Canadian society. This new generation not only identifies more closely with Canada as 'home,' but also with a pan-Latina/o rather than a nation-based identity.

Hazelton's pioneering 2007 study *Latinocanadá: A Critical Study of Ten Latin American Writers of Canada* was the first comprehensive attempt in the English language at bringing together the work of Canadian writers of various Latin American descents.[4] In his survey of Latina/o Canadian literature, many texts testify to the lived experiences of Latina/o Canadians as perpetual crises, or states of emergency, moving from resistance to dictatorships, civil strife, poverty, and social injustice to emigration, exile, and loss of identity and status. In spite of these rather bleak experiences, most texts offer utopian gestures towards a future that is vastly different from the status quo, and imagine a Canada that lives up to its multicultural promise; it is here where I locate literary *Latinocanadá*'s embrace of a utopian ideal of Canada as what I call 'el otro norte.'[5]

Latin American Exiles and the Continuity of a Chicana/o Tradition in *Latinocanadá*

Given the current political climate in the United States, which is characterized by an anti-Mexican rhetoric reminiscent of the 1930s, and the much friendlier immigration and asylum policies of the Trudeau administration, Canada has emerged as an increasingly attractive country of immigration for Latin American as well as US-Latina/o writers. In the wake of such historical continuities and new trends, the study of Latina/o Canadian literature is becoming increasingly important to a global understanding of Latina/o Studies beyond the United States.

Since Latina/o Studies has historically focused on the United States, the production of Latina/o literature, and by extension *latinidad,* in Canada offers unique insights not only in the multiple dimensions of this critical category, but also in Canadian Latina/o writers' efforts to face and overcome the difficulties that led to emigration and the crises experienced in the new home country due to xenophobia and cultural alienation. Narratives by Latina/o Canadian authors such as the Salvadoran-Canadian Alfonso Quijada Urías, the Argentinian-Canadian Nela Rio, and the Chilean-Canadian Carmen Rodríguez celebrate the creative imagination as a source of both personal joy and political resistance, and offer an often marginalized yet crucially important counterpoint to US-based Latina/o stories of migration and exile. Equally important are the specifically Canadian experiences of immigration and exile that offer alternatives to failing US-American models of immigration policy and cultural integration.

Born in Córdoba, Argentina, in 1938, Nela Rio grew up in Mendoza, a booming city full of immigrants and refugees from Spain, Italy, Belgium, the Soviet Union, and Eastern Europe. Her own grandparents had been immigrants from Italy, and Rio therefore emphasizes time and again that she always identified with the immigrant experience both in Argentina and in Canada. Groomed as an early member of grassroots movements opposed to the Peronist dictatorship, Rio became active in Amnesty International upon her move to Canada, and focused especially on the plight of refugee women from Central and South America who, after having experienced unimaginable physical and psychological violence, sought refuge in Canada. Her work was anthologized in the aforementioned anthology *Latinocanadá*, which established Latina/o Canadian texts as a specific category of inquiry. Excerpts from and discussions of her work also appear in two more recent Spanish language anthologies, *Lumbre y relumbre: Antología selecta de de la poesía hispano canadiense* (Torres-Recinos/Feliciano 2012)[6] and *Retrato de una nube: Primera antología del cuento hispano canadiense* (Molina Lora/Torres-Recinos 2008), which was also translated into English as *Cloudburst: An Anthology of Hispanic Canadian Short Stories* (Molina Lora/ Torres-Recinos 2013).

In *Latinocanadá*, Hazelton asserts that "what distinguishes Rio's work dealing with repression is the power of her imagination" (Hazelton 2007, 133) and it is here where I detect a utopian impulse in Latina/o Canadian writing that gestures beyond the crisis. Every poem in Rio's debut collection is dedicated to women resistance fighters in Guatemala and Argentina, and Hazelton asserts: "The book is a cry of resistance, defiance, and mourning, a cry that the speaker wants to 'resound like thunderbolts' through the world." (Hazelton 2007, 133) Rio's speaker's defiance is palpable, and reminiscent of the earliest stages of Chicana/o writing that emerged during the Chicana/o Civil Rights movement, showcasing the continuity between Chicana/o political poetry in the US and Chilean exilic poetry in Canada.

Rio's most recent collection of poetry, *El laberinto vertical/Vertical Labyrinth*, was published in a bilingual edition by Broken Jaw Press in New Brunswick in 2014. In these poems Nela Rio offers an alternative to Judeo-Christian creation narratives, in a move that is in direct conversation with Chicana/o theorists and writers such as Alicia Gaspar de Alba, whose own rewriting of the more *risqué* poems by the 17th century *criolla* nun, scholar, playwright, poet, and, to some, proto-feminist Sor Juana Inés de la Cruz, is echoed in Rio's poem "The Mystics":

> They asked if it was wrong to love man
> saying "love is sacred"
> as well as "that's the way it is."
> The women returned and loved with their hearts,
> letting the flesh delight
> in exquisite prayers. (Rio 2014, 28)

While Rio's mystics eschew sexual fulfillment and embrace a spiritual ecstasy instead, Gaspar de Alba concludes her historical novel *Sor Juana's Second Dream* with a poem entitled "Litany in the Subjunctive," which allows us at least to imagine a physical as well as spiritual same-sex union:

> If I could turn myself
> Into a bee and free
> This soul, those bars
> Webbed across your window
> Would be vain, that black
> Cloth, that rosary, that crucifix –
> Nothing could save you
> From my sting. (Gaspar de Alba 1999, 457)

The poem "Rivalidades" by Nela Rio offers gestures towards queering the history of conquest and evokes the work of Chicana feminist historians and philosophers Emma Perez and Gloria Anzaldúa:

> And there began to be many gods
> and rivalries
> and to outdo one another
> they created norms and modes and laws.

And they went even further, inventing punishments,
and spoke of obedience and disobedience
and of slippery planes of restless backs,
a land of condemnation or invincible pleasure.

And there was no longer understanding among people
for they spoke different languages
and loved the same things, but exclusively.

Unity was then filtered through the centuries
And love had to *disguise* itself as many things
to survive. (Rio 2014, 57; my emphasis)

Minorities need to "*disguise*" themselves "as many things" in order to survive in a conquest-induced Babel that promotes Puritan values and Manichaean binaries. This practice of 'masking' the self can be productively read not only as disavowal but also as hybrid performance – as an exercise in queering history. Rio thus participates in a discourse that is central to Chicana/o and Latina/o writing South of the border, which privileges the importance of *mestizaje* and the adaptability of syncretic spirituality in the Americas. The discursive production of a narrative of 'unity' is exposed and critiqued by the lyrical 'I' as a historical process that does not allow for what the queer Chicano poet and memoirist Rigoberto González has called "piedritas" in his *Autobiography of My Hungers* (2013, 4) – the small irregular pieces of dissenting individuality that are sifted out in any process that ultimately aims at creating conformity. And yet, the poem does not end in defeat, but with endurance and survival.

Latinocanadá's Utopian Responses to the Anti-Immigrant Crisis in the Unites States

Nela Rio's contemporary, Alfonso Quijada Urías, is one of the foremost poets and prose writers from El Salvador working in Canada. Quijada Urías is an experimental writer who, in his *minificciones*, or flash fictions, employs what José Esteban Muñoz has called a "queer utopia," which he defines as "a modality of critique that speaks to quotidian gestures as laden with possibility" (Muñoz 2009,

91); Quijada Urías imagines such a world full of possibility, beyond the crisis, and, to engage Žižek (2010), beyond the apocalypse. The short story "Florencia Sánchez," for example, begins with the subjugation of indigenous Central Americans, but ends in the utopian promise of the arrival of the "hour of the jaguar" (Hazelton 2007, 122). This ending is not the apocalypse as in a biblical universe or in Žižek's perception of the "end times," but rather an indigenous alternative to a binary system of good and evil. The hour of the jaguar promises the return of the fifth sun and hints at renewal rather than destruction. Latina/o authors in Canada and in the United States thus embrace neither Žižek's focus on an impending global apocalypse nor Fukuyama's overly optimistic, Eurocentric notion of "the end of history" (1992) after the fall of the Berlin Wall. Instead, they offer what Foucault has termed a "history of the present" (Foucault 1977, 34), in which a cyclical genealogy replaces linear archaeology as the most productive form of historiographic inquiry and epistemology. This approach is utopian because it looks beyond the limitations of the present moment and entertains multiple possibilities.

This revolutionary view of history and time requires a revolutionary language, and Alfonso Quijada Urías has suggested that he is "always looking for a new style, experimenting as I went, working toward a revolution in language" (Hazelton 2007, 104). One example of this effort is his humorous political poem "Pobres de Nosotros/Poor Us."

> We'll die along with Capitalism,
> we've been sentenced.
> Poor us
> and without ever having enjoyed it. (Quijada Urías 1991, 25)

The poem's sarcastic tone actually offers a meaningful commentary on the very role of ethnic literature in the Americas. As Elena Machado Sáez and Raphael Dalleo (2007, 5) have pointed out, post 1960s Latina/o literature actively engages with the commodification of ethnicity on the literary market. Rather than repudiating capitalism altogether, Latina/o authors, according to Machado Sáez and Dalleo (2007, 25), claim their stake and voice in the production of literary discourses on *latinidad*. And yet in spite of their best efforts at capitalizing on the global market that commodifies their ethnic difference, most Latina/os continue to be excluded from the profits reaped by the commodification of their cultures. In fact, one could argue that capitalism itself is nearing its end, in an almost anachronistic use of Marxist-infused postmodern perspective. In this respect, the contemporary Latina/o Canadian poem differs substantively from a Nuyorican poem from the 1960s, with which it is otherwise in conversation. This poem draws on an aesthetics of resistance from the 1960s reminiscent of Pedro Pietri's Nuyorican poem "Puerto Rican Obituary" (2015), in which the poet laments the fate of his people, without betraying a faith in the possibility of the end of capitalism itself.

The Evolution of a Canadian Pan-Latina/o Identity: The Latino Theatre Group (LTG) in Vancouver and the PUENTE Theatre in Victoria, British Columbia

Rio, Rodríguez, and Quijada Urías are important representatives of the first phase of Latina/o Canadian literary production which is, indeed, dominated by the experience of exile. Starting in the mid-1990s, the focus began to shift from an exilic literature to an often multilingual and pan-Latina/o Canadian literature that reflects and gives voice to an emerging Latina/o Canadian identity. Among the most powerful expressions of this emerging work by mostly Canada-born Latina/os are the performances of the Latino Theatre Group in Vancouver. Founded in 1994 by Carmen Aguirre, a Chilean exilic poet, playwright, and activist, the group is truly pan-Latina/o, featuring Canadian-born children of Argentinian political exiles, first-generation immigrants from El Salvador, and second-generation Mexican Canadians. Similar to the Quijada Urías's debt to Nuyorican Poetry, and Nela Rio's nod to Chicana spirituality, the theatre group is an heir to and practitioner of both Luis Valdez's *Teatro Campesino* and Augusto Boal's "Theatre of the Oppressed" in the United States. Drawing on traditional themes and performance elements in Valdez' *Actos* (1990), Chicana/o political theatre performed in the fields of California, and on the method developed in the favelas of Rio de Janeiro, the Latino Theatre Group draws on hemispheric forms of critical artistic expression and brings them together in improvised scenes that draw heavily on the productive tensions and experiences among the members of the group. Lived experience as theatrical performance is a key component of theatre as well as a tool for social change. The group's pastiche-like performances draw on a Latin American aesthetics of resistance and *testimonio* as well as on popular culture such as comics, vintage rock'n'roll, Puerto Rican reggaeton, and Afro-Caribbean hip-hop. It is here where I locate the most promising sites of resistance and endurance of what Anishinaabe writer and scholar Gerald Vizenor (2008) has called, in the context of Native-American literature, "survivance" in a community's culture of resistance.

The PUENTE Theatre was founded by Lina de Guevara, like Carmen Aguirre a Chilean exile. Similar to the LTG, PUENTE is based in British Columbia and prides itself on a pan-Latina/o ensemble and repertoire. The theatre's current artistic director is Mercedes Bátiz-Benét, a "multi-disciplinary artist, writer and award-winning director," and a recent immigrant from Mexico.[7] Their recently added program "Worldplay" branches out into plays and theatrical traditions that move beyond Latin America.[8] As its name indicates, the PUENTE Theatre strives to build bridges between a multicultural Canadian audience and its pan-Latina/o ensemble, many of whom are immigrants themselves. Because of its reliance on non-verbal communication and by mixing Latina/o and non-Latina/o narratives, the theatre offers, as Rachel Adams (2008, 313) has suggested in a different context, a particularly productive venue to perform a truly hemispheric Latina/o experience that moves beyond a discourse that is "often framed in terms of a dichotomy between the United States (or the more amorphous North America) and Latin America" (Alvarez 2013, 314). In 2014, a production of *Cruel Tears/ Lágrimas Crueles: A Tex-Mex Musical Based on Shakespeare's Othello* set an excellent example of such efforts at transcending divisive binaries via humor, mimicry, and camp. The play comes with an appropriate warning: "Some Spanish," but immediately reassures the audience with "English subtitles."[9] In doing so, the PUENTE theatre facilitates a theatrical encounter with *latinidad* that invites audience members of diverse ethnic, cultural, educational, and linguistic backgrounds into a space that merges the familiar with the new. While Natalie Alvarez argues in her introduction that "the critical appropriation of the moniker 'Latina/o' during the civil rights movement in the US" (2013, 5-6) was used as a "positive designation of social place" (Velez-Ibáñez/Sampaio 2002, 2 in Alvarez 2013, 6), I would add that this invocation of a much less politically charged pan-*latinidad* in Canadian theatre also performs what Arlene Dávila has termed "Latinos, Inc." or the creation of *latinidad* as a marketing category that consciously participates in the commodification of its ethnicity (Dávila 2001, 3). Rather than reflecting a crisis in socially conscious theatre, this strategy showcases, in my view, the success of Latina/o playwrights, actors, and directors to effectively manipulate the literary market in their favor.

Transforming US-Immigration Crises into Transnational Pan-Latina/o Cultural Production in Canada

Latina/o Canadian literature is an exciting emerging field that further foregrounds the intrinsically transnational character of Latina/o literature in Canada, in the United States, and beyond. The literary production of exilic Latin American writers of the 1970s and 1980s in Canada is akin to the evolution of nation-based fields of Chicana/o Studies, Puerto Rican/Boricua Studies, and Cuban-American Studies in the United States, to name but a few, in the 1960s. Given Canada's different historical, economic, and political relationship with the nations of the Southern hemisphere, and due to its greater acceptance and appreciation of a multilingual literary archive, a transnational, pan-Latina/o literary identity, and collective consciousness has emerged in Canada much faster than in the United States. In stark contrast to identity politics and an ongoing nation-based model of Latina/o identification in the United States that is grounded in an anti-immigration crisis, this shift to a pan-Latina/o identity is not immediately conceived as a conflation of all things 'Latina/o' and the threat of obliterating important historical, cultural, and political differences among Canadians of Latin American descent. Mexican Canadians, Salvadoran Canadians, Chilean Canadians, and Argentinian-Canadians have not been pitted against each other in ideological terms the way, for example, Cuban Americans and Mexican Americans have. As a result, studying Latina/o Canadian literature allows us to open up the possibility for a transnational discourse of solidarity. According to Daniel Alarcón, a Peruvian American novelist, radio journalist, and self-described "transnational" writer who publishes in English and in Spanish and resides in both the United States and Peru,

> [t]he future is all about impurities, mestizaje, and so if I write about the neighborhoods of Lima, created through internal migration – because these are global processes at work – I am by implication also writing about

> New York, San Jose, Atlanta, Cleveland, Madrid, London… (Anderson/
> Moreno 2014, 187)

I venture to add Montreal, Toronto, and Vancouver to this list of locations where powerful, transnational Latina/o stories are told.

1   Habell-Pallán (2005) herself acknowledges in "'Call Us Americans, 'Cause We Are All from the Américas': Latinos at Home in Canada," the epilogue to her book *Loca Motion*, that her shift in perspective was the direct result of her move from Los Angeles to Seattle to start a tenure track job at the University of Washington – without personal exposure, it seems, awareness of *latinidad* is still vastly limited to the United States.

2   I am using numbers from the 2011 census, since the immigration and ethno-cultural diversity results of the 2016 census will not be available until October 25, 2017: http://www12.statcan.gc.ca/nhs-enm/2011/dp-pd/dt-td/Rp-eng.cfm?TABID=2&LANG=E&APATH=3&DETAIL=0&DIM=0&FL=A&FREE=0&GC=0&GID=1118296&GK=0&GRP=0&PID=105396&PRID=0&PTYPE=105277&S=0&SHOWALL=0&SUB=0&Temporal=2013&THEME=95&VID=0&VNAMEE=&VNAMEF=&D1=0&D2=0&D3=0&D4=0&D5=0&D6=0 (accessed 24/05/2017).

3   'Latinidad' is a term that is notoriously difficult to define. I consider Arlene Dávila's definition to be the most productive for my purposes here: "I treat Latinization as the 'out-of-many, one people' process through which 'Latinos' or 'Hispanics' are conceived and represented as sharing one common identity. These processes are not properly seen as a top-down development, resulting from the commodification and appropriation of Latino culture from self-agency; rather, they stem from the contrary involvement of and negotiations between dominant, imposed, and self-generated interests […]. [T]he ensuing enactments, definitions, and representations of Hispanic or Latino culture from such continuing processes are what I define as 'Latinidad'." (Dávila 2001, 16-17)

4   Another early English language contribution to the study of Latina/o Canadian literature is an edited collection by Lorena M. Gajardo entitled *Melting the Ice: Latinocanadá Voice, Culture, and Creativity*. It was published by Zurita, the Latina/o Canadian imprint of Tightrope Books, in 2006 and is out of print.

5   I coin the term 'el otro norte' by connecting two commonly used terms, 'el norte' and 'the other America' to challenge a facile and false conflation of 'el norte' with the United States only. First, the common colloquial reference to the United States is 'el norte' by Mexican and Central American immigrants and migrants (cf. also Gregory Nava's award-winning 1983 feature film on two Guatemalan siblings escaping the civil war, *El Norte*). Second, I draw on Michael J. Dash's use of the term 'the other America' in his eponymous monograph (published by the University of Virginia Press, 1998) to emphasize the fact that the term 'America' has been falsely connoted with the United States only. In doing so, I wish to highlight that 'el norte' can and has also been Canada, not only the United States, to immigrants and refugees from the Southern hemisphere, Mexico, and the Caribbean.

6   *Cloudburst: An Anthology of Hispanic Canadian Short Stories*, 2013. The insistence on the term 'Hispanic' results from a focus on the Spanish language as well as on the inclusion of Enrique Fernández, an author from Spain.

7   http://www.puentetheatre.ca/mercedes.html (accessed 23/03/2017).

8   http://www.puentetheatre.ca/worldplay.html (accessed 23/03/2017).

9   http://www.puentetheatre.ca/plays_current.html (accessed 25/05/2017).

Bibliography

Acuña, Rodolfo: *Occupied America: A History of Chicanos*. New York: Longman, 2007.

Adams, Rachel: "The Northern Borderlands and Canadian Latino Diaspora." In: Levander, Caroline F. / Levine, Robert S. (eds): *Hemispheric American Studies*. New Brunswick: Rutgers University Press, 2008, 313-327.

Alvarez, Julia: *Something to Declare: Essays*. New York: Plume, 1998.

Alvarez, Natalie (ed.): *Latina/o Canadian Theatre and Performance*. Toronto: Playwrights Canada Press, 2013.

Anderson, Thomas / Moreno, Marisel: "I Am an American Writer: An Interview with Daniel Alarcón." In: *MELUS* 39,4 (2014), 186-206.

Anzaldúa, Gloria: *Borderlands – La Frontera: The New Mestiza*. San Francisco: Aunt Lute, ²1999.

Berlant, Lauren: *Cruel Optimism*. Durham: Duke University Press, 2011.

Caminero-Santangelo, Marta: *On Latinidad: U.S. Latina/o Literature and the Construction of Ethnicity*. Gainesville: University of Florida Press, 2009.

Cervantes, Lorna Dee: *Emplumada.* Pittsburgh: University of Pittsburgh Press, 1981.

Dalleo, Raphael / Machado Sáez, Elena: *The Latina/o Canon and the Emergence of Post-Sixties Literature.* New York: Palgrave Macmillan, 2007.

Dash, Michael J.: *The Other America: Caribbean Literature in a New World Context.* Charlottesville: University of Virginia Press, 1998.

Dávila, Arlene: *Latinos, Inc.: The Marketing and Making of a People.* Berkeley: University of California Press, 2001.

Foucault, Michel: *Discipline and Punish: The Birth of the Prison.* Translated by Alan Sheridan. New York: Pantheon, 1977.

Fukuyama, Francis: *The End of History and the Last Man.* New York: The Free Press, 1992.

Gajardo, Lorena M. (ed.): *Melting the Ice: Latinocanadá Voice, Culture, and Creativity.* Toronto: Tightrope Books, 2006.

Gaspar de Alba, Alicia: *Sor Juana's Second Dream.* Albuquerque: University of New Mexico Press, 1999.

Gómez, Mayte: "Healing the Border Wound: *Fronteras Americanas* and the Future of Canadian Multiculturalism." In: *Theater Research in Canada/Recherches théâtrales au Canada* 16,1-2 (1995), https://journals.lib.unb.ca/index.php/tric/article/view/7169/8228 (accessed 20/03/2017).

González, Rigoberto: *Autobiography of My Hungers.* Madison: University of Wisconsin Press, 2013.

Gutierrez, Leopoldo: *Blue Jay: Notes from Exile.* Cinema Libre, 2001. DVD.

Habell-Pallán, Michelle: *Loca Motion: The Travels of Chicana and Latina Popular Culture.* New York: New York University Press, 2005.

Hazelton, Hugh / Geddes, Gary (eds): *Compañeros: An Anthology of Writing About Latin America.* Dunvegan: Cormorant, 1990.

Hazelton, Hugh: *Latinocanadá: A Critical Study of Ten Latin American Writers of Canada.* Kingston/Montreal: McGill-Queen's University Press, 2007.

Hazelton, Hugh: "September 11, 1973: Latin America Comes to Canada." In: Mezei, Kathy / Simon, Sherry / Von Flotow, Luise (eds): *Translation Effects: The Shaping of Modern Canadian Culture.* Kingston/Montreal: McGill-Queen's University Press, 2014, 182-196.

Molina Lora, Luis / Torres-Recinos, Julio (eds): *Retrato de una nube: Primera antología del cuento hispano canadiense.* Ottawa: Editorial Lugar Común, 2008.

Molina Lora, Luis / Torres-Recinos, Julio (eds): *Cloudburst: An Anthology of Hispanic Canadian Short Stories*. Translated by Hugh Hazelton et al. Ottawa: University of Ottawa Press, 2013.

Molina Lora, Luis: "A Look into *Cloudburst*: The Central Themes." Translated by Susan Cruess. In: Molina Lora, Luis / Torres-Recinos, Julio (eds): *Cloudburst: An Anthology of Hispanic Canadian Short Stories*. Translated by Hugh Hazelton et al. Ottawa: University of Ottawa Press, 2013, 15-19.

Muñoz, José Esteban: *Cruising Utopia: The Then and There of Queer Futurity*. New York: New York University Press, 2009.

Nava, Gregory: *El Norte*. The Criterion Collection, 1984. DVD.

Nómez, Naín (ed.): *Chilean Literature in Canada/Literatura chilena en Canadá*. Ottawa: Cordillera, 1982.

Pietri, Pedro: "Puerto Rican Obituary." In: Flores, Juan / López Adorno, Pedro (eds): *Pedro Pietri: Selected Poetry*. San Francisco: City Lights Books, 2015, 3-12.

Quijada Urías, Alfonso: "Pobres de Nosotros/Poor Us." In: Quijada Urías, Alfonso: *They Come and Knock on the Door*. Translated by Darwin J. Flakoll. Willimantic, CT: Curbstone Press, 1991.

Quijada Urías, Alfonso: "Florencia Sánchez." In: Hazelton, Hugh: *Latinocanadá: A Critical Study of Ten Latin American Writers of Canada*. Kingston/Montreal: McGill-Queen's University Press, 2007, 119-122.

Ramirez, Pablo: "Collective Memory and the Borderlands in Guillermo Verdecchia's *Fronteras Americanas*." In: Yovanovich, Gordana / Huras, Amy (eds): *Latin American Identities After 1980*. Waterloo: Wilfrid Laurier University Press, 2010, 273-286.

Rio, Nela: *El laberinto vertical/Vertical Labyrinth*. Translated by Sophie M. Lavoie and Hugh Hazelton. New Brunswick: Broken Jaw Press, 2014.

Rodríguez, Carmen: "I Live in a Language That's Not Mine." In: Silvera, Makeda (ed.): *The Other Woman: Women of Color in Contemporary Canadian Literature*. Toronto: Sister Vision, 1995, 208-218.

Ruprecht, Alvina / Taiana, Cecilia (eds): *Reordering of Culture: Latin America, the Caribbean and Canada in the Hood*. Ottawa: Carleton University Press, 1995.

Siemerling, Winfried / Casteel, Sarah Phillips: "Canada and Its Americas." In: Siemerling, Winfried / Casteel, Sarah Phillips (eds): *Canada and Its Americas: Transnational Navigations*. Montreal: McGill-Queen's University Press, 2010, 3-28.

Torres, Luis: "Writings of the Latin-Canadian Exile." In: *Revista Canadiense de Estudios Hispánicos* 26,1-2 (2001), 179-198.

Torres-Recinos, Julio / Feliciano, Maria (eds): *Lumbre y relumbre: Antología selecta de la poesía hispano canadiense*. Ottawa/Toronto: Editorial Lugar Común/Editorial Antares, 2012.

Valdez, Luis: *Early Works: Actos, Bernabe, and Pensamiento Serpentino*. Houston: Arte Público Press, 1990.

Velez-Ibáñez, Carlos G. / Sampaio, Anna: "Processes, New Prospects, and Approaches. Introduction." In: Velez-Ibáñez, Carlos G. / Sampaio, Anna (eds): *Transnational Latina/o Communities: Politics, Processes, and Cultures.* Lanham: Rowan and Littlefield, 2002, 1-37.

Vizenor, Gerald (ed.): *Survivance: Narratives of Native Presence*. Lincoln: University of Nebraska Press, 2008.

Žižek, Slavoj: *Living in the End Times*. New York: Verso, 2010.

Les auteur(e)s – The Authors

DAVID BOUCHER

Doctorant au Département des littératures de langue française à l'Université de Montréal (thèse portant sur les représentations dystopiques de la société dans le nouveau roman d'anticipation francophone chez Nelly Arcan, Michel Houellebecq et Antoine Volodine) et chercheur à l'IIS (Institut international de sociocritique). Participation à plusieurs colloques internationaux et publication de plusieurs textes et articles scientifiques.

MARIE CARRIÈRE

Director of the Canadian Literature Centre at the University of Alberta, where she also teaches English. A comparatist by training, she has published books, articles, and edited collections on Canadian and Quebec literatures in English and French, migrant literature, postcolonialism, mythocriticism, the ethics of care, as well as feminist theory and literature. Monographs: *Writing in the Feminine in French and English Canada: A Question of Ethics* (UTP, 2002); *Médée, protéiforme* (POU-UOP, 2012). Edited volumes and journal issues, among them *Ten Canadian Writers in Context* (UoAP, 2016); *Medea Nunc Sum. Refiguring the Myth of Medea / Refigurer le mythe de Médée* (*MuseMedusa*, 2015); *Regenerations: Canadian Women's Writing / Régénérations : écriture des femmes au Canada* (UoAP, 2014, with Patricia Demers). She is presently working on a book on metafeminism, namely the new faces of feminism in women's writing in English Canada and Quebec.

NICOLE CÔTÉ

Professeure à l'Université de Sherbrooke, a publié de nombreux articles et chapitres, co-dirigé trois ouvrages, *The Legacies of Jean-Luc Godard* (WLUP, 2014), *Expressions culturelles des francophonies* (Nota bene, 2008) et *Varieties of Exile* (Peter Lang, 2002). Elle a également dirigé deux recueils de nouvelles qu'elle a aussi traduites, *Vers le rivage* et *Nouvelles du Canada anglais* (L'instant même, 2002, 1999). Ses recherches actuelles portent sur les questions de genre/sexe, d'espace, liées à la minorisation, ainsi que sur les récits de la Crise.

PIET DEFRAEYE

Professor at the University of Alberta, where he teaches contemporary theatre. He also directs for the stage and does production dramaturgy. His critical publications include essays on Shakespeare and film, Quebec and Canadian theatre, German and Austrian theatre, gender theory and Reception Aesthetics, and more recently, theatre of genocide and cultural discourse on Patrice Lumumba. He is a graduate of the University of Louvain, U.C. Dublin, and the University of Toronto, and taught in Belgium (Louvain, Antwerp), Austria (Innsbruck), Germany (Munich), and Canada (Toronto, Fredericton, Edmonton).

NICOLETTA DOLCE

Chercheure du CRILCQ, enseigne au DLLM de l'Université de Montréal. Elle a publié des essais et des articles dans divers collectifs au Canada et à l'étranger. Son livre *La porosité au monde : l'écriture de l'intime chez Louise Warren et Paul Chamberland* (Nota bene, 2013) a été finaliste au prix Gabrielle-Roy 2012.

DANIELLE DUMONTET

A enseigné les littératures française et francophones au Département d'études romanes de l'Université Johannes Gutenberg. Ses travaux portent sur la littérature française de l'extrême contemporain et les littératures francophones, les littératures des Antilles (Haïti, Martinique et Guadeloupe) ainsi que du Canada (Québec et Acadie). Elle a beaucoup publié sur les auteurs des ‹ écritures migrantes › au Québec, entre autres sur l'auteur haïtien G. Étienne et l'écrivaine R. Robin. Elle travaille actuellement sur les poétiques de la mémoire et postmémoire dans les documentaires, films et romans.

ANA MARÍA FRAILE-MARCOS

Associate Professor of English at the University of Salamanca, where she teaches Canadian Literature. Her publications and research have focused mostly on African American and African Canadian literature. She is the editor of *Literature and the Glocal City: Reshaping the English Canadian Imaginary* (Routledge, 2014), and a member of the research project funded by the Spanish Ministry of Science and Innovation, "The City, Urban Cultures and Sustainable Literatures: Representations of the Anglo-Canadian Post-Metropolis."

ANDREA KROTTHAMMER

Études à l'Université d'Innsbruck (BA, MA ; semestre d'échange à l'Université de Montréal). Actuellement, elle travaille à l'*Innsbrucker Zeitungsarchiv*, au CEC Innsbruck (assistance rédactionnelle) et enseigne le français et l'allemand dans le secondaire. Pour son mémoire de master *La vie d'une femme, c'est la marche sur un fil. « L'écriture funambule » de Louise Dupré à l'exemple des relations mère-fille* (2015), elle a obtenu le Prix du Canada du CEC Innsbruck 2015 et le Prix d'Excellence du Gouvernement du Québec 2017.

MARION KÜHN

Détentrice d'un doctorat de l'Université de Passau, stagiaire postdoctorale au CRILCQ de l'Université Laval. Son projet de recherche actuel sur les enjeux de la narration problématique dans le roman historique du 21e siècle au Québec, en France et en Allemagne, est financé par le CRSH.

HANS-JÜRGEN LÜSEBRINK

Professeur à l'Université de la Sarre (depuis 1993), Chaire d'Études Culturelles Romanes et de Communication Interculturelle. Doctorats en philologie romane (Bayreuth, 1981) et en histoire (EHESS, Paris, 1984). Prix Diefenbaker du Conseil des Arts du Canada (2001), directeur de la section canadienne-française de la *Gesellschaft für Kanada-Studien* ; co-directeur de l'École Doctorale Internationale « Diversity » (Montréal-Trèves-Sarrebruck). Domaines de recherche : transferts culturels ; littératures et cultures francophones, théorie de la communication interculturelle. Derniers livres e.a. *« Le livre aimé du peuple ». Les almanachs québécois depuis 1777 à nos jours* (PUL, 2014) et, avec M.-A. Bernier et C. Donato (éds), *Jesuit Accounts on the Colonial Americas* (UTP, 2014).

CARMEN MATA BARREIRO

Professeure titulaire à l'Universidad Autónoma de Madrid ; professeure invitée à l'Université de Montréal (1999-2000, 2000-2001, 2001-2002). Ses recherches portent sur la littérature et la civilisation françaises et francophones (et particulièrement sur la culture et la littérature francophones du Canada) et sur la civilisation espagnole. Elle a publié des livres en Belgique, Espagne et France, et est auteure de nombreux articles. Elle a participé, au Québec, à 8 ouvrages collectifs ainsi qu'aux tomes 7 et 8 du *DŒLQ*. Elle a publié *Espagnes imaginaires du Québec* (PUL, 2012), et a coordonné un numéro de *Globe* (10,1 [2007]). Elle a été membre du Conseil d'administration de l'AIEQ.

URSULA MATHIS-MOSER

Professeure émérite au Département de langues romanes de l'Université d'Innsbruck et directrice du Centre d'études canadiennes (1997-). Elle a fondé et dirigé, pendant de longues années, le centre de recherche Cultures en contact, le Centre d'étude de la chanson québécoise (1995) et les archives Texte et musique (1985) de l'Université d'Innsbruck. Ses domaines de recherche sont les littératures française et francophones, la transculturalité, les littératures de la migration, les théories postcoloniales et l'intermédialité. Elle co-dirige la revue électronique *ATeM*. Publications (choix) : *Dany Laferrière : La dérive américaine* (vlb, 2003) ; plus de 25 ouvrages dirigés, dont *Acadiens et Cajuns. Politique et culture de minorités francophones en Amérique du Nord* (iup, 2009) ; *Passages et ancrages en France. Dictionnaire des écrivains migrants de langue française (1981-2011)* (avec Birgit Mertz-Baumgartner, Honoré Champion, 2012) ; *Die Krise schreiben. Writing Crisis. Écrire la crise* (iup, 2016).

DUNJA M. MOHR

Assistant Professor, English Department, Erfurt University. Studied in London (UK), Marburg, and in Montreal. PhD at Trier University (BMBF doctoral scholarship); DFG postdoctoral fellowship, Erlangen University; Margaret Atwood Award for Best PhD Thesis for *Worlds Apart? Dualism and Transgression in Contemporary Female Dystopias*

(McFarland, 2005). Editorial board *M. Atwood Studies*; Officer M. Atwood Society; Liaison Officer Hans-Böckler-Foundation, Düsseldorf. Editor: *Embracing the Other: Addressing Xenophobia in the New Literatures in English* (Rodopi, 2008); co-editor *9/11 as Catalyst: American and British Cultural Responses* (*Zeitschrift für Anglistik und Amerikanistik*, 2010); co-editor *Radical Planes? 9/11 and Patterns of Continuity* (Rodopi, 2016).

ÉMILIE NOTARD

Pour sa thèse intitulée *La traversée des sens : Trajectoire féministe dans l'œuvre de Nicole Brossard de 1977 à 2007*, publiée en 2016 chez LIT Verlag, Émilie Notard a reçu le Prix d'Excellence du Gouvernement du Québec en 2014. Actuellement, elle enseigne le français et l'allemand dans le secondaire à Berlin, travaille pour les éditions Accents Poétiques et écrit des poèmes.

DANIEL POITRAS

Après avoir consacré ses premières recherches sur le rapport à l'histoire, au temps et à la narrativité au Québec et en France au 20ᵉ siècle, Daniel Poitras effectue présentement un postdoctorat à l'University of Toronto sur l'histoire des étudiants étrangers au Canada. Il s'intéresse particulièrement aux expériences interculturelles sur les campus après 1945 et aux stratégies narratives déployées par les différents acteurs des milieux universitaires.

VÉRONIQUE PORRA

Professeure de Littératures française et francophones à l'Université Gutenberg de Mayence depuis 2002. Elle est spécialiste des littératures francophones hors d'Europe et des écritures migrantes. Elle travaille actuellement sur l'Atlantique francophone et sur le discours mémoriel dans les littératures et les cinémas français et francophones. Auteure de nombreux articles et ouvrages collectifs, elle a également publié en 2011 (Olms) un ouvrage intitulé *Langue française – langue d'adoption. Une littérature « invitée » entre création, stratégie et contraintes (1946-2000).* En 2015 (Olms), elle a coédité *Les lieux d'oubli de la Francophonie* (avec D. Dumontet, K. Kloster et Th. Schüller) et *L'Atlantique littéraire : Perspectives théoriques sur la constitution d'un espace translinguistique* (Olms ; avec J.-M. Moura).

SRILATA RAVI

Professor of French at the University of Alberta. Her research interests are in comparative literary and cultural studies, Francophone postcolonial studies and Indian Ocean studies. Her publications include *Sport, modernité et réseaux impériaux : Napoléon Lajoie, Kumar Shri Ranjitsinhji, baseball et cricket au tournant du XXᵉ siècle* (PUL, 2017, co-authored); *Translating the Postcolonial in Multilingual Contexts* (PULM, 2017, co-ed.); *Autour de l'œuvre de Gérard Bouchard. Histoire sociale, sociologie historique, imaginaires collectifs et politiques publiques* (PUL, 2015, co-ed.); *Rethinking Global Mauritius: Critical*

Essays on Mauritian Literatures and Cultures (La Librairie Mauricienne Numérique, 2013); *Rainbow Colors – Literary Ethno-Topographies of Mauritius* (Lexington, 2007); *Écritures mauriciennes au féminin: penser l'altérité* (L'Harmattan, 2011, co-ed.); *Asia in Europe, Europe in Asia* (Institute of Southeast Asian Studies, 2004, co-ed.).

MARION CHRISTINA ROHRLEITNER

PhD (University of Notre Dame, 2007), Associate Professor of English at The University of Texas at El Paso, where she teaches contemporary literature of the Americas focusing on Chicana/o, Latina/o, and Caribbean diasporic fiction. She is co-editor of *Dialogues Across Diasporas* (Lexington, 2012) and has published research on Latina/o and Caribbean literature in, for example, *American Quarterly, Antipodas, Interdisciplinary Humanities, Latino Studies,* and *Oxford Bibliographies* in Latina/o Studies.